POLITICAL GEOGRAPHY OF THE UNITED STATES

ERRATUM

POLITICAL GEOGRAPHY
OF THE UNITED STATES

Fred M. Shelley, J. Clark Archer,
Fiona M. Davidson, and Stanley D. Brunn

The maps (but not the keys to the maps) on pages 275 and 279 (Figures 9.1 and 9.3) were transposed in the printing of the above volume, i.e., the map keys explaining the percentage of the popular vote are presently situated below the wrong map.

Political Geography of the United States

Fred M. Shelley, J. Clark Archer,
Fiona M. Davidson, and Stanley D. Brunn

THE GUILFORD PRESS
New York   London

© 1996 The Guilford Press
A Division of Guilford Publications, Inc.
72 Spring Street, New York, NY 10012

Marketed and distributed outside North America
by Longman Group UK Limited

Printed in the United States of America

This book is printed on acid-free paper.

Last digit is print number: 9 8 7 6 5 4 3 2 1

Library of Congress Cataloging-in-Publication Data

Political geography of the United States / by Fred M. Shelley . . . [et
    al.].
        p.   cm.
    Includes bibliographical references and index.
    ISBN 1-57230-047-7 (hardcover). —ISBN 1-57230-048-5 (pbk.)
    1. Political geography.   2. Human geography—United States.
    3. Regionalism—United States.   4. United States—Politics and
    government.   I. Shelley, Fred M., 1952–   .
    JC319.P587   1996
    320.973—dc20
                                                            96-10814
                                                               CIP

CONTENTS

PREFACE

This book is intended as an examination of the political geography of the United States. Recognizing that an understanding of U.S. political geography today requires reference to historical developments, we devote considerable attention to a historical perspective on the geography of U.S. politics. The book thus has several purposes: to summarize recent research on the geography of U.S. politics, to provide an integrated and historical perspective on the development of the U.S. political system, and to serve as a springboard for future research on this vast and fascinating topic. It is intended to complement existing textbooks on political geography written from a global perspective.

Over the past twenty years, the subdiscipline of political geography has undergone a remarkable transformation. Once geography's backwater, political geography has emerged since the late 1960s to occupy the discipline's center stage. One of the landmark events of the early renaissance of political geography was the publication of Stanley Brunn's *Geography and Politics in America* in 1974. *Geography and Politics in America* was the first book-length examination of the politics of the United States from a geographic perspective.

In the two decades since *Geography and Politics in America* was published, both the subdiscipline of political geography and the U.S. political economy themselves have undergone major changes. The energy crisis of the 1970s, the Watergate scandal, the end of the Vietnam War, the increased globalization of the U.S. economy, and the end of the Cold War are but a few of the significant events that have affected the U.S. political economy over the past two decades. Thus, it is appropriate not only to update some of the major themes developed in *Geography and Politics in America* but also to develop a more explicitly historical narrative that provides a contemporary examination of the political geography of the United States at the end of the twentieth century.

The book comprises ten chapters. Chapter 1 provides the basic context underlying the book. We discuss the subdiscipline of political geography, show the value of approaching U.S. politics from a geographic perspective, and lay the groundwork for the substantive analyses presented in the ensuing chapters.

Chapter 2 is devoted to discussion of America's colonial era, the American Revolution, and the drafting and ratification of the Constitution. During the nearly two centuries following the establishment of Jamestown, Virginia, in 1607, what is today the United States grew from a series of lonely British outposts on the shores of the Atlantic Ocean to a full-fledged, independent country. It was during the colonial era that the basic institutions of U.S. democracy emerged and, in many cases, diverged significantly from their European antecedents. After the American Revolution, the U.S. Constitution was written and ratified. The Constitution established the basic framework of U.S. democracy, and this framework remains in place today.

Chapter 3 focuses on the political geography of the United States in the nineteenth century. During the nineteenth century, the United States assumed sovereignty over all of its present fifty states. Areas from the Appalachian Mountains to the Pacific Ocean and from the 49th parallel to the Rio Grande were annexed, settled, and successively admitted to the Union. The U.S. economy expanded steadily, and by the end of the nineteenth century, the United States had become the world's leading industrial power. The politics of the nineteenth-century United States were dominated by two-party competition across three major sections: the Northeast, the South, and the West.

In Chapter 4, we examine the development of U.S. political geography from the 1890s to the 1960s. The period began with the Populist Revolt and the Progressive Era. Despite the major changes in U.S. life occurring during this period, the basic geography of U.S. politics changed little until after World War II. After the war ended, however, U.S. politics began to undergo a fundamental transformation. Democratic dominance of the South eroded as the national Democratic Party espoused positions on civil rights and foreign policy that were increasingly unpopular among white Southerners. The Republicans began to make inroads into the South, while Democratic strength increased in the Northeast. By the 1960s, the Northeast was the most Democratic section of the country, while the once volatile West had become dominated by the Republicans.

In Chapter 5, we turn our attention to the political geography of state and local governance in the United States. The United States, like other large and heterogeneous countries throughout the world, is a federal state. The Constitution divides governmental responsibilities between the federal government and the states. The administrative structures of the fifty states vary markedly, and the more than 80,000 units of local government in the United States vary widely in terms of structure, taxing authority, and power. In recent years, some critics have charged that U.S. government is characterized by excessive fragmentation of governmental responsibility, especially in metropolitan areas. A variety of proposals to reform the governance of metropolitan areas have been suggested, although to date none have been implemented successfully across wide areas.

In 1962, the U.S. Supreme Court declared malapportionment unconstitutional in the celebrated case of *Baker v. Carr. Baker* initiated the so-called reapportionment revolution, and since the case was decided, both federal and state courts have decided thousands of cases in which the constitutionality of districts drawn to elect members of the House of Representatives, state legislators, and local officials has been challenged. The *Baker* decision and subsequent redistricting decisions dealt with fundamental issues concerning the nature of representative democracy as practiced in the United States. These controversies form the basis for discussion in Chapter 6, which is devoted to the issue of representation, reapportionment, and redistricting in the United States. Our discussion traces the most significant cases on redistricting from the outset of the reapportionment revolution in the 1960s to decisions handed down by the Supreme Court in the early summer of 1995.

In Chapter 7, we turn our attention to the role of the United States in the world economy. Over the course of U.S. history, foreign policy decision making in the United States has oscillated between periods of introversion and periods of extroversion. During introvert cycles, the United States has tended to avoid foreign entanglements. During extrovert cycles, on the other hand, the United States has taken a more active role in international affairs. The debate between isolation and intervention has a geographic as well as a temporal dimension. During the early twentieth century, the Northeast and the South emerged as the most strongly interventionist sections of the United States, while isolationism was strongest in the Middle West and the West. By the late 1960s, this pattern had faded. In its place arose a pattern characterized by interventionism in the Sunbelt and isolationism in the Rustbelt. This pattern began to emerge during the antiwar movement of the 1960s, and it remains today.

Chapter 8 is devoted to a discussion of recent changes in the U.S. position in the world economy. The energy crisis of the 1970s marked the beginning of profound changes in the organization of the U.S. economy. Over the past two decades, the tertiary and quaternary sectors have become much more important, while many manufacturing jobs have left the United States as employers seek cheaper labor elsewhere. During the same period, the organization of production has changed dramatically. Smaller, more flexible, and more globalized production systems have replaced the concentration on assembly line production in large factories that had characterized the mid-twentieth century. The transition to a post-Fordist economy occurred in conjunction with the end of the Cold War. Today, Americans continue to ponder their country's place in the uncertain new world order.

These changes have affected the recent political history of the United States. Since 1976, U.S. presidential politics have been characterized by the so-called Conservative Normal Vote. The Northeast remains the most Democratic area of the country while the West remains strongly Republican. The once Solid South, on the other hand, has emerged as the pivotal section of the United States. Will this pattern continue to hold in the 1996 and subsequent presidential elections?

In Chapter 9, we discuss the analysis of presidential elections in historical and geographic perspective. Techniques for analyzing elections in historical sequence are described. T-mode and S-mode factor analyses have proven to be especially powerful methods for identifying important spatial and temporal trends from large quantities of electoral data. An S-mode analysis of U.S. presidential elections at a state level between 1872 and 1992 illustrates the importance of sectionalism to U.S. political history and geography. The Northeastern, Southern, and Western sections emerge as clearly distinct electoral regions of the United States, and, with only a few exceptions, the fifty states load most highly on the appropriate sections.

We then turn to T-mode factor analyses of the United States as a whole. T-mode analyses of the three major regions are then presented, with each yielding a distinctive electoral history. Indeed, we find that the pattern of critical elections identified in the political science literature conforms closely to the electoral history of the Northeast but is quite distinct from the electoral histories of the South and the West. Yet a true understanding of electoral history can be attained only by considering all three sections in combination.

The final chapter considers the political geography of the United States in the twenty-first century. How will the dramatic changes in the world economy and the global political map, along with equally dramatic changes in technology, affect U.S. politics after the turn of the century? In the final chapter, we undertake the admittedly hazardous task of prediction. Not only are changes in the Constitution possible, and even likely, but the prospect of adding new states, thus expanding the scope of U.S. democracy and otherwise restructuring the democratic process in the United States, is indeed real. Our purpose in the concluding chapter is to stimulate thoughtful discussion on the future of the U.S. polity.

In completing this project, we wish to acknowledge the numerous family members, colleagues, students, and friends who contributed to our efforts in a wide variety of ways. We especially wish to thank a few of these many persons who provided us with particularly valuable assistance. Seymour Weingarten, Editor-in-Chief of Guilford Press, laid the initial groundwork that enabled us to begin the project. Later, Peter Wissoker, editor, gave us steadfast support and valuable advice throughout the course of the project. We also benefited greatly from the efforts of two external reviewers, our friends Kenneth Martis of West Virginia University and Gerald Webster of the University of Alabama. Ken and Jerry provided us with very useful feedback, both formal and informal, on an earlier draft of this manuscript, and these comments were instrumental to our preparation of the final draft.

POLITICAL GEOGRAPHY OF THE UNITED STATES

Chapter I

INTRODUCTION

The Durability of U.S. Democracy

The United States is the oldest functioning democracy in the world. "We the People of the United States," to quote the Preamble to the federal Constitution that went into effect in 1789, have indeed formed "a more perfect Union," one that has already celebrated its bicentennial anniversary.

There are, of course, many reasons for the success of the United States as a federally unified entity. Among those that come to mind are the iconography and political pageantry of the United States—for example, the flag, Uncle Sam, the questionably accurate but inspiring tales about George Washington and other patriots told to generations of U.S. public school pupils, and the Fourth of July as an annual celebration of American independence. The importance of such celebrations was early attested by John Adams, the second president of the United States, who, as an advocate of "publick happiness," asserted in a letter to Abigail Adams that the anniversary of the Declaration of Independence "ought to be commemorated with . . . Shews, Games, Sports, Guns, Bells, Bonfires and illumination from one End of this Continent to the other from this Time forward forever more."

Yet even brief reflection will soon demonstrate that "Shews, Games, Sports," and other forms of pageantry and iconography cannot for long maintain a flawed political entity. The once massive May Day parades through Red Square in Moscow, for example, have been discontinued. Countless portraits of Lenin and Stalin have been pulled down throughout the former Soviet Union since the dramatic revolution of 1991. In Prague, capital of the new Czech Republic, a large colorful pendulum now occupies the conspicuous hilltop site where a huge and somber statue of Lenin once stood. Slogans, portraits, statues, and parades were not enough to overcome the self-destructive internal contradictions of a "dictatorship of the proletariat." Indeed, the end of the Soviet regime was forced by Gdansk shipwrights, Ukrainian farmers, Russian coal miners, and other workers who no longer supported a system supposedly formed to advance their interests.

The U.S. political system has been tested many times during the first two centuries of its independence. Undoubtedly, the U.S. system will continue to be tested in the future. Differences in status, class, ethnicity, and culture guarantee that there will continue to be differences in attitudes and interests among U.S. citizens and that these differences will vary from one locality or region to another. With every passing decade, fundamental changes in the global economy, in technology, in culture, and in social life bring new issues to the forefront of the U.S. political agenda. As the U.S. electorate articulates these issues, new coalitions of voters and politicians form and new patterns of support and opposition to political leaders and parties emerge at the national, state, and local levels.

Not only will honest differences in public opinion continue to manifest themselves within the U.S. polity, but efforts to reform the political system itself will continue. By the mid-1990s, for example, many Americans had expressed support for a constitutional amendment limiting the number of terms to which members of Congress could be elected. Others advocated implementing a greater degree of direct as opposed to representative democracy. For example, some want to increase citizens' opportunities—through the use of new technology, such as cable television and interactive computers—to vote directly on proposals to levy taxes or legislate public policy. Still others have questioned the U.S. tradition of territorial representation, advocating in its place a system of delineating representative constituencies that would give greater weight to ethnic identity.

Geography and the U.S. Political System

Seldom if ever has the U.S. public been in agreement on the appropriate direction of public policy. In recent years, controversies such as the civil rights movement, the Vietnam War, the conduct of the Cold War, the legality of abortion, and the North American Free Trade Agreement have aroused deep and passionate feelings on the part of supporters and opponents across the United States. Yet despite fundamental disagreement concerning the direction of public policy, the U.S. political system itself represents a monument of durability.

When the United States is compared with less durable governmental and political entities, it becomes clear that a distinctive feature of U.S. governance has been the extent to which individuals and groups of citizens with different or even conflicting opinions have been able to approach and command the attentions of various decision-making bodies and officials. The U.S. tradition of access to these decision-making bodies dates from well before the United States became an independent country in the late eighteenth century. Many of the institutions of representative democracy that have proven their durability throughout the more than two centuries of U.S. independence have their origins in the colonial era, the nearly two centuries between the earliest English settlement of North America in the early seventeenth century and the Peace of Paris in 1783.

What accounts for the durability of U.S. democracy? We contend that one of the most important reasons the success of the U.S. system of government is its inherently geographic qualities. Ease of access to governmental officials and policy-making bodies was an important feature of American democracy long before the American Revolution. Residents of the Thirteen Colonies, who were scattered in often isolated outposts along the Atlantic coast from Georgia to New Hampshire, demanded that the institutions of representative government be set up in such a way as to ensure accessibility. The capitals of the colonies were located centrally, and many were moved westward as the Anglo-American population moved westward. Counties were small enough that any resident of a county could journey to the seat of government on horseback or by stagecoach, transact business, and return home before nightfall.

Profound cultural and economic differences within the Thirteen Colonies were evident long before the American Revolution. Despite regional differences, however, many eighteenth-century residents of the Thirteen Colonies began to see themselves not only as citizens of the individual colonies, but as Americans—that is, as members of a polity derivative of yet distinct from the British Isles. Leaders throughout the Thirteen Colonies advocated the maintenance of government based on the philosophy of particular representation, with each legislator regarded as accountable primarily to the residents of a territorially defined constituency.

The philosophy of particular representation underlay many of the grievances that residents of the Thirteen Colonies harbored against British rule. The famous slogan "No taxation without representation" is recalled even today as a symbol of American support for a territorial orientation in politics and government. Once independence was achieved, the philosophies of accessibility and particular representation strongly influenced the development of the U.S. Constitution and of the constitutions of the individual states. To a considerable extent, the system of checks and balances associated with the Constitution and therefore with the practice of U.S. representative democracy can be regarded as an outgrowth of the importance that colonial Americans placed on geography as an organizing principle of governance.

Because of the importance of geography to U.S. democracy, as well as to the political economy of the United States and its relationships with the world economy, we must consider U.S. governance from a political–geographic perspective. This book is intended to examine the U.S. political system in theory and practice from an explicitly political–geographic perspective, which will contribute much to our understanding of how the U.S. political system works and how the U.S. polity is likely to evolve as society, the economy, culture, and technology change.

What, then, is political geography? How can the perspective of political geography inform our understanding of the U.S. political system? The subdiscipline of political geography examines the interaction between location and political activity. Such a perspective is especially valuable for studying the development and the future of an explicitly geographic political system, such as that of the United States.

In examining the interaction between political activity and location, we are asserting that place and location affect the outcomes of political conflict and vice-versa. Fundamentally, the purpose of any political system is the resolution of conflict. It is because people disagree about laws, policies, and regulations that political systems are organized, and it is through organized political institutions that conflicts over public policy are articulated and resolved.

The institutionalized process of conflict resolution is characterized by an inherently geographic dimension. Policy decisions affect people in places. Where people live, work, shop, visit, and interact can and frequently do influence their views on public policy issues.

Among the strengths of the political–geographic perspective is its explicit recognition of relationships between the global economy, governmental decision making, and local places. Thus, political geography links the global, national, and local spheres of human activity. Americans, like people throughout the world, live in an interdependent global economy. Any supermarket, shopping mall, or department store contains goods for sale from all over the world. Moreover, events in particular places have significant effects around the globe. For example, cold snaps in Brazil can cause the price of coffee to double in New York, the threat of armed conflict in the Middle East is felt by consumers, who pay higher prices for gasoline, the easing of Cold War tensions results in layoffs in communities whose economies depend on defense-related industries, and so on.

Political institutions in the United States, as in other countries, give Americans the opportunity to respond to changes in the world economy. For example, higher gasoline taxes can discourage people from driving and so reduce consumption of petroleum products. These taxes might be welcomed in areas where gasoline is in short supply but opposed in oil-producing regions. The U.S. political system allows representatives of the different places that may be particularly affected by such proposals to participate in the policy making that will impact their regions.

The purpose of the book, then, is to provide a geographic perspective on U.S. politics and government. Of necessity, such an approach involves examination of the historical, social, political, cultural, and economic forces that have influenced the development of the U.S. polity. Thus we begin our discovery of the political geography of the United States with a journey into the colonial era. Having traced the historical development of U.S. political geography from its origins in the colonial period through the present, we will then turn to specific issues involving the operation of U.S. democracy today, including discussions of federalism, representation, elections, and the U.S. place in the post–Cold War global economy. Finally, we will use the historical and contemporary geographic analysis of the political geography of the United States to provide a basis for projecting into the political geography of the United States in the twenty-first century.

Chapter 2

BUILDING THE FOUNDATIONS

Our discovery of U.S. political geography begins during the period between the establishment of the first permanent English settlement in North America in 1607 and the drafting and ratification of the U.S. Constitution in the late 1780s. During the nearly two centuries that comprise the colonial era, the Thirteen Colonies that would become the original thirteen states of the United States were founded and settled. By the late eighteenth century, the Thirteen Colonies had achieved sufficient economic and political maturity to become an independent country.

In this chapter, we trace the political geography of colonial America. Many of the important characteristics of modern U.S. democracy emerged during the colonial era. The dramatic developments of the late eighteenth century—the Declaration of Independence, the American Revolution, and the drafting and ratification of the Constitution—were the culmination of the colonial era: In Abraham Lincoln's immortal words, "our fathers brought forth on this continent, a new nation, conceived in Liberty and dedicated to the proposition that all men are created equal." Thus, the U.S. Constitution of 1787 was the fruit of nearly two centuries of experience in self-government among European settlers in North America. This chapter surveys American political geography from the outset of European settlement until the ratification of the Federal Constitution.

Colonialism and the World Economy

The European settlement of North America that occurred during the colonial era was part of a much larger process that spread European civilization throughout the world. Colonialism was the means by which Europeans achieved military, governmental, commercial, and cultural domination of non-European areas of the world. During the same period, millions of Europeans moved to other parts of the world. By the twentieth century, the entire earth had become incorporated into a European-based world economy.

The Age of Exploration and the European Discovery of America

The contemporary world economy is characterized by global economic interdependence, while the earth's surface is divided politically into independent, sovereign countries. Resource extraction, industrial production, and commercial markets now connect producers and consumers in widely separated locations throughout the world.

The modern world economy began to emerge in western Europe during the Renaissance. Earlier, returning Crusaders had introduced a variety of foreign luxury goods into Europe, including silk and lace for fine clothing from China and peppers, cloves, nutmeg, and other spices from south and southeast Asia. Trade in these and other non-European items was dominated by merchants from the city-states of Italy, which controlled the very profitable trade routes between Europe and the Middle East and Asia.

Every increase in European demand for silk, spices, and other items of Oriental trade brought greater wealth to Italian merchant traders. In response, members of the political and economic elite classes in northern and western Europe desired to undercut Italian and Islamic dominance of the lucrative trade between Europe and Asia by discovering their own trade routes to the sources of Asian luxury goods. Their search for alternate trade routes spurred the Age of Exploration, prompting major innovations in sailing and navigation, weapons and warfare, and banking and commerce.

As the Age of Exploration began, Europeans began to consider the possibility of circumnavigating the globe in a westerly direction in order to reach Asia. Most educated Europeans by the end of the fifteenth century knew that the earth is spherical, not flat. The ancient Greeks, of course, knew that the world is round. About 1400, Ptolemy's *Geography* was rediscovered and translated into Latin, thus reintroducing the important concept of the spherical earth to literate Europeans (Boorstin, 1983, pp. 152–53).

Christopher Columbus was not only a seaman, but a cartographer who had carefully studied the maps and writings of his contemporaries and predecessors. Long before he set sail across the Atlantic, he became familiar with Ptolemy's work. Yet Columbus was unaware that Ptolemy had miscalculated the circumference of the earth. Ptolemy's erroneous calculations led Columbus to believe that the earth's circumference was several thousand miles less than it actually is. Had Columbus known the actual distance from Spain to China, he might have been less eager to set sail, and his backers might have balked at financing his voyages.

Moreover, those who sought to reach the Far East by sailing westward were unaware that the Americas and the Pacific Ocean were located in between. Upon sighting the islands of the Caribbean, Columbus believed that he had reached the "Spice Islands" off the coast of Asia. He called the islands the "Indies" and their inhabitants "Indians." Not for several decades did Europeans fully realize that the westward route to Asia was blocked by two entire continents and that the circumference of the earth is about 7,000 miles greater than Ptolemy had calculated.

The Political Geography of Pre-Columbian America

The Americas at the time of Columbus were inhabited by several million Native Americans who were descended from Asian migrants who had journeyed eastward from Siberia into present-day Alaska across the Bering Strait. At various times during the Pleistocene, lowered sea levels allowed a low-lying land bridge between Asia and North America to emerge. Anthropologists believe that the earliest ancestors of today's Native Americans began their travels some 40,000 years ago. Long before the arrival of Columbus, Native Americans had settled all of North and South America and had established a great variety of cultures throughout these continents.

Contemporary anthropologists believe that, at the time of Columbus, one to three million Native Americans lived in what is now the United States. Their cultures were diverse and complex, but they had developed in isolation from the rest of the world. That Vikings from Norway and Iceland attempted to colonize northeastern North America is undisputed, and sporadic contacts between Native American societies and other societies elsewhere might have occurred as well. But none of these contacts had a significant impact on the social organization of pre-Columbian North America. After the European discovery of North America, however, the world economy spread across the Atlantic. Native American cultures underwent radical transformation. Many were eliminated entirely, and others were modified greatly in response to the arrival of the Europeans.

European Settlement of North America

Long before Europeans were fully aware that the Americas were separated from Asia by thousands of miles of ocean, they began to colonize North and South America. Within a few decades of Columbus's initial discoveries, the Spanish had discovered and exploited lucrative deposits of gold and silver throughout upland Central and South America. Exploitation of these mineral resources made Spain the wealthiest and most powerful country in the world at the time.

During the sixteenth century, Spanish and Portuguese settlements in Latin America prospered. North America, on the other hand, was largely ignored by sixteenth-century Europeans. Spanish explorers such as Francisco Coronado, Hernando de Soto, and Alvar Núñez Cabeza de Vaca tramped deep into the interior of North America in search of the fabled Seven Cities of Cibola. Disappointed in their failure to find gold on the North American mainland, the Spanish soon retreated southward and concentrated on colonizing mineral-rich Latin America.

By 1600, Spanish and Portuguese settlements such as Rio de Janeiro, Mexico City, Buenos Aires, and Lima had already emerged as important world cities. Few could have predicted that, less than four centuries later, South America would be regarded as an economic backwater whereas North America, which in the early 1600s lacked European settlement almost entirely, would have become the most powerful and wealthiest part of the world.

The Spanish established highly profitable commercial and mining enterprises in Latin America decades before Spain's European competitors were ready to attempt to establish their own presence in the New World. By the middle of the sixteenth century, however, English fishing vessels were harvesting cod from the Grand Banks off the coast of Newfoundland, and English pirate ships were preying on Spanish galleons in the Caribbean. In 1577–1580, Francis Drake seized a fortune from Spanish settlements along the west coast of South America. Drake then sailed his ship, the *Golden Hind,* across the Pacific in order to avoid capture by Spanish forces in the Atlantic. The dramatic English victory over the Spanish Armada in 1588 encouraged English explorers to attempt systematic colonization of the New World (Morison, 1971). After several failed attempts, Jamestown, Virginia, was established in 1607 as the first permanent English settlement in North America.

The English were not alone in attempting colonization of the eastern seaboard of North America. Other early European settlements included the establishment of a Dutch trading post on Manhattan Island, in what is now New York, in 1610. An early Swedish settlement, called Christianaham, was established in 1638 at a site that is now within the city limits of Wilmington, Delaware. Gradually, the British Empire absorbed these and other non-English colonial ventures. New Sweden's forts on the Delaware Bay were captured by the Dutch West India Company in 1655. In turn, the Dutch New Netherlands were ceded to the authority of the British Crown in 1664. Within sixty years of the establishment of Jamestown, the British controlled most of the eastern seaboard of North America between Maine and Georgia. By 1733, all of the Thirteen Colonies had been founded.

Regions within the Thirteen Colonies

Long before the end of the seventeenth century, the Thirteen Colonies formed three distinctive regions: New England, the Middle Atlantic colonies, and the South. Each region was characterized by a distinctive economic base and a distinctive political–economic relationship with Europe. These early economic differences were crucial to the development of distinctive political cultures in the three regions, as we will see in detail in Chapter 3.

The Southern Colonies

The Southern colonies (Maryland, Virginia, North Carolina, South Carolina, and Georgia) established economies based on the production of crops for export to European markets. The warm, humid subtropical climate of the South permitted the cultivation of crops unsuitable for cultivation in Europe. Large quantities of cotton, tobacco, rice, indigo, and other crops were exported across the Atlantic.

Southern agricultural production was organized according to a plantation system. Thus, much of the productive agricultural land of the South was owned by a small minority of the population. Southern plantation agriculture was labor-intensive. Labor was provided by indentured servants and by slaves. Indeed, millions of Africans were captured and sold into slavery in the United States before the Constitution outlawed the importation of slaves effective in 1808.

Most trade in Southern crops was handled by merchants in London or in the northern colonies. Moreover, disease spread rapidly in the warm, humid Southern climate under the primitive eighteenth-century sanitation conditions. Thus, there was little incentive to develop cities and towns. Community life in the colonial South revolved around individual plantations, not urban centers.

New England

In contrast to the South, the colonies of New England (Massachusetts, Connecticut, New Hampshire, and Rhode Island) offered their settlers little incentive to establish large-scale commercial farms. Colonists settling in New England "found the terrain hilly, the soil stony and acid, and the growing season short" (Whittlesey, 1956, p. 246). Many of the crops best suited to New England's cool climate and infertile soils, such as barley or potatoes, were already produced in northwestern Europe. Thus, most of New England's agricultural output was consumed locally.

New England's settlers soon realized that they could not hope to prosper through the export of agricultural products. Instead, they turned to other pursuits to generate revenue. At first, furs, timber, and naval stores (turpentine, resin, etc.) were extracted, but local supplies soon diminished as more and more land was cleared for cultivation. Many New Englanders turned to the sea for a livelihood. New England had excellent access to the rich and lucrative fishing grounds of the North Atlantic, and New England fish were soon in demand throughout North America and Europe. Trading became a New England specialty, and shipbuilding encouraged many colonial New England communities to begin to specialize in small-scale manufacturing activities.

Whereas the isolated farm or plantation was the basic social unit of the South, the basic social unit of the New England colonies was the town. Many New England towns were founded by Puritans and other religious dissenters who were intent on creating self-sufficient communities of believers free of worldly external influences. Towns were often arranged around a central pasture or "commons," which was flanked by a church and a meeting hall. The spatial organization of New England towns reinforced the communal spirit characteristic of their residents.

The Middle Atlantic Colonies

The Middle Atlantic colonies (New York, New Jersey, Pennsylvania, and Delaware) enjoyed the most favorable geographic position of the Thirteen Colonies. The Middle Atlantic region was blessed with productive soils and a mild climate. By the 1700s, the Middle Atlantic was recognized as one of the major granaries of Europe, with large quantities of wheat, corn, and other basic foodstuffs exported across the Atlantic. Moreover, its central location and fine harbors made the Middle Atlantic region the natural center of commerce and industry within British North America.

In contrast to the South and New England, the Middle Atlantic colonies were characterized by substantial ethnic and cultural diversity. For example, Dutch settlers founded the city of New York as New Amsterdam and settled the Hudson Valley to the north. Swedish settlements were established in Delaware, and German settlers were numerous in Pennsylvania and New Jersey. Whereas the South was dominated by Anglicans and New England by Puritans, the Middle Atlantic colonies were known for religious diversity and tolerance. Roman Catholics, Quakers, Dutch Reformed, Lutherans, and Mennonites settled in substantial numbers in various areas of the Middle Atlantic. Persons in these and other religious communities "found it possible to live under the same laws and in the same habitats, so long as they were allowed to think and believe as they wished" (Whittlesey, 1956, p. 250). With their ethnically varied populations and diversified economies, New York City and Philadelphia grew rapidly to become the largest and most cosmopolitan cities in British North America. These urban commercial centers would play a leading role in the struggle for independence, although ongoing friction between urban commercial and rural agricultural interests proved critical to the development of many of the institutions of representative government that are still in place in the United States today.

Law and Government in the
Thirteen Colonies

During the colonial era, the North American colonists established a variety of practices that would later evolve into the unique institutions of U.S. democracy. For the most part, U.S. legal and political institutions were modified from English antecedents. Yet the process of applying English legal and governmental institutions to the vast and sparsely settled North American continent created a uniquely American system of law, politics, and government.

In 1619, the House of Burgesses—the earliest legislative assembly in the Thirteen Colonies—convened for the first time at Jamestown, Virginia. Although the initial meeting of the House of Burgesses lasted only six days, its establishment set an important precedent. Government throughout British North America would be based on the rule of law and would involve the will of the people.

During the seventeenth century, most of the Thirteen Colonies followed Virginia's lead and established assemblies of elected legislators. For several decades, these local colonial governments operated with little interference from the British Crown. As the seventeenth century drew to a close, however, the commercial success of the colonies encouraged England to exercise a more active role in colonial governance. Beginning in 1650, Parliament passed a series of laws known as the Navigation Acts. The basic intent of the Navigation Acts was to enhance the commercial profitability of English commerce by regulating trade between England and the colonies.

The Navigation Acts required that trade between the colonies and England be conducted on English ships. Colonial products could be exported only to England, where they were subject to English taxation. This was especially burdensome to farmers and merchants in New England and the Middle Atlantic colonies, whose surplus food products were valued on Caribbean islands that specialized in plantation production of sugar. Under one of several forms of "triangular trade," American merchants shipped corn and wheat to feed Caribbean plantation workers, Caribbean planters shipped sugar to sweeten English tea, and English industrialists shipped manufactured products to American merchants. Since American corn and wheat usually attracted a higher price in, say, Kingston, Jamaica, than in London, the British subjects in North America were inclined to regard the Navigation Acts as unjust and unreasonably burdensome.

English officials soon recognized that the colonial assemblies would neither support nor enforce the Navigation Acts. Enforcement of the Navigation Acts thus required more direct supervision of the colonial assemblies. Some of the colonial charters were revoked and replaced with governments more directly responsive to the British Crown. In 1685, King James II attempted to combine the governments of the New England colonies, New York, and New Jersey into a single Dominion of New England. James believed that organizing these colonies under a single government would facilitate enforcement of the Navigation Acts. The colonial assemblies were abolished, and James appointed a single governor to supervise the entire area.

After James was overthrown in the Glorious Revolution of 1688, the Dominion of New England was abolished. The charters of the colonies within the Dominion of New England were amended or revoked, however. In each case, the king and Parliament were given expanded authority at the expense of the colonial assemblies. Over the course of the eighteenth century, British-imposed limits on colonial self-government in conjunction with increasing population and prosperity would create a climate ripe for independence. Especially after 1763, English efforts at strict enforcement of the Navigation Acts heightened tensions between the colonists and the British. As the colonies continued to prosper, more and more colonists began to object to British efforts to expand control over the colonies.

The American Revolution

By the 1760s, several generations of colonists had been born and raised in North America. Colonists increasingly regarded themselves as Americans rather than as British subjects. At the same time, a series of grievances against British rule on the part of Americans crystallized into sentiment favoring full-scale American independence. During the last third of the eighteenth century, these sentiments came to fruition. The Thirteen Colonies broke free of British rule and became an independent country sovereign over most of eastern North America from the Atlantic Ocean to the Mississippi River.

Underlying Causes of the American Revolution

Both Great Britain and France had made extensive claims in North America by the early eighteenth century. French settlements were concentrated along the St. Lawrence River in what is now eastern Canada, but French fur traders ranged widely throughout the Great Lakes area and the Ohio and Mississippi River systems. Friction increased as frontier English settlements spread inland in New England, New York, and Pennsylvania. Elsewhere, France and England emerged as colonial rivals in India and the Far East. France and Great Britain also gravitated toward opposing sides in central and eastern Europe, as France allied with Austria and Russia while Great Britain allied with Prussia.

Growing hostilities between English settlers and French traders in interior North America and between English and French rivals in India erupted into open warfare by mid-century. Great Britain and France declared war on each other in 1756, inaugurating the Seven Years' War—a conflict known in North America as the French and Indian War.

Battles in North America, including the seizure of the city of Quebec in 1759 by a British army that included many residents of the Thirteen Colonies, were critical to the eventual British and Prussian victory in the Seven Years' War. Under the terms of the Treaty of Paris in 1763, most French territory in North America was ceded to Great Britain. Once Great Britain had gained uncontested supremacy over eastern North America (Figure 2-1), the British government strengthened its efforts to exert greater and more direct control over the local affairs of the Thirteen Colonies. One of its objectives was to minimize the risk of incurring additional military outlays in conflicts with Spanish or Native American opponents in North America. Toward this end, the British government issued the Proclamation of 1763 forbidding American colonists to settle west of the crest of the Appalachian Mountains. The vast territory between the Appalachian crest and the Mississippi River was to be reserved for Native Americans and for fur traders who formed the North-West Fur Company of Montreal. The fur trade was highly profitable to British merchants and to the British government, but most colonists regarded the Proclamation Line as an infringement on their rights. Colonists were further enraged in 1774 when Parliament passed the Quebec Act, which formally included most of the territory between the Great Lakes and the Ohio and Mississippi Rivers within the Province of Quebec. The Proclamation of 1763 and the Quebec Act were largely ignored. By the time of the American Revolution, nearly 100,000 colonists had settled west of the Proclamation Line (Meinig, 1986).

Because the Seven Years' War had left the British government deeply in debt, members of Parliament were eager to extract more revenues from the North American colonies. The Sugar Act of 1764 established stiff import duties on sugar, wine, and other imported products. The intent of the Sugar Act was to restrict the trade in sugar and sugar products between the colonies and the West Indies, most of which were French or Spanish colonies. The Stamp Act of 1765 required that all official documents, deeds, newspapers, and pamphlets published in the colonies bear stamps issued and sold by the British government. This tax was intended to help pay for the maintenance of a permanent force of British troops in order to control hostilities between colonists and Native Americans living along the western frontier. The Stamp Act provoked fierce opposition in the Thirteen Colonies. Many colonists objected to the tax and regarded the Stamp Act as "taxation without representation." As public outcry over the Stamp Act increased, a more fundamental question arose: What authority did Parliament have over the legislatures of the colonies? More generally, what political rights did American colonists enjoy independent of their rights as British subjects?

The Proclamation of 1763, the Sugar Act, and the Stamp Act also promoted a sense of unity and common purpose among the Thirteen Colonies. Merchants in New England and the Middle Atlantic states suffered from restrictions on commerce, tariffs, and the closing of the West to land

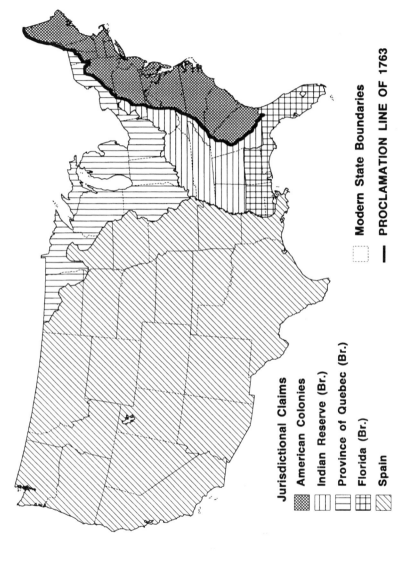

FIGURE 2-1. North America in 1775. Data from Hewes and Gannett (1883), Plate 12; U.S. Geological Survey (1987).

Jurisdictional Claims

American Colonies

Indian Reserve (Br.)

Province of Quebec (Br.)

Florida (Br.)

Spain

Modern State Boundaries

━━ **PROCLAMATION LINE OF 1763**

speculators and fur traders. Manufacturing had been restricted so that industries in the colonies would not compete with the rapidly growing industries of Great Britain. Meanwhile, Southern planters and small farmers throughout British North America were subject to higher taxes, while the restriction on western settlement drove the price of land upward.

In October 1765, representatives from nine of the Thirteen Colonies met in New York to protest the Stamp Act. This Stamp Act Congress asserted that Parliament had no right to tax the unrepresented colonists. With the support of many American merchants, it also organized a boycott of British goods. So effective was this boycott that commerce between Great Britain and North America was brought to a virtual standstill until Parliament repealed the Stamp Act in 1766.

The colony of Massachusetts had taken a leading role in the opposition to the Stamp Act. Indeed, the Massachusetts Assembly circulated a letter to the other colonial assemblies urging them to resist taxes imposed by Parliament. Soon afterward, advisers to the British King George III decided to make Massachusetts an example for the other colonies. In 1768, a garrison of British troops was stationed in Boston. The "redcoats" were bitterly resented by many of the colonists, who frequently taunted and harassed the soldiers. On March 5, 1770, British soldiers shot and killed five American colonists. The "Boston Massacre" fueled anti-British sentiment throughout the Thirteen Colonies.

Virtual and Particular Representation

The debate over the legality of the Stamp Act and the hostilities in Boston brought the issue of representation to a head. By the time the Revolution began, American leaders had developed a philosophy of democracy that was quite distinct from that held by the British.

Territoriality as the explicit basis of representation emerged as a basic principle of American democracy during colonial times. Each of the colonies was divided into legislative districts, with each district electing one or more delegates to the colonial assembly. Thus, each legislator was regarded as accountable primarily to the residents of the district. This territorial link between representative and constituent remains a fundamental component of U.S. democracy, as we shall see in Chapter 6.

Accessibility to the seat of government was an important corollary of the American philosophy of territorial or particular representation during colonial days (Zagarri, 1987). In colonial days, of course, transportation and communication between places were far slower and more laborious than is the case today. Thus, colonial Americans were far more concerned about physical proximity to the seat of government than is usually the case today. Poor roads and communication often made it impossible for residents of outlying districts to convey their views to legislators in distant capitals. In fact, sometimes the representatives themselves were unable to make the difficult journeys to distant capitals in time to participate in legislative sessions. Because "Americans believed that it was a matter of right, not simply of personal comfort, to have a centrally located capital" (Zagarri, 1987, p. 17), the capitals of many of the states were moved to more central locations. (Similarly, the capitals of other states, states that were established in the nineteenth century, were moved to central locations once settlement proceeded westward. For example, the capital of Iowa was moved from Burlington on the Mississippi River to Iowa City and subsequently to Des Moines in the center of the state.)

The American tradition of particular representation contrasts with the English tradition of virtual representation. The philosophy of virtual representation implies that it is the duty of each legislator to represent the interests of the entire polity, regardless of where the legislator resides. Thus, under a system of virtual representation, it is not necessary that each citizen has the right to vote for members of the legislature. The British government cited the philosophy of virtual representation to defend its refusal to allow representation in Parliament for the American colonists. A British member of Parliament, Thomas Whateley, defended the Stamp Act by stating that all subjects of the British Crown, including the American colonists, "are virtually represented; for every Member of Parliament sits in the House [of Commons], not as Representative of his own Constituents but as one of that august Assembly by which all of the Commons of Great Britain are represented" (Wood, 1969, p. 3).

Apologists for virtual representation pointed out that many people within Great Britain itself were not represented in Parliament during the eighteenth century. As many as a quarter of the seats in Parliament were held by representatives of "rotten boroughs," that is, districts delineated during medieval times and subsequently depopulated. At the same time, growing industrial cities such as Liverpool, Birmingham, and Manchester had no representation in Parliament. Not until Parliament enacted the Great Reform Bill in 1832 did the British abandon the philosophy of virtual representation.

Underlying the debate between supporters of particular and virtual representation in the Thirteen Colonies was the issue of ultimate sovereignty. The philosophy of virtual representation implied that Parliament had the inherent right to legislate for the entire British Empire. Thus, the Crown and Parliament were the sole ultimate authority. American supporters of particular representation, on the other hand, argued for a division of sovereignty. Colonial assemblies would be responsible for the enactment of laws affecting the colonies themselves. The British commitment to the philosophy of virtual representation led the Americans to begin to recognize that they must eventually choose between complete subordination to England and complete independence.

The American Revolution

Although overt hostilities eased during the early 1770s, many Americans grew increasingly resentful of British assertion of direct control over the Thirteen Colonies. The spark that eventually started the revolutionary flame was the Tea Act of 1773. The Tea Act gave the British East India Company a monopoly on the tea trade between England and the colonies. Many Americans regarded the Tea Act as a new tax, and they responded by boycotting British tea. In December 1773, colonists disguised as Native Americans sneaked aboard British ships moored in Boston Harbor and dumped their cargoes of tea into Massachusetts Bay.

By the time of the Boston Tea Party, leaders throughout the Thirteen Colonies had begun to call for joint action against the British. The First Continental Congress, which met in Philadelphia in September, 1774, consisted of representatives from all of the Thirteen Colonies except Georgia. The Congress did not seek complete independence from Britain; rather, it sought ways to effect a reconciliation with Great Britain while asserting colonial rights. By the time the Second Continental Congress met the following year, the famous battles of Lexington and Concord had been fought. The American Revolution was under way.

More than a year later, the Continental Congress adopted the Declaration of Independence. The Declaration asserted that the colonies "are, and of right ought to be FREE AND INDEPENDENT STATES . . . absolved from all allegiance to the British Crown." Thus, "all political connection between them and the State of Great Britain, is and ought to be totally dissolved." The Declaration of Independence was approved by Congress on July 4, 1776—a date recognized ever since as the day of the birth of the United States.

The revolutionary effort was supported by a substantial majority of America's population, although many Loyalists, or Tories, opposed it. Geographically, an important feature of the American Revolution was that "it was not primarily concerned with the methodical investment of fortified strongholds, or even with the outcome of great, set piece battles; it was a war of movement" on a continental scale (Harley et al., 1978, p. 19). Key land battles in North America occurred from Quebec to Georgia and from the Atlantic to the Mississippi. Because of the geographic scale and the importance of geographic intelligence, "[m]ilitary commanders throughout the Revolution held maps of the right sort and quality in high esteem as potentially useful, even indispensable aids to warfare" (Harley et al., 1978, p. 105). George Washington's cartographic training as a land surveyor helped in planning American strategy, though a desperate shortage of copies of maps for everyday use in campaigning was a hindrance to the American cause, especially early in the war.

By 1778, American military success coupled with effective diplomatic overtures by Benjamin Franklin and other envoys convinced the European powers that the colonists stood a good chance of winning the war (Bemis,

1957; Ferrell, 1969). France, which still resented the British victory in the Seven Years' War, recognized American independence and provided military and economic assistance to the new nation. French and Spanish support for the Americans threatened to draw the British into a major European war.

The threat of a larger war led many in Great Britain to advocate abandoning the military effort in America. Armed hostilities in North America culminated in 1781 with the British surrender to American and French forces at Yorktown, Virginia. Two years later, the Treaty of Paris was signed. Great Britain recognized the independence of her former colonies as the United States of America and acknowledged U.S. sovereignty over the Thirteen Colonies as well as the territory westward to the Mississippi River, northward to Canada, and southward to the Spanish territory of Florida (Figure 2-2).

American Democracy and the Constitution

As we have seen, American democratic traditions began to diverge from their English antecedents long before the Revolution began. The debate over the Stamp Act forced the colonists to distinguish "between what was legal and what was constitutional" (Hall, 1989, p. 57). That the Stamp Act, the Proclamation of 1763, and other objectionable actions of Parliament were within the scope of Parliament's authority under the English common law tradition could not be doubted. Yet Americans argued that "Parliament was not the embodiment of sovereign authority and that the fundamental principles of government had to be in writing if they were to have meaning" (Hall, 1989, p. 57). Thus, the principles of governance had to be separated from the products of its actions.

Under English common law, there was no written constitution. "The English constitution was not a written document, nor was it a fixed set of unchangeable rules. It was a general sense of the way things were done, and most people in England were willing to accept evolutionary changes in it" (Brinkley, 1993, p. 104). Yet Americans had witnessed changes in British policy that appeared to have been justified by no more than the whims and caprices of the king and Parliament. Hence the American philosophy of democracy emphasized the fundamental importance of a written constitution that specified and when necessary limited the authority of governmental institutions.

Once independence from Britain was achieved, this philosophy was put into practical effect through the drafting and ratification of the Constitution as a document superior to and separate from the laws passed by Congress and the state legislatures. Yet the process of drafting and ratifying the Constitution was laborious, fraught with opposition, and linked closely to sectional differences among the colonies (Libby, 1894; Wilson, 1908; Turner, 1932; Zagarri, 1987). During the Revolution, regional economic and political differ-

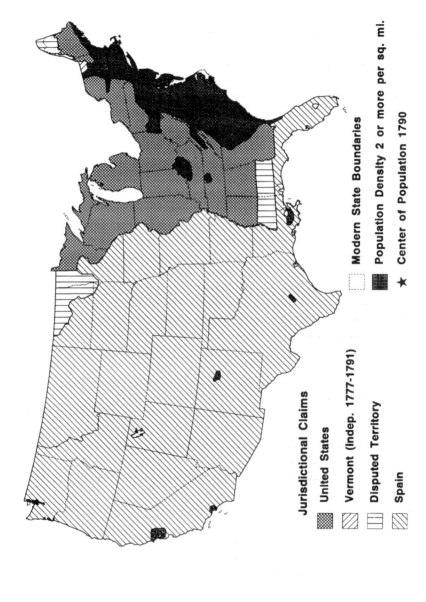

FIGURE 2-2. United States in 1790. Data from Gannett (1898), p. 11 and Plate 3; Marschner (1959), p. 29; U.S. Geological Survey (1987).

Jurisdictional Claims

United States

Vermont (Indep. 1777-1791)

Disputed Territory

Spain

Modern State Boundaries

Population Density 2 or more per sq. mi.

★ Center of Population 1790

ences among residents of the Thirteen Colonies were sublimated to the common goal of achieving independence from the British. Once the Treaty of Paris was signed, however, the colonists were faced with the task of resolving sectional disputes concerning the structure of the new American government. For more than a decade, leaders of the former Thirteen Colonies wrestled with this perplexing question. The end result of this debate was the Constitution—a document that established the basic principles of U.S. democracy and that remains in force today.

The Articles of Confederation

The first efforts to provide for a union of the Thirteen Colonies resulted in the Articles of Confederation, which were drafted in 1777 and went into effect on March 1, 1781. Under the Articles, the national government of the United States was weak and in fact subordinate to the governments of the states. Congress under the Articles was composed of delegates from each state. Each state had one vote, and disagreement within any state's delegation would be settled by majority vote of the delegation.

The Articles granted Congress the power to conduct foreign affairs, provide for defense, coin money, and establish a postal system. Yet any measure passed by Congress required the consent of at least nine of the thirteen states. Moreover, Congress could not collect taxes, control foreign commerce, or force the states to comply with its laws. Thus, the central government was dependent on the willingness of the individual states to carry out its mandates. Without the power to levy taxes, Congress was forced to rely on voluntary financial contributions from the states. Few of the states volunteered more than token contributions to support the national government's activities. Nor did the Articles establish federal executive or judicial branches of the government.

Despite the general failure of the Articles of Confederation, Congress under the Articles did deal with one question of fundamental importance: the issue of "western lands" outside the formal boundaries of the Thirteen Colonies. Prior to the Revolution, several of the colonies had (in violation of the Proclamation of 1763) claimed territory between the Appalachians and the Mississippi River. During the 1780s, however, these colonies ceded their western claims to the federal government. By 1786, Congress was in full possession of the "Old Northwest" between the Ohio and Mississippi Rivers.

In its efforts to administer the Old Northwest, Congress enacted two laws that remained fundamental to U.S. land policy long after the Constitution replaced the Articles. The Land Ordinance of 1785 established the township-and-range system of public land surveying (Box 2-1). This system of land surveying was later used throughout the United States. The Old Northwest, the Louisiana Purchase, and other nineteenth-century territorial acquisitions would eventually be surveyed in accordance with the township-and-range system.

The Northwest Ordinance, enacted in 1787, provided for a system of self-government in the "Northwest Territory." The Northwest Territory, which would later become the states of Ohio, Indiana, Illinois, Michigan, and Wisconsin, was to be divided eventually into three to five states. The ordinance provided for a three-step process by which the Old Northwest—and

---

Box 2-1. The Township-and-Range System of Land Surveys

Although the Articles of Confederation proved unsuccessful, one of the key actions of Congress under the Articles was the establishment of the U.S. system of land surveys. This system was used in surveying not only the lands acquired from the British after the American Revolution but also the lands acquired during the nineteenth century (see Chapter 3).

Many members of Congress realized that an orderly survey of newly acquired lands would be critical to the process of distribution and settlement. Orderly and precise survey procedures would prevent the haphazard division of land into irregular parcels. Thus the Land Ordinance of 1785 provided for the partitioning of territory into systematic, rectangular parcels. Settlers could then select and occupy and improve previously surveyed parcels of land (Brown, 1948; Marschner, 1959; Johnson, 1976; Thompson, 1987).

This land survey system required the identification of an initial point. The parallel of latitude passing through this initial point was termed the *base line*, and the meridian of longitude intersecting that parallel at the initial point was known as the *principal meridian* (Figure 2-B1-1). Once the initial point was determined, surveyors identified range lines along meridians of longitude at six-mile intervals east and west of the principal meridian. Township lines were surveyed along parallels of latitude at six-mile intervals north and south of the base line.

Township lines and range lines thus divided the territory being surveyed into tracts of approximately six-by-six miles. Each of these areas of approximately thirty-six square miles was termed a "township." Each township was then divided into sections of one square mile. Each section was then numbered according to its position within the township. Sections were often divided into halves, quarters, or even smaller units. In many areas, sections 16 and 36 were reserved for the construction of public schools, and the remaining sections were sold or given to settlers.

The township-and-range system thus made it possible to locate unfamiliar territory without ambiguity. Even today, legal descriptions of land titles refer to the township, range, and section number of the parcel in question. The township-and-range system has remained the basic principle of U.S. land survey since 1785. Yet its application has not always been accurate. Surveying errors, ambiguities in record keeping, corrections necessitated by the curvature of the earth, unusual physical features on the landscape, and many other factors have distorted the actual use of the township-and-range system.

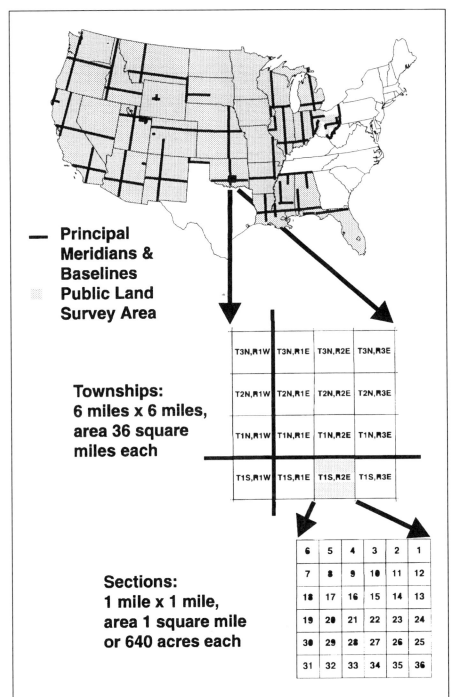

Principal Meridians & Baselines

Public Land Survey Area

Townships:
6 miles x 6 miles, area 36 square miles each

Sections:
1 mile x 1 mile, area 1 square mile or 640 acres each

FIGURE 2-B1-1. U.S. Public Land Survey System. Data from Thompson (1987), pp. 82–83; Marschner (1959), p. 16.

eventually other territorial acquisitions—would proceed from territory to statehood (Meinig, 1993, p. 432). First, Congress would organize a territorial government headed by an appointed governor. Once the population of free adult males reached 5,000, territorial residents were granted the right to elect a territorial legislature and a nonvoting delegate to Congress. When the free population of the territory reached 60,000, the territory would be eligible for admission to the Confederation on an equal basis with established members. With minor modifications, the Northwest Ordinance provided the blueprint for the orderly progression of the western three-quarters of the United States to statehood.

Despite the success of the Articles in dealing with the controversial question of western lands, their inherent weaknesses became more and more evident as the 1780s wore on. Between 1781 and 1786, Congress raised only half a million dollars a year, barely enough to cover the day-to-day expenses of government and not nearly enough to pay back war loans and foreign debts (Morison et al., 1980, p. 239). The requirement that the individual states approve treaties with foreign powers hindered the efforts of American diplomats abroad.

Recognizing that these and other problems had become acute, Congress on February 21, 1787, formally invited each of the states to send delegates to a convention in Philadelphia in May to discuss possible revisions to the Articles. Fifty-five delegates, representing twelve of the thirteen colonies, participated in the meeting. As deliberations began, some of the delegates suggested that the Articles should be abandoned entirely. In their place, the delegates drafted an entirely new document: the U.S. Constitution. The Constitution, as amended over the years, remains the cornerstone of U.S. democracy.

The Legislative Branch under the Constitution

The Constitution provides for three branches of government: legislative, executive, and judicial. Legislative power is vested in Congress, which consists of two houses, the Senate and the House of Representatives. The Senate is composed of two senators from each state, elected for six-year terms. The House of Representatives consists of representatives elected from districts within each state, with the number of representatives apportioned among the states on the basis of population. Each representative is elected for a two-year term. A bill proposed in either house of Congress becomes law when passed by majority votes in the Senate and the House and signed into law by the president.

The organization of Congress under the Constitution was a compromise between small-state and large-state interests. At the outset of the constitutional convention, Governor Edmund Randolph of Virginia proposed the establishment of a congress of two houses, with members of the lower house to be elected directly by the people and members of the upper house to be elected by the lower house. Seats in the lower house would be apportioned to the states on the basis of population. This "Virginia Plan" was opposed by delegates from the smaller states, who were concerned that political power would become concentrated in the larger states. In response, delegates from New Jersey proposed an alternative, with a single-house legislature whose seats would be apportioned among the states equally.

For more than a month, the delegates debated the merits of the two plans. Eventually, they agreed upon what is known to history as the Great Compromise (or the Connecticut Compromise after its author, delegate Roger Sherman of Connecticut). Sherman recognized that the smaller states preferred that each state have an equal voice in the national government, while the larger ones wanted representation on the basis of population. Representatives of small states, which tended to contain compact and homogeneous populations, tended to support statewide rather than strictly territorial representation within their states (Zagarri, 1987, p. 5). Residents of larger states tended to support "electing their congressmen and presidential electors from districts whose boundaries were drawn according to population" (Zagarri, 1987, p. 6).

Under the Great Compromise, the Constitution provided for a bicameral legislature. Members of the lower house, the House of Representatives, were to be elected by the people and seats were to be apportioned among the states on the basis of population. Senators, on the other hand, were to be selected by the legislatures of the respective states. Two seats in the Senate were afforded each state, regardless of size.

While representatives were elected for two-year terms, senators were to be chosen for terms of six years. The six-year term of office for members of the Senate was "meant to be a brake on hasty action" (Morison et al., 1980, p. 253). Thus, the framers of the Constitution also intended to protect the interests of the propertied class against the public. Not until after the Seventeenth Amendment was ratified in 1913 were senators elected directly by the people.

The Constitution imposes only three qualifications for membership in Congress. Members of the House must be at least 25 years of age and must have been citizens of the United States for at least seven years, and members of the Senate must be at least 30 years old and must have been citizens of the United States for at least nine years. Members of both houses are required to reside in the states they represent. Members of the House are not required to live in the specific districts that they represent, but they usually do so.

Should a vacancy occur in the House through death, retirement, or resignation, the governor of the state calls a special election to fill out the balance of the term. Some states also require special elections to fill vacant seats in the

Senate, whereas in others the state's governor is empowered to fill the vacancy through appointment.

In recent years, a large majority of congressional elections have been won by incumbents seeking reelection. During the 1980s, for example, over 94 percent of House incumbents seeking reelection were successful. Incumbents are often successful in seeking reelection for several reasons: Incumbency guarantees publicity, which is reinforced by mailings, radio and television appearances, and press releases. Incumbents can also take advantage of their positions to ensure that federal dollars flow into their districts. Moreover, incumbent members of Congress are often able to build up large campaign treasuries. Typically, an incumbent will outspend his or her challenger by a considerable margin.

So overwhelming are the advantages of incumbency that many potential challengers are discouraged from committing themselves to campaigns that will probably prove futile. Of course, the advantages of incumbency are reinforced by the absence of strong opposition. As a result, many Americans are concerned that Congress has become less responsive to the public. In reaction to this belief, eighteen states have imposed term limits on members of Congress and other elected officials (Box 2-2).

The Executive Branch

The executive authority of the United States is vested in a president, who along with the vice president is elected for a four-year term. The president appoints the chief executive officers of each of the governmental departments, or the cabinet, subject to majority confirmation by the Senate. Formally, the president is elected by the Electoral College. Seats in the Electoral College are apportioned among the states; each gets one seat for each member of Congress. For example, Alabama, with two senators and seven representatives, has nine seats in the Electoral College.

The electoral system as originally outlined in the Constitution afforded each member of the Electoral College the right to vote for two individuals. The candidate receiving a majority of electoral votes would be elected president, with the vice presidency going to the runner-up. As we shall see in Chapter 3, difficulties with this system soon became apparent, and it was revised less than two decades after the Constitution was ratified.

Article II of the Constitution enumerates the powers granted to the president. These powers are surprisingly few, given the enormous power and prestige of the office today. The article states that the president "shall take Care that the Laws be faithfully executed." The president serves as Commander in Chief of the armed forces; is empowered, with the advice and consent of the Senate, to make treaties; and is empowered to appoint ambassadors, judges, diplomats, and heads of executive agencies. The president is required to

---

Box 2-2. *Term Limits*

The Twenty-second Amendment to the Constitution, adopted in 1951, limits the president of the United States to two, four-year terms. Yet the Constitution does not limit terms of members of Congress or other legislative officials. We have seen that the Constitution imposes only three qualifications—age, citizenship, and state of residence—on members of Congress.

In recent years, however, several states have adopted laws restricting the length of service of their congressional delegations (Figure 2-B2-1). Term limits for state legislatures were adopted by the voters of California, Colorado, and Oklahoma in 1990. Two years later, twelve additional states adopted term-limit laws. The specific content of term-limit laws varies considerably from one state to another, but most limit senators to two consecutive six-year terms and representatives to six to twelve years of consecutive service (DeCarli, 1993). By 1993, 186 of the 435 representatives were subject to term limits, as were nearly a third of U.S. senators.

Public opinion polls taken throughout the early 1990s revealed strong support for term limits (Fett and Ponder, 1993). Term-limit amendment initiatives passed easily in most of the states in which they appeared on the ballot. Why have term-limit initiatives proven so popular in recent years? What are the arguments for and against term limits? What are the long-run implications of the term-limit movement for the legislative branch of our government?

In recent years, turnover rates in Congress have declined considerably (Will, 1992). Since the 1930s, in most elections less than 20 percent of congressional seats have changed hands. Evidence of increasingly lengthy congressional careers is used to buttress arguments that Congress is increasingly out of touch with the public. Thus, proponents of term limits argue that Congress is composed of career politicians who are overly influenced by special interests. Some have called for a return to the tradition of the citizen legislator, whose short but productive career as a representative is followed by a return to private life. Will the presence of term limits mean a return to the citizen as legislator? Or will it mean that career politicians will rotate offices on a more frequent basis?

On the other hand, opponents of term limits point out that legislative clout increases with seniority. States that limit terms of legislative service may have less influence than those states that have not enacted similar initiatives. Fett and Ponder (1993, p. 215) have predicted bluntly that "states with term limits will effectively diminish their voice in Congress."

Other opponents have argued that the qualifications clauses in the Constitution preclude the states from imposing additional restrictions, such as limiting years of service. Indeed, the Nevada Supreme Court refused to allow a term-limit initiative to appear on that state's ballot in 1992 because the court concluded that the state's voters had no right to constrain congressional membership further (*Stumpf v. Lau*, 839 P.2d. 120 [Nevada, 1992]). Yet some legal analysts have concluded that "while Congress is prohibited from adding to the qualifications required for Congressional membership, [the Constitution] does not indicate that the people of the states similarly lack this power" (DeCarli,

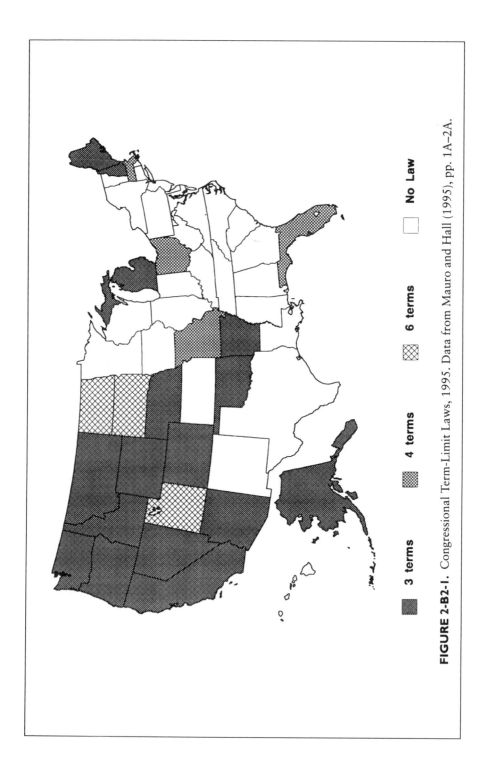

FIGURE 2-B2-I. Congressional Term-Limit Laws, 1995. Data from Mauro and Hall (1995), pp. 1A–2A.

3 terms 　 4 terms 　 6 terms 　 No Law

1993, p. 867). Thus, the distinction between congressional limitations on its membership and limitations enacted by the states may be a corollary to the Tenth Amendment. Because the Constitution makes no mention of a *state's* right to further limit the length of a legislator's service, the states and the people retain this right.

In May 1995, the U.S. Supreme Court ruled by a vote of 5 to 4 that term-limit laws, as applied to Congress, were unconstitutional. The majority advanced the argument that term-limit laws created an unconstitutional qualification for membership in Congress; the minority, on the other hand, stated that the term-limit laws should be considered constitutional because nothing in the Constitution prohibits the states from imposing additional qualifications on congressional representation. Because the majority opinion overturned term-limit laws for members of Congress, supporters of term limits realized that they would be required to enact an amendment to the Constitution permitting states to impose term limitations. Shortly after the Court's decision was announced, supporters of term limits introduced four proposed constitutional amendments, but none of these proposals received the two-thirds majority in the House of Representatives needed to progress. Nevertheless, continued public outcry may increase the pressure on Congress and the states to further limit the length of congressional and legislative service.

provide information on the state of the union to Congress on a periodic basis and has the right to convene special sessions of Congress when this is deemed necessary. Presidential approval is required in order to enact legislation, although the president's veto may be overridden by a two-thirds majority of each house of Congress.

The president serves several important functions simultaneously. The president is the "chief legislator," responsible for placing a legislative agenda before Congress. The president's constitutional mandate to serve as Commander in Chief and to make treaties, subject to the advice and consent of the Senate, also gives the president a dominant role in foreign policy. The president is also head of state and is normally recognized as the leader of his or her political party.

The Cabinet and the Federal Bureaucracy

In upholding the Constitution's mandate to "faithfully execute the laws" of the United States, the president is assisted by a vast, complex federal bureaucracy whose power and influence have grown enormously during the twentieth century. Executive administration is undertaken by federal executive departments and a large variety of other federal agencies. Heads of federal executive agencies are appointed by the president, subject to majority approval of the Senate. Each serves at the pleasure of the president. Collectively, the heads of the federal executive agencies form the president's cabinet (Box 2-3).

In 1789, the First Congress authorized George Washington to appoint four cabinet officers: secretary of state, secretary of the treasury, secretary of war, and attorney general. The U.S. Post Office was created in 1792, and the Department of the Navy six years later. The Department of the Interior was created in 1849, and the Departments of Agriculture, Commerce, and Labor were founded between 1881 and 1910. In contrast to earlier cabinet-level departments, these agencies were founded in order to regulate and to provide service to these important sectors of the economy.

Since World War II, the size of the cabinet has increased significantly. In 1947, the Department of War and the Department of the Navy were merged into the Department of Defense. The Department of Health, Education, and

---

Box 2-3. *Where Do Cabinet Officers Come From?*

Where do cabinet officers come from? Over the years, the selection of cabinet members has been influenced by both political and geographic considerations.

Many cabinet posts have gone to persons who played key roles in the president's election. Thus, many have come from states that had been important battlegrounds in previous elections. Although some presidents have reached across party lines to select cabinet officers, the large majority of cabinet officers are members of the president's political party. Hence, heavily Democratic states or regions are unlikely to contribute many cabinet members to Republican administrations, and vice versa.

Despite these political considerations, various cabinet positions have come to be associated with particular sections of the United States (Figure 2-B3-1). For example, most secretaries of state and secretaries of the treasury have come from the Northeastern industrial core. Indeed, nearly half of the twenty-five twentieth-century secretaries of state have come from the state of New York alone. Thus, many presidents have considered that experience in the legal, financial, and diplomatic communities of the Northeast is an important qualification for these positions.

The Department of Agriculture, on the other hand, is often headed by a secretary from an agricultural state or region. Recent secretaries of agriculture, for example, have come from Mississippi, Nebraska, Indiana, Illinois, and Minnesota. The Department of the Interior has jurisdiction over federal land, and federal land ownership is concentrated in the Western states; thus, the secretary of the interior usually comes from a Western state. Over the past three decades, secretaries of the interior have come from Arizona, New Mexico, Wyoming, Idaho, and Alaska.

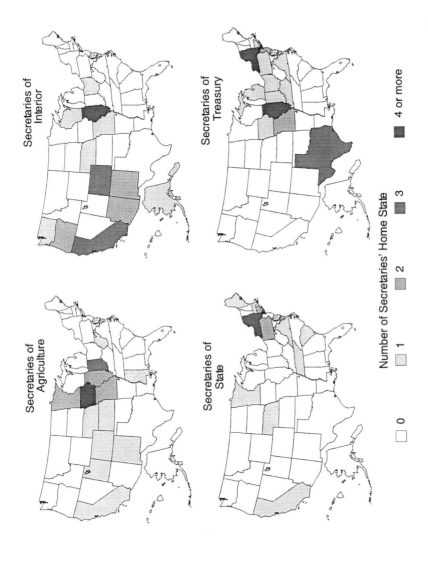

FIGURE 2-B3-1. Home States of Secretaries of Agriculture, Interior, State, and Treasury, 1900–1994. Data from Famighetti (1994), pp. 98–102.

Secretaries of
Agriculture

Secretaries of
Interior

Secretaries of
State

Secretaries of
Treasury

Number of Secretaries' Home State

☐ 0   ▨ 1   ▨ 2   ▨ 3   ■ 4 or more

Welfare was established in 1953, and its responsibilities were later split between the Department of Health and Human Services and the Department of Education. Since the 1960s, the Departments of Housing and Urban Development, Transportation, Energy, and Veterans' Affairs have been created and afforded cabinet status, while the Post Office was reorganized as the U.S. Postal Service and downgraded from cabinet rank. Other executive officers, including the president's chief of staff and the budget director, have been given cabinet status by many recent presidents.

In addition to the cabinet departments, the federal bureaucracy includes a large number of independent agencies and regulatory commissions. These agencies, although headed by presidential appointees, operate outside the jurisdiction of the federal departments. Some of the most powerful and influential agencies within the federal bureaucracy, including the Central Intelligence Agency, the Environmental Protection Agency, and the National Aeronautics and Space Administration, are independent agencies.

Independent regulatory commissions have been established to regulate important sectors of the economy. Examples include the Federal Trade Commission, the National Labor Relations Board, the Civil Rights Commission, and the Interstate Commerce Commission. Each regulatory agency is governed by a commission consisting of presidential appointees. In contrast to cabinet officers, commission members serve for fixed terms and may not be fired by the president.

The Judiciary

According to the Constitution, the primary judicial power in the United States is the U.S. Supreme Court. The Supreme Court consists of a Chief Justice and eight Associate Justices. In addition, Article III of the Constitution empowers Congress to establish "inferior" federal courts. There are two levels of "inferior" federal courts: circuit courts of appeals and federal district courts (Figure 2-3). All federal judges, including members of the Supreme Court, are appointed for life terms by the president, subject to majority confirmation by the Senate.

The lowest level of the federal judiciary consists of federal district courts. Each has jurisdiction over all or part of a particular state. The eighty-nine federal district courts in the nation are staffed by about six hundred federal district judges. District court judges hear cases involving interpretations of federal laws. By the early 1990s, U.S. district courts were hearing an average of 200,000 cases per year (Bibby, 1992).

Between the federal district courts and the Supreme Court are the circuit courts of appeals. Appellate court judges hear cases appealed from federal district courts. The fifty states are divided into eleven circuits. An additional

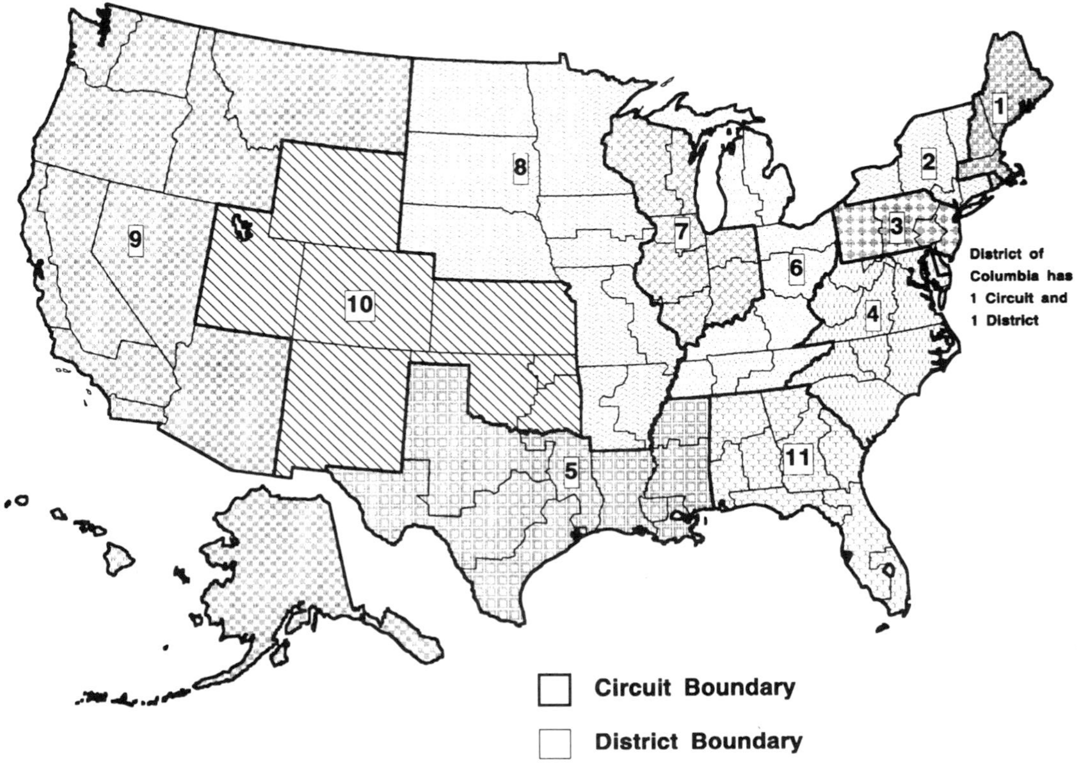

FIGURE 2-3. Federal Judicial Circuits and Districts, 1992. Data from U.S. Geological Survey (1970), p. 278; Finn and Jellison (1993).

circuit is based in Washington, DC. The primary function of the Circuit Court of the District of Columbia is to hear cases that directly affect the federal government and its operations. The twelve courts of appeals are served by 168 judges.

Supreme Court justices and the judges of the circuit courts of appeals and federal district courts are appointed by the president for life terms, subject to majority confirmation by the Senate. Because judicial decisions can and often do have profound effects on U.S. life, the selection and confirmation of Supreme Court justices and lower court judges has become highly politicized in recent years. Since the late 1960s, four nominees to the Supreme Court have been rejected by the Senate.

Checks and Balances

The framers of the Constitution were concerned that none of the three major branches of the government exercise undue authority over the others. In order to forestall such a possibility, the framers designed a complicated system of checks and balances, carefully dividing authority among the executive, legislative, and judicial branches. For example, legislation enacted by Congress must be signed into law by the president, but Congress has the right to override a presidential veto. The Supreme Court has the right to determine the constitutionality of legislation and to declare null and void any piece of legislation it deems in conflict with the Constitution. The Senate must approve treaties and presidential appointments, and only Congress has the right to declare war on another country. Impeachment of the president, judges, and federal executive officers is conducted by Congress, with an impeachment trial to be held by the Senate and presided over by the Chief Justice.

Of particular concern to many of the delegates to the constitutional convention was the issue of centralizing federal power. Some delegates expressed concern that the Constitution, once adopted, would require the states to cede their authority to a distant federal government that would usurp the rights of the individual states. Thus, the delegates took care to ensure that the Constitution expressly limits the power of the federal government. The relationship between federal and state authority was further clarified by the Tenth Amendment, which provides that "the powers not delegated to the United States by the Constitution, nor prohibited by it to the States, are reserved to the States respectively, or to the people."

The framers of the Constitution looked ahead to the future in their deliberations by providing a procedure to amend the Constitution and to provide for the admission of new states into the Union. To become part of the Constitution, an amendment must be ratified by a two-thirds majority in each house of Congress and then by three-quarters of the state legislatures. To date, twenty-seven amendments have been added to the Constitution.

The constitutional convention also settled the issue of unassigned lands obtained as a result of the Treaty of Paris. In general, the Constitution followed the lead of the Articles of Confederation, reaffirming the right of new territories to become states on an equal basis with the existing states and confirming the right that had been granted to Congress under the Articles of Confederation to control and dispose of unassigned lands. The federal government was given the right to create new territories and to provide for their eventual admission to the Union as states. As Sherman stated to the Convention, "[W]e are providing for our posterity, for our children and grandchildren, who will be as likely to be citizens of the new Western states as of the old states" (Peters, 1987).

Ratification of the Constitution

Article VII of the Constitution states that the Constitution would go into effect once ratified by nine of the Thirteen Colonies. For a time, it was doubtful whether the Constitution would in fact be ratified at all. More than a year elapsed from the time that the constitutional convention adjourned until the Constitution was ratified by the requisite nine states.

In general, support for the Constitution was strongest in the more developed and commercially oriented regions of the fledgling republic, particularly in the Middle Atlantic colonies and in urban areas. Opposition was concentrated inland, in rural areas, and in parts of New York, New England, and the South. Much of the opposition centered on the issue of federal authority. Representatives of the poorer and less developed states feared that a stronger central government would usurp power and increase imbalances in wealth and development, and on these grounds many opposed the new document.

Leaders of the colonies coalesced into two factions: the "Federalists," who supported ratification, and the "Anti-Federalists," who opposed it (Figure 2-4). Federalists commanded the support of large majorities in several states. On December 7, 1787, Delaware became the first state to ratify the Constitution. The First State was followed by Pennsylvania five days later, and by New Jersey, Georgia, Connecticut, Massachusetts, and Maryland in early 1788.

The debate over ratification then shifted to Virginia and New York. These were the two largest and most populous colonies, and it was clear that the success of the Constitution hinged on their ratification. Anti-Federalist sentiment was strong in both states, but both ratified the Constitution by narrow margins in mid-1788. New Hampshire and South Carolina also ratified

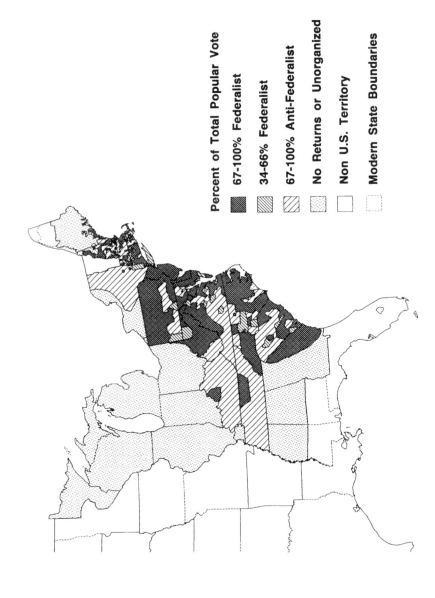

FIGURE 2-4. Popular Vote on Ratification of the United States Constitution, 1787–1788. Redrawn from Libby (1894).

the Constitution before it went into effect in 1789. Not until 1791 did North Carolina and Rhode Island ratify the Constitution.

The first ten amendments to the Constitution, the Bill of Rights, were drafted and submitted in response to opposition to ratification. In particular, advocates of retaining state power supported the Tenth Amendment, which states that all powers not specifically given to the federal government in the Constitution are reserved to the states or to the people. The Tenth Amendment ensures that the government of the United States is to be construed as a covenant among the states, and it restricts federal authority to those spheres of activity specifically identified in the Constitution. The Bill of Rights was enacted by the First Congress on September 25, 1789. After approval by the states, it took effect in 1791.

Choosing the Nation's Capital

Early in 1789, George Washington was unanimously elected by the first Electoral College as the first president of the United States. Shortly afterward, Washington began a journey from his estate in Mount Vernon, Virginia, to New York City. Along the way, numerous celebrations and festivities were held in honor of the nation's first president. Upon arriving in New York, Washington took the oath of office as president in a ceremony at Federal Hall on April 30, 1789.

Although New York had been designated as the nation's temporary capital, few expected that the city would remain the new country's capital indefinitely. The question of determining the permanent site for the federal government had been an important issue of public debate since the end of the Revolution. Many Americans regarded the selection of the capital as an extremely important decision. As we have already seen, physical access to the seat of representative government was regarded by eighteenth-century Americans as an important corollary of particular representation. Moreover, Americans had an economic interest in the location of their capital city. Property values near the capital site would rise, employment opportunities would abound, transportation would improve, and farmers would profit from an increased number of consumers for their produce (Bowling, 1991, p. 3).

The debate over locating the nation's capital was also influenced by sectional considerations (Bickford and Bowling, 1989). Northerners, Southerners, and Westerners in and outside of Congress argued for locating the capital city in their respective sections. Yet even the most ardent advocates of particular sections recognized that locating the nation's capital involved more than regional interests. "Properly located, a capital would cement the North, South and West, thus insuring the survival of the Union and the prestige and respect

Congress so desperately sought to establish for itself at home and abroad" (Bowling, 1991, p. 4).

At the same time, many Americans were uneasy about the prospect that their capital would be a major commercial center. The republican philosophy expressed in the Declaration of Independence and in the Constitution regarded the centralization of political and economic power as dangerous. European capitals such as London and Paris and their residents were regarded by Americans as excessively materialistic, slothful, dissipated, corrupt, and lazy. In contrast, the U.S. capital "would reflect such American ideals as liberty, union and republican empire" (Bowling, 1991, p. 4).

The first session of the First Congress convened in New York on March 4, 1789, eight weeks before Washington's arrival from Mount Vernon. The Pennsylvania delegation in the House of Representatives immediately proposed to adjourn to Philadelphia. The Virginia delegation, led by James Madison, managed to persuade Congress to postpone debate over the capital question until the end of the session, so that the Congress could tackle other fundamental issues, including the organization of the executive and judicial branches of the government and the Bill of Rights. The Pennsylvanians reluctantly agreed to postpone the debate (Bowling, 1991, p. 105).

On August 27, Representative Thomas Scott of Pennsylvania introduced a resolution to establish a permanent seat of government. Scott's bill proposed that the capital site be "as near the center of wealth, population, and extent of territory" as possible (Bowling, 1991, p. 137). Although this information was not available to Congress at the time, the actual population center of the United States in 1790 was located in Maryland, twenty-three miles east of Baltimore (Figure 2-2).

For nearly a month, members of the House debated the merits of various sites along the Delaware, Susquehanna, and Potomac Rivers. Although the Potomac was the closest of the three rivers to the centers of territory and population of the United States at the time, representatives from New England and the Middle Atlantic states preferred a site along the Susquehanna. Representative Benjamin Goodhue of Massachusetts proposed that Congress remain in New York "until the completion of suitable buildings at a permanent seat on the east bank of the Susquehanna River in Pennsylvania" (Bowling, 1991, p. 139).

On September 22, Goodhue's motion was adopted by a vote of 31 to 17. Three days later, the Senate passed a similar but slightly different measure. Because the two bills were slightly different, the House was required to reconsider the issue to resolve the differences between them. James Madison, who supported a site along the Potomac, pointed out that once Congress assumed jurisdiction over the capital territory, that territory would be without benefit of law. He then moved to amend the Senate bill to provide that the laws of Pennsylvania would remain in effect until the new capital was completed. The Senate then voted to table the issue until the following year.

By the time the debate resumed in 1790, another important issue had arisen. Secretary of the Treasury Alexander Hamilton called for the federal government to assume the Revolutionary War debts of the states. Hamilton's proposal was generally supported in the North but opposed in the South. Many Southerners regarded such an assumption of debt as "an unconstitutional seizure of state authority which might lead to a consolidation of the states in a unitary or national government" (Bowling, 1991, p. 169). The Northern states had, for the most part, contracted larger debts than had the Southern states.

On June 20, 1790, Hamilton dined with Madison and Thomas Jefferson. The three discussed the issues of assumption and capital relocation. Madison and Jefferson agreed to provide enough Southern votes for assumption in return for Northern support for a capital on the Potomac. The Compromise of 1790 was soon ironed out. A bill was introduced to locate the capital in Philadelphia for ten years; it would then be moved to a site on the Potomac upstream from the mouth of the Anacostia River. Both houses passed the bill by narrow margins, 14 to 12 in the Senate and 32 to 29 in the House of Representatives. President Washington, who strongly supported a Potomac site, signed the Seat of Government Act into law shortly thereafter.

For the remainder of his life, Washington devoted a great deal of attention to siting and constructing the new capital city that would eventually bear his name. On January 24, 1791, Washington issued a proclamation announcing the location of the capital district. Contrary to the Seat of Government Act, Washington's site was located four miles downstream from the mouth of the Anacostia. Thus, Washington's proposal required passage of a supplemental act to include land south of the Anacostia, in Maryland, along with Alexandria on the Virginia side of the Potomac. Washington's critics charged the president with self-interest, because his relatives owned extensive amounts of property in the area. His supporters pointed out that the city's location along the fall line would be most advantageous for industrial and commercial development as well as for political activity. Washington's prestige helped the supplemental act pass both houses of Congress by a comfortable majority.

Conclusion

The colonial era was the formative period of U.S. politics. The political institutions that have underlain U.S. democracy to the present day owe their origins to the period of British colonialism in North America.

During the same period, the sectional divisions and political cultures of the United States also came into being. Once the United States became an independent country, these divisions would intensify. The upcoming nineteenth century would be characterized by ongoing tension between the forces of U.S. nationalism on the one hand and the competing interests of the country's various sections on the other.

Chapter 3

THE UNITED STATES IN THE NINETEENTH CENTURY

When George Washington took the oath of office as the first president of the United States in 1789, the newly independent republic consisted of thirteen former British colonies containing about three million people. In barely a hundred years, the United States became a major world power. By the end of the nineteenth century, it stretched across North America and contained over 75 million residents.

The nineteenth century was a dramatic period in the development of the political geography of the United States. Political parties were formed and battled for supremacy in the White House and Congress, while sectional tensions continued to mount until a bloody civil war was fought. By the end of the century, the American frontier had closed and the process of transition from an agrarian to an urbanized, industrial society was under way. The transitions characteristic of nineteenth-century U.S. politics continue to have profound implications for U.S. politics even today.

Westward Expansion of the United States

During the first half of the nineteenth century, the United States acquired the territory that today forms the forty-eight contiguous states (Figure 3-1). The territories acquired by the United States in the half century between 1803 and 1853 would be admitted as states by 1912 under the provisions that had been established during the eighteenth century.

The Louisiana Purchase

As we saw in Chapter 2, Americans had begun to move westward across the Appalachians in large numbers even before the Revolution. After the Revo-

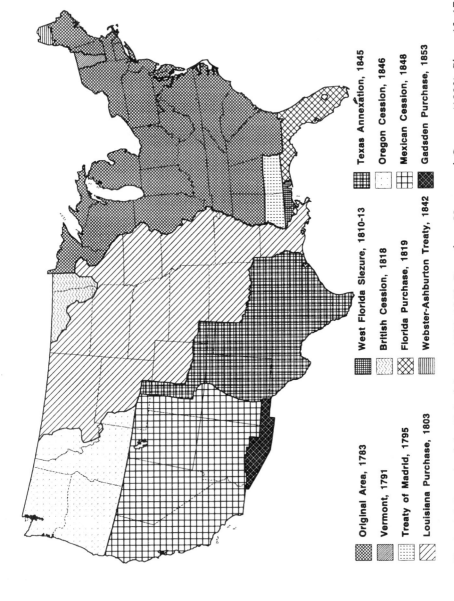

FIGURE 3-1. Territorial Growth of the United States, 1783–1853. Data from Hewes and Gannett (1883), Plates 12–17; Faulkner and Kepner (1944), p. 227; U.S. Geological Survey (1987).

Legend:

Original Area, 1783

Vermont, 1791

Treaty of Madrid, 1795

Louisiana Purchase, 1803

West Florida Siezure, 1810-13

British Cession, 1818

Florida Purchase, 1819

Webster-Ashburton Treaty, 1842

Texas Annexation, 1845

Oregon Cession, 1846

Mexican Cession, 1848

Gadsden Purchase, 1853

lution ended, more and more Americans settled in the western territories. Vermont, Kentucky, and Tennessee were admitted to the Union in the 1790s, and Ohio, Indiana, Illinois, Alabama, and Mississippi were admitted before 1820.

The rapidly growing trans-Appalachian states depended on the Mississippi River and its tributaries in order to trade with the Eastern states and foreign countries. Yet New Orleans, the principal port at the mouth of the Mississippi, remained under foreign control. After the Seven Years' War, Spain obtained New Orleans and the Louisiana Territory between the west bank of the Mississippi and the Rocky Mountains. Trade between the American interior and other parts of the world was thus controlled by Spanish and, later, French officials in New Orleans.

In 1801, Thomas Jefferson was inaugurated as the third president of the United States. After taking office, Jefferson began to express concern about the dangers associated with continued European control of New Orleans. He believed that "as long as a foreign country controlled the mouth of the Mississippi, the United States was in danger of being drawn into every European war" (Morison et al., 1980, p. 339).

Early in 1803, Jefferson sent James Monroe and Robert Livingston to Paris with instructions to negotiate the purchase of New Orleans from the French government. Monroe and Livingston offered Napoleon Bonaparte six million dollars for the city. After a few weeks of negotiation, Napoleon's foreign minister, Charles-Maurice de Talleyrand, responded with an astounding counteroffer: France would sell not only the city of New Orleans but the entire Louisiana Territory to the United States for fifteen million dollars. Monroe and Livingston quickly concluded negotiations before Napoleon changed his mind. The signing of a treaty transferring Louisiana from French to U.S. sovereignty was announced publicly on July 4, 1803—the twenty-seventh anniversary of the Declaration of Independence.

The announcement of the treaty created a constitutional crisis. The Constitution was silent about the acquisition of foreign territory. Could the executive branch of the government expand "what was basically a compact among states" (Meinig, 1993, p. 12)? Jefferson believed that a constitutional amendment would be needed in order to justify the Louisiana Purchase. His advisers, still fearful that Napoleon would back out of the agreement, persuaded Jefferson that the Constitution's treaty-making powers would ensure the constitutionality of the agreement. Eventually, Jefferson decided that the practical benefits of the purchase would outweigh any legalistic concerns. He maintained that "the nation's best interests demanded the extension of the empire for liberty" and that "the people approved of such expansionism and that therefore Louisiana's acquisition would strengthen his party and administration" (DeConde, 1976, p. 185).

Shortly after the Eighth Congress convened on October 17, 1803, Jefferson submitted the treaty to the Senate for approval. Opposition was expressed by some New Englanders, who "feared most that the incorporation of Louisiana would alter the original balance between the states by permitting the South and West to dominate the Union" (DeConde, 1976, p. 191). Other opponents of territorial expansion argued that Louisiana should be reserved for Native Americans. Despite such opposition, the Senate ratified the Louisiana treaty by a vote of 24 to 7.

The overall level of support for the Louisiana Purchase was substantial, but there were notable regional variations in approval, as revealed by the final Senate roll-call vote on October 26, 1803, on a formal "bill to enable the President of the United States to take possession of the territories ceded by France to the United States" (*Proceedings and Debates of the Senate of the United States, Eighth Congress, First Session,* October 26, 1803, p. 26). In 1803, Federalists represented several Northeastern states in the U.S. Senate, while Democratic-Republicans usually represented Southern or Western states (Martis, 1989) (Figure 3-2). The Senate vote on the enabling act was 26 in favor, 6 opposed, and 2 not voting. All 23 Democratic-Republican senators who cast ballots approved President Jefferson's request to take possession of the Louisiana Territory, but Federalists split 3 for and 6 against. All of the opposition votes were case by Federalists from New England states (Figure 3-3). Several New England Federalists also opposed the appropriations bill, which originated in the House of Representatives, to provide $11.25 million in funds for the Louisiana Purchase, though the measure was passed by a comfortable margin in each chamber. On December 20, Louisiana was formally transferred from France to the United States.

Louisiana Joins the Union

The acquisition of the Louisiana Territory created a new set of controversies. One important question involved the citizenship rights of the residents of New Orleans. Prior to the Louisiana Purchase, the territories occupied by the United States had been either uninhabited or populated only by Native Americans, who were not regarded by Americans of European ancestry as citizens. By purchasing Louisiana, the United States for the first time expanded into territory already occupied by "civilized" people of European ancestry. New Orleans alone contained thousands of residents of French and Spanish descent. Were these people, who were French citizens prior to the Louisiana Purchase, now to be regarded as U.S. citizens, with the same rights and privileges as other U.S. citizens?

Moreover, the transfer of Louisiana from France to the United States had been undertaken without the consent of its residents. The issue of consent was troubling to members of Congress, who still remembered the importance of the issue of "no taxation without representation" during the Revolution. A further problem involved the integration of Louisiana's laws with the laws of the United States. Louisiana law was based on French and Spanish law, which in turn were derived from the Roman rather than the Anglo-American legal

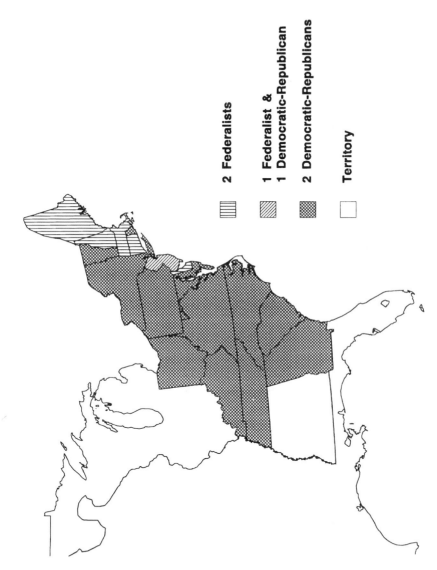

FIGURE 3-2. U.S. Senate Party Affiliation, 1803. Data from Martis (1989), p. 77.

2 Federalists

1 Federalist &
1 Democratic-Republican

2 Democratic-Republicans

Territory

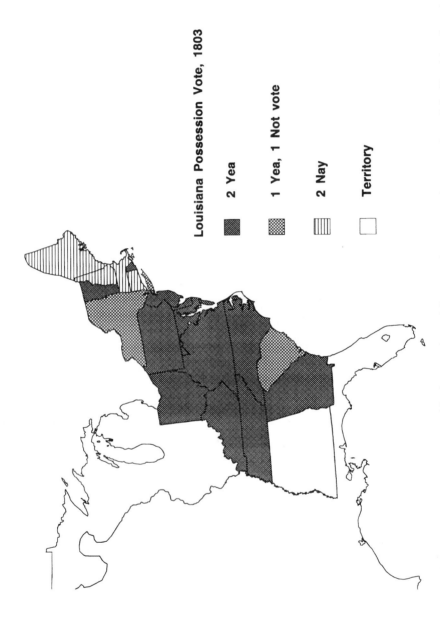

Louisiana Possession Vote, 1803

⬛ 2 Yea

▨ 1 Yea, 1 Not vote

▥ 2 Nay

☐ Territory

FIGURE 3-3. U.S. Senate Vote on "An act to enable the President of the United States to take possession of the [Louisiana] territories ceded by France," October 26, 1803. Data from *Proceedings and Debates of the Senate of the United States, Eighth Congress, First Session* (1852), p. 26.

Box 3-1. *The Anglo-American Legal System*

The transplantation of English legal institutes to a new continent resulted in the development of Anglo-American law. Anglo-American law is still the basis of the U.S. legal system today, and it is recognized as one of the great legal traditions of the modern world (Easterly, 1977).

The two major legal traditions in Western civilization are Anglo-American law and Roman law. Anglo-American law underlies the legal systems of the United States as well as of the United Kingdom, Canada, and the British Commonwealth; Roman law forms the basis of law in France, Spain, Italy, and their former colonies. In the United States today, Roman law influences the laws of several states that were once French or Spanish possessions. For example, the law of Louisiana is based on French law, and the legal codes of Texas, California, and other southwestern states are influenced by the Spanish legal tradition, including the Spanish Law of the Indies. Of course, these local legal traditions are sublimated by the U.S. legal tradition, which is based squarely on English law.

Several characteristics distinguish Anglo-American from Roman law. Under Anglo-American law traditions, persons accused of crimes are presumed innocent until proven guilty. The state is responsible for proving guilt beyond a reasonable doubt if the accused is to be convicted. In criminal trials, the role of the judge is that of an impartial arbiter between the prosecution and the defense. Judges play no role in attempting to establish the guilt of the accused. Under Roman law traditions, in contrast, the accused is considered guilty until proven innocent, placing the burden of proof on the individual rather than on the state. In criminal trials, the judge plays an adversarial role, taking an active part in building the state's case against the accused.

Roman law is based on civil law, or law as written in civil codes. The philosophy of civil law regards the law as a rational, written body of rules intended to apply to any situation. The task of lawyers and judges under civil law is to identify and apply the appropriate provisions in the code to particular situations. On the other hand, Anglo-American law rests on the foundation of common law. Common law is in turn based on the evolving values and attitudes of citizens, with considerable attention paid to local customs. Thus, common law is "judge-made law—molded, refined, examined, and changed in the crucible of active decision and handed down from generation to generation in the form of reported cases" (Friedman, 1973, p. 17). The judiciary under Anglo-American law must consider both statutes enacted by legislative councils and previous court decisions in evaluating legal disputes. Care is taken to distinguish the facts of the case in question from the situations covered in previous cases. Thus, a primary role of the Anglo-American judiciary is the interpretation, and not merely the application, of the law.

Unlike in England, however, in the United States there are also written federal and state constitutions, against which both statutes and precedents can be tested. But because the federal and state constitutions were mainly written using generalized language to promote and achieve collective goals and well-being, U.S. judges must also seek to understand and to interpret the aims of these important documents. Thus, U.S. jurisprudence has been built upon two important foundations: English common law and U.S. constitutional law. But it cannot be forgotten that if English common law traditions are found to be inconsistent with the provisions of the U.S. Constitution, then it is the U.S. Constitution that serves as the supreme law of the land. It is important to remember that England's reliance on a vague, "unwritten constitution" was a source of great irritation to the English subjects in North America at the time of the American Revolution.

tradition (Box 3-1). How would this distinction affect the integration of Louisiana into U.S. legal and political culture?

Most Americans assumed that the residents of Louisiana would welcome the opportunity to join the United States, but the residents of Louisiana were "a people speaking a foreign tongue and steeped in foreign ways, exhibiting unusual and even questionable values and behavior . . . used to authoritarian government, unlettered in representative institutions, following strange legal customs and laws" (Meinig, 1993, p. 15). To the surprise of many Americans, some influential residents of New Orleans expressed strong reservations about the Louisiana Purchase. Shortly after Louisiana was formally transferred to U.S. control, a delegation of prominent Louisianans traveled to Washington "to plead for immediate statehood on terms that would provide equality of treatment with other states but at the same time ensure the integrity of Louisiana laws and customs" (Meinig, 1993, p. 16). The delegates' plea was accepted. In 1808, the United States formally recognized Louisiana's Digest of Civil Laws—a document that had been modeled on the Napoleonic Code—as the basic law of Louisiana. Three years later, Louisiana was admitted to the Union.

The War of 1812 and the Acquisition of Florida

In purchasing Louisiana, Jefferson hoped to reduce the possibility that the United States would be drawn into a European war. Within a decade after the Louisiana Purchase, however, the United States found itself at war with Great Britain once again.

The War of 1812 broke out for several reasons. The westward movement resulted in continued pressure on Native Americans, who began to mobilize against the influx of settlers. Some Native Americans attempted to forge alliances with the British in the Northwest and with the Spanish, who still controlled Florida, in the South. Many Northerners favored expansion into British-held Canada. Southerners, recognizing that Great Britain and Spain were allies, supported conflict with the British in the hopes that military success would allow the United States to capture Florida.

On June 18, 1812, President James Madison approved a declaration of war against Great Britain. Military operations were inconclusive, with both sides claiming notable successes and dismal failures. The War of 1812 was perhaps the most unpopular of U.S. wars, including the Vietnam War (Hickey, 1989). The war was especially unpopular in New England, and many New Englanders believed that its underlying motivation was to advance the fortunes of the Democratic-Republican Party, which was popular in the expanding South and West. Federalists in New England, who remained that region's majority party, pondered dissolution of the Union. Some "began to dream of creating a separate nation in that region, which they could dominate and in which they could escape what they saw as the tyranny of slaveholders and backwoodsmen" (Brinkley, 1993, p. 204).

On December 15, 1814, delegates from the New England states met in Hartford to discuss the region's grievances against the federal government. The delegates to the Hartford Convention proposed several constitutional amendments intended to protect the influence of New England against the growing South and West. One proposed amendment would require that declarations of war, trade embargoes, or admission of new states be approved by a two-thirds majority of Congress. Another called for the end to the practice of counting three-fifths of slaves in apportioning seats in the House of Representatives, thus increasing the power of New England and the North at the expense of the slaveholding South. A third would bar the election of consecutive presidents from the same state.

The Hartford Convention appointed a delegation to present its resolutions to Madison. Unfortunately for the New Englanders, the delegation arrived while the city of Washington was celebrating the news that Andrew Jackson had routed British forces at the Battle of New Orleans and that the U.S. and British had concluded negotiations ending the war. Suddenly, "these New England dissensions now seemed not only an embarrassment but scandalous, indeed traitorous . . . as defensive Southern congressmen would never let their Yankee colleagues forget in the rancorous days ahead" (Meinig, 1993, p. 463).

The Expansions of the 1840s

The War of 1812 ended in a stalemate. Yet the war reaffirmed U.S. control of the Mississippi drainage basin. Once hostilities ended, the United States began to cast covetous glances at other European-controlled territories, including Florida, Texas, Mexico, and the islands of the Caribbean. Florida, which included all of the territory south of the 31st parallel of latitude westward to the Mississippi, was partly occupied by U.S. forces in 1818 and was formally acquired from Spain in 1819. Following the acquisition of Florida, U.S. boundaries remained unchanged until the 1840s. Between 1845 and 1853, the remaining territory that would eventually become the forty-eight contiguous United States was acquired.

By the 1840s, many Americans believed that it was the destiny of the

United States to expand westward, from sea to shining sea. The philosophy of continued U.S. expansion is known as "manifest destiny." This view rested on "the idea that America was destined—by God and by history—to expand its boundaries over a vast area . . . that included but was not necessarily restricted to North America" (Brinkley, 1993, p. 326). To some, manifest destiny meant expansion to the Pacific. Others took a broader view, arguing that manifest destiny implied nothing less than the eventual takeover of Canada, Mexico, the Caribbean, and Latin America.

Manifest destiny underlay the three great territorial expansions of the 1840s. In 1845, the Republic of Texas voluntarily joined the United States. Many Anglo-Americans moved to Texas during the early nineteenth century. By 1830, nearly three-quarters of the European-descended population of Texas was of Anglo-American rather than of Spanish or Mexican origin (Meinig, 1993, p. 38). The Mexican government's efforts to require Anglo-American immigrants into Texas to speak Spanish and practice Catholicism were largely ignored. Once Mexico formally refused to grant concessions to Anglo-American Texans analogous to those given to Louisianans by the United States, outright rebellion began. The independent Republic of Texas was proclaimed on March 1, 1836, and its sovereignty was assured following victory in the Battle of San Jacinto on April 21.

Many U.S. settlers in Texas soon pushed for the annexation of the Lone Star Republic. In part because some Northerners believed that the annexation of Texas would result in the further spread of slavery and upset the already delicate sectional balance between North and South, Congress refused to address the issue, and Texas remained independent for several years. The question of annexation was reopened, however, during the presidential election campaign of 1844. The activities of British agents in Texas gave rise to fears that "Great Britain might convert disgruntled Texas into a cotton-growing colony" (Whittlesey, 1939, p. 486). Southern expansionists within the Democratic Party secured the nomination of the first "dark-horse" presidential candidate, James Knox Polk of Tennessee. Polk's strong advocacy of annexation helped to secure him the presidency, and Texas was formally admitted to the Union in 1845.

The following year, hostilities broke out between the United States and Mexico, engendered in part because of the Texas issue. Like the annexation of Texas, the Mexican War was opposed by many antislavery Northerners but supported in the South and the West. Within two years, the United States won the war. The Treaty of Guadalupe Hidalgo, signed in 1848, granted sovereignty over all of California, Nevada, and Utah and much of Arizona, New Mexico, Colorado, and Wyoming to the United States.

During the same year, the United States settled a long-standing border dispute with Great Britain concerning the Oregon country. The British insisted that the 42nd parallel, or what is today the border between Oregon and California, be the boundary, whereas the United States insisted that the boundary be established at 54°40' north latitude, or the southern boundary of what is now Alaska. Some Americans, under the slogan "fifty-four forty or fight" advocated war with Great Britain over the Oregon country. Cooler heads prevailed, however, and a compromise that established the 49th parallel as the northern boundary of the United States was agreed upon by both sides.

By the end of the first half of the nineteenth century, the United States had expanded to more than three million square miles of territory. The acquisition of what would become the forty-eight contiguous states was completed by the Gadsden Purchase, including much of southern Arizona and New Mexico, from Mexico in 1853.

The Nineteenth-Century U.S. Economy

For many Americans, the philosophy of manifest destiny implied not only that new territories should be acquired but also that the newly acquired lands should be settled and "civilized" as quickly as possible. Thus the nineteenth century was marked not only by the rapid westward movement of the U.S. population but also by the rapid maturation of the economy.

During colonial days, internal economic activity had been limited to very local production and exchange of basic consumer goods (Bruchey, 1975). The small scale of the economy was further enhanced by the very independence of the colonies from one another. Each colony was established to trade with Great Britain, and each was relatively independent of the others. Moreover, British policy discouraged active trade among the colonies. As a result, trade and distribution within British North America were highly localized.

The relative economic independence of the colonies was reinforced by poor internal transportation. Concerned primarily with trade between each colony and the mother country, the British paid little attention to constructing transportation systems and other networks that could have increased trade among the colonies themselves. The importance of trade between the individual colonies and Great Britain is evident from the fact that all of the ten largest cities of the newly independent United States in 1790 were ports. The list includes not only major cities such as New York, Boston, and Philadelphia but also smaller ports such as Gloucester, Massachusetts, and Newport, Rhode Island, which today are only minor components of the U.S. urban system. Over the course of the nineteenth century, however, cities in the interior, such as Chicago, St. Louis, Pittsburgh, Cleveland, and Cincinnati, took their places among the nation's leading metropolitan areas, while older seaports such as Gloucester and Newport declined.

The National Road

Settlement, economic growth, and industrialization were all dependent upon transportation. Transportation routes and facilities were critical to the burgeoning westward movement of the United States in the nineteenth-century. Not surprisingly, the issue of developing and financing roads, canals, and rail-road lines was one of the great political controversies of the period.

During the first third of the nineteenth century, a vigorous debate over the desirability of federal financing of transportation improvements occurred. Controversy erupted along sectional lines. The West, which of course would be the primary beneficiary of new transportation routes, was strongly sup-portive of a national transportation program. Representatives of the South and the Northeast, on the other hand, were generally lukewarm if not openly hostile to the idea of federally financed internal improvements, especially if their home sections would be bypassed by newly constructed transportation routes.

As early as 1808, a national system of roads and canals was proposed by Thomas Jefferson's secretary of the treasury, Albert Gallatin. Congressional action on Gallatin's plan was delayed by the impending international crisis that would lead to the War of 1812. During the war itself, U.S. military lead-ers experienced great difficulty in moving troops, supplies, and weapons to battle stations in various parts of the country. Others viewed a national road network as an important step toward replacing localism and sectionalism with a broader, more national outlook. Thus, many began to call for direct federal intervention into the construction of highways, bridges, canals, and other internal improvements.

Opponents of federally financed internal improvements argued against them on several grounds. Southerners pointed out that federally financed road construction would contribute to the development of the West at the ex-pense of the South. Others doubted that Congress had the authority to redis-tribute revenues for the specific benefit of a few states or regions.

Specific proposals varied widely among the bills introduced in Congress for transportation improvements, but most of them focused on the National Road. The National Road had originally been authorized by Congress in 1802 in order to connect the Potomac and Ohio Rivers. A road was built con-necting Cumberland, Maryland, on the Potomac with Wheeling, Virginia (now West Virginia), on the Ohio.

In 1817, an internal improvements bill containing a substantial appropri-ation for the National Road was enacted by Congress. The bill was vetoed by President James Monroe, however, on the grounds that Congress lacked the constitutional authority to initiate systems of internal improvements. Monroe suggested, however, that specific internal improvements could be justified if the benefits associated with them were "of a national character." On these grounds, a more modest bill providing funds to repair the National Road and extend it west of the Ohio River was enacted shortly thereafter.

A financial panic in 1819 delayed the actual implementation of the im-provements to the National Road until 1822. In that year, Congress passed a bill authorizing the government to collect tolls on the National Road, with the revenues to be used to improve it further. The bill passed the House by a vote of 87 to 68, with the vote divided along sectional lines. The bill was supported nearly unanimously west of the Appalachians and in Pennsylvania and Maryland (which would benefit most directly from their positions at the eastern end of the road), whereas a large majority of representatives from New England, New York, Virginia, and the Carolinas voted against it. Monroe again vetoed the bill, but he called for a constitutional amendment to authorize Congress to fund internal improvements.

In 1830, President Andrew Jackson vetoed a bill to construct a road to Maysville, Kentucky. Jackson's veto meant the end of early-nineteenth-century efforts to provide federally financed transportation. Once the federal government finally refused to fund further construction of the National Road and other transportation projects, their development was undertaken by state and local governments and by private enterprise. The National Road itself was turned over to the states through which it ran in 1834, and it was completed soon afterward. Today, Interstate Highway 70 follows much of the original route of the National Road between Washington, DC, and St. Louis, Missouri.

The Erie Canal

In the long run, state initiative and private enterprise would have important implications for U.S. political geography. For example, the Erie Canal, whose construction was financed by the State of New York and by private investment, was instrumental in allowing New York City to establish itself firmly as the commercial and financial center of the United States.

As the nineteenth century dawned, Jefferson, Gallatin, and other prominent Americans recognized that the most efficient and cost-effective way to transport people and goods in the interior was by water. The Mississippi River, its tributaries, and the Great Lakes provided a vast natural network of transportation arteries extending from Pittsburgh to Louisiana to the Dakotas. What was lacking, however, was a navigable water connection between the Mississippi drainage basin and the Atlantic seaboard. The Erie Canal, which connected the Hudson River to Lake Erie, would provide this vital link.

Gallatin's report called for the construction of canals to connect the Atlantic coast with the interior. Shortly afterward, the invention of the steamboat by Robert Fulton provided an added incentive for the creation of artificial waterways. By 1815, steamboats were operating on the Chesapeake Bay, the Hudson River, and other navigable streams along the eastern seaboard (Meinig, 1993, p. 317). Although the eastern steamboat runs were profitable, Fulton and his associates soon recognized that the potential for profit was even greater in the interior. By the early 1820s, more than seventy steamboats provided regular freight and passenger service among the principal Mississippi ports, including New Orleans, St. Louis, Cincinnati, and Pittsburgh.

In the fall of 1825, the Erie Canal was completed and opened to steamboat traffic. In constructing the canal, New York officials and financiers had taken advantage of the only wide natural break in the Appalachian Mountains. Yet the canal builders were careful to connect the Hudson with Lake Erie rather than with Lake Ontario, thus bypassing Niagara Falls. Indeed, cities along the canal route such as Rochester and Syracuse soon became boomtowns, eclipsing cities on Lake Ontario itself (Meinig, 1993, p. 322).

The canal was an immediate financial success, and its success encouraged New York's commercial rivals to attempt canal-building projects of their own. In 1826, for example, Pennsylvania appropriated funds to build a canal between the Susquehanna River and Pittsburgh. Both Maryland and the federal government contributed to the construction of the Chesapeake and Ohio Canal. Yet none of these other projects were nearly as successful as the Erie Canal, in part because the rugged topography outside New York made canal construction difficult and expensive, and in part because the profitability of water transportation was soon eroded by the development of the railroad.

Economic Development Following Independence

The development of the National Road, the Erie Canal, and other internal improvements was accompanied by rapid growth in the U.S. economy. At the outset of the nineteenth century, the U. S. economy was still based primarily on providing raw materials for European industry, and the nation imported most of its manufactured products. By the middle of the century, however, the United States had emerged as a major industrial power in its own right.

Between 1805 and 1815, U.S. capitalists began to invest in the cotton mills of New England and the iron forges of western Pennsylvania. During this short period, domestic consumption of cotton increased from 1,000 to 90,000 bales per year, and production of woolen manufactures increased fivefold (Field, 1984). The trade embargo with Great Britain that had been implemented before and during the War of 1812 halted British exports to the United States, encouraging the growth of U.S. manufacturing.

After the end of the War of 1812, the reopening of trade with Great Britain brought a flood of cheap British manufactured goods back onto the U.S. market. The presence of British industrial products seriously damaged the infant U.S. manufacturing sector. The wave of imports prompted a swift legislative response in the form of a series of tariff acts. Protective tariffs were supported strongly by the new industrial barons of the Middle Atlantic states but resisted by trade-oriented New England merchants and Southern planters (Field, 1984).

At the same time, British textile technology was being rapidly diffused to the United States. Many skilled artisans from Great Britain moved to the United States. Soon, numerous spinning mills developed along rivers and streams in New England. These were soon joined by mills incorporating technology to produce woolen cloth. The Blackstone Valley of Massachusetts and Rhode Island has been called "the nation's nursery of manufacturing" (Meinig, 1993, p. 376). By the mid-1830s, the fledgling nation had its first integrated industrial region, encompassing southern New England and the eastern Middle Atlantic states.

Other industries, still largely craft-based and relying heavily on skilled artisans, also developed along the river sites. These included concentrations of silverware, cutlery, hardware, and armaments producers. The production of armaments was particularly influential in U.S. industrialization, for it was here that the idea of the interchangeability of parts and machine tooling developed. These ideas would be carried over into many other industries.

Nonetheless, until the development of steam power, U.S. manufacturing remained craft-oriented and small scale, with production still tied to relatively simple technology. Steam power and the opening of high-quality coal sites was to change that by the 1850s. A local supply of iron ore and a plentiful supply of wood for charcoal gave western Pennsylvania a start in the iron industry. This region developed a complex of small, dispersed ironworks that produced iron for the local markets. At first, however, these ironworks were local, small-scale enterprises. Not until after the discovery of coal deposits in western Pennsylvania did the western sites gain their first real advantage over those of the eastern seaboard. Because of limited transportation technology, access to a coalfield site became paramount for ironworks. A new wave of immigration from Great Britain brought skilled ironmasters, miners, and new machinery into this region (Meinig, 1993).

As these initial advantages were realized, the major industrial region of the United States began to expand westward. The cities of the Great Lakes joined southern New England and the Middle Atlantic region as the major industrial region in the United States. Stretching from New York to Pittsburgh and then west to Cincinnati and Chicago, the region became a "'culture hearth of industrialization'" (Meinig, 1993). The core region not only had an initial advantage based on its material resources, but it also rapidly developed a culture of entrepreneurship and competition that enhanced the concentration of innovation and industrialization and led to ever-increasing industrial growth in the region. At a time when transportation was difficult, it was necessary for entrepreneurs, investors, and skilled workers to be located near one another. This concentration allowed the North to become the nation's first agglomerate economy. Well before the Civil War, industrialization in the North had created an economy fundamentally distinct from and often at odds with the economies of other parts of the United States.

Political Culture and the Westward Movement

In Chapter 2, we pointed out that the New England, Middle Atlantic, and Southern colonies were each characterized by distinctive political economies.

By the time of the American Revolution, these differences would be reflected in emerging differences in political culture. The concept of political culture refers to the set of prevailing attitudes and beliefs about the appropriate nature of government and politics.

The three major political cultures of the United States were traditionalistic political culture, which arose in the South; moralistic political culture, which originated in New England; and individualistic political culture, which flourished in the Middle Atlantic states (Elazar, 1984, 1994). According to Elazar's model, styles of government and citizens' attitudes toward major aspects of politics vary substantially among the three major political cultures. Other aspects of culture also can be found to vary by region, such as linguistic dialect, religious affiliation, architectural style, and even dietary preferences (Table 3-1).

TABLE 3-1. Elazar's Political Culture Theory: A Summary

Issue	Traditionalistic political culture	Moralistic political culture	Individualistic political culture
Role of Government			
How viewed?	Means of maintaining existing order	Means of bettering the commonwealth	Means of achieving marketplace efficiency
Appropriate sphere?	Mainly areas securing traditional lifestyles	Any realm enhancing the collective community	Mainly areas promoting economic development
Role of Politics			
How viewed?	Elite privilege	Civic responsibility	Demeaning activity
Appropriate participants?	Small elite	All citizens	Professional politicians
Style of political competition?	Between elite factions over traditional value maintenance	Between citizens over policy alternatives	Between party regulars over tangible rewards
Culture Hearth Features			
Location?	Southern colonies	New England colonies	Middle-Atlantic colonies
Dialect?	Southern	Northern	Midland
Early religion?	Anglican, Baptist	Congregational	Methodist, Roman Catholic
Folk Architecture?	Tidewater cottage, dogtrot cabin	Cape Cod, salt box	Cumberland, classic I-house

Sources: Brunn, 1974; Rooney et al., 1982; Elazar, 1984; Archer and Shelley, 1986.

Characteristics of U.S. Political Cultures

Traditionalistic political culture is based on the philosophy that the underlying purpose of politics and government is the preservation of the traditional social order. In the colonial South, the established social order was dominated by plantation owners, who despite being a small minority of the population controlled a large share of the region's land and resources. Preservation of the established social order implied that government and politics were to be dominated by the elite and that political participation by persons of lower social standing was discouraged or suppressed. Government under traditionalistic political culture is limited and restricted to those activities that primarily benefit the interests of the governing elite. Politics under traditionalistic political culture are more personalized, with competition taking place between factions of the elite within a dominant political party. Traditionalistic political culture regards public administration as the province of the elite and thus discourages formalized bureaucracy.

Moralistic political culture is based on the philosophy that the purpose of politics and government is the promotion of the common good. Political activities are viewed as a means toward the establishment and maintenance of the good and just society. Political participation is encouraged and, indeed, is regarded as a civic duty, while politicians are expected to serve the public interest rather than to profit from their activities. Government officials are expected to become active in noneconomic as well as economic spheres of life. Under moralistic political culture, political parties are weak, and voters tend to respond to issues rather than to party labels. Public administration under moralistic political culture emphasizes a strong, nonpartisan bureaucracy staffed by professionally trained civil servants.

Individualistic political culture emphasizes the relationships between politics and the private good. Under individualistic political culture, the political order is regarded as a marketplace. Politics are a means by which social and economic status can be increased, and political participation is undertaken in order to benefit individuals, regions, economic classes, or ethnic groups. For the most part, government activity emphasizes economic development and regulation and pays less attention to noneconomic considerations. Thus, individualistic political culture emphasizes strong party organization, with long-term party loyalty expected of voters and political office seekers.

The Westward Movement and Political Culture

Over the course of the nineteenth century, these three major political cultures spread westward across North America. Millions of Americans moved westward during the nineteenth century. In 1790, much of the original territory of the United States remained unsettled by Americans of European origin. By 1840, however, the frontier of settlement had reached as far west as southern

Michigan and Wisconsin, Iowa, Missouri, Arkansas, and Texas. Fifty years later, the U.S. Bureau of the Census officially declared the frontier to be closed (Figure 3-4).

Generally, migration occurred in a latitudinal fashion from east to west (Hudson, 1988). Migrants typically moved directly westward to areas near the frontier one or two states to the west. By 1800, New Englanders had already settled much of upstate New York, northeastern Pennsylvania, and the Western Reserve of northeastern Ohio (Meinig, 1986, p. 348). Migrants from the Middle Atlantic colonies, meanwhile, moved in large numbers to southern and western Ohio, Indiana, Illinois, and Missouri. The Ohio River and its tributaries were an important migration route, but settlers also journeyed overland along the National Road. Southerners were responsible for much of the settlement of Alabama, Mississippi, and Arkansas. Over the course of two or three generations, a South Carolina family might move from the Atlantic seaboard to Georgia, Alabama, or Mississippi. Soon the letters GTT—"Gone to Texas"—would appear on storefronts and houses, indicating the intended destination of their owners.

Many westward migrants were motivated by the availability of cheap land. Throughout the nineteenth century, government policy encouraged the distribution, settlement, and improvement of the land. Land within the original Thirteen Colonies was distributed by the states. Land in the Old Northwest, the Louisiana Purchase, and other newly acquired territories was distributed by the federal government. Federal land sold for $2 per acre in 1800, and this price was reduced to $1.25 per acre by 1820.

Land prices and distribution policies were controversial issues, however. For the most part, residents of the Middle Atlantic states and of the West itself favored the wide distribution of cheap or free land, while Southerners and New Englanders opposed it. Before the Civil War, proposals to distribute government land free to settlers were blocked by Southern members of Congress, who feared that the large-scale distribution of free or cheap lands would undermine Southern plantation agriculture. After the secession of the South, Congress passed the Homestead Act in 1862. The Homestead Act offered free government land in the West to native-born and immigrant settlers, although a clause restricting the right to free land to those "who had never taken up arms against the United States" precluded homesteading on the part of Confederate veterans. The Homestead Act dramatically increased the pace of westward expansion and reinforced migration patterns.

Not everyone benefited from laws intended to promote the westward movement. Native Americans were driven further and further west. The Indian Removal Act of 1832, for example, was intended to open lands in the Southeast occupied by the Cherokee, Choctaw, Creek, Chickasaw, and Seminole Nations for white settlement, but opening these lands to Anglo-American settlers required the extermination or expulsion of resident Native Americans. Thousands were forcibly removed from their homelands and resettled along the "Trail of Tears" to Indian Territory in what is now eastern

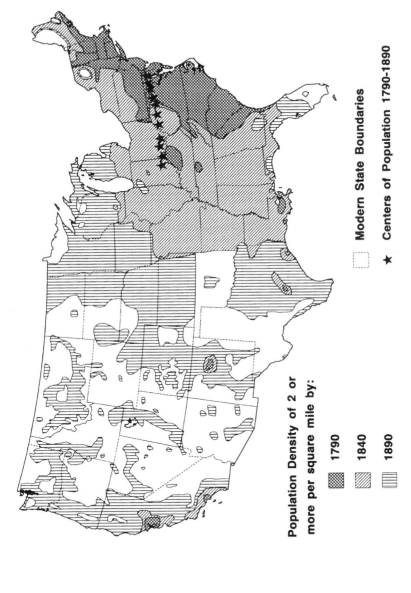

Population Density of 2 or more per square mile by:

1790

1840

1890

☐ Modern State Boundaries

★ Centers of Population 1790-1890

FIGURE 3-4. Settlement Expansion, 1790–1890. Data from Gannett (1898), pp. 11–15 and Plates 3–6; Marschner (1959), p. 29.

Oklahoma. Although the Native American nations suffered great hardship in the nineteenth century, the government rationalized their removal on the grounds that their lands were not productive in the hands of their "savage" occupants and were needed by Anglo-American settlers. Between 1816 and 1836 alone, most of Michigan, Indiana, and Illinois, along with substantial areas of Georgia, Alabama, Mississippi, Tennessee, Missouri, and Iowa were taken, usually by force, from various Native American tribes by the federal government.

Few westward-moving Americans possessed great wealth. Many, in fact, journeyed west with little more than the clothes on their backs and a few dollars in their pockets. Yet the westward movement resulted in the spread of far more than material possessions. A culture that was increasingly identified as American yet that was possessed of regional overtones diffused from east to west across North America.

Many homesick travelers named new cities, counties, and villages after their native communities. For example, natives of Champaign County, Ohio, gave that name to a newly settled county in Illinois, and the county seats of both counties are named Urbana. The city of Portland, Oregon, was named after the city in Maine, allegedly after a Downeaster won a coin flip with a native of Boston. Community names such as New Philadelphia, Ohio, Pittsburg, Kansas, and Rochester, Minnesota similarly reflect the nineteenth-century westward movement.

The westward movement also resulted in the spread of moralistic, individualistic, and traditionalistic political cultures across the United States (Figure 3-5). Moralistic political culture spread with the westward movement of New Englanders. Thus, moralistic political culture spread to upstate New York and the states of the upper Middle West, including Michigan, Wisconsin, Minnesota, Iowa, and the Dakotas. New England settlers also played an important role in the settlement of the Pacific Northwest. The traditionalistic political culture of the South eventually spread from its origins in the South Atlantic states to Oklahoma and Texas. Individualistic political culture spread from the Middle Atlantic states to the southern Great Lakes states, including Ohio, Indiana, and Illinois, and eventually to California. Of the three, this political culture is most attuned to circumstances in urban areas. Hence, individualistic political culture has become the dominant political culture in the contemporary United States. Nevertheless, moralistic and traditionalistic political culture remain important in their own areas. Especially in the western half of the United States, other distinctive political cultures have arisen (Box 3-2).

Nineteenth-Century U.S. Political Geography

The nineteenth century witnessed a series of important political conflicts, many of which stemmed from historical currents of migration, settlement,

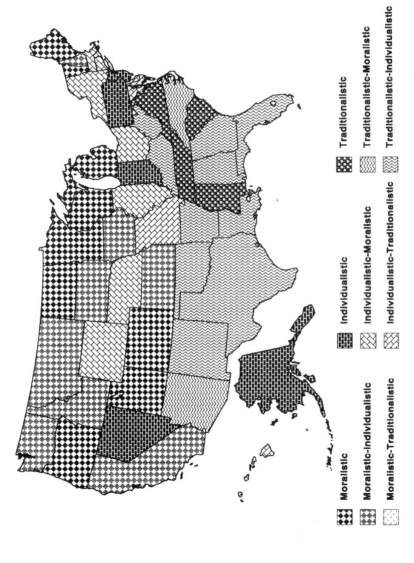

Legend:

- Moralistic
- Moralistic-Individualistic
- Moralistic-Traditionalistic
- Individualistic
- Individualistic-Moralistic
- Individualistic-Traditionalistic
- Traditionalistic
- Traditionalistic-Moralistic
- Traditionalistic-Individualistic

FIGURE 3-5. Elazar's Political Culture Classification. Data from Elazar (1984), pp. 135–36.

Box 3-2. *Political Culture in the Great Plains*

As we have seen, moralistic, individualistic, and traditionalistic political cultures followed the prevailing migration patterns westward across the United States during the nineteenth century. As settlers moved farther and farther west, however, they began to encounter environments very different from those of the eastern United States in which they had originated. Distinctive local political cultures have arisen in response to interaction with these new environments.

The Great Plains is one region whose political culture is derived from and yet distinct from the major political cultures of the East. The semi-arid, grass-covered Plains region stretches across the United States from North Dakota and Montana to Texas. More than sixty years ago, Webb (1931) described the eastern margin of the Plains region as an "institutional fault." West of this unseen barrier, Eastern cultural, economic, and political institutions had to be modified in order to fit an environment characterized by unreliable and unpredictable physical conditions and economic dependency.

Today, the Plains region remains isolated from the mainstream of the now metropolitanized U.S. political economy. Agriculture and other primary-sector activities continue to dominate the economies of the Plains states, despite the dwindling importance of these activities elsewhere. Many parts of the region have experienced decades of depopulation, and some counties now contain fewer than half as many people today as they did in the early 1900s (Archer, 1992).

The distinctive physical and economic characteristics of the Plains have contributed to a political culture that stresses the role of government in stabilizing the uncertain physical and economic environment (Elazar, 1980; Shelley, 1993). Elazar (1980) recognized the uniqueness of the political culture of the Plains states, writing that the Plains states "are the last bastions of the old agrarian ethic in the United States, which sees the good society as one composed of communities of self-reliant, God-fearing individuals and families who cooperate with one another on an equal basis to achieve common goals while eschewing collectivism in all forms" (Elazar, 1980, pp. 266–67).

The Plains political culture implies that the region's politics are characterized by unusually high levels of political participation, opposition to large-scale government, resentment of bureaucracy, and a preference for local rather than state or federal solutions to local problems (Shelley, 1993). Opposition to large-scale bureaucracy can be traced to the region's economic dependency, its isolation, and consequently to a belief that local conditions are ignored or poorly understood by officials in distant power centers. Hence, many residents of the Great Plains tend to regard government regulation as unnecessary or inappropriate for local conditions, and local management of problems is generally strongly preferred to nonlocal administration.

In state and national politics, voters in the Plains are often quick to oppose the party in power. The Republican Party, which has traditionally been seen as representing the interests of small farmers in the North, has usually fared well in the Plains states. Yet opposition to Republican policy has generated sharp increases in support for Democrats when agricultural conditions are especially depressed, as, for example, in 1956 and 1988. In addition, third-party movements have often garnered extensive support in the Plains. From the Populists of the 1890s to the Ross Perot campaign of 1992, third-party candidates who have argued for policies consistent with the political culture of the Plains have been rewarded with high levels of support throughout the region.

and industrialization in association with concomitant changes in the global economy. The nineteenth century was also a period in which the political institutions first established by the Constitution were put into practice. Many have endured to the present day, but others were reformed as practical experience disproved the initial expectations of the framers of the Constitution.

Sectionalism in the Nineteenth-Century United States

As we saw in Chapter 2, conflict between three major sections dominated the politics of colonial America. Conflict between the divergent interests of New England, the Middle Atlantic states, and the South was critical to the development of American political institutions (Wilson, 1908; Whittlesey, 1956). During the nineteenth century, however, the colonial sectional alignment of New England, Middle Atlantic, and South was replaced by the modern alignment of Northeast, South, and West (Turner, 1932; Whittlesey, 1956; Archer and Taylor, 1981; Martis and Elmes, 1993).

Although some of their contemporaries regarded the delegates to the Hartford Convention as traitors, many of the delegates were aware that New England, in contrast to the Middle Atlantic colonies and the South, could not benefit directly from westward expansion. By 1800, population pressure had driven the cost of land upward. New England farmland of even moderate quality cost fifty dollars or more per acre—far more than the cost of better-quality land in the West (Billington, 1960, p. 247). Many New Englanders decided to take advantage of cheap land in the Old Northwest. Thus, the steady depopulation of northern and central New England began. Numerous towns in New Hampshire, Vermont, and Maine contain fewer people today than they did in the early nineteenth century.

As New England's population and political influence declined compared to that of the West, its economic and political interests coalesced with those of the more powerful and prosperous Middle Atlantic and Great Lakes states. Meanwhile, the distinctive political interests of the pre-Revolutionary frontier evolved into a third full-scale section, the West. Thus, by the time of the Civil War, the Northeast, the South, and the West had emerged as the major sections of the United States. These remain the three major sections in U.S. politics today.

Sectional Conflict in the Early Nineteenth Century

Throughout the nineteenth century, persons from the Northeast, the South, and the West expressed increasingly divergent views about public policy and economic development. Slavery was a major issue of conflict between the Northeast and the South. By the early nineteenth century, slavery had been abolished in the North, but it flourished in the South. The invention of the cotton gin and other technological improvements, along with the settlement of fertile lands in Alabama, Mississippi, Louisiana, and Texas, increased the economic value of slaves. By the Civil War, millions of slaves lived throughout the South (Figure 3-6).

The Northeast and the South disputed whether slavery should be allowed in the newly settled territories of the trans-Mississippi West. On these grounds, many in the Northeast (including Abraham Lincoln in his only term in the House of Representatives) opposed the Mexican War, for they believed that the acquisition of new territory from Mexico would not only increase available land for the extension of slavery but would also encourage the further southward expansion of the United States into Mexico, increasing the power of the South relative to the North.

Meanwhile, the industrializing North began to increase in population more rapidly than the South. By the 1830s, the Northern states contained considerably more people than did the Southern states. Thus representatives of Northern states, in which slavery was prohibited, formed a majority in the House of Representatives. Only by maintaining a balance of power in the Senate could the South block the passage of legislation favorable to Northern interests (Martis and Elmes, 1993).

The increasing population and economic strength of the North was already evident before 1820. By 1819, the United States comprised twenty-two states—eleven slave states and eleven free states. The following year, Missouri applied for admission to the Union. Slavery was well established in Missouri, but its admission would give the slave states a majority in the Senate.

After two years of acrimonious debate, the issue of slavery in Missouri resolved itself when Maine, which had previously been part of Massachusetts, applied for statehood. The Missouri Compromise called for the admission of Missouri as a slave state and Maine as a free state, with slavery prohibited in the remaining portions of the Louisiana Purchase located north of the southern boundary of Missouri.

Following the Missouri Compromise, states were admitted to the Union in pairs, one slave state and one free state. This ensured that the South would hold half of the seats in the Senate. Hence, the South could veto any Northern

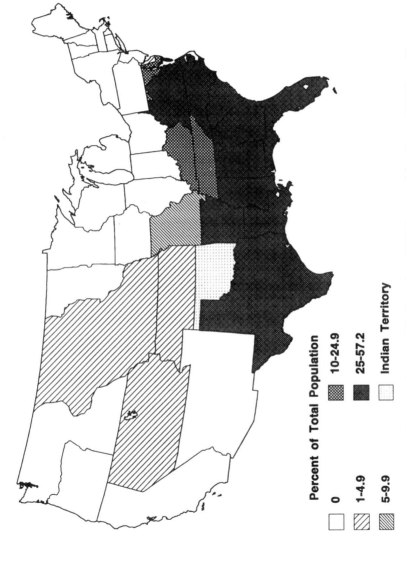

Percent of Total Population

☐ 0	▦ 10-24.9
▨ 1-4.9	■ 25-57.2
▧ 5-9.9	▒ Indian Territory

FIGURE 3-6. Slave Population, 1860. Data from U.S. Bureau of the Census (1918), p. 57.

effort to eliminate slavery, promote free distribution of land, or otherwise en-act national legislation unacceptable to the region.

Sectionalism Following the Missouri Compromise

The Missouri Compromise muted the growing sectional tensions between North and South for a generation. Yet the competing interests of the two sections created tension that would eventually lead to civil war.

Underlying the debate over the extension of slavery was a more fundamental dispute between the Northeast and the South concerning how the economy was to be organized (Agnew, 1987a). During the early nineteenth century, the nation's primary contribution to the world economy was cotton and other Southern agricultural products. Southern planters used profits from cotton exports to purchase foodstuffs from the agricultural West, while the Northeast supplied manufactured goods to the other two sections (Agnew, 1993a).

By the middle of the nineteenth century, industrialization in the Northeast had caused the Northeastern economy to grow faster than those of the other two sections. The value of manufactured goods produced in the United States rose from less than 500 million dollars in 1840 to nearly two billion dollars by 1860. Most of this increase occurred in New England and the Middle Atlantic states, where most industrial employment was concentrated (Figure 3-7).

Industrialization in the Northeast caused the balance between Southern cotton exports, Western agricultural production, and Northeastern industry to unravel. The Northeast became less dependent on Southern markets for its products, while its growing population demanded more and more agricultural products from the West. Farm prices rose as demand for farm products increased in the Northeast as well as in the industrial centers of Europe. The growth of agriculture in the West paralleled the expansion of industry in the East. "Hence a strong economic relationship was emerging between the two regions that was profitable to both—and that was increasing the isolation of the South within the Union" (Brinkley, 1993, p. 282).

After the Mexican War, leaders from both North and South debated the legality of slavery in the newly acquired Mexican Cession and the Oregon Territory. In 1849, the balance between free and slave states was still in effect. Florida, Arkansas, and Texas had been admitted as slave states, and Michigan, Wisconsin, and Iowa had been admitted as free states. Soon additional territories would demand admission—California, in fact, already had more than 100,000 residents. All but one of the Northern state legislatures adopted resolutions demanding that slavery be prohibited in the territories (Brinkley, 1993, p. 241). Southerners, meanwhile, feared that this would soon make slave states a minority. In the minds of many Southerners, failure to preserve a sectional balance in the Senate could only mean secession.

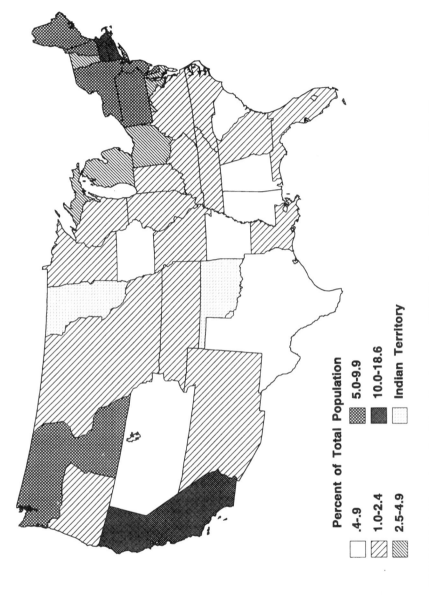

Percent of Total Population

.4-.9	5.0-9.9	
1.0-2.4	10.0-18.6	
2.5-4.9	Indian Territory	

FIGURE 3-7. Manufacturing Wage Employment, 1860. Data from Dodd (1993), pp. 313–38.

Early in 1850, Henry Clay attempted to patch together a compromise between sectional interests. The compromise of 1850 called for the admission of
California as a free state. Territorial governments in the remaining areas acquired from Mexico could be formed without restrictions on slavery. The
Compromise also included provisions for a stronger fugitive slave law, enrag-
ing Northern abolitionists, who were already active in helping runaway slaves
escape to the North. After nearly a year of debate, the compromise was enacted.

Hopes that sectional tensions would ease following the Compromise of
1850 were short-lived. Tensions resurfaced four years later, again because of
the issue of slavery in the territories. In January 1854, Senator Stephen Douglas of Illinois introduced a bill organizing the territory of Nebraska. Although the proposed Nebraska Territory (which included both Nebraska and
Kansas) was located north of the southern boundary of Missouri, the bill
would authorize the territorial legislature to determine the status of slavery. In
response to Southern objections, Douglas proposed two changes: First, Nebraska would be divided into two territories, Nebraska and Kansas, allowing
for the possibility that Kansas would choose to become a slave state. And second, the Missouri Compromise would be repealed.

Passage of the Kansas-Nebraska Act reinforced sectional and political
tensions throughout the United States. Supporters and opponents of slavery
established rival governments at separate sites in Kansas, each claiming to be
the only legitimate authority over the territory. In the Northeast, the Republican Party was founded. The new party was explicitly opposed to slavery and
its extension into the territories.

The Civil War and Its Aftermath

The Civil War began in the spring of 1861 and continued until the South surrendered at Appomattox in 1865. Northern victory in the Civil War ensured
the dominance of the Northeastern industrial core over the Southern agrarian
periphery.

Northeastern industrial interests firmly supported and, after the Civil
War, increasingly controlled the Republican Party. The Republicans encouraged policies that promoted further economic development in the West, including the Homestead Act, the completion of transcontinental railroads,
high protective tariffs, and federal control over banking and currency structures intended to promote industrial expansion (Agnew, 1993a).

Industrial Development Following the Civil War

Despite the development of industry in the Northeast, the United States on
the eve of the Civil War was still largely an agrarian economy. The Civil War

was the catalyst that transformed a fledgling industrial economy into the economic giant of the twentieth century. The huge mobilization of capital and manpower, particularly in the Northeast, imparted a tremendous boost to the iron, railroad, armaments, textile, and leather industries (Kennedy, 1987). A combination of this increased war productivity, the opening of the western Middle West and the Great Plains states to farmers via the Homestead Act, and rapid improvements in communications technology led to a boom in consumer demand for manufactured goods in the 1870s.

The increased demands associated with this boom were accommodated not by an expansion of the number of industrial centers in the country but by an expansion of production in the existing industrial centers. Improvements in transportation technology enabled existing industrial centers to expand their markets while retaining an advantage over potential competitors. The introduction of steel rails allowed the railroads to carry substantial loads, enabling industrial firms to export to a national rather than a regional market. Cities began to specialize in particular products, and, given a national market, factories grew to meet demand and in the process developed economies of scale and scope that gave them further advantages over potential newcomers. Thus, the industrial hegemony of the Northeast was consolidated.

Much of that hegemony was based on the region's dominant position in steel production, a crucial component of almost all industrial production at the time. Steel was the specialty of western Pennsylvania, developing out of the iron industry that had been established there during the early years of the Republic. Iron production required the raw materials, ore, and first wood (for charcoal) and then coal of the Alleghenies. It also required skilled ironmasters, many of whom were immigrants from the blast furnaces of England. These immigrants brought to the United States knowledge of the improved Bessemer process for manufacturing steel from molten pig iron, a process that was invented in England in 1856. Bessemer steel was first produced in the United States in Michigan in 1864, but it was the J. Edgar Thompson Works in Pittsburgh that gave western Pennsylvania its dominance in steelmaking. Staffed by experienced steelmakers from the Cambria Iron Works in Johnstown, Pennsylvania, Andrew Carnegie's J. Edgar Thompson Works opened in August 1875, and by the end of the decade it had become the primary producer of Bessemer steel in the United States (Bridge, 1903). In 1901, when Carnegie Steel was sold to the United States Steel Corporation, the company was producing more steel than all the steel mills in England combined (Barraclough, 1967).

With steel as its base, the economy of the United States grew with astounding speed. Between 1865 and 1900, annual production of steel ingots grew from 20,000 to over 9,000,000 long tons. Coal production increased by 800 percent. Steel rails increased by 523 percent, and by the end of the century the United States had more miles of railway track than the rest of the world combined. Thus, by the end of the nineteenth century, the United States had emerged as the world's leading industrial nation.

Box 3-3. *The Prime Meridian Conference*

In the contemporary world economy, movement and communication over long distances on the earth's surface is routine. Thousands of Americans cross the Pacific Ocean between the United States and East Asia every day. In doing so, Americans must remember that they "gain" a day in going to Asia and "lose" one in returning to the United States. Why?

Absolute location on the earth's surface is determined by latitude and longitude. As the earth revolves around the sun, it rotates on its axis. The axis of rotation provides a reference point for determining absolute location. The endpoints of the axis of rotation are the North and South Poles. The equator, whose latitude is 0 degrees, is halfway between the poles. The latitude of any other place on the earth's surface is determined by its distance from the equator.

Straight-line movement along the earth's surface between the North Pole and the South Pole defines half-circles that intersect the equator at right angles. These half-circles are called "meridians." Meridians are used to determine the distance east or west of a given reference meridian known as the "prime meridian."

Today, longitude is routinely given in degrees east or west of Greenwich, England. The expressions "west of Greenwich" and "east of Greenwich" refer to the fact that the prime meridian is that meridian that passes through the Royal British Observatory at Greenwich, a suburb of London. From a scientific point of view, however, there is no reason why any particular meridian should be chosen as the prime meridian. During the nineteenth century, in fact, maps and nautical charts prepared in different countries showed the longitudes of places as determined from different reference meridians. Many U.S. maps, for example, were based on reference meridians passing through Washington, DC.

By the late nineteenth century, the use of maps and charts drawn from different meridians had become increasingly confusing. The volume of international trade had increased dramatically, while railways and other transportation improvements made rapid east–west travel possible. The Age of Exploration had ended, and geographers and other scientists possessed accurate information about the size and shape of the earth. Recognizing these developments, scientists and diplomats within the international community began to consider the advantages of international agreement on a single meridian as the prime meridian.

The United States took a leading role in settling this question. In 1882, Secretary of State Frederick T. Frelinghuysen invited delegates of countries throughout the world to attend an international conference "for the purpose of fixing a Prime Meridian and a universal day" (*Protocols of the Proceedings,* 1884, p. 1). Delegates from twenty-eight countries attended the conference, which began in Washington on October 1, 1884.

Where, then, should the prime meridian be located? The delegates recognized that "from a purely scientific point of view, any meridian may be taken as the prime meridian. But from the standpoint of convenience and economy there is undoubtedly much room for a choice" (*Protocols of the Proceedings,* 1884, p. 39). Two distinct points of view were soon expressed by the delegates.

Some argued that the prime meridian should be one of the major national meridians already in use. The American delegation supported the Greenwich meridian, pointing out that more than 70 percent of international shipping and a majority of nautical charts then in use had been drawn based on this meridian (*Protocols of the Proceedings*, 1884, p. 40).

The French delegation argued vigorously against the Greenwich meridian proposal. Instead, the French argued for a "neutral" meridian, which did not cross through national territory. A neutral meridian would be one passing through the oceans, away from populated areas. The meridians passing through the Azores and through the Bering Strait were proposed as candidates. The French delegation reminded their colleagues that the metric system of weights and measures was a comparable example of a "neutral" system. Indeed, the Spanish delegate, Juan Valera, argued that it was incumbent on Great Britain and the United States to accept the metric system in exchange for the placement of the prime meridian at Greenwich (*Protocols of the Proceedings*, 1884, p. 84). After continued discussion, however, the French proposal was voted down. Shortly afterward, a large majority of the delegates voted in favor of the U.S. resolution to establish Greenwich as the prime meridian (*Protocols of the Proceedings*, 1884, p. 99). The international date line was established as the 180th meridian, adjusted slightly in some areas so as not to divide countries. Thus, all of Alaska is east of the international date line even though the westernmost Aleutian Islands are actually less than 180 degrees east of Greenwich.

As U.S. industrial strength increased, the influence of the nation's industry in the world economy also expanded. The United States began to play a more and more important role in the coordination of production and distribution worldwide. For example, the conference at which the international community agreed to the establishment of the prime meridian and the international date line was held in Washington in 1884 (Box 3-3).

The Electoral Geography of the United States in the Nineteenth Century

The dramatic changes in U.S. cultural and economic geography that occurred throughout the nineteenth century had profound effects on the nation's political geography. These effects included a critical modification of the procedure by which presidents were elected, the rapid democratization of the franchise, and the emergence of ongoing competition between two major parties. The result of these effects was the so-called Sectional Normal Vote, a geography of election results that would influence the U.S. polity for much of the twentieth century.

Political Parties and the Twelfth Amendment

During the nineteenth century, many of the institutions established by the Constitution were modified or amended to meet the needs of the rapidly growing population. The nineteenth century also witnessed the birth of the two major political parties and the development of the basic geographical cleavages that remain characteristic of contemporary U.S. politics.

The first presidential election was held in 1789. George Washington, who had been the commander of the American forces during the Revolution and president of the constitutional convention, was regarded by most Americans as the leading citizen of the new republic. Washington was the logical choice to be the first president of the United States, and he was elected unanimously by the first Electoral College.

Washington believed that the office of president should be conducted above partisan politics. Yet organized political factions had already come into existence long before Washington's second term came to an end. In disputes among his cabinet and Congress, Washington often sided with those who advocated increasing the strength of the central government, who had formed the Federalist faction during the debate over ratification of the Constitution. Supporters of increased federal power coalesced into the Federalist Party, while Anti-Federalists formed the nucleus of the Republican Party, the ancestor of today's Democratic Party.

In 1796, Washington announced his intention to retire at the end of his second term. The leaders of the two newly formed political factions soon emerged as the leading contenders for the presidency. Vice President John Adams was supported by many Federalists, while Thomas Jefferson, who had served as secretary of state, led the Republicans. In the election, Adams received the most electoral votes and became president. Jefferson finished second and became vice president. Thus, the presidency and vice presidency were held by political opponents. Political and personal animosity between the two men impaired the success of the Adams administration.

Four years later, the Republicans enjoyed a clear majority in the Electoral College. The Republican leadership intended that Jefferson should be elected president, with Aaron Burr of New York as vice president (Figure 3-8). Yet every Republican elector voted for both Jefferson and Burr, who consequently finished in a tie. According to the Constitution, because the election was tied the House of Representatives was empowered to select the president. Some of the Federalist members of the House despised Jefferson and were inclined to vote for Burr. Only the intervention of Alexander Hamilton, a leading Federalist who disliked Jefferson but loathed Burr, assured that Jefferson would assume the presidency as the Republicans had intended.

After Jefferson took office, leaders of both parties realized that reform was necessary. The Twelfth Amendment, which incorporated these reforms, was ratified in 1804. The Twelfth Amendment separated the contests for president and vice president. Each member of the Electoral College was empow-

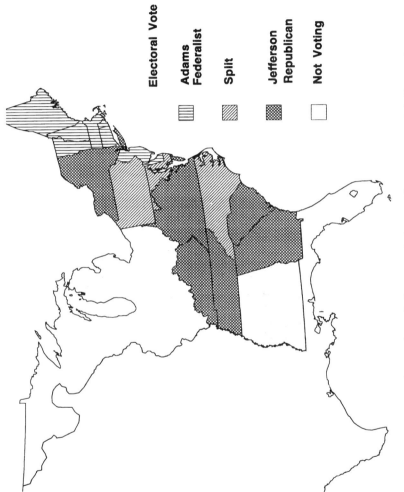

FIGURE 3-8. U.S. Presidential Election, 1800. Data from Peterson (1963), p. 13.

ered to vote for one candidate for president and another for vice president, subject only to the stipulation that both candidates could not come from the same state as the elector.

In effect, the Twelfth Amendment legitimized partisan politics in national elections. Parties could now nominate slated tickets of candidates to run for the presidency and the vice presidency. The House of Representatives was empowered to elect the president only if no candidate achieved a majority of presidential votes in the Electoral College. Since the adoption of the Twelfth Amendment, this has happened only once, in 1824. On only one other occasion did the president-elect fail to receive a popular plurality: In 1888, Republican Benjamin Harrison defeated the incumbent Democratic president, Grover Cleveland, although Cleveland won the popular balloting by a small margin. Thus, the Electoral College has usually ratified the public will, although throughout U.S. history there have been arguments for eliminating it (Peirce and Longley, 1981).

Nineteenth-Century Political Parties

Two-party competition has been characteristic of U.S. politics since Jefferson's day. By legitimating party competition for the presidency, the Twelfth Amendment reinforced the tendency toward two-party politics in the United States.

During Jefferson's administration, the Republicans came to be known as "Democratic-Republicans." Three different parties competed with the Democratic-Republicans for political supremacy during the nineteenth century. The Federalists, who had been so critical to the ratification of the Constitution and the establishment of a strong central government, began to decline in importance after Jefferson's election. The Federalists were increasingly identified with the wealthy, who were outnumbered by the small farmers and workers who formed the core of Jefferson's constituency. By 1810, the Federalist Party was strong only in New England. The failure of the Hartford Convention hastened its demise and by 1820 it was defunct.

Between the 1820s and the 1850s, the Whig Party became the nation's second major political party, opposing the Democrats (who by now had dropped "Republican" from their name). The two parties coalesced around the controversial figure of Andrew Jackson, who served as president from 1829 to 1837. Jackson's supporters were Democrats, and his opponents were Whigs. The Whigs included persons representing a great variety of sectional and commercial interests, but opposition to Jackson provided common ground.

In general, Whigs were supported by commercial and industrial interests and by wealthier planters and farmers, while the Democrats were strongest among smaller farmers and laborers. The Whigs "wished to use the national government in order to further capitalistic enterprise" (Morison et al., 1980,

p. 508). They supported a national banking system, a protective tariff, and the use of federal funds to construct roads, railroads, and canals. The Democrats, on the other hand, supported decentralization and states' rights and preferred that internal improvements be paid for by the states rather than by the federal government.

The Whigs won only two presidential elections, in 1840 and 1848. By the mid-1850s, the party had split into Northern and Southern wings, and it had been eclipsed by the Republican Party. The Republican Party arose in the Great Lakes states during the 1850s. Some Republicans argued for the outright abolition of slavery, and most agreed that slavery should not be extended to newly settled territories. At the same time, most Republican leaders supported economic policies favorable to the burgeoning industries of the North.

The new party soon spread across the North, attracting antislavery Whigs and Democrats. In 1856, the Republican Party nominated its first presidential candidate, the well-known explorer John C. Fremont. Fremont ran a strong campaign but lost narrowly in a three-way race to Democrat James Buchanan. Four years later, Abraham Lincoln swept the Northern states and secured the presidency. Although Lincoln's campaign was aided by fragmentation among his opponents in a four-way election, he was elected despite receiving few popular and no electoral votes from south of the Mason–Dixon Line (Figure 3-9).

After the Southern states seceded, the Republicans became established as the nation's dominant political party. The Republicans championed the Northern cause during the Civil War and for decades thereafter Republican orators and candidates continued to "wave the bloody shirt" to reinforce the allegiance of Northern voters. After the Southern states returned to the Union, the Republican Party continued to dominate many parts of the North. So successful were the Republicans in dominating the political agenda of the late nineteenth century that only two Democrats—Grover Cleveland and Woodrow Wilson—won presidential elections between 1860 and 1928.

The Democratization of the Franchise

Over the course of the nineteenth century, popular interest and participation in presidential elections increased steadily. Neither the Constitution nor the Twelfth Amendment specifies how the individual states are to choose their representatives to the Electoral College. By the 1830s, however, nearly all the states selected slates of electors pledged to the presidential candidate who won a plurality of the state's popular votes. The winner-take-all system has been all but universal since the time of the Civil War. Recently, however, Maine and Nebraska have voted to afford one electoral vote to the winner of a popular plurality within each congressional district, with the two remaining votes given to the statewide winner.

Popular selection of Electoral College members became standard by the

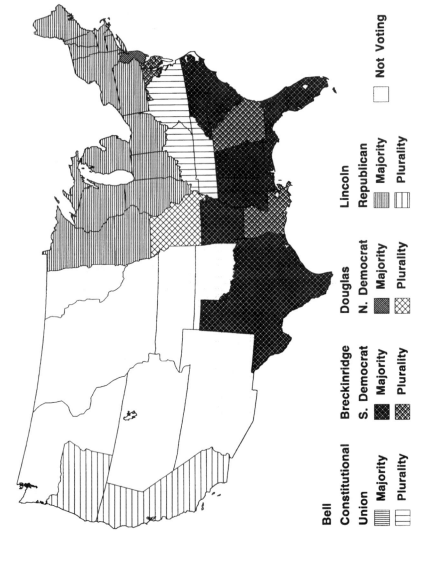

FIGURE 3-9. U.S. Presidential Election, 1860. Data from U.S. Bureau of the Census (1975), p. 1080.

Bell
Constitutional
Union

Breckinridge
S. Democrat

Douglas
N. Democrat

Lincoln
Republican

▦ Majority

■ Majority

▨ Majority

▥ Majority

▤ Plurality

▨ Plurality

▨ Plurality

▥ Plurality

☐ Not Voting

1830s. Levels of popular participation in presidential elections had previously been low, since electors were chosen by state legislatures in many parts of the United States during the late eighteenth and early nineteenth centuries. To be sure, it is difficult to estimate nineteenth-century voter turnouts with great accuracy, since analysis is complicated by nonuniform election procedures, missing returns, and vote tallies of dubious validity for numerous counties and even some states in early elections. Despite these difficulties, it is interesting to examine general trends in voter turnout over time in different parts of the United States.

Slightly over one-third of a million popular votes were cast in eighteen states in the presidential election of 1824. This election was ultimately decided in the House of Representatives (the last time that the House has decided a presidential election). Four candidates—John Quincy Adams, Henry Clay, William Crawford, and Andrew Jackson—received electoral votes, but none won a majority. Early in 1825, the House resolved the Electoral College deadlock in favor of Adams, even though Jackson had received more popular votes. Although the size of the potential electorate is quite difficult to estimate for so early an election, it appears that only about one-fourth of adults who might have been eligible to vote did so in 1824.

Voter participation expanded greatly for the elections that followed the controversial 1824 contest. Nationwide turnout increased to over 50 percent in the elections of 1828, 1832, and 1836. Turnout levels exceeded 70 percent for several states in the interior South, Middle West, and New England during this important formative era. This was the period when mass-based popular electoral politics were quite literally being invented by U.S. politicians. Canals, steamships, and railroads were extending and speeding travel. Higher rates of literacy and advances in printing technology were opening new frontiers of mass print communications. Popularly based political parties were being mobilized by ambitious political leaders who applied the new technologies and organizational methods to gain electoral advantages over their opponents.

National party conventions, partisan newspapers, coordinated campaign canvassing of eligible voters, buttons and badges, torchlight parades, and other tools for mobilizing and rallying voters were used and refined in the "Log Cabin and Hard Cider" campaign of 1840. Intense and enduring party loyalties were kindled and reinforced as "masses of people, including some normally distrustful, set aside their caution and threw themselves into the secular revivalism of log cabins and Tippecanoe. They . . . believed at least briefly that government, with the right leaders in command, could 'redeem' their morally wayward and economically stagnant society" (Formisano, 1993, p. 682).

Nearly 2.5 million voters—over 80 percent of the potential electorate—swarmed to the polls in 1840, when Whig William Henry Harrison ousted Democrat Martin Van Buren. Ironically, the Whigs who represented the wealthier commercial and planting interests relied on mass appeal to defeat

Van Buren, the political heir of Jackson. "The rich and wellborn had at last learned that in politics the votes of the humble were not to be despised" (Roseboom and Eckes, 1979, p. 56). Mass-based partisan electoral politics had arrived on the political stage. Indeed, mass political parties emerged in the United States decades before they appeared in European democracies (Taylor and Johnston, 1979).

Voter participation rose even higher after mid-century. National turnout rates exceeded 75 percent in two out of every three presidential elections from 1852 until the close of the nineteenth century. During this period, the number of active voters doubled, from 3.2 million in 1852 to 5.7 million in the first post–Civil War presidential election of 1868, and then doubled again, to over 13.9 million in the election of 1896.

The increase in voter turnout coincided with a general trend toward democratization of electoral participation throughout the nineteenth century. Before 1800, many of the states restricted the franchise to property owners, although property qualifications were generally eliminated prior to the Civil War. Universal white male suffrage was the norm by 1850, but women, African-Americans, Native Americans, and others were ineligible to vote. Not until the twentieth century would these restrictions be fully lifted.

Ironically, U.S. citizenship was not necessarily regarded as a prerequisite to voting. Adult white male aliens were eligible to vote at various times in more than a dozen states in the nineteenth century. For example, the Wisconsin constitution of 1848 gave adult males who had lived in the state for one year and had declared their intention to become U.S. citizens the right to vote (Wyman, 1968, p. 270). Alien voting was especially common in newly settled interior Western states. In fact, U.S. citizenship was not a universal requirement for voting throughout the United States until 1928.

The Sectional Normal Vote

During the 1850s, sectional tensions dominated U.S. electoral politics. Sectional conflict culminated in the election of Abraham Lincoln in 1860, followed by the secession of the slaveholding Southern states and eventually by the Civil War. Northern victory in the Civil War upheld not only the primacy of industrial capitalism in U.S. society but also the dominance of the Northeast in the political arena.

Once armed hostilities ended, the victorious Northerners came to be deeply divided concerning the reconstruction of the South. Lincoln preferred to pursue a moderate course, but more radical elements came to dominate the Republican Party after Lincoln was assassinated in 1865. The radical Republicans advocated harsh reconstruction measures, including military government. Southerners bitterly resented the presence of army troops and the arrival of Northern carpetbaggers.

Reconstruction ended with the disputed election of 1876, in which Republican Rutherford B. Hayes defeated the Democratic nominee, Samuel Tilden, by a single electoral vote in the face of widespread allegations of electoral fraud and corruption in the South. Hayes promised to remove U.S. troops from the South once elected. The end of Reconstruction gave Southern planters the opportunity to reassert control over local politics in that region. Still fiercely opposed to the party of Lincoln, Southern leaders gravitated to the Democratic Party. By 1880, the "Solid South" was safely in Democratic hands. Between 1880 and 1916, in fact, all of the former Confederate states gave their electoral votes to the Democratic nominee in every single presidential election.

The very uniformity of the Solid South rendered this section impotent in national elections. Both parties conceded the region to the Democrats and competed for votes elsewhere (Shelley and Archer, 1995). In order to win elections, Republican strategists realized the need to combine strength in the Northeast with that in the West. The degree of attachment to the Republican Party varied, however, throughout these sections (Figure 3-10). New England, Minnesota, Iowa, Wisconsin, and Michigan were heavily Republican. The West leaned toward the Republicans in most elections, but, especially after the 1870s, it embraced progressive and agrarian-oriented reforms that were increasingly antithetical to the interests of Republicans and industrialists in the Northeastern core.

As a result, the growing industrial states of the Middle Atlantic and Great Lakes regions became the key battlegrounds in most elections. New Jersey, New York, Ohio, Indiana, and Illinois were especially critical states. Between 1868 and the 1950s, whichever party won these states was almost certain to win the election. In all but one of the presidential elections held between 1860 and 1956, in fact, at least one of the two major-party presidential candidates came from one of these five states.

The general pattern of Democratic dominance in the South, Republican domination of the northern tier and the West, and intense competition in the industrializing central states characterized presidential elections throughout the late nineteenth century. Because sectional conflict remained clearly evident in presidential and congressional elections during this period, this pattern has been termed the Sectional Normal Vote (Archer and Taylor, 1981; Archer and Shelley, 1986).

The Republican Party had been founded on the basis of two underlying principles: the abolition of slavery and the promotion of Northern industrial interests. Northern victory in the Civil War, followed by the ratification of the Thirteenth, Fourteenth, and Fifteenth Amendments, fulfilled the former objective. Hence, the Republican Party came to be dominated by Northeastern industrial interests. Like their Federalist and Whig predecessors, the Republicans came to depend on the votes of farmers and small businessmen, especially in the Middle Atlantic region, the Great Lakes states, and the West. Republican strength in rural areas of the North was often needed to offset the Democratic loyalties of immigrants and industrial workers in the cities (Kleppner, 1979).

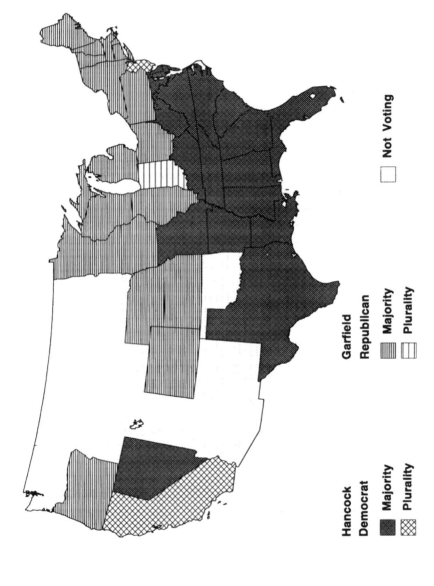

Hancock
Democrat

▮ Majority

▨ Plurality

Garfield
Republican

▥ Majority

▢ Plurality

☐ Not Voting

FIGURE 3-10. U.S. Presidential Election, 1880. Data from U.S. Bureau of the Census (1975), p. 1079.

Ethnicity played a major role in the voting behavior of many nineteenth-century Americans. The nineteenth-century Republican Party can be regarded as a manifestation of New England's moralistic political culture, which, as we have seen, spread rapidly across the northern tier of states. Thus, the Republicans believed in governmental activism to promote the common good. Republicans advocated not only abolition but also other reforms that were associated with the virtues of Puritan New England, including prohibition, Sabbath observance, and conformity with religious values in civil society.

Republican Yankee emphasis on these "moral" issues offended many voters of Continental European ancestry. Many Roman Catholic voters were offended by Republican emphasis on Protestant virtues, while both Protestants and Catholics of German ancestry objected to Republican advocacy of prohibition. Hence, many immigrants and their descendants gravitated to the Democrats. Although the Republicans won a large majority of statewide and local elections in the North in the late nineteenth century, these and other cultural issues sometimes engendered sufficient opposition to swing various states to the Democrats. Occasionally, in fact, a combination of national and local issues worked against Republican dominance.

As the nineteenth century drew to a close, the Sectional Normal Vote, which depended on an alliance between the industrial Northeast and the agrarian West, began to break down. The Populist Revolt of the 1890s was the culmination of increasing tension between these sections, and it resulted in the restructuring of both major parties, as discussed in detail in the next chapter.

Chapter 4

THE UNITED STATES
IN TRANSITION

n 1890, the U.S. Census Bureau declared that the frontier was closed. The census of 1890 revealed that the transition from the rural and agrarian United States of the nineteenth century to the highly industrialized metropolitan United States of today was in full swing. By 1900, the value of U.S. industrial products had become considerably greater than that of U.S. agricultural products. By 1920, a majority of Americans were residing in urban areas.

As its economy continued to prosper and its population continued to expand, the United States began to play an increasingly important role in the world economy. After the Spanish–American War of 1898, the United States became a colonial power. Well before World War I broke out, the United States had become the world's leading industrial producer. By mid-century, the United States was the world's leading political and economic power.

All of these developments had profound consequences for the political geography of the United States in the twentieth century. In this chapter, we examine the major impacts on U.S. political geography during the first two-thirds of the twentieth century, beginning with the 1890s and continuing into the late 1960s.

Immigration, Settlement, and Demography
in the Twentieth-Century United States

In 1900, the population of the United States was about 76 million people, with about 60 percent living in rural areas. By the 1960s, the population had reached 200 million, with over two-thirds living in urban areas. Large-scale migration of Americans from rural to urban areas has had a profound impact on the twentieth-century political geography of the United States.

The Transition to an Urbanized Society

During the nineteenth century, the U.S. Census Bureau defined a "settled" area as one containing a minimum of two persons per square mile. The Census Bureau's declaration that the frontier was closed was prompted by evidence that most parts of the United States contained more than two people per square mile (see Figure 3-3). Despite the closing of the frontier, there remained large tracts of unsettled land throughout the West. In fact, the government would give away more acres between 1890 and 1930 than it had between the passage of the Homestead Act in 1862 and 1890 (Brinkley, 1993, p. 448). Yet the idea that the frontier was closed had a profound influence on U.S. society and politics at the end of the nineteenth century.

Over the course of the nineteenth century, millions of Americans moved from farms to cities and towns. Yet the movement of farm youths to urban areas attracted little attention compared to migration to the western frontier. After 1890, however, rural-to-urban migration began to eclipse the westward movement. Migration from rural origins to urban destinations became one of the most important demographic processes of the twentieth century. In 1920, 31 million Americans lived on farms. By 1990, the rural farm population of the United States numbered only 5 million—only 1.9 percent of the total population of the country.

Why has the farm population declined so dramatically and consistently? Paradoxically, the very success of U.S. agriculture has proven to be detrimental to the agricultural sector (Fite, 1981). A farmer's profit is determined by the difference between the cost of producing a crop and the price received from its sale. Because individual farmers cannot influence prices, they can increase their profits only by reducing production costs or producing more crops. These goals can be accomplished by obtaining technological improvements. New technologies have enabled farmers to increase crop production dramatically, yet increased production expands the supply of agricultural produce, driving prices downward.

Declining prices increased incentives for farmers to identify and implement additional new technologies, so that yields continued to increase and prices continued to drop. Farmers unable to keep pace with this technological treadmill abandoned farming. As a result, production has become increasingly concentrated on high-quality lands, with fewer and fewer farmers producing more and more food on larger and larger farms (Hart, 1991). As the number of profitable farms declined, more and more residents of rural areas moved to cities in search of employment.

Migration of Indigenous Ethnic Groups in the Twentieth Century

The rapidly growing cities absorbed people from a wide variety of origins. The children of farmers who moved to cities during the late nineteenth and early twentieth centuries encountered many immigrants from other parts of the world (Box 4-1) as well as members of indigenous ethnic groups whose migration patterns were also changing.

Changes in the distribution of immigrants and their descendants paralleled changes in the distribution of indigenous ethnic groups. African-Americans, Hispanics, Native Americans, and other nonwhite Americans moved in large numbers throughout the United States.

Although African-American slaves had been emancipated during the Civil War, a large majority of their descendants continued to live in the rural South. After World War I, however, large numbers of African-Americans began to migrate to Northern industrial cities. Rapid industrial expansion coupled with newly enacted restrictions on foreign immigration during the 1920s made plenty of industrial jobs available in the Northeast. Manufacturing concerns sent recruiters to rural areas of the South in order to persuade African-Americans to move northward. At the same time, many African-Americans saw a move to the North as an opportunity to escape the poverty and institutionalized racism of the rural South.

Between the 1920s and 1960s, millions of African-Americans streamed northward to New York, Philadelphia, Detroit, Cleveland, Washington, Baltimore, Chicago, and many other Northern cities. Like nineteenth-century European immigrants, many moved to areas where they had friends and relatives, who could help them get jobs and housing. As a result, the northward migration of African-Americans followed several distinct streams: Natives of Virginia, the Carolinas, and Georgia moved to the large cities of the East Coast. Natives of Alabama and Mississippi tended to settle in Detroit, Chicago, and other Great Lakes cities, while those from Louisiana and Texas often moved to cities on the West Coast.

The Hispanic-American population of the United States also grew rapidly throughout the twentieth century. Hundreds of thousands of immigrants from Mexico poured across the border, legally or illegally, between the 1920s and 1960s despite restrictions on immigration. After Fidel Castro took over the government of Cuba in 1959 and aligned that former U.S. colony with the Soviet Union, thousands of Cubans—primarily middle-class business executives and professionals—moved to southern Florida, less than two hundred miles away. By the 1980s, Cuban-Americans had become a dominant ethnic group and political faction in the Miami area. Puerto Ricans in search of higher wages and better job opportunities streamed into Florida, New York, and elsewhere throughout the twentieth century. The Hispanic-American population of the United States rose even more dramatically after restrictions on foreign immigration were lifted in 1965. Hispanic-Americans are especially numerous in Sunbelt states, including California, Arizona, Texas, and Florida.

By 1900, centuries of persecution and genocide had nearly wiped out the Native American population. Native Americans made an impressive comeback during the twentieth century. Many migrated from reservations to cities

Box 4-1. *Twentieth-Century Immigration Patterns*

On October 28, 1886, President Grover Cleveland traveled to New York to dedicate the Statue of Liberty. The famous poem by Emma Lazarus engraved on a tablet at the base of the statue, including the immortal words "Give me your tired, your poor, your huddled masses yearning to breathe free" has long symbolized the role of immigration into the United States. Even as Cleveland dedicated the statue, however, patterns of immigration into the United States were undergoing a fundamental transformation. During the twentieth century, patterns of immigration into the United States would undergo several more fundamental changes.

For most of the nineteenth century, northern and western Europe provided the preponderance of immigrants into the United States. By the 1890s, however, immigrants from southern and eastern Europe began to outnumber those from northern and western Europe. Whereas only 1.4 percent of all immigrants into the United States between 1861 and 1870 came from southern or eastern Europe, this percentage rose to 51.9 between 1891 and 1900 and to 70.8 a decade later (Morison et al., 1980, p. 108).

Between 1891 and 1920, over 11 million Italians, Poles, Russians, Bohemians, and natives of other countries in southern and eastern Europe booked passage on ships across the Atlantic. Most settled in industrial cities, in neighborhoods containing friends, relatives, and other compatriots from the "old country."

Neighborhoods of people of eastern and southern European origin soon became prominent in Detroit, Cleveland, Chicago, Pittsburgh, and other major U.S. cities. Industrial cities and neighborhoods such as New York's Little Italy, Detroit's Hamtramck, Chicago's Back of the Yards, and Sugar Hill in St. Louis teemed with immigrant families and their children. Immigrants in these neighborhoods continued to speak their ancestral languages and established churches, schools, and newspapers, enabling them to preserve their European cultural heritage while adjusting to a new and unfamiliar society.

Immigration to North America reached a peak in the period in the years before World War I. After the war ended, however, the U.S. government began to restrict immigration. In 1917, Congress established the Asiatic Barred Zone. This law specified that no immigrants would be admitted to the United States from China, India, or Southeast Asia. The Immigration and Naturalization Act of 1924 limited the total numbers of immigrants from other parts of the world. Quotas were established for each country of origin. Quotas were based on national origins in 1890, when the percentage of Americans originating in southern and eastern Europe had been much lower than was the case by 1920. Thus, the largest quotas were granted to the United Kingdom, Ireland, and Germany. Eastern and southern European countries were granted much smaller quotas.

As a result of the Immigration and Naturalization Act, levels of immigration declined sharply. A 1929 amendment restricted entry to 150,000 immigrants per year, but "immigration officials seldom permitted even half that number to actually enter the country" (Brinkley, 1993, p. 645). The quota system ensured that the pattern of origin countries would not change. Although there were fewer, the flow of immigrants continued to be dominated by people of European origin.

The period of restricted immigration into the United States lasted until 1965, when immigration laws were liberalized and national quotas and the Asiatic Barred Zone were abolished. In their place came two hemispheric quotas, 170,000 per year for the Eastern Hemisphere and 120,000 per year for the Western. Also established was a comprehensive refugee policy that accommodated persons fleeing from "political oppression." Numerous refugees from Vietnam, Laos, Haiti, Cuba, and other countries immigrated to the United States. Determination of political refugee status was controversial at times, however. During the Cold War, U.S. officials routinely accepted natives of the Soviet Union and Communist Eastern Europe as political refugees, while they tended to deny applications from natives of Third-World countries fleeing political oppression.

The revised immigration laws triggered a dramatic shift in the geography of immigration into the United States. By 1980, a large majority of immigrants into the United States came from Asia and Latin America. Between 1981 and 1991, nine million legal immigrants moved to the United States. Over 85 percent came from Asia or Latin America. Indeed, over 2.5 million immigrants came from Mexico alone—more than three times as many as arrived from all of Europe during the decade.

Meanwhile, the principal immigrant destinations changed dramatically. While the industrial cities of the Northeast and the Great Lakes states were the principal destinations of immigrants prior to 1924, a large majority of post-1965 immigrants settled in the Sunbelt. Cities such as Los Angeles, Atlanta, Miami, Houston, New Orleans, and Washington, DC, along with their suburbs, attracted especially large numbers of "new" immigrants. Today, more than a third of all foreign-born Americans live in California, with another third living in Florida, Texas, and New York. Thus, only four of the fifty states account for nearly two-thirds of all foreign-born Americans.

in search of better economic opportunities. Minneapolis, Denver, Los Angeles, and several other major cities boast thriving Native American communities.

During the late nineteenth and early twentieth centuries, many conceptualized U.S. society as a "melting pot." It was generally believed that distinctions of culture, language, religion, and demography would gradually disappear, to be replaced by a single, homogeneous North American culture. Proponents of the melting pot idea pointed to the development of transcontinental communication and transportation, industrialization and the emergence of national commercial markets, and the rapid mobility of the population as indicators of increasing homogeneity.

By the late twentieth century, however, it had become evident that the United States is not a melting pot at all. Rather, U.S. culture is characterized by increased heterogeneity and pluralism. U.S. society today may be more accurately described as a "salad bowl" than as a melting pot: The richness and variety of U.S. culture is best described by analogy with a salad, whose ingredients retain their individual and distinctive flavors while contributing to the quality of the whole.

Distinctions among the various ethnic and cultural groups that comprise the contemporary American "salad bowl" are important to the understanding of the political geography of the United States. By the end of the twentieth century, in fact, issues of cultural identity and cultural pluralism have become very important in the political geography of the United States.

Industrial Development in the Twentieth Century

As we have seen, the Civil War was the catalyst that triggered unparalleled economic expansion in the United States throughout the late nineteenth century. By the early twentieth century, the United States had become the world's leading industrial nation.

Industrial Expansion between 1900 and World War II

In 1914, the United States was the world's largest producer of coal, oil, pig iron, and steel, with production of these commodities exceeding the combined production of the next three largest producers (Britain, Germany, and France). The United States also produced 90 percent of the world's motor vehicles and consumed more energy than Great Britain, France, Germany, Russia, and Austria-Hungary combined (Barraclough, 1967). During the late nineteenth century, the United States increased its overseas exports of industrial products dramatically. Between 1860 and 1914, in fact, the volume of U.S. overseas exports increased sevenfold. Huge amounts of European capital were funneled into the United States economy to pay for the exports (Kennedy, 1987).

This accumulation of capital contributed to the continued rapid growth of the U.S. economy after World War I. Not only was the United States the world's greatest exporter of both agricultural and industrial commodities, but it was also the world's largest creditor nation. The huge and wealthy U.S. domestic market could absorb a seemingly endless increase in production of manufactured goods, automobiles, office equipment, agricultural machinery, electrical goods, and other products. With industrial output greater than that of the six next-ranked industrial powers combined, the United States also became manufacturer to the world (Kennedy, 1987).

Most industrial concerns founded in the late nineteenth and early twentieth centuries were located near the centers of cities. The industrialization of the 1920s saw the first major round of decentralization in U.S. industrial history. Increased population and wealth created markets for consumer items, and U.S. industry began to shift from capital-goods production to consumer-goods production. Factories in which these consumer goods were produced came to be located at the edges of cities in the Northeast, where the necessary markets, capital, and entrepreneurship were located. As the consumer-durables economy grew and corporations increased in size and organizational efficiency, the groundwork for future decentralization was being laid.

The U.S. Economy during the Great Depression and World War II

The 1930s proved a significant setback to the U.S. economy. In an attempt to protect domestic agricultural markets, Congress enacted the Smoot-Hawley Tariff in 1929. The Smoot-Hawley Tariff generated a round of retaliatory tariffs abroad that decimated U.S. export markets and contributed greatly to the severity of the depression in the United States. By 1933, unemployment in large industrial cities such as Detroit and Pittsburgh was running at 50 percent. Even in more diversified centers such as Philadelphia, unemployment rates were between 20 and 30 percent.

Despite high unemployment and economic misery during the depression, productivity and efficiency within the U.S. industrial economy continued to increase. By the late 1930s, there was a huge amount of unused capacity in the U.S. economy (Kennedy, 1987). World War II provided the stimulus needed to unleash this unused capacity. In fact, there was enough labor, raw materials, and industrial capacity that industry could not only supply the growing war economy, it could also meet increases in civilian consumption until late into 1941 (Cochran, 1972). By 1945, the U.S. economy was operating at full capacity turning out war material, and there had been a 35 percent increase in both employment and real gross national product since the beginning of the war, despite the enlistment of nearly fifteen million Americans in the armed services.

World War II also initiated fundamental changes in the distribution of U.S. industrial activity. Prior to the war, manufacturing employment was concentrated in the Northeastern states (Figure 4-1). Only in New England and the large industrial states of New Jersey, Pennsylvania, Ohio, and Michigan was as much as a third of the working population employed in manufacturing. As World War II approached, however, the federal government began to invest heavily in the construction of industrial plants in order to manufacture needed war supplies. Seventeen billion dollars, or nearly half of the previous total investment of $40 billion, were invested in war production by the federal government between 1940 and 1945. Much of this money was invested outside the traditional manufacturing belt (Figure 4-2). After the war ended, this investment would play a crucial role in stimulating the refocused growth of the postwar economy.

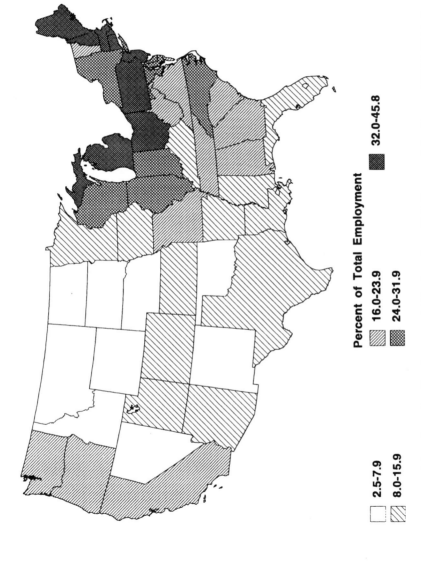

Percent of Total Employment

2.5-7.9

8.0-15.9

16.0-23.9

24.0-31.9

32.0-45.8

FIGURE 4-1. Manufacturing Employment, 1940. Data from U.S. Bureau of the Census (1947), Table 1.

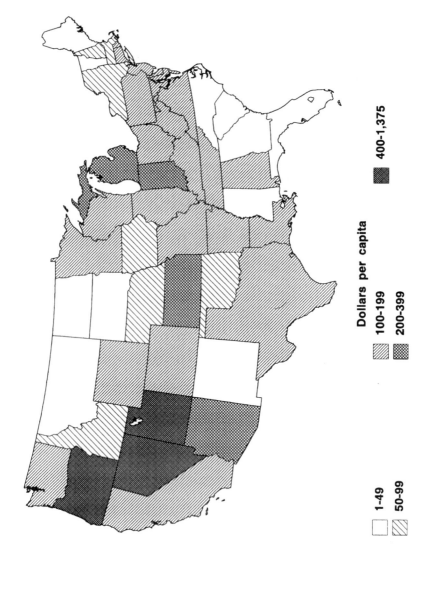

FIGURE 4-2. Industrial War Facilities Projects, 1940–1945. Data from U.S. Bureau of the Census (1947), Table 1.

U.S. Politics from 1890 to 1945

Reconstruction and industrialization fixed the geographic pattern of U.S. politics for several decades following the Civil War. As we saw in Chapter 3, the South became heavily Democratic while the Republicans dominated the Northeast and the West. As the nineteenth century drew to a close, however, the economic interests of the Northeast and West diverged. Farmers in the West complained of economic exploitation on the part of Northeastern industrial interests.

By the 1890s, agrarian protest in the West had reached a crescendo. This political explosion, in conjunction with the important demographic and economic changes sweeping U.S. society, would have a significant impact on the geography of U.S. politics throughout the first half of the twentieth century.

The Populist Revolt

As we saw in Chapter 3, one of the founding principles of the Republican Party was the promotion of Northern industrial interests. By the 1890s, however, many U.S. workers and many outside the Northeast had begun to view industrialization as a mixed blessing. The increasing concentration of capital in industrial cities was viewed with alarm. Northeastern capital had financed the development of railroads and other projects that had expedited the settlement of the West, but the Western economy remained dependent on the Northeast as a market for its minerals and agricultural products and as a source of capital and manufactured items.

Increased dependency generated protest. Throughout the 1870s, 1880s, and 1890s, a series of agrarian protest movements and third parties arose in the farming areas west of the Mississippi River. The West had remained Republican in most presidential elections following Reconstruction, but Northeastern and Western Republicans in Congress espoused radically different views on important public issues. During the administration of Benjamin Harrison, from 1889 to 1893, Republicans secured the admission of North Dakota, South Dakota, Wyoming, Montana, Idaho, and Washington to the Union. The new states promptly elected twelve Republicans to the Senate, but the newly elected Republican senators often voted in opposition to their Northeastern colleagues. Instead, many Western Republicans in Congress voted with the Democrats in opposition to the entrenched financial interests of the Northeast.

Meanwhile, a period of sustained expansion in the agricultural sector came to an abrupt end in the late 1880s. Droughts in many areas, coupled with low prices, resulted in unusually hard times for Western farmers. The hard times of the late 1880s and early 1890s coincided, moreover, with the closing of the frontier. Previously, farmers faced with hard times had had the option of pulling up stakes and establishing new farms in the West. After

1890, however, "with the lands all taken and the frontier gone, this safety valve was closed.... The restless and discontented voiced their sentiments more and fled from them less" (Hicks, 1931, p. 95). As the agricultural depression deepened, farmers began to blame hard times on the concentration of wealth in the Northeast. Banks, railroads, grain milling companies, and other interests affecting the agricultural economy of the West had their headquarters in the Northeast, and Western farmers had no control over grain prices, freight charges, or interest rates.

In the late 1880s, the People's, or "Populist," Party was founded. The People's Party called for currency expansion, government regulation or ownership of railroads, reform of the banking system, and other measures intended to ease the lot of the small farmer (Box 4-2). The new party soon became an important political force in the Western states. The Populist Party held its first national nominating convention in 1892. James B. Weaver of Iowa was selected as the party's presidential candidate. Weaver won the electoral votes of Kansas, North Dakota, Colorado, Idaho, and Nevada, while scores of Populist candidates were elected to state and local offices.

Shortly after Grover Cleveland's reelection in 1892, the Panic of 1893 began. Farm prices dropped and unemployment rose. At the same time, sectional controversy engulfed both the Republican and Democratic Parties. The immediate issue was the gold standard, supported by Easterners and opposed in the West by those favoring free and unlimited coinage of silver. The Republican convention of 1896 was dominated by Northeastern supporters of the gold standard. William McKinley of Ohio was nominated for the presidency on a "sound-money" platform with a minimum of opposition. The Cleveland administration favored a similar approach to the money policy issue, but the Democratic convention repudiated Cleveland. Instead, the delegates selected William Jennings Bryan of Nebraska, who had electrified the convention with his famous "Cross of Gold" speech. Shortly afterward, Bryan also received the nomination of the People's Party.

In his campaign, Bryan attempted to fuse Western and Southern agrarian interests in opposition to Northeastern financial and industrial power. While Bryan received considerable support in the Middle West and the West, his populist-oriented campaign received little support in the industrialized Northeast. Northern industrialists warned workers that Bryan's election was likely to cost them their jobs. In a record voter turnout, Bryan lost decisively to McKinley (Figure 4-3). The Republicans swept the Northeast, including the large industrial states that had been so closely contested in previous elections. McKinley combined support in the Northeast with sufficient strength elsewhere to win the election.

The Political Impacts of Populism

Following Bryan's defeat, the populist movement faded into history. Bryan's dream of forming a coalition between the South and the West against the in-

Box 4-2. *The Populist Party Platform of 1892*

The following resolutions appeared in the "Report of the Populist Party's Committee on Platform and Resolutions," presented in Omaha in 1892.

1. Resolved, That we demand a free ballot and a fair count in all elections, and pledge ourselves to secure it to every legal voter without Federal intervention, through the adoption by the States of the unperverted Australian or secret ballot system.
2. Resolved, That the revenue derived from a graduated income tax should be applied to the reduction of the burden of taxation now levied upon the domestic industries of this country.
3. Resolved, That we pledge our support to fair and liberal pensions to ex-Union soldiers and sailors.
4. Resolved, That we condemn the fallacy of protecting American labor under the present system, which opens our ports to the pauper and criminal classes of the world and crowds out our wage-earners; and we denounce the present ineffective laws against contract labor, and demand the further restriction of undesirable emigration.
5. Resolved, That we cordially sympathize with the efforts of organized workingmen to shorten the hours of labor, and demand a rigid enforcement of the existing eight-hour law on Government work, and ask that a penalty clause be added to the said law.
6. Resolved, That we regard the maintenance of a large standing army of mercenaries, known as the Pinkerton system, as a menace to our liberties, and we demand its abolition; and we condemn the recent invasion of the Territory of Wyoming by the hired assassins of plutocracy, assisted by Federal officers.
7. Resolved, That we commend to the favorable consideration of the people and the reform press the legislative system known as the initiative and referendum.
8. Resolved, That we favor a constitutional provision limiting the office of President and Vice-President to one term, and providing for the election of Senators of the United States by a direct vote of the people.
9. Resolved, That we oppose any subsidy or national aid to any private corporation for any purpose.
10. Resolved, That this convention sympathizes with the Knights of Labor and their righteous contest with the tyrannical combine of clothing manufacturers of Rochester, and declare it to be the duty of all who hate tyranny and oppression to refuse to purchase the goods made by the said manufacturers, or to patronize any merchants who sell such goods.

dustrial interests of the Northeast had failed. Yet the Populist Revolt resulted in lasting changes in the orientation of both major parties. The long-run impact of these changes would be to reinforce the Sectional Normal Vote for another half-century.

In response to the Populist Revolt, conservative Southern Democrats

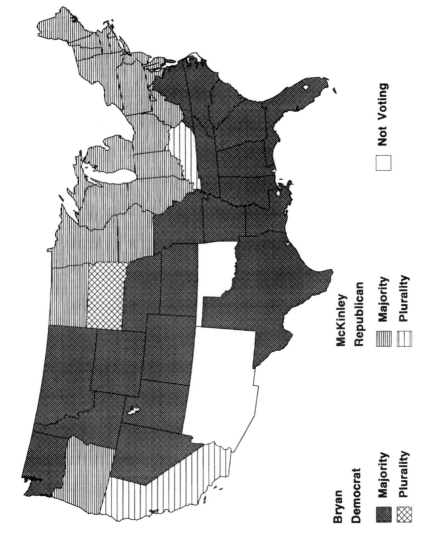

FIGURE 4-3. U.S. Presidential Election, 1896. Data from U.S. Bureau of the Census (1975), p. 1079.

Bryan
Democrat

■ Majority

▨ Plurality

McKinley
Republican

▦ Majority

▥ Plurality

☐ Not Voting

pushed for laws that greatly restricted political participation on the part of low-income whites and African-Americans. It was at this time that "Jim Crow" laws were enacted; these laws forbade African-Americans to vote or participate in politics, and they institutionalized racial segregation in housing, employment, education, and social life. Not until the civil rights movement of the 1960s would these laws be invalidated or repealed. The Republicans, meanwhile, recognized that they could not expect to win elections without Western support. Thus, they began to make a more concerted effort to gain support west of the Mississippi. In particular, the Republicans supported expansion of U.S. influence overseas. President McKinley was advised by many influential party members to support a war with Spain as a response to "the common fear, still meaningful in 1898, that the Democrats would go into the next presidential election [in 1900] with the irresistible slogan of Free Silver and Free Cuba as its battle cry" (Hofstadter, 1960, p. 90). After the Spanish–American War, Spain ceded Cuba, Puerto Rico, and the Philippines to the United States. By de-emphasizing policies of primary interest to Northeastern industrialists, the Republicans tried to cement an alliance between the North and the West against the Democratic-dominated South.

The Progressive Era

By the first decade of the twentieth century, both parties had begun to embrace some of the reforms demanded by the Populists a decade earlier. Theodore Roosevelt, a progressive Republican who succeeded McKinley after the latter was assassinated in 1901, made "trust-busting," that is, deconcentration of economic power, a priority of his presidency. Many of the reforms advocated by the Populists were enacted into law in the early twentieth century, but it would take an urban-based political coalition to achieve them.

The Populists "looked backward with longing to the lost agrarian Eden, to the republican America of the early years of the nineteenth century." They wanted "to restore the conditions prevailing before the development of industrialism and the commercialization of agriculture" (Hofstadter, 1960, p. 62). As the twentieth century dawned, however, a new Progressive movement appeared. The Progressives emphasized economic efficiency along with acceptance of and adjustment to the increasingly urbanized and industrialized twentieth-century United States. During this period, numerous reforms in electoral procedure, business regulation, education, and other spheres of human activity were enacted into law.

The Progressive ascendancy coincided with rapid growth in the manufacturing sector. Income generated from industry surpassed that amassed from agriculture by 1890. Ten years later, industrial income was twice that generated by agriculture. Cities grew rapidly, with the number of U.S. cities with populations of more than 50,000 increasing from 16 in 1860 to 109 by 1910 (Schlesinger, 1933). Demands for reform, including various reforms that the Populists had proposed, began to spread from the agricultural community to the urban middle class. While populism was concentrated in the South and West, progressivism was a nationwide movement. "A working coalition was forged between the old Bryan country and the new reform movement in the cities, without which the broad diffusion and strength of Progressivism would have been impossible" (Hofstadter, 1960, p. 133).

Many of the reforms embraced by the Progressives involved representation and electoral process. The Progressives scorned the urban political machines of the larger cities. The urban machines and their bosses depended on votes from immigrant communities that had little experience with the traditions of U.S. democracy. Thus, the Progressives concentrated on enacting reforms in the electoral process. They supported the initiative and referendum as a means of allowing public decisions to be made directly rather than by legislators who were frequently the targets of corrupt political bosses. The right of recall allowed the public to remove incompetent or crooked public officials, and the direct primary election reduced the bosses' control of nominating candidates for public offices.

By the second decade of the twentieth century, Progressive ideas had achieved wide circulation throughout the United States. Theodore Roosevelt was a strong supporter of the Progressive tradition. After defeating a conservative Democrat, Alton Parker, in 1904 (Figure 4-4), Roosevelt declined to run again in 1908. Roosevelt's secretary of war, William Howard Taft, was elected to the presidency by a substantial margin over William Jennings Bryan, who lost the presidential election for the third time.

The new Taft administration began to steer a more conservative course than had its predecessor. Roosevelt began to actively oppose Taft's policies, and he sought to wrest the Republican nomination from Taft in 1912. When the Republican convention renominated Taft, Roosevelt bolted the party and ran a third-party campaign. The conservative Taft won only two states, while the remaining states were divided between the two more progressive candidates, Roosevelt and the victorious Democrat, Woodrow Wilson (Figure 4-5).

The Progressives, like the Populists, were strongest in the Western United States. In the 1912 election, Roosevelt outpolled Taft throughout the West. A second Progressive ticket, headed by the veteran Progressive leader Robert LaFollette of Wisconsin, sought the presidency twelve years later. LaFollette carried only his native state (Figure 4-6), yet he ran ahead of the Democratic nominee, John W. Davis, in many western states. By the mid-1920s, however, the Progressive movement had effectively ended. Roosevelt had died in 1918, and LaFollette and Bryan both died in 1925. With their passing went the most effective leadership of Progressive forces in U.S. presidential politics, while sustained industrial expansion throughout the 1920s encouraged many Americans to pursue more conservative approaches to governance.

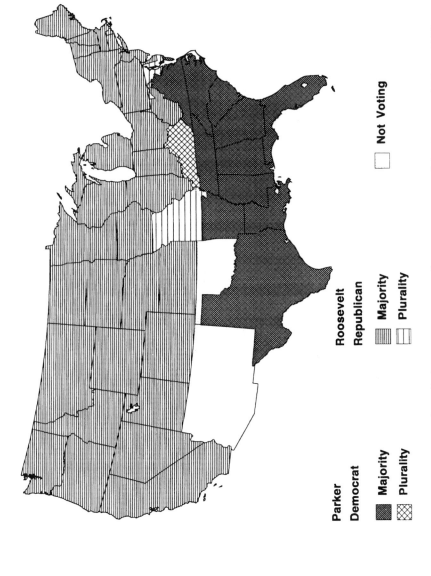

Parker
Democrat

■ **Majority**

▨ **Plurality**

Roosevelt
Republican

▥ **Majority**

▯ **Plurality**

☐ **Not Voting**

FIGURE 4-4. U.S. Presidential Election, 1904. Data from U.S. Bureau of the Census (1975), p. 1079.

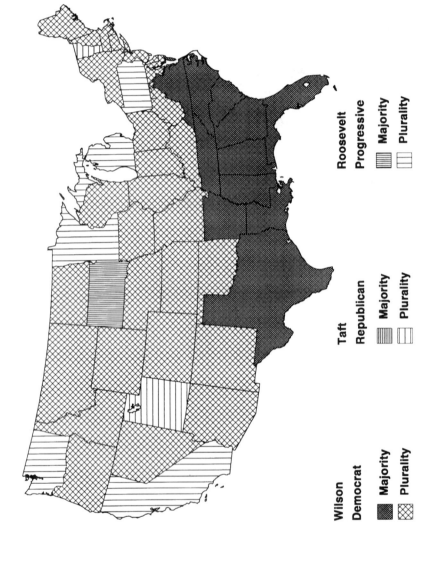

FIGURE 4-5. U.S. Presidential Election, 1912. Data from U.S. Bureau of the Census (1975), p. 1078.

Wilson
Democrat
Majority
Plurality

Taft
Republican
Majority
Plurality

Roosevelt
Progressive
Majority
Plurality

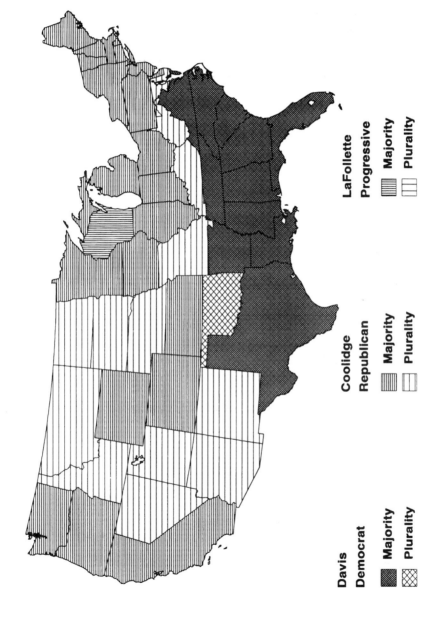

Davis
Democrat

■ Majority

▨ Plurality

Coolidge
Republican

▥ Majority

☐ Plurality

LaFollette
Progressive

▥ Majority

☐ Plurality

FIGURE 4-6. U.S. Presidential Election, 1924. Data from U.S. Bureau of the Census (1975), p. 1078.

The Politics of the Depression and the New Deal

Although industrialization and Progressive reforms wrought profound changes in U.S. life, the pattern of sectional conflict in the political arena changed little during the first three decades of the twentieth century. The South remained solidly Democratic, although Republicans carried some Southern states in the presidential elections of 1920 and 1928. The Northeast remained dominated by the Republican Party, and the electoral votes of the West were Republican in most presidential elections. In Wisconsin, Minnesota, and North Dakota, populist-oriented third parties became the Republicans' chief competition for state and local offices.

During the 1930s, the United States remained in the throes of the Great Depression. The depression began in earnest following the collapse of the New York stock market in October 1929, although agriculture and some other sectors of the economy had been in poor shape throughout the otherwise prosperous 1920s. By 1932, numerous banks had failed, and unemployment had risen to unprecedented levels. No longer could nineteenth-century economics and public policy deal with the crisis.

In response to the depression, the U.S. electorate turned in large numbers from the Republicans to the Democrats. Democrat Franklin D. Roosevelt won a landslide victory over his Republican opponent, President Herbert Hoover, in 1932 (Figure 4-7). Roosevelt promised a "New Deal" for the people of the United States. Aided by a heavily Democratic Congress, Roosevelt initiated an unprecedented series of reforms during his first hundred days in office. The Federal Deposit Insurance Corporation, the Tennessee Valley Authority, and the Federal Emergency Relief Administration were among the agencies created during the Hundred Days (Barone, 1990, Chapter 10). The Securities and Exchange Commission, the Social Security Administration, and the Rural Electrification Administration were established by the end of Roosevelt's first term. These and other new federal programs and agencies began to affect life in the United States profoundly.

The New Deal resulted in a substantial increase in federal responsibility and federal spending. Previously, levels of federal spending had approached levels of state and local government spending only during wartime. During the 1930s, much of this increase in spending was directed to the interior West, a region where support for the Democrats was weak. Roosevelt's strongholds in the South and the Great Lakes states, on the other hand, received only modest amounts of federal monies (Figure 4-8).

The electorate heartily approved of the New Deal, rewarding Roosevelt with a landslide reelection victory in 1936. Only Maine and Vermont supported Roosevelt's Republican opponent, Alf Landon. Scores of Democratic senators, representatives, governors, and state and local officials were swept into office on Roosevelt's coattails, making the Democrats the nation's majority party for the first time since before the Civil War. Indeed, recent historians

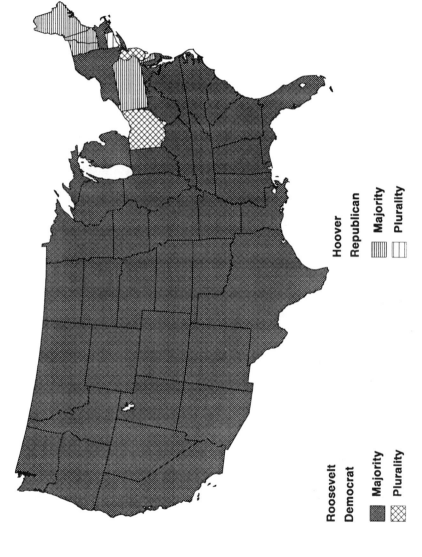

FIGURE 4-7. U.S. Presidential Election, 1932. Data from U.S. Bureau of the Census (1975), pp. 1077–78.

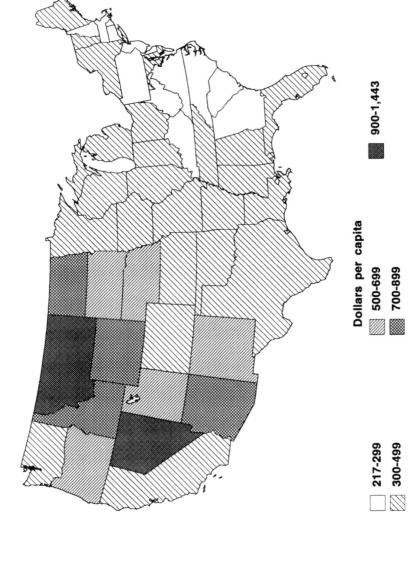

Dollars per capita

217-299

300-499

500-699

700-899

900-1,443

FIGURE 4-8. New Deal Expenditures and Loans, 1933–1939. Data from Reading (1973), pp. 808–9.

have claimed that Roosevelt's legacy has influenced the two major political parties and, indeed, the presidency itself ever since (Leuchtenberg, 1993).

While the New Deal permanently transformed U.S. politics, it had little immediate effect on the *geography* of U.S. elections. The shift toward the Democrats was relatively uniform across the United States. The South remained overwhelmingly Democratic, while New England and the Northeast were still the most heavily Republican areas of the country. Not until after World War II would major changes come about in the geography of partisan support in presidential elections.

U.S. Political Geography after World War II

Many Americans, following President Woodrow Wilson, believed that World War I was "the war to end all wars." Two decades later, most Americans recognized that another major international conflict was possible and, indeed, likely. Roosevelt's second term was increasingly overshadowed by the threat and eventually the reality of a second global war.

During the late 1930s, Americans were deeply divided about the U.S. role in the conflict. Some favored involvement, while others preferred neutrality and isolation (see Chapter 7). Debate and division came to an abrupt end, however, with the bombing of Pearl Harbor on December 7, 1941. For nearly four years, U.S. energies were devoted to winning the war. The United States emerged from the war as the unquestioned leader of the free world and by far the world's leading economic producer. Yet the decades following the war would bring major changes to U.S. life and society, changes that, in contrast to the effects of the Populist and Progressive eras and the New Deal, would result in substantial and permanent sectional realignment of the electorate.

Industrial Growth after World War II

When World War II ended, the United States again found itself in a very favorable economic situation. As had been the case in 1918, the United States was the only nation to come out of the war with an intact industrial capacity. The United States was therefore in a unique position not only to rebuild the economic base of Europe and Japan but also to use its enhanced economic power to expand export markets. Many industrial plants that had been run by the government during World War II were sold to private investors, often for prices far less than their actual market value. These sales spurred continued industrial development in areas that had experienced relatively little industrial activity prior to the war. Thus, World War II provided the initial basis for the rapid development of Sunbelt metropolitan areas. This process was reinforced by the Korean War of the early 1950s, which encouraged additional investment in the Pacific Coast states.

It was these advantages that laid the foundations for the economic expansion of the 1950s and 1960s. For twenty years after the end of World War II, the United States was the undisputed economic giant of the Western world. The United States provided investment capital, technology, and consumer goods for the reconstruction of the other Western economies, and in return it received interest, profits, employment, and the highest standard of living in the world.

The economic expansion could not have taken place without substantial improvements in communications technology and changes in the organizational structure of U.S. companies. Large corporations started to become a feature of the U.S. economic landscape during the early part of the twentieth century. Not until the postwar expansion of the 1950s, however, was technology sufficiently advanced to permit the large-scale functional decentralization of U.S. manufacturing firms. The development of interstate transportation, air travel, computer technology, and satellite communication during and after World War II enabled U.S. managers to control production facilities on a global scale.

Yet technological ability alone did not lead to the geographic dispersion of facilities. There also needed to be changes in the way the U.S. economy was organized. During the nineteenth century, the productive capacity of the United States was concentrated primarily in small, single-product, competitive firms. Large industrial organizations, such as the giant United States Steel Corporation, accounted for only a very small proportion of industrial output (Bluestone and Harrison, 1982).

The process of concentration of industrial capacity began in earnest during the merger wave of the 1920s (Knox et al., 1988). However, until World War II, only specialized heavy industries—such as automobiles, heavy machinery, and electrical equipment—tended to be highly concentrated. The vast majority of consumer goods industries were still in the hands of small independent manufacturers. During the postwar period, the degree of concentration increased for almost all domestic manufacturing sectors.

Increased concentration in turn generated a need for ever more complex managerial structures to administer the increasing size and complexity of multiplant, multinational, and multiproduct companies. It was these managerial structures that capitalized on new technology in communication and transportation to facilitate the expansion of their corporate empires. It was now possible for U.S. corporations to greatly expand the process of separating their operations both functionally and spatially.

The mode of production that developed as a result of this spatial fragmentation became known as "Fordism." While Fordism refers specifically to the process of using automated assembly lines to mass-produce products, the process also facilitated the separation of divisions of a corporation. The stage of automated production, requiring large amounts of low-skilled labor, could now be separated from the higher order functions of research and development and higher management. Production could now be decentralized to meet a variety of goals, including market penetration, tariff avoidance, and cost reduction. The decentralization of production would prove important in the transition from a Fordist to a post-Fordist economy, as documented in subsequent chapters.

Changing Electoral Patterns after World War II

The sectional pattern of the early twentieth century began to break down after World War II. During his presidency, Franklin D. Roosevelt straddled an effective but uneasy coalition between Southern conservatives and Northern liberals. This coalition secured Roosevelt's election to unprecedented third and fourth terms in 1940 and 1944.

By 1948, however, Roosevelt's New Deal coalition was beginning to fragment. The immediate issue underlying the breakup of the New Deal coalition was civil rights. Northern and Southern delegates to the 1948 Democratic National Convention in Philadelphia disputed whether or not to include a strongly worded statement in favor of civil rights for African-Americans in the party platform. Civil rights supporters, with the support of President Harry Truman, who had succeeded to the Oval Office following Roosevelt's death in 1945, won a narrow victory.

Southern conservatives objected, however, and many walked out of the convention. Under the label of the States' Rights Democratic Party, the "Dixiecrats" nominated Governor Strom Thurmond of South Carolina for the presidency. While Thurmond took thirty-nine electoral votes away from Truman in the still Solid South, Truman's strong support of civil rights legislation was critical to his support among African-Americans, liberals, and labor union members in the Northeast. Indeed, African-Americans, who had moved northward in large numbers before and during the war years, composed important blocs of votes in large Northern cities such as New York, Chicago, Cleveland, and Detroit. These votes proved critical to Truman's upset reelection over his Republican challenger, Thomas Dewey. At the same time, Truman ran an active and energetic campaign, criticizing the Republican-controlled "do-nothing" Eightieth Congress and comparing prosperity under the New Deal with the earlier depression years under Republican administrations. These considerations were critical to Truman's success in the Middle West and the West, giving him the election (Figure 4-9).

Transitions after 1948

The 1948 election ushered in a period of important geographical transition. By the 1960s, the once Solid South had become increasingly Republican in presidential politics. The Northeast, on the other hand, shifted toward the Democrats while the West became the most dependably Republican area of the country.

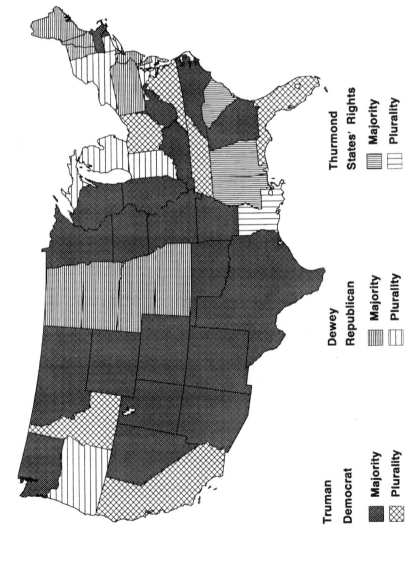

FIGURE 4-9. U.S. Presidential Election, 1948. Data from U.S. Bureau of the Census (1975), pp. 1077–78.

The Democrats backed away from a strong pro–civil rights position during the 1950s, but made civil rights a major issue in the 1960s. The Voting Rights Act and other major pieces of civil rights legislation were passed with the strong support of Northeastern and Western Democrats, along with numerous Republicans from these sections, although most Southern Democratic members of Congress opposed them. Continued Democratic adherence to a strong civil rights policy has cost the party substantial support among many white voters in the South.

Changes in U.S. foreign policy also contributed to the erosion of Democratic support in the South. Throughout the twentieth century, Southerners have tended to support an activist, intervention-oriented foreign policy, along with substantial military expenditures. By the 1960s, however, the Democrats had moved away from foreign policy activism and they became identified increasingly with opposition to U.S. military involvement in Vietnam.

Both civil rights and foreign policy had strong effects on the changing geography of presidential politics during the post–World War II era. In the 1950s, Republican Dwight D. Eisenhower's victories over his Democratic opponent Adlai Stevenson were due in part to a strong Republican performance in the Southern border states. Neither Eisenhower nor Stevenson took a strong stand for or against civil rights. During the 1960s, however, the civil rights movement and the Vietnam War polarized the nation, leading to a fundamental shift in the geography of presidential politics. The Republicans made inroads in the South and dominated the West, while the Democrats gained strength in the Northeast (Figure 4-10).

During this same period, suburbanization began to affect the geography of U.S. politics. Although suburbanization began in the late nineteenth century, large-scale movement of Americans to suburban areas began in earnest after World War II (Muller, 1981). Since World War II, the suburbs have grown at a much faster rate than have either central cities or rural areas. In fact, the 1990 census revealed that suburban areas now contain nearly half of the entire U.S. population.

Along with suburban growth has come political polarization within many metropolitan areas, especially in the Northeast. In general, central cities are far more Democratic than are their suburbs. A variety of factors, particularly demography and income, explain the tendency of central cities to vote Democratic: Median per capita incomes are higher in suburbs than in central cities. Ethnic minorities in many metropolitan areas are concentrated in central cities. And central cities generally contain fewer traditional families and larger numbers of young singles, elderly, and persons living in nontraditional households.

On the other hand, Republicans have dominated the suburbs since World War II, and suburban support has been critical to Republican victories in many national, state, and local elections since that time. Although differences between urban, rural, and suburban status influence voting outcomes, in most recent elections these differences have been outweighed by distinctions between the Northeast, the South, and the West (Murauskas et al., 1988).

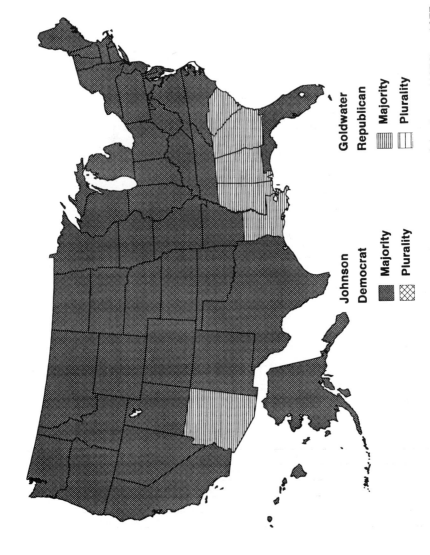

FIGURE 4-10. U.S. Presidential Election, 1964. Data from U.S. Bureau of the Census (1975), p. 1077.

Citizenship and Voter Turnout in the Twentieth Century

Over the course of the twentieth century, the concept of U.S. citizenship has changed dramatically. Since 1900, there has been an increased commitment to full political equality among Americans, along with a greatly expanded role for the federal government in enforcing equal citizenship rights.

Law in Twentieth-Century United States

The expanded right of citizenship was accompanied by several fundamental changes in the law. Prominent among these changes have been the increased importance of government regulation, the expansion of federal as opposed to state and local influence on the law, and increased emphasis on civil rights and civil liberties.

During the nineteenth century, U.S. law had been primarily distributive in character. A major objective had been to ensure the orderly distribution of the nation's vast resources for the maximum benefit of its growing population. As the nineteenth century drew to a close, Americans began to recognize that the land and resource bases of the United States were not unlimited. With this recognition came a shift in emphasis from distributive to regulatory law. Both the Populists and the Progressives supported expanded government regulation of economic activity. Western farmers depended on railroads in order to market their produce, and railroads that enjoyed monopoly status in particular areas frequently were guilty of setting prices at levels far in excess of market value.

Meanwhile, as more and more Americans began to work for wages in factories, workers demanded protection from discrimination, wage cuts, safety hazards, and other abuses. The Progressives were in the forefront of the movement to regulate economic enterprise. Reforms adopted in the early twentieth century included restrictions on child labor, enactment of regulations assigning employer liability in industrial accidents, inspection of meat and other agricultural products, and occupational licensing for doctors, lawyers, teachers, and other professionals. Other laws established minimum wages for workers, provided compensation for injured workers, regulated work hours, and gave state protection to labor union activities. Increasingly, government accepted the responsibility of regulating the economy in order to protect the rights of individuals.

The New Deal, which as we have seen was enacted in response to the Great Depression of the 1930s, set the stage for increased federal regulation. Much of the original impetus to regulate the economy during the Progressive Era had come at the state level. During and after the New Deal, however, the federal government began to become more active in economic regulation. By the 1960s, most efforts to enact and enforce economic regulation and laws for worker protection were undertaken at the federal level.

Civil Rights and Civil Liberties

During the twentieth century, the judiciary began to pay more attention to civil rights and civil liberties. To be sure, the Bill of Rights provides U.S. citizens with guarantees of freedom of speech, freedom of the press, freedom of religion, and so on. During the eighteenth and nineteenth centuries, however, these rights were often interpreted rather narrowly by the judiciary. Indeed, in 1833 the U.S. Supreme Court interpreted the Bill of Rights as applying only to the national government, and not to state governments. In the twentieth century, however, the judiciary began to interpret the Bill of Rights, and other fundamental rights enjoyed by Americans, more broadly.

The broadening of civil rights and civil liberties is based on interpretation of the Fourteenth Amendment. The Fourteenth Amendment, which was added to the Constitution in 1868, establishes that no state shall "deprive any person of life, liberty, or property, without due process of law; nor deny to any person within its jurisdiction the equal protection of the laws." This clause of the Fourteenth Amendment has been interpreted to apply to the rights protected in the Bill of Rights and elsewhere in the Constitution, as well as other rights implicit although unstated explicitly in that document.

A long series of court cases placed specific rights enumerated in the Bill of Rights under federal protection through the Fourteenth Amendment (Bibby, 1992, pp. 100–101). These include the right to freedom of speech, freedom of peaceable assembly, freedom of the press, and the free exercise of religion. Several important Fourteenth Amendment decisions have focused specifically on criminal law and the rights of the accused. For example, the Court has reinforced the right of the accused to protection from self-incrimination, the right to legal counsel, and the right to a speedy trial. The "rights" statements read to criminal suspects arrested by police officers, familiar to any viewer of police dramas in the movies and on television, are similarly derived from the Supreme Court's recent broadening of the Bill of Rights.

In some cases, the judicial extension of the Bill of Rights has proven highly controversial. For example, the Eighth Amendment bans states from inflicting "cruel and unusual punishment" on persons convicted of crimes. Some prominent judges, including members of the Supreme Court, have suggested that capital punishment is cruel and unusual and hence unconstitutional. In addition, the controversial case of *Roe v. Wade* bases a woman's right to have an abortion on a right of privacy, or the right of a woman to control her body—a right that is not stated explicitly in the Constitution but is implicit in several constitutional amendments.

Legal and judicial activity also proved critical to the success of the civil rights movement in enhancing the social, economic, and political status of members of racial and ethnic minority groups in the United States. As we saw earlier in this chapter, Jim Crow laws were enacted by many of the Southern states in response to the threat of populism. Segregation was given constitutional status in *Plessy v. Ferguson* (1896), which upheld the right of states to enact legislation that was segregated by race so long as facilities available to each race were "equal." The "separate-but-equal" doctrine underlay segregated housing, education, service provision, and many other spheres of governmental activity, especially in the South. Of course, the separate facilities for minority Americans were very seldom "equal." For example, per-pupil expenditures for white children in the South during the first half of the twentieth century were several times greater than for African-American pupils.

Only after World War II did the federal government begin to act to protect the civil rights of African-Americans against such legalized discrimination. As we have seen, the Democratic Party adopted a pro–civil rights position in the 1948 campaign, while President Truman ordered the integration of the armed services at the same time. Yet political expediency dictated a retreat from these positions during the early 1950s. In response, civil rights organizations relied on the judicial system to establish a framework for eliminating racial discrimination.

In 1954, the Supreme Court addressed the issue of legalized segregation directly. Many Southern and border states had maintained laws forbidding integrated education. In the landmark case of *Brown v. Board of Education* (347 U.S. 483), a unanimous Court held that racially segregated public schooling violated the Fourteenth Amendment by denying equal protection of the laws to African-American and other minority children. In *Brown,* the Court overturned the "separate-but-equal" principle, arguing, instead, that "separate educational facilities are inherently unequal." *Brown* was followed by a series of additional decisions banning segregation in other spheres of state activity.

Despite *Brown,* many white Southerners opposed the integration of schools and other public facilities, and steps were taken to prevent or delay its implementation. As years went by, African-Americans began to protest centuries of injustice and discrimination with more and more vigor. In 1963, a massive demonstration in Washington, DC, where civil rights leader Dr. Martin Luther King, Jr., gave his famous "I Have a Dream" speech, brought nationwide attention to the civil rights movement. The following year, the Civil Rights Act of 1964 was passed by Congress and signed into law by President Lyndon Johnson. The Civil Rights Act banned racial discrimination in all places of public accommodation, federally funded programs, and public and private employment. It also authorized the Department of Justice to initiate lawsuits against school systems to enforce compliance with *Brown.* A year later, the Voting Rights Act was enacted. The Voting Rights Act has had far-reaching consequences for contemporary U.S. politics, as we will see in detail in Chapter 6. This was followed in 1968 by the Fair Housing Act, which prohibited discrimination in the sale or rental of residential property.

The extension of federal protection to civil rights and civil liberties has by no means been limited to race and ethnicity. Title IX of the Higher Education Act of 1972, for example, bans discrimination based on sex in federally funded higher education programs. Other laws have prohibited gender-based discrimination in housing, employment, and transportation. A proposed Equal Rights Amendment to the Constitution failed of ratification during the late 1970s, but sixteen of the states have since adopted equal rights amendments to their state constitutions (Bibby, 1992, p. 128). In 1990, Congress passed the Americans with Disabilities Act, which bans discrimination against those with physical and mental handicaps in most spheres of public activity. These and many other pieces of legislation enacted during the past three decades are all within the twentieth-century tradition of expanding the scope of federal protection and enforcement of civil rights.

The Expansion of Citizenship

Citizenship can be defined as an individual's right to participate fully in the political life of the community in which he or she lives (Shklar, 1991). In general, the course of U.S. history has been one of steady expansion of citizenship. As we saw in Chapter 2, the Constitution was the world's first attempt to initiate a democratic form of government on a large scale. Yet the rights to vote, to hold public office, and to otherwise participate as a full citizen in the community was restricted at that time to white, male property owners.

Over the course of the past two centuries, the right to participate in political activity has steadily expanded. The Thirteenth, Fourteenth, and Fifteenth Amendments, added to the Constitution after the Civil War, upheld the citizenship rights of African-Americans (although these amendments were not universally enforced until the 1960s). In 1920, the Nineteenth Amendment guaranteed women the right to vote.

Other twentieth-century amendments to the Constitution have also expanded popular democracy. The Seventeenth Amendment, ratified in 1912, provided that senators be elected directly by the voters. The franchise was extended to residents of the District of Columbia by the Twenty-Third Amendment in 1961 and to citizens between 18 and 21 years of age by the Twenty-Sixth Amendment in 1971.

The Twenty-Fourth Amendment, ratified in 1962, forbade poll taxes. Literacy requirements were eliminated by the Supreme Court in the mid-1960s, and residency requirements were reduced during the late 1960s and early 1970s.

Voter Turnout in the Twentieth Century

Over the course of the twentieth century, the number of voters participating in national, state, and local elections has continued to increase. In fact, overall voter turnout exceeded 100 million for the first time in the presidential election of 1992. The continued expansion of the electorate is the result of population growth due to natural increase and immigration along with the effects of steady expansion of citizenship rights throughout the century (Figure 4-11).

The increased number of voters over the course of the twentieth century has not, however, been accompanied by an increase in the *percentage* of eligible voters who participate in elections. Indeed, the election of 1896 represents the high-water mark of the percentage of popular participation in U.S. politics. During the twentieth century, rates of voter participation have declined substantially, although the absolute number of voters has continued to increase.

By the end of the nineteenth century, party activists were effectively using railroad transport between cities and trolley transport within cities, as well as national telegraph and local telephone communications, to coordinate increasingly sophisticated election efforts. In 1896, most voters could read their own copies of Democrat/Populist William Jennings Bryan's "Cross of Gold" speech and Republican William McKinley's counterpledge of a "full dinner pail." By the time of this election, the adult illiteracy rate had fallen to barely 10 percent, and newspaper circulation was nearing 10 million copies per day.

Nationally, 79 percent, or nearly four out of five potential voters, cast ballots in 1896. Voters in Illinois, Indiana, Iowa, Michigan, Ohio, and West Virginia exhibited astonishing turnout rates of 90 percent or more. The state-level median in 1896 was 75.0 percent, a level exceeded by states as geographically separated as New Hampshire, Texas, Idaho, and California (Figure 4-12). On the other hand, turnout rates in such Deep South states as Georgia, Mississippi, and South Carolina were 34 percent or less. Most Southern states had turnout rates well below the national average.

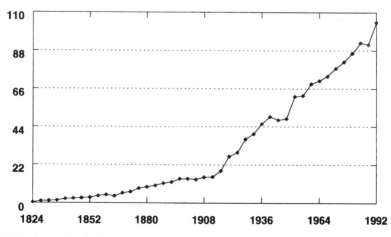

FIGURE 4-11. Total Numbers of Voters Casting Ballots in U.S. Presidential Elections, 1824–1992. Data from U.S. Bureau of the Census (1975), pp. 1073–74; U.S. Bureau of the Census, *Statistical Abstract* (various years).

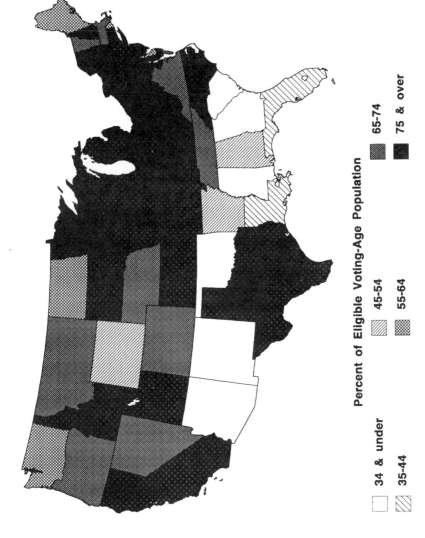

FIGURE 4-12. Voter Turnout, 1896. Data from U.S. Bureau of the Census (1975), pp. 1071–72.

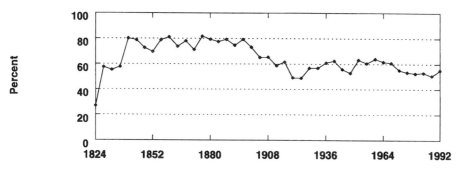

FIGURE 4-13. Voter Turnout in U.S. Presidential Elections as Percentage of Potentially Eligible Voting-Age Population Casting Ballots, 1824–1992. Data from U.S. Bureau of the Census (1975), p. 1071; U.S. Bureau of the Census, *Statistical Abstract* (various years).

During the early twentieth century, voter turnout rates began to fall (Figure 4-13). In 1919, the Nineteenth Amendment guaranteed women the right to vote. In the 1920 presidential election, more than 25 million votes were cast for the first time, but the rate of voter turnout fell below 50 percent. Evidence from Chicago suggests that female voter participation trailed male voter participation by about 20 to 30 percent in 1920 (Nie, Verba, and Petrocik, 1979, p. 77). This gap was even larger in the South, where poll taxes and a lack of electoral competition discouraged many families from casting two ballots.

Over the course of the twentieth century, however, the rate of female voter participation has risen steadily. By the late twentieth century, female and male voter participation rates have become similar. Because adult women outnumber adult men, more women than men now cast votes in presidential elections. Although the voting decisions of women in the early twentieth century usually mirrored those of men, by the 1980s there was clear evidence of a "gender gap" in U.S. politics. Since then, women have been more inclined to vote for Democrats. The gender gap has been attributed to Democratic Party support for civil rights, feminism, a pro-choice position on abortion, and opposition to military buildups.

The Geography of Twentieth-Century Voter Participation

The 1924 election warrants attention for having set the low-water mark of voter participation, even though it followed the high-water election of 1896 by less than three decades. Nationally, 29 million voters out of an eligible electorate of 59 million voters cast ballots in 1924, for an overall turnout rate just under 49 percent. The state-level median in 1924 was 57.8 percent. The highest turnout, 75 percent, was reached in West Virginia, and the lowest turnout, just 6 percent, occurred in South Carolina (Figure 4-14).

All but two Southern states had voter participation rates below 35 percent, and fewer than 20 percent of adults cast presidential ballots in 1924 in Alabama, Arkansas, Florida, Georgia, Louisiana, Mississippi, South Carolina, and Virginia. Poll taxes, "grandfather" clauses, rigged literacy tests, and outright physical intimidation were among the tools that had come to be used to eviscerate the suffrage guarantees of the Fifteenth Amendment, which had been ratified in 1870. Although suffrage restrictions had been adopted in some southern states as early as the 1870s, it was not until after the 1896 election that they were enforced rigidly in most of the South. As a result, turnouts declined dramatically between 1896 and 1924 in the South. In Virginia, for example, the turnout rate was over 60 percent for each presidential election from the 1870s to the 1890s; then Virginia's turnout rate plummeted from 71 percent in 1896 to 28 percent in 1904, before dropping even further to just 18 percent in 1924.

After dropping below 50 percent in 1920 and 1924, the national rate of voter turnout rebounded to nearly 57 percent in 1928 and 1932, and then further rose to over 60 percent for the New Deal era elections of 1936 and 1940. The participation of new voters, including women, contributed to Democrat Franklin Roosevelt's victory over Republican Herbert Hoover in 1932, but the fact that the voter participation had already increased four years earlier, when Hoover defeated Democrat Alfred E. Smith, argues that both the mobilization of new voters and the conversion of old voters played a role during this important period in U.S. politics.

National voter participation rates have fluctuated within a relatively narrow range since the end of World War II. Between 1952 and 1968, the turnout rate remained above 60 percent, with a postwar high of 64 percent in 1960. Participation rates declined thereafter, to a low of slightly less than 51 percent in 1988.

Voter turnout rates have risen dramatically among African-Americans since 1960 in response to the civil rights movement. As late as 1960, less than 15 percent of African-American citizens were registered to vote in Alabama, Mississippi, and South Carolina. On the average, only 30 percent of Southern African-Americans were registered in 1960, as compared to 64 percent of whites. Expanded African-American voter registration was one of the major goals of the civil rights movement during the 1950s and 1960s. Efforts to pursue this goal, which were part of Democrat John Kennedy's vision of a "New Frontier," intensified after Lyndon Johnson became president following Kennedy's assassination. During Johnson's administration, several notable measures dealing with housing, education, and civil rights were enacted. Johnson described the Voting Rights Act of 1965 as "one of the most monumental laws in the entire history of American freedom."

The Voting Rights Act empowered the federal government to send officials into localities where less than 50 percent of citizens were registered to

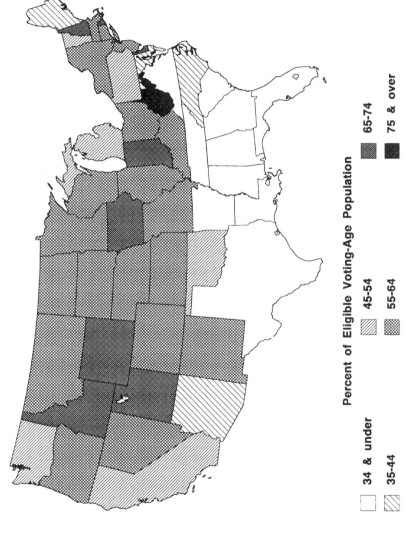

FIGURE 4-14. Voter Turnout, 1924. Data from U.S. Bureau of the Census (1975), pp. 1071–72.

Percent of Eligible Voting-Age Population

34 & under

35–44

45–54

55–64

65–74

75 & over

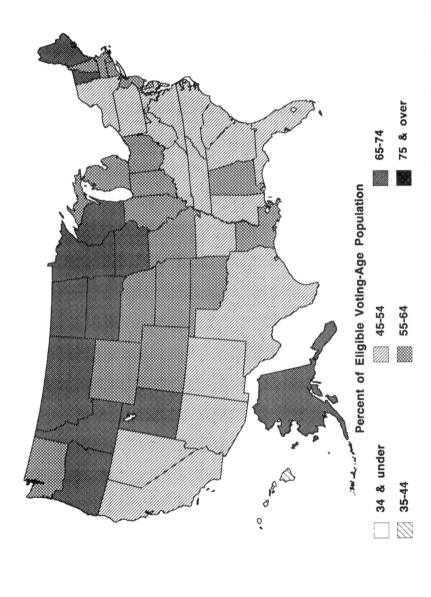

Percent of Eligible Voting-Age Population

34 & under   45-54   65-74

35-44   55-64   75 & over

FIGURE 4-15. Voter Turnout, 1992. Data from U.S. Bureau of the Census, *Statistical Abstract of the United States, 1993*, p. 285.

vote. The effect was dramatic. It took only three years for the rate of African-American voter registration in the South to double, to 62 percent. By 1992, 65 percent of African-Americans and 69 percent of whites were registered to vote in the South. In the North and West, 63 percent of African-Americans and 71 percent of whites were registered to vote in 1992.

In 1992, voter turnout rose to 55 percent—the highest figure in two decades. For the first time, more than 100 million Americans voted in a presidential election. The increased turnout rate undoubtedly received a boost from the third-party candidacy of Ross Perot. There seems to be little doubt that many of the 19 million citizens who cast Perot's popular votes would have stayed home during the election had he not entered the race as the strongest third-party challenger since Progressive Theodore Roosevelt in 1912. Perot's challenge may well have boosted the turnout for the other candidates as well, perhaps adding to George Bush's 38 million popular votes and to Bill Clinton's 44 million popular votes. Closer, more dramatic elections tend to draw more voters to the polls than do dull, one-sided elections.

The state-level median voter turnout in 1992 was 58.9 percent, only slightly greater than the 1924 median of 57.8 percent. But these averages disguise great differences in the statistical range between the two elections. In 1924, it may be recalled, the range was from a turnout rate of 6 percent in South Carolina to a turnout rate of 75 percent in West Virginia, so that 69 percentage points separated the lowest from the highest state. In 1992, in contrast, the range was from 42 percent in Hawaii to 72 percent in Maine, so only 30 percentage points separated the lowest from the highest state (Figure 4-15).

An examination of the state-level geographic pattern of voter turnout in 1992 helps to clarify the significance of the greatly diminished range in state-level turnout rates for the 1992 election compared to the 1924 election (compare Figures 4-14 and 4-15). Most important, the Southern states no longer have voter turnout rates dramatically lower than those of states elsewhere. To be sure, states with comparatively high turnout rates remain concentrated in New England and along the Canadian border from the western Great Lakes to the Pacific Coast. The lowest voter participation rates are still found in the South, but Southern voter participation rates now are much higher than they were early in the twentieth century.

Chapter 5

STATE AND LOCAL POLITICAL GEOGRAPHY

T he late Thomas P. "Tip" O'Neill, who served as Speaker of the House of Representatives during the administrations of Jimmy Carter and Ronald Reagan, once said that "all politics is local." Under the U.S. system of governance, place plays a particularly important role in the outcome of elections and the development of public policy.

One of the unique qualities of U.S. governance is the role played by state and local government in the United States. The process of governing the more than 260 million Americans is divided between three levels of government: the federal government, the governments of the fifty states, and the more than 80,000 units of local government. In this chapter, we discuss various elements of U.S. federalism that affect the geography of state and local government in the United States.

The U.S. Federal Structure

The framers of the Constitution took pains to establish relationships between the government of the United States and those of the individual states. The basic principles of federal–state relations established in the Constitution continue to govern relationships between the federal government and the governments of the states today, although the powers of the federal government in relation to those of the state governments has increased dramatically over the course of the twentieth century.

Unitary and Federal Countries

Throughout the world, functions of governance are divided between national and subnational governments. In a majority of countries, subnational government owes its very existence and authority to the national government. This type of structure characterizes a unitary country.

Unitary countries tend to be small or culturally homogeneous. A majority of countries in the Arab cultural realm, Latin America, and Africa are unitary countries. Other examples of unitary countries include France, Sweden, Japan, the Philippines, and New Zealand.

The highly centralized structure of France is typical of a unitary country. France is divided into ninety-six units of local government called "departments." The government of each department is responsible for carrying out the mandates of the national government in Paris. Governors and local officials are appointed by the national government, and they have no authority to develop policy initiatives independently. Services such as education, health care, and police protection are provided uniformly throughout the entire country, with no local variation in service standards or requirements.

In other countries, power is formally divided between the national government and subnational governments. This type of country is called a federal country. Many of the world's large and ethnically diverse countries, including the United States, are federal countries. Other examples of federal countries include Canada, Mexico, Germany, Switzerland, India, Brazil, Nigeria, and Australia.

The United States is a federal country. The United States Constitution explicitly divides authority between the federal government and the state governments. The Tenth Amendment to the Constitution specifies that all governmental powers not specifically delegated to the federal government are reserved to the states. Because services such as education and health care are not mentioned in the Constitution, these services are legally the responsibility of the individual states.

Because the structure of federal countries grants specific authority to subnational governments, one of the responsibilities of a federal country is to resolve conflict between subnational governments. The U.S. Supreme Court has frequently been called on to resolve disputes between various states. For example, the Court has often ruled on the allocation of water from the Colorado River, the Arkansas River, and other rivers among the states through which they flow.

State Constitutions

Each of the fifty states is also governed by its own constitution. State constitutions are fundamentally different, however, from the Constitution of the United States. As we have seen, the U.S. Constitution is a document of restricted authority and limited powers. On the other hand, state constitutions place limits on governmental powers that are otherwise construed to be unlimited. Thus, while the federal government may only do what it is specifically empowered to do, the government of a state may do whatever is not specifically prohibited by its own constitution or by the U.S. Constitution.

Because state constitutions must spell out specifically how governmental powers are limited, most tend to be somewhat longer and much more detailed than the U.S. Constitution. Americans' preference for written constitutions—a preference that contributed to the drive for independence from Great Britain, whose tradition was of an unwritten constitution—has prompted a considerable amount of constitutional revision at the state level. In general, state constitutions tend to be more directly responsive to electorates than is the U.S. Constitution. Consequently, it is much easier to amend the constitution of most states than to amend the U.S. Constitution. Seventeen of the states allow amendment by initiative, while all but Delaware permit the legislature to propose constitutional amendments that are then submitted for the approval of the electorate. Majority vote of the people is often sufficient to amend state constitutions, although constitutional amendments in some states require approval by larger percentages of voters.

Because it is generally easier to amend state constitutions than it is to amend the U.S. Constitution, the number of amendments to state constitutions is much greater than those to the U.S. Constitution. The 146 constitutions that have been ratified by the fifty states have been amended more than 5,300 times since 1775. The Constitutions of South Carolina and California have been amended over 450 times each. In contrast, the U.S. Constitution includes only twenty-seven amendments, with only seventeen having been enacted since 1791.

Not only are most state constitutions longer, more detailed, and more frequently amended than the U.S. Constitution, but state constitutions are also often more explicit than the U.S. Constitution in protecting individual rights. For example, some state constitutions contain more detailed and specific equal protection clauses than the Fourteenth Amendment. Others contain guarantees of equal rights for women. California affords greater protection to individuals from police searches than is required by the Fourth Amendment to the U.S. Constitution. That individual states may require stricter scrutiny of rights violations than those required at the federal level is an established principle of U.S. constitutional law. Finally, in contrast to the federal government, nearly all the states require government officials to balance their operating budgets by limiting current government outlays to the level of current tax and other revenues. (However, long-term financing of capital improvements such as parks, buildings, or roads through the issuance of bonds is usually permitted.)

Although the specifics of each state constitution are different, several distinct types can be identified (Elazar, 1988). Which type of constitution a state has adopted generally depends on where the state is located and when the constitution was adopted. A distinctive type of constitution has been identified with each of the three major political cultures. The moralistic states of New England adopted constitutions based on the commonwealth pattern, which institutionalizes the state's goal of providing positive direction to civil society and providing for the common good. The constitutions of the individualistic Middle Atlantic states establish "commercial republics," and they represent compromises among competing interest groups identified along ethnic, economic, and regional lines. The constitutions of the traditionalistic Southern states are contractual, establishing explicit norms governing the relationship between the established social order and the government. After the Civil War, the Southern states were required to redesign their constitutions, explicitly renouncing secession from the United States.

Three other types of constitutions are found in other parts of the United States. The constitutions of most of the Western states were written in the late nineteenth and early twentieth centuries. Many were heavily influenced by populism and progressivism (see Chapter 4). The intent of these state constitutions was to promote efficient conduct of state business while preventing excess concentration of government power. The Constitution of Louisiana is unique because its structure is based on the French civil code, which, as we saw in Chapter 3, had governed the state before the Louisiana Purchase. Louisiana's many constitutions have all been long and explicit codes spelling out the functions of the state in considerable detail. Finally, the states of Alaska and Hawaii adopted constitutions characteristic of post–World War II managerial approaches to federalism. They grant broad powers to the executive branch, place few restrictions on legislative activity, and stress the importance of government responsibility for welfare and natural resources.

The Distribution of Elected Officials

Interestingly, the classification of state constitutions is associated with regional variations in the proportion of government employees who are elected officeholders. Nationally, there were a total of 510,497 popularly elected state and local officials in 1992, or an average of 19.7 elected officials for every 10,000 persons. Regional variation was considerable, however. The number of state and local elected officials per 10,000 persons in 1992 ranged widely, from fewer than 2 in Hawaii to 244 in North Dakota (Figure 5-1).

It might be expected that variations in numbers of elected officials simply reflects variations in overall numbers of state and local government employees, including nonelected government workers. However, this expectation is clearly not supported by the evidence. Nationally, there were about 525 state and local workers per 10,000 persons in 1992. In Hawaii, there were about 570 state and local workers per 10,000 persons, while North Dakota, with a hundred times as many elected officials per capita, reported approximately 560. Thus, it is evident that geographic variations in the rate at which state and local officials are chosen by voters cannot be accounted for merely by noting geographic variations in overall numbers of state and local government workers.

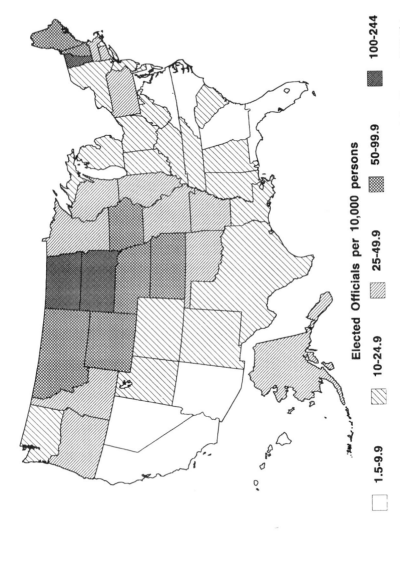

Elected Officials per 10,000 persons

1.5-9.9	10-24.9	25-49.9	50-99.9	100-244

FIGURE 5-1. Elected State and Local Officials, 1992. Data from U.S. Bureau of the Census (1994b), p. 5.

How, then, can we explain the distribution of elected officials per capita across the United States? In general, the distribution of elected officials per capita reflects differences in political culture, which are also reflected in differences among state constitutions. States along the Atlantic seaboard exhibit differences in rates of elected officials that are reminiscent of the early distinctions between New England, Middle Atlantic, and Southern colonies. The Southern colonies generally had more centralized local governments than did the New England colonies. Today, the Atlantic seaboard states south of the Mason–Dixon Line average fewer than 8 elected state and local officials per 10,000 persons. In contrast, the New England states average more than 57 elected state and local employers per 10,000 persons. In between, the Middle Atlantic states of New Jersey, New York, and Pennsylvania exhibit an average of slightly over 17 elected state and local officials per 10,000 persons. Thus, early differences of political culture are found to persist in the extent to which state and local officials are chosen by voters.

States located between the Appalachian Mountains and the Mississippi River generally show moderate degrees of emphasis on the selection of state and local officials by popular ballot. States located between the Mississippi River and the Rocky Mountains, states that were formed later in the frontier era, tend to elect larger numbers of state and local government officials. Indeed, the states of Kansas, Nebraska, South Dakota, and North Dakota average over 132 elected state and local officials per 10,000 persons. In these states, in fact, nearly one out of every five state and local government officials is an elected official.

States in the Southwest are less likely to emphasize electoral procedures for choosing their state and local employees. In Arizona and California, for example, there are fewer than 10 elected state and local officials per 10,000 persons. The northwestern states of Idaho, Oregon, and Washington, however, average slightly more than 32 elected state and local officials per 10,000 persons. The pattern along the Pacific Coast, therefore, echoes the pattern along the Atlantic seaboard, which can be linked to north-to-south differences in political culture. Yet the pattern is also influenced by the timing of settlement and admission to the Union.

The Administrative Structure of the States

States have often been called "laboratories of democracy"—a term recognizing the fact that states retain considerable flexibility in their administrative structures and procedures. Individual states are permitted, and in some cases encouraged, to experiment with novel social and economic programs, which, if successful, are adopted elsewhere. Many current federal programs are based on ideas that were generated by state or local governments.

Although administrative procedures and structures vary considerably across the states, certain regularities can be identified and analyzed. The chief executive officer of each state is the governor, and in each state he or she is elected by popular vote. The specific electoral procedures and powers of the governor vary somewhat among the states. Governors are elected for four-year terms in forty-seven of the fifty states, while the governors of New Hampshire, Vermont, and Rhode Island serve two-year terms. Eighteen of the states allow governors to serve an unlimited number of terms, while others restrict them to only one or two consecutive terms (Figure 5-2).

The power afforded to the state's governor under its constitution also varies considerably from state to state. For example, some states permit the governor to appoint important state officials, while in others these officials are appointed by independent corporations or elected by the public. Some states give their governor the dominant role in setting the state's budget, whereas others require the governor to share this power with the legislature. All but North Carolina permit the governor to veto laws proposed by the legislature, and many permit the governor to exercise a line-item veto over specific expenditures associated with appropriations bills.

Recently, an index has been developed to compare the formal powers of the office of governor across the fifty states (Figure 5-3). The index was based on the governor's tenure potential, power of appointment, budgetary authority, and veto power. Powerful governors were elected for four-year terms, were eligible for more than two terms, had the right to appoint major state officials, were charged with submitting executive budgets, and were granted the right of line-item veto.

Throughout the United States, a variety of other state officials are elected by the public. The lieutenant governor is elected by voters in forty-two states, and the state attorney general—an appointive position at the federal level—is elected in forty-three states. In many states, voters also elect a state treasurer, a secretary of state, and a state auditor. Other offices that are elective in some states include the state superintendent of education; the commissioners of agriculture, insurance, labor, and public utilities; and boards of education and state university regents.

Some critics of state government have claimed that the higher number of elected executive offices in the states is a hindrance to the process of governance. Candidates for governor and lieutenant governor, like those for president and vice president, run in tickets in the primary election in some states, such as Maryland and Florida. Voters cast their ballots for tickets including candidates for each office. In some other states, candidates for lieutenant governor run campaigns independently of gubernatorial candidates. The lieutenant governor, attorney general, and other state officials can and often do belong to a different political party or faction than does the governor. Moreover, the lieutenant governor, the attorney general, and other officers often harbor their own political ambitions—in many cases, aiming for the governor's chair themselves. Critics have argued that this fact hinders efficient governance of the states.

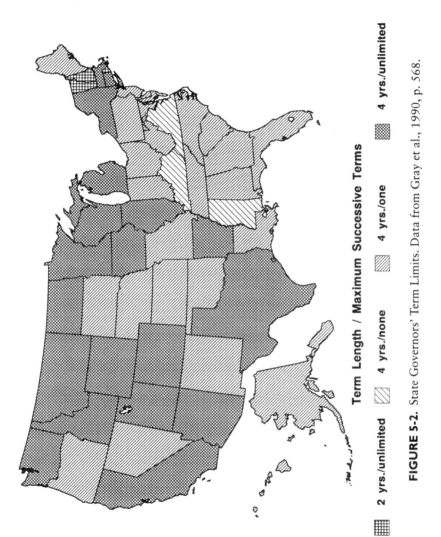

Term Length / Maximum Successive Terms

2 yrs./unlimited   4 yrs./none   4 yrs./one   4 yrs./unlimited

FIGURE 5-2. State Governors' Term Limits. Data from Gray et al., 1990, p. 568.

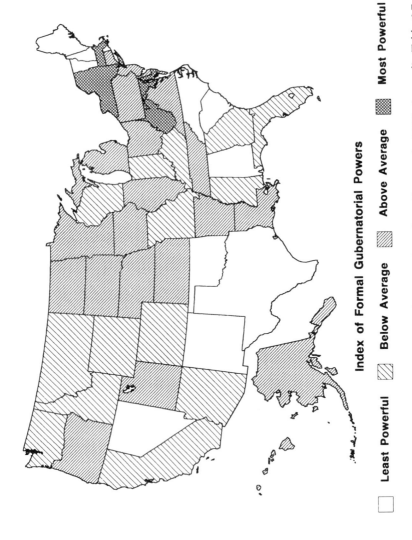

Index of Formal Gubernatorial Powers

Least Powerful   Below Average   Above Average   Most Powerful

FIGURE 5-3. State Governors' Formal Powers. Data from Gray et al., 1990, Appendix Table 6.7.

U.S. Federalism Today

Perhaps the greatest contribution of the New Deal to the political geography of the United States has been a permanent increase in the importance and presence of the federal government in U.S. life. The federal government's sheer size and scope has continued to increase ever since the New Deal.

Dual and Cooperative Federalism

The federal bureaucracy's influence on U.S. life has increased steadily over the course of U.S. history. During the nation's first century, most government officials subscribed to a philosophy of dual federalism, which suggests that responsibilities be divided clearly and unambiguously between the states and the federal government. The Tenth Amendment limited the power of the federal government under the philosophy of dual federalism to those powers enumerated specifically in the Constitution (for example, those powers enumerated in Article I, Section 8, such as the power to coin money, regulate foreign and interstate commerce, maintain armed forces, and so on). During the early nineteenth century, the U.S. Supreme Court addressed the controversial issue of how the Constitution's description of federal power should be interpreted. In the 1819 case of *McCulloch v. Maryland,* Chief Justice John Marshall established the doctrine of implied powers, which states that the federal government may "exercise powers that can be reasonably implied from its delegated powers" (Bibby, 1992, p. 72). Over the years, the doctrine of implied powers has been used to justify the assertion of federal power over numerous spheres of U.S. life.

Over the course of the nineteenth century, the philosophy of dual federalism was supplanting by a philosophy of cooperative federalism, which, in contrast to the philosophy of dual federalism, implies that responsibility for various governmental functions is shared by the national government and the states. The philosophy of cooperative federalism was initially developed in response to the recognition of the importance of the national government in developing the resources of the expanding United States. The Louisiana Purchase, the Mexican cession, and other territorial acquisitions (see Chapter 2) gave the United States title to vast amounts of land. At various times and in various places, federal land was granted to the states, to individuals, and to corporations. For example, federal land grants to the states were used to establish the many land-grant colleges and universities located throughout the United States. The Homestead Act of 1862 enabled large-scale transfer of federal lands in newly settled territories to individual farmers; other lands were granted to canal authorities and railroads, which used them to construct the infrastructure needed to promote effective settlement and development.

During the late nineteenth and early twentieth centuries, two important developments paved the way for the increased federal authority characteristic of modern U.S. society. During the nineteenth century, most federal officials were political appointees. Both political parties subscribed to the old maxim "To the victor belongs the spoils." The "spoils" awarded to the winning party were government jobs, and much of the federal bureaucracy was replaced with each new administration. After the Civil War, many criticized the federal bureaucracy as corrupt and inefficient, while presidents were besieged by office seekers hoping to receive presidential appointments to federal positions. In 1881, President James Garfield was assassinated by a disappointed office seeker, Charles Guiteau. Outrage over the president's assassination expedited congressional passage of the Civil Service Reform Act in 1883. This law placed the large majority of federal jobs under civil service protection, with appointments and promotion based on merit rather than on political considerations.

In 1913, the Sixteenth Amendment to the Constitution was ratified. The Sixteenth Amendment authorized the federal government to levy income taxes, assuring the federal government of a steady flow of revenues. Previously, the federal government had relied on tariffs and the sale of federal lands to raise funds. The Sixteenth Amendment paved the way for the federal government to raise far more money than state and local governments could. By the 1940s, the federal government had begun to spend far larger amounts of money than did the subnational governments. After the Sixteenth Amendment was ratified, the federal government inaugurated the concept of grants-in-aid, that is, direct cash grants to state and local governments for specific purposes. The Highway Act of 1916 was the first major law to provide grants-in-aid, in this case for the construction of paved highways in rural areas.

The power of the federal bureaucracy increased enormously in response to the Great Depression of the 1930s. Destitute state and local governments turned to Washington for help. The New Deal of the 1930s established numerous federal programs intended to alleviate the stresses of the depression and provide for public welfare, and the federal bureaucracy began to grow rapidly. In 1927, for example, federal assistance to state and local governments totaled $123 million, of which two-thirds was earmarked for highway construction. In contrast, the Federal Emergency Relief Act of 1933 alone provided $3 billion to the states in emergency relief aid between 1933 and 1936.

Since the depression, federal grants-in-aid have increased fairly steadily. By 1933, federal grants-in-aid to state and local governments totaled nearly $200 billion, or about 14 percent of state and local government revenues. At the state level, federal grants-in-aid received in 1993 ranged from $453 per capita in Virginia to $1,583 per capita in Alaska; in Washington, DC, federal aid reached $3,393 per capita (Figure 5-4). States as different in character and as widely separated geographically as Louisiana, New York, and Wyoming joined Alaska in receiving more than $1,050 per capita in federal grants-in-aid in 1993. In contrast, Colorado, Florida, Nevada, and Vermont joined Vir-

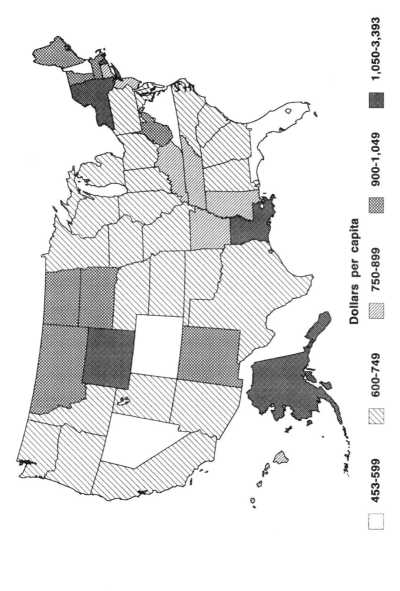

Dollars per capita

453-599 | 600-749 | 750-899 | 900-1,049 | 1,050-3,393

FIGURE 5-4. Federal Grants to State and Local Governments, Fiscal Year 1993. Data from U.S. Bureau of the Census (1994a), Table 8.

ginia in receiving less than $600 per capita in federal grants in 1993. Much federal aid is disbursed on the basis of formulas that reflect such need indicators as population numbers or poverty levels, but state or local matching funds are required by many programs, so that the overall geographic pattern is the outcome of complex social, economic, and political forces that involve and interact across all levels of the U.S. federal system.

Recent Changes in the Federal System

Not only has the amount of money granted to states and local governments increased steadily over the years, but the granting process has also changed substantially on several occasions. In response to particularly rapid increases in federal spending during the 1950s and 1960s, many observers became concerned that federal granting programs were inefficient, uncoordinated, and subject to rapid proliferation. Many critics also complained that the power of the federal bureaucracy over state and local governments had increased too much.

In response to these criticisms, President Richard Nixon promoted reform of the grants-in-aid process, a program that he called the "New Federalism." The New Federalism included two innovations. First, federal grants to local communities under the Community Development Block Grant program were distributed on an entitlement basis, with the specific amount of money determined by formulas that take into account population, poverty incidence, and other relevant variables. In this way, the grant application procedure was simplified and streamlined. In addition, Congress passed a revenue-sharing program in 1972 in which the federal government donated an entitlement to each state and each general-purpose local government every year, without earmarking the grant for specific purposes. The revenue-sharing program was eventually eliminated in 1986.

The New Federalism was less than successful, however, in achieving its stated objective of reducing federal intervention into state and local government. In fact, during the late 1960s and early 1970s, numerous federal statutes were enacted regulating state and local government activity. It was during this period that the federal government asserted expanded authority over environmental protection, education, and other spheres of activity that had previously been managed at the state or local level. The Coastal Zone Management Act, the Clean Air Act Amendments, the Family Educational Rights and Privacy Act, the National Environmental Policy Act, the Occupational Health and Safety Act, and the Equal Employment Opportunity Act were among the many federal regulatory laws enacted during Nixon's administration.

Ronald Reagan assumed the presidency in 1981 with the stated objective of reducing the size and power of the federal bureaucracy. During Reagan's first term, the government authorized a massive tax cut, eliminated or consolidated many federal grant programs, streamlined grant program administration, and promoted the deregulation of many programs. The result of Reagan's reforms has been a reduction in state and local dependence on federal aid, and state and local governments have turned to alternative sources of revenue or have reduced spending on various services.

Over the years, the increased size and scope of federal authority has resulted in increased federal intervention in various matters traditionally recognized as within the purview of the individual states. States and localities have become more and more dependent on federal funding to maintain their programs, and hence federal regulations linking funding to particular policies have influenced state and local policy in many cases. For example, in 1983 a presidential commission recommended that the legal drinking age be raised to 21. Determining the drinking age is a state rather than a federal responsibility, and many states had within the previous decade lowered their drinking ages to 18. In order to enforce compliance, Congress responded to the commission's recommendation and passed a law mandating that highway funds be withheld from states that did not raise their drinking ages to 21. Because states depend heavily on federal funds to maintain their highway systems, all soon complied.

The Geography of State Spending

Not only do administrative and political structures vary considerably among the fifty states, but patterns of revenue collection and spending are also very different from one state to another above and beyond differences in levels of federal spending. As we have seen, one of the major purposes of state government in the United States is the provision of a wide variety of public services to the population. Several factors influence the relative importance of various aspects of service provision across the fifty states.

In general, to examine spending on public service provision we must pay attention to three factors: inputs, outputs, and outcomes. Inputs are revenues raised for the purpose of providing services. Thus, inputs include various types of taxes, revenues raised from other sources such as user fees and lotteries, and grants from the federal government. Outputs are specific items purchased with inputs, whereas outcomes are the improvements in welfare associated with spending in inputs. For example, tax revenues raised by school districts (inputs) are used to purchase outputs such as teacher salaries, school buildings, textbooks, buses, supplies, and so on. The outcome, of course, is education. Although most people assume that higher levels of output translate to higher levels of outcome, this proposition is by no means universally true. Those who oppose raising taxes for improved services typically argue that the increased output spending associated with higher taxes will not contribute adequately to higher quality outcomes.

The states vary markedly in spending per capita. For the most part, states in the South and the Great Plains spend less per capita than the national average, whereas high levels of per capita spending are reported in the Northeast. Wealth and political culture appear to be the critical determinants of state tax effort and spending levels (Figure 5-5). The states also vary according to the relative proportion of revenues spent by states and revenues spent by local governments (Figure 5-6). In general, the ratio of state to local spending is higher in the Northeast than in the South.

States draw on many different sources for their tax revenues. Prior to the twentieth century, most states relied heavily on property taxes. During the early twentieth century, state and local governments began to impose taxes on income and sales. Today a large majority of the states impose both types of taxes on their residents. Only New Hampshire among the fifty states imposes neither an income tax nor a sales tax. Collectively, sales and income taxes account for nearly half of all state government revenues in the United States.

Some have criticized sales taxes as regressive. Regressive taxes affect the poor to a greater degree than the wealthy, because the poor spend larger percentages of their income on food and other taxable goods and services than do the rich. Yet sales taxes may represent more stable sources of revenue than other types of taxes, in part because consumption of food, gasoline, and other essential items is relatively independent of the state of the economy at any given moment. Also, sales taxes can be collected from nonresidents who purchase goods and services in a particular state. Many states and localities levy taxes on hotels, motels, restaurants, alcoholic beverages, and luxury items likely to be purchased by out-of-state residents. Reliance on such methods of raising revenue is especially prevalent in those states and communities that depend on tourism as a major component of their economic bases, such as Florida and Nevada.

How is this revenue spent? Salaries represent the largest cost in most state and local government programs. The distribution of state and local employment illustrates the relative importance of government service to each state's overall employment structure. The number of full-time equivalent state and local government employees per 10,000 population ranges from 390 in Pennsylvania to 770 in Alaska. Despite their lower tax bases, many southern and western states report relatively high numbers of state and local employees, in part because of the lack of alternative employment and in part because many employees such as teachers, highway patrol officers, and county clerks serve small and dispersed populations.

The Nature and Function of Local Government

Despite the dramatic growth in federal and state governments since the New Deal, local governments remain responsible for the provision of many public services and for the administration of many federally, state, and locally funded programs. The more than 80,000 organized local government units in the

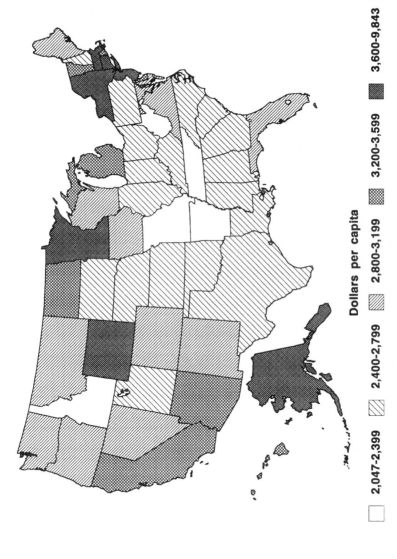

Dollars per capita

2,047-2,399   2,400-2,799   2,800-3,199   3,200-3,599   3,600-9,843

FIGURE 5-5. State and Local Government Outlays, 1989. Data from Tax Foundation (1992), pp. 166–67.

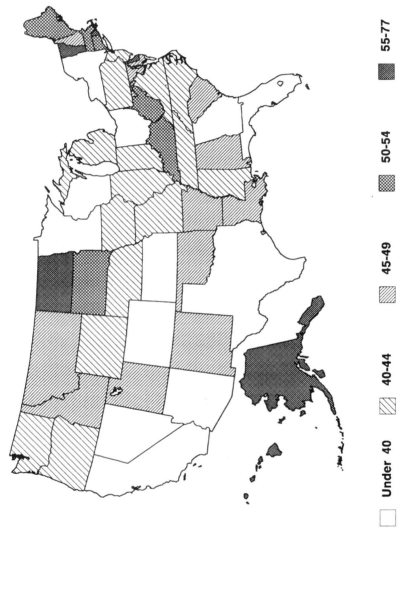

FIGURE 5-6. Percentage of Total State and Local Government Outlays Spent by State Governments, 1989. Data from Tax Foundation (1992), pp. 166–67.

Under 40   40-44   45-49   50-54   55-77

contemporary United States include general purpose and special purpose districts. General purpose districts include more than 3,000 counties, along with thousands of incorporated cities, towns, villages, and townships throughout the country. General purpose districts are responsible for providing a wide variety of local services to their residents, although their specific responsibilities vary considerably throughout the United States. A special purpose district, on the other hand, is a local government unit organized for the purpose of providing one or more particular services to its population. Special purpose districts include school districts, water management and quality districts, police and fire protection districts, among many other types.

The more than 3,000 counties in the contemporary United States range in size from twenty-three-square-mile New York County, which contains the Borough of Manhattan in New York City, to San Bernardino County, California, which covers more than 20,000 square miles of land and is in fact larger than several of the states. In population, U.S. counties range from Los Angeles County, California, with over eight million residents, to Loving County, Texas, with only 107 people in 1990. During the twentieth century, county boundaries in the United States have generally remained stable, although municipal boundaries have changed dramatically.

Regardless of purpose, all units of local government share several features. Each has jurisdiction over a specific area marked by boundaries, and most have the authority to levy taxes in order to provide services. Legally, however, local governments are the creation of the states in which they are located. Thus, any changes in local government authority or jurisdiction requires state approval. In some cases, in fact, such changes are initiated at the state level. Although local self-government is a deeply embedded component of U.S. political culture, local communities have no inherent right to self-government under the federal system. Thus, local governments are "subject to the obligations, privileges, powers and restrictions that state governments impose upon them" (Dye, 1985). In effect, the relationships between state and local governments in the United States is analogous to that between national and subnational governments in unitary countries.

Legally, incorporated cities in the United States are known as "municipal corporations." A municipal corporation is established through a charter from the state granting powers of local self-government to the community. While municipal corporations are often responsible for the enforcement of state law within their boundaries, they are also granted the power to enact local ordinances or laws effective only within their boundaries. In general, however, the power of a municipality to exercise independent self-government is very limited. "Dillon's Rule," a principle frequently invoked in court decisions concerning conflict between state and local power, expresses this limited interpretation. In conflict between the state and the municipal corporation, "any fair, reasonable, substantial doubt concerning the existence of power is resolved by the courts against a [municipal] corporation, and the power is denied" (Dillon, 1911, p. 448).

Because of Dillon's Rule, many city charters are extremely long and detailed. The charter must spell out in detail exactly what the municipal corporation can and cannot do. The charter of New York City, for example, is several hundred pages long (Dye, 1985). The effect of Dillon's Rule is to grant state legislatures considerable power over local issues, because any change in the charter must be approved by the state legislature. In some states, city charters are specific to each municipal corporation. Any change in an individual city charter in such states must be approved by the legislature through the passage of a bill referring to that city specifically.

In other states, "general act" charters are provided to municipal corporations. Usually, a state's cities are grouped into classes according to size, with separate municipal laws applying to all cities in the same class. For example, a state may apply one set of municipal laws to cities with populations of more than 100,000 people, another for cities whose populations are between 25,000 and 100,000 people, and so on. Of course, the practice of dividing cities by size enables a legislature to single out individual large cities for specific legislation. If the Michigan legislature, for example, were to pass a law affecting municipal corporations whose population exceeds one million, it would be obvious that the intent of the law would be to affect the population of Detroit because the Motor City is the only city in Michigan with that large a population.

Some states have attempted to reverse Dillon's Rule by granting home rule charters to municipal corporations. In contrast to Dillon's Rule, a home rule charter grants the municipal corporation the right to do anything not specifically prohibited by the charter. Of course, local ordinances may not violate state or federal law either. In some states, conflict between urban and rural interests has restricted the degree to which large cities have been granted home rule by their states. Legally, conflict over jurisdiction between home rule cities and the state is resolved in favor of the latter. The legislature may take a role in local affairs simply by identifying the matter in question as an issue of statewide rather than purely local concern.

Changes in City Boundaries

In the twentieth century, the boundaries of many municipal corporations have changed, often dramatically. Whether a municipal corporation may expand its boundaries to encompass additional territory varies considerably among the states. The issue of annexation is often highly politicized, especially when cities seek to annex adjoining high-income territory. In large metropolitan areas, many suburban residents vociferously oppose efforts to annex their communities to central cities. Suburban opposition to annexation is based on a variety of factors, including bias against racial minorities who may dominate a city's population and fear that annexation will result in a lower property tax base, poorer services, and higher taxes. On the other hand, annexation may also be opposed by some central-city residents, particularly members of ethnic minority groups who fear that their influence on city politics may be diluted by annexation procedures that add to the expanded city's nonethnic populations.

Whether annexation efforts are successful often depends on the differences in social and economic status between central cities and surrounding suburban areas. Nevertheless, annexation procedures vary considerably among the states. Some states, such as Texas, Florida, Georgia, and Oklahoma, grant broad annexation powers to local municipal corporations, but the power of annexation is extremely limited in many other areas, especially in the Northeast and the Great Lakes states. As a result, central cities such as Boston, Philadelphia, and St. Louis have come to be ringed by suburban municipalities.

Types of Municipal Administrative Structures

Although the specific administrative structure of municipal corporations varies widely throughout the United States, three basic types of administrative structure can be identified. About half of U.S. cities maintain the mayor–council plan of government. Most of the others have the council–manager plan, and about 3 percent are administered by city commissions. Under the mayor–council plan of government, voters elect the city's mayor and city council separately. In many cases, other officials (which may include, for example, the city attorney, assessor, or auditor) are also elected. The mayor is ultimately responsible for appointing and supervising heads of administrative departments, which are in turn responsible for providing services to the population.

Under the council–manager plan, voters elect a city council. The council in turn appoints a city manager, who is responsible for supervising administration. Under this plan, policy making and administration are considered separate functions, with the council responsible for the former and the manager—whose appointment is usually based on training and merit rather than on political considerations—is responsible for the latter. In some council–manager cities, the mayor is chosen by the council members from among themselves, whereas in others the voters elect the mayor directly. The mayor is responsible for presiding over meetings of the city council, but in contrast to the mayor–council plan, the mayor's office is usually more a ceremonial than a politically powerful office.

Under the city commission plan, a board of commissioners is elected by the voting public. The elected commissioners are directly responsible for the administration of city services. Typically, each commissioner assumes responsibility for specific services or agencies. Although many cities adopted the commission plan in the early twentieth century, conflict between agencies resulting from political discord has impeded the effective provision of services and has led to the decline of this system in recent years. Reformers who once advocated the city commission plan in response to the concentration of political power in the hands of the city's mayor have shifted their allegiance to the council–manager plan.

What factors determine which of the administrative plans is adopted by a particular city? Typically, very large and very small cities prefer the mayor–council plan, whereas the council–manager plan is more popular in medium-sized cities. In fact, nearly two-thirds of U.S. cities whose populations are between 25,000 and 250,000 people have adopted the council–manager plan. Smaller cities, in contrast, usually do not have the resources or the administrative problems to justify hiring a professionally qualified expert to serve as city manager. In large cities, the degree of policy consensus necessary for professional administration of city government is usually lacking. Two other factors predicting city government structure include growth rate and socioeconomic structure (Dye and McManus, 1976). The council–manager plan is more typical of cities that are growing rapidly and have large middle-class and professional populations. On the other hand, mayor–council cities are more likely to be growing slowly and are more likely to contain larger blue-collar, ethnic, and minority populations. For these reasons, council–manager governments are relatively more common in the Sunbelt and the West, whereas mayor–council governments are more typical of the Northeast and Midwest.

Cities vary considerably according to electoral procedure, and the nature of the procedure used to elect city officials is often itself a source of conflict. In some cities, mayors, council members, and other officials are elected on nonpartisan ballots, whereas others elect their officials on partisan ballots. In general, nonpartisan elections are more typical of council–manager cities, and partisan elections are typical of mayor–council cities, although there are notable exceptions. For example, the mayors of Detroit, Boston, and Cleveland are elected on nonpartisan ballots. Of course, mayors and mayoral candidates do not disguise their partisanship when running for office. In 1972, Boston's Mayor Kevin White was considered for the Democratic nomination for vice president, and Ohio's Republican Governor George Voinovich once served as the officially nonpartisan mayor of Cleveland.

Problems of Local Governance in Metropolitan Areas

Does the United States maintain too many local governments? In recent years, many social scientists have argued the affirmative, especially for large metropolitan areas, which may contain hundreds of local government units. Today more than half of all Americans reside in metropolitan areas of over one million people. Would their needs be served better by fewer local governments?

The question of reducing the number of general purpose and special purpose districts in large metropolitan areas is linked intimately with the issue of the contrast between central cities and suburbs in the United States. Since World War II, the suburbs have grown much faster than either central cities or nonmetropolitan areas. Particularly since 1970, the spectacular growth in suburban populations has been accompanied by large-scale movement of industries, retail opportunities and commercial centers to suburban locations. In most of the nation's large metropolitan centers, only a minority of the metropolitan area population can be found within the boundaries of the central city. Moreover, the rapid shift of the nation's population to the suburbs has left behind the dispossessed and the impoverished. Many central-city populations are dominated by ethnic minorities, the poor, and people whose lifestyles are at variance with suburban norms: gays, transients, present and former residents of mental health institutions, and the homeless, for example. Although gentrification (the purchase and renovation of urban property by upwardly mobile and high-income young professionals) has contributed to the restoration of inner-city neighborhoods in some metropolitan areas, its impact on the overall socioeconomic structure of most large metropolitan neighborhoods has been minimal. Of course, not all suburbs are equally wealthy. Many inner suburban municipalities are beset by poverty, unemployment, and physical and economic decline. Yet the contrast between central cities and suburbs in general is critical to the understanding of problems facing local governments in U.S. metropolitan areas.

As wealthy Americans continue to desert the central cities, central-city tax bases have declined compared to those of the surrounding suburbs. On the other hand, central-city dwellers are much more likely to need government-funded social services than are suburban residents. Hence, central cities are characterized by more service demands, but they are less able to meet these demands by raising taxes. The suburbs, on the other hand, contain wealthier populations whose demands for government services may be less extensive. The contrast between central-city and suburban tax bases and service quality is known as "fiscal disparity."

Without state or federal intervention, fiscal disparities within metropolitan areas tend to increase over time. Many people prefer suburban to central-city residence precisely because the quality of services is higher while taxes are lower. As wealthy people and revenue-producing industries continue to desert the central cities, the contrast between central cities and suburbs continues to increase. In some states, efforts to alleviate fiscal disparity have been enacted. For example, Minnesota law requires all jurisdictions in the Minneapolis–St. Paul metropolitan area to contribute 40 percent of their locally raised revenues to a common fund, whose monies are distributed throughout the metropolitan area on a need basis.

Fiscal disparity often influences land-use competition within metropolitan areas. Local governments compete for land uses that will expand their tax bases, while competing to avoid being saddled with those that will reduce their tax bases or increase service demands. Land uses that increase local tax bases without a corresponding increase in local service demands are known as "revenue-generating land uses." Examples of revenue-generating land uses include high-technology industry, shopping malls, and high-income housing developments. By attracting revenue-generating land uses, a municipality can increase its tax base and provide higher quality services without a corresponding increase in taxes. On the other hand, land uses that cause a reduction in the tax base compared to service demands are called "revenue-absorbing land uses." Examples of revenue-absorbing land uses include sewage treatment plants and polluting industries. Halfway houses for paroled prisoners or former mental patients have been placed in this category as well. The presence of revenue-absorbing land uses may result in reduced property values, exacerbating their negative impact on local tax bases.

In the competition for revenue-generating land uses, wealthy jurisdictions usually have the advantage over poor jurisdictions. Not only is a favorable balance between tax base and services often attractive to business owners and developers, but wealthy jurisdictions can devote more resources to attracting revenue-generating land uses. At the same time, wealthy communities tend to have more political clout and can use this influence to avoid revenue-absorbing land uses. Hence, the competitive process tends to reinforce the already considerable disparity between central cities and suburbs.

Some experts, aware of the continuing problem of fiscal disparity and land-use competition, have argued that the fragmented nature of metropolitan government has impeded effective governance of U.S. metropolitan areas. Large metropolitan areas now include dozens and sometimes hundreds of local government units. Some experts, in fact, believe that this has contributed to the social and economic problems of the metropolitan regions, which now contain nearly 80 percent of the U.S. population.

Advocates of reform have advanced several arguments in favor of consolidating local governments. Some argue that consolidation can enable services to be provided to the public more efficiently and effectively, in part by improving coordination between competing jurisdictions. Such coordination is especially important in the case of services that extend across existing jurisdictional boundaries, such as mass transit and fire protection. Others argue for reformed metropolitan governmental structure on the grounds of equity. According to this view, the continued presence of fiscal disparity is inequitable and deprives central-city residents of needed public services.

Opponents of metropolitan government consolidation point out that the present fragmented system, while by no means perfect, nevertheless has several advantages: It has been argued that fragmented local government increases local control over local affairs and provides local residents with better access to decision-making structures. Individual and interest-group access to service provision would be lessened under larger, more centralized, and more bureaucratized units of government. Thus, fragmented, decentralized metropolitan governance provides local residents with more influence over local government. In addition, its advocates point out that it allows local residents the opportunity to sort themselves into communities of people with similar values and lifestyles, who presumably will support similar levels of expenditures on various public services.

Advocates of reformed metropolitan governance have proposed several types of strategies to achieve the goal of eliminating governmental fragmentation in metropolitan areas. Although some have recommended territorial annexation, we have already seen that annexation is opposed by residents of both central-city and suburban areas. Others have proposed the consolidation of city and county governments. During the 1960s, city–county consolidation was undertaken in Indianapolis, Nashville, Virginia Beach, Jacksonville, and Columbus, Georgia. More recent efforts to promote consolidation have failed, however. Opponents of consolidation, like opponents of annexation, have often resisted the possibility of diluted political influence. Others have proposed the increased use of special districts in order to provide those services that are subject to problems of interjurisdictional coordination, yet opponents have argued that reliance on special districts gives excessive power to professionals in the function in question while reducing local control and influence.

Two less controversial and more successful approaches used in recent years include interjurisdictional agreements and councils of government. Many local governments effect formal or informal agreements with one another in order to streamline service provision. For example, two municipalities may agree to share the costs of police or fire protection or to operate a sewage treatment facility or refuse collection service jointly. Such agreements allow improved service efficiency without threatening local control. Councils of government are associations consisting of representatives of local governments who meet to discuss and recommend solutions to metropolitan-wide problems. Yet councils of government have no direct authority, and their recommendations are not binding on the local governments that they serve.

Sectionalism at a State and Local Level

Sectionalism between different regions of the United States is an important component of U.S. political geography at the federal level. Sectional cleavages are also characteristic of politics within state and local governments. Local sectional distinctions are important to an understanding of electoral competition for a variety of state and local offices, including governors, mayors, senators, representatives, and many others.

The politics of many states are characterized by endemic conflict between distinct regions. The politics of some states hinge on competition between major metropolitan areas and "downstate" or "outstate" areas outside the metropolitan orbit. Metropolitan versus nonmetropolitan competition is characteristic of the politics of New York, Illinois, Maryland, Minnesota, and Georgia, for example. In New York State, many Polish-American and Italian-American voters in upstate New York, who would elsewhere probably identify with the Democratic Party, are Republicans in opposition to Democratic dominance in New York City. In other states, rivalry between two major metropolitan areas is evident in state and local politics, for example, between Los

Angeles and San Francisco in California, between Tulsa and Oklahoma City in Oklahoma, and between Pittsburgh and Philadelphia in Pennsylvania.

Other states cut across two distinct physical environments and encompass widely divergent economic bases. Washington, for example, is divided between the humid, urbanized lands west of the Cascades and the sparsely populated, arid steppes to the east. Conflict within California between the well-watered northern regions and the heavily populated but water-deficient southern region is well known. In Louisiana, large-scale conflict is defined along religious and ethnic lines, with the Protestant, Anglo-Saxon population in the north opposing the Catholic Cajun population of French origin in the south. Competition for statewide office often follows these long-standing conflicts.

Many Southern states, including the Carolinas, Kentucky, Tennessee, Alabama, and Arkansas, contain extensive highland areas as well as large lowlands. In these states, conflict between the highlands and the lowlands is a basic feature of local politics. These conflicts, which originated prior to the Civil War, are linked directly to political culture. Plantation agriculture is a lowland phenomenon, as is traditionalistic political culture. The highlands of the South, in contrast, are unsuited for plantation agriculture. The hilly lands are suited only for small subsistence farms, and few highland farmers maintained plantations or owned slaves. Residents of these highland areas tended to support Republican candidates during the traditional Solid South period, and many continue to do so today.

State Iconography

Although regional differences characterize the politics of many states, most states are also characterized by a variety of centripetal forces that encourage persons to identify with their state of residence. In most states, public policy gives preference to state residents. For example, state residents are usually given preference in admission to colleges and universities, with out-of-state students being required to pay higher fees or being subject to stricter admissions policies. Out-of-state hunters and fishermen pay higher license fees and may be forbidden to hunt certain species that are available to state residents.

Most states reinforce their residents' loyalties through a variety of symbols. Nearly all recognize state birds, flowers, and trees. Typically, these symbols are chosen because of their association with the state's culture, history, or physical environment. Examples of state birds that typify the natural environments of the states that recognize them include the roadrunner of New Mexico, the scissor-tailed flycatcher of Oklahoma, the loon of Minnesota, and the Baltimore oriole of Maryland.

Each state has a state flag. Colors, emblems, and mottoes on state flags reinforce state iconography. Each state recognizes one or more songs as its state song, and state songs also reflect the culture, history, and image of their states. Well-known examples include "Deep in the Heart of Texas," "My Old Ken-

---

Box 5-1. *Controversy over the Confederate Battle Flag*

Over the past several years, several Southern states have experienced consider-able controversy over the use of the Confederate Battle Flag as a component of their states' flags and other symbols. One of the most acrimonious controver-sies has taken place in recent years in Georgia (Leib, 1995).

In 1956, the Georgia legislature enacted a bill to create a new state flag that included the Confederate battle emblem (a blue "X" on a red field with white stars embedded within the "X"). In 1992, however, Georgia's Governor Zell Miller called for the legislature to remove the Confederate battle emblem from the state's flag. The Confederate emblem was identified by many African-Americans as a symbol of Georgia's slaveholding past and, thus, as a symbol of segregation and racism. Others argued that the continued use of the emblem would be harmful to business, particularly with the state preparing for interna-tional exposure during the upcoming Olympic Games in 1996. While Miller's supporters regarded the Confederate battle emblem as a symbol of hate, those who preferred to keep it as part of the state's flag regarded it as a tribute to Georgia's Confederate heritage.

The heritage–hate debate raged in the legislature and among ordinary Georgians throughout the early months of 1993. Miller's proposal to remove the Confederate battle emblem from the state flag was introduced into both houses of the legislature. The bills were bottled up in committees of both cham-bers, perhaps to the relief of many legislators who therefore were able to avoid taking public positions on the flag issue in roll-call votes. Less than half ex-pressed a public opinion on the flag bill. While the flag issue was independent of partisan considerations, African-Americans strongly supported Miller's posi-tion. Most white Democrats who represented African-American constituencies also supported his position (Leib, 1995). Thus, the continued debate over Georgia's flag implies that the flag as a symbol of Georgia is a centrifugal or di-visive as opposed to a centripetal or unifying force.

---

tucky Home," "Home on the Range" (Kansas), "Old Folks at Home" (Flori-da), and "Oklahoma!" (although some Oklahoma legislators recently argued that this song, which was written by New Yorkers Richard Rodgers and Oscar Hammerstein for the well-known Broadway musical, should be replaced by a song written by an Oklahoma native). State nicknames also reflect efforts to promote particular images and values. Thus, Wyoming's nickname, the Equal-ity State, commemorates the fact that it was the first state to grant women the right to vote; Delaware, the first state to ratify the Constitution, is called the First State.

Although many state symbols have been used for decades, if not for cen-turies, some continue to generate controversy. For example, controversy over the continued use of the Confederate Battle Flag is currently raging in several Southern states (Box 5-1).

The Geography of U.S. Laws

The states' laws vary dramatically, and explaining why such variation occurs is a fascinating exercise for the student of U.S. politics. Some laws vary in accordance with the different political cultures (see Chapter 2). For example, laws encouraging or requiring individuals to participate in environmental protection efforts are most commonplace under moralistic political culture, which emphasizes the role of government in promoting the common good. The states that require customers purchasing soft drinks or beer to pay deposits on returnable containers, for example, are concentrated in the North (Figure 5-7).

Variation in other types of laws, while related to political culture, may be independent of the moralistic, individualistic, and traditionalistic political cultures of the eastern United States. For example, ten of the fifty states have enacted laws that restrict or prohibit corporate ownership of agricultural land (Figure 5-8). All of them are located in the agricultural regions settled between the Civil War and the closing of the frontier in 1890. It is in these states that the prevalent political culture demands government action to counteract the vagaries of an uncertain economic and physical environment. Whereas corporate farm ownership is commonplace in some areas, notably Florida and California, only a small percentage of farmland in the Plains states is actually owned by nonfamily corporations. Yet many Plains residents regarded corporate farmland ownership as a threat to their lifestyles, and they pushed for the enactment of laws to restrict it.

The distribution of support for the proposed Equal Rights Amendment to the U.S. Constitution in the 1970s followed a somewhat similar pattern. In fact, this pattern was reminiscent of the spread of female suffrage prior to and during the ratification of the Nineteenth Amendment in the early twentieth century (Figure 5-9). Wyoming became the first state to grant full voting rights to women in 1869. By 1900, three other interior Western states—Colorado, Utah, and Idaho—had followed suit. Between 1900 and 1919, full voting rights were granted to women in eleven other states, of which all but two were in the West. Partial women's suffrage, which was sometimes limited to the right to vote only in local school elections, became available in many states around the turn of the century. Only nine states, all in the South and East, allowed no voting at all by women prior to the ratification of the Nineteenth Amendment (Figure 5-10).

The proposed Equal Rights Amendment was quickly ratified by several Western and Middle Western states. In keeping with its tradition, the Wyoming legislature in fact ratified the amendment only a few minutes after it was passed by both houses of Congress. The more populous states of the eastern and central parts of the country were slower to ratify it, and most of the Southern states refused to ratify the proposed amendment at all. Eventually, the proposed amendment failed of ratification by three of the necessary thirty-eight states.

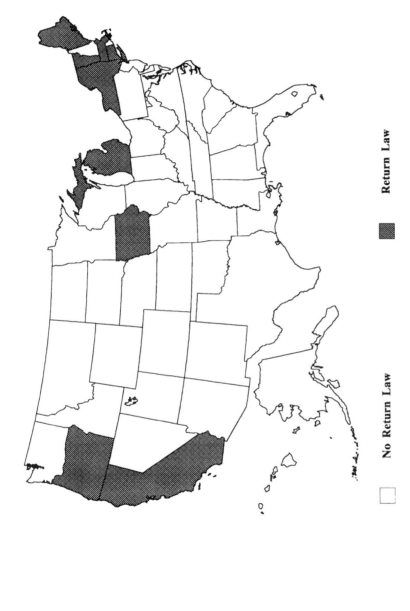

FIGURE 5-7. Beverage Container Return Laws, 1995. Data from "La Croix Natural Lime Flavored Sparkling Water," 12 fl. oz. aluminum can top.

No Return Law   Return Law

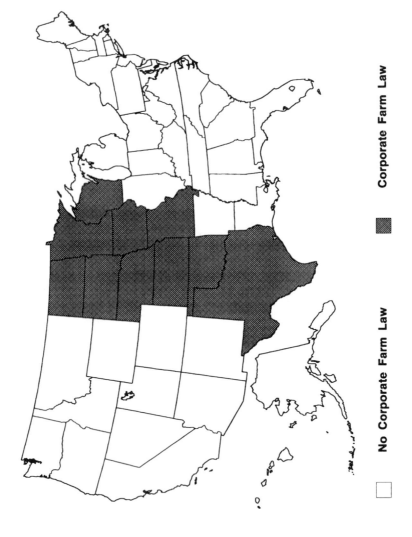

No Corporate Farm Law   Corporate Farm Law

FIGURE 5-8. Corporate Farm Restriction Laws, 1995.

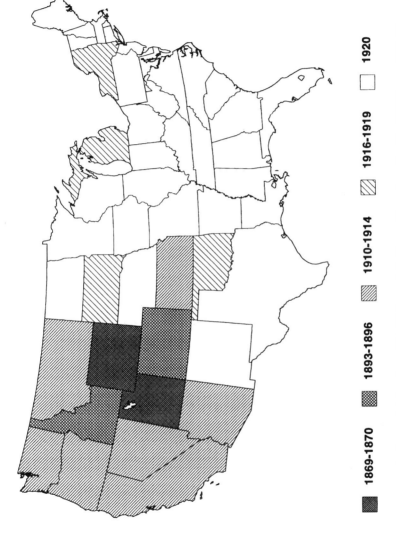

■ 1869-1870   **▓** 1893-1896   **▒** 1910-1914   **▨** 1916-1919   **□** 1920

FIGURE 5-9. Date of Adoption of Full Women's Suffrage. Data from Paullin (1932), pp. 127–28.

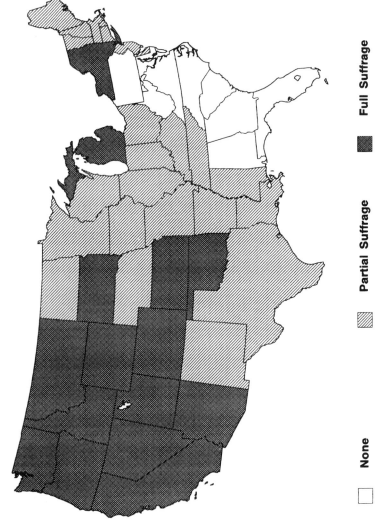

None   Partial Suffrage   Full Suffrage

FIGURE 5-10. Women's Suffrage, 1919. Data from Paullin (1932), pp. 127–28.

Clearly, political equality for women has been most strongly supported in the West and Middle West. Support was lukewarm in the Northeast, and generally absent in the South. Why? Some have argued that support for political equality for women was strongest in recently settled and agricultural areas, where a woman's contribution to the economic success of her family could be observed most easily. On the other hand, the geographic separation of the Northeastern industrial workplace from the home hindered support for female economic and political equality in the industrial core of the country.

Water Law

In other cases, variations in the law can be explained on the basis of physical geography. The United States is a country characterized by a tremendous range of physical environments: from the deserts of Arizona to the cool, rainy forests of New England, and from the snowy wastes of Alaska to the semitropical environment of peninsular Florida, for example. Such variability implies that laws appropriate to some areas may be useless in others. For example, the tendency for smog to form in basins in mountain regions means that large Western cities, notably Los Angeles, Phoenix, and Denver, are particularly subject to smog. Air pollution and emissions standards are enforced more strictly in these areas by both federal and state law. Thus, California has stricter emissions control standards for new and used vehicles than do other states, and as a result, a new car costs somewhat more in California than in other states.

Water law typifies the role of physical geography in the development of the law. Settlers moving to the Thirteen Colonies from England brought British water law across the Atlantic. The water law of Great Britain is based on the riparian principle. Like Great Britain, the eastern United States is endowed with abundant rainfall.

The riparian principle grants ownership of water in streams, ponds, and other bodies of water to the owners of the lands adjacent to them; that is, a person owning land adjacent to a stream has the right to divert that water for whatever purpose may suit his or her needs. During colonial days, the law distinguished "natural" from "artificial" uses of water. Water used for drinking, farming, and watering livestock was considered natural, whereas its diversion for mining, manufacturing, or other similar purposes was considered artificial. During the nineteenth century, on the other hand, this distinction disappeared. The importance of diverted water for economic development was soon recognized—for example, the profitable textile industry of New England required the construction of large and complicated dams—and the law soon afforded "artificial users" the same rights as "natural users" (Hall, 1989, pp. 115–16). The extension of riparian rights to artificial uses was justified on the grounds that the entire community benefited from the productive development of water resources.

The riparian principle is appropriate in the eastern half of the United States, where rainfall is generally plentiful. As settlers moved westward, they soon discovered that the lands west of the 100th meridian of longitude were arid. Many learned from bitter experience that the land could not produce profitable crops on a sustained basis without irrigation. Only in those places where water could be obtained and developed was successful settlement possible.

In response to movement into the arid West, Americans west of the 100th meridian developed the principle of prior appropriation. The prior appropriation principle assigns the right to use water to the first person to identify and develop that water, regardless of location. Someone who diverts a stream channel and builds an irrigation ditch to a farm several miles away, for example, has appropriated the right to that water, even if a second potential user lives adjacent to the stream channel itself.

The phrase "first in time, first in right" has often been used to describe the principle of prior appropriation. Water rights are allocated by Western states to users on a first come, first served basis. Yet the appropriation principle also implies that the user has the duty to use the water efficiently and productively. The state regulates how much water may be taken by each user, and each user has the responsibility to prove that the water is not being wasted. A water right that is not used productively or that is abandoned reverts to the state. Today, the prior appropriation principle underlies the water law of most of the Western states, whereas the riparian principle is the basis for water law east of the 100th meridian. Interestingly, the water laws of California and Texas, which each contain large areas of both humid land and arid land, are based on blends of both systems.

Border Effects

The fact that state and local laws vary from one place to another creates an interesting geography along the boundaries between political jurisdictions. When certain activities are legal in one jurisdiction and illegal in another, the activity in question is often found immediately adjacent to the border.

Visitors driving into Nevada, for example, find casinos and other places in which legalized gambling occurs right on the Nevada border. Indeed, because casino gambling is illegal in neighboring states, most of the major gambling resorts of Nevada are found near its borders, and each is oriented to a nearby metropolitan area from which it draws a large number of visitors. Thus, Las Vegas is strongly oriented to Los Angeles, while Reno is oriented toward the San Francisco Bay area. Laughlin, at the southern tip of Nevada, draws heavily from the Phoenix area, while Jackpot is oriented to Boise and West Wendover to Salt Lake City (Figure 5-11).

In Oklahoma in the early 1980s, voters approved a referendum permitting the construction and operation of a horse-racing track at which pari-mutuel betting, previously illegal, would be allowed. Debate subsequently centered on where the track should be located. The initial proposal was to locate the track at Marietta in south-central Oklahoma. Although Marietta is far removed from the population centers of Oklahoma, it is only sixty miles north of the Dallas–Fort Worth metropolitan area, whose population rivals that of the entire state of Oklahoma. Shortly thereafter, however, voters in Texas legalized pari-mutuel betting. Recognizing that they would probably no longer be able to tap into the Dallas–Fort Worth market, Oklahoma officials then authorized the construction of Remington Park in Oklahoma City, the state's capital and largest city.

Border effects are also evident at a local level. Laws governing the sale and consumption of alcohol, for example, are uniform in some states and variable in others. Some states have adopted "county-option" legislation, giving the voters of each county the right to decide whether to permit the sale of alcoholic beverages. Such was the case in Oklahoma, which in the early 1980s

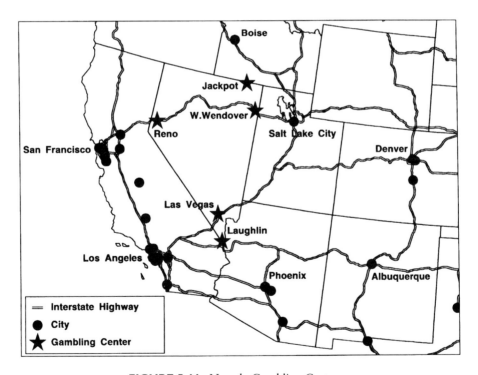

FIGURE 5-11. Nevada Gambling Centers.

authorized each county to decide whether to permit the sale of intoxicating beverages. All of the state's urbanized counties did so, while most of those that voted against alcohol sales are rural and sparsely populated.

A similar pattern has prevailed in most other states that allow liquor sales by county option. Not only are urban residents less likely to refuse alcohol themselves for personal or religious reasons, but many also regard alcohol sales as critical to a community's efforts to attract tourists and other out-of-town visitors, whose presence contributes to that community's economy. An analogous urban–rural distinction occurred in Iowa, which authorized those counties located on the Mississippi and Missouri Rivers to vote on whether they would legalize gambling on riverboat casinos. The measure was rejected by voters in several rural counties, but it passed by substantial majorities in those counties that contain urban areas.

Geography plays a critical role in the outcome of many gubernatorial elections. Some states are characterized by long-standing political disputes between regions distinguished on the basis of physical geography, culture, economy, or settlement patterns. For example, many elections in Louisiana involve competition between the Cajun-dominated, Catholic southern part of the state and the Anglo-dominated, Protestant north. Similar competition has been evident between northern and southern California, eastern and western Washington, and northern and southern Florida.

In other states, gubernatorial politics involve competition between a major metropolitan area and the rest of the state. New York, Illinois, Michigan, Minnesota, and Georgia typify this metropolitan versus nonmetropolitan political division. Candidates from outside the metropolitan areas of their states often campaign against what rural voters may consider to be undue outside influence in state politics. In some states, it is difficult for residents of state capitals or major metropolitan areas to achieve statewide office. Until recently, for example, no resident of Little Rock had been elected governor of Arkansas.

Especially in the traditionalistic South, gubernatorial politics have often been characterized by "friends-and-neighbors" voting. In such cases, support for a gubernatorial candidate tends to be greatest in and near the candidate's home county. Most Southern states require runoff elections between the two leading candidates if no candidate receives a majority of votes cast in the primary election. The runoff requirement forces the successful candidate to broaden his or her appeal beyond the home area and to address issues of concern to a statewide constituency.

In summary, the federal structure of the United States has generated an interesting and diverse pattern of state and local governance throughout the country. The unique characteristics of politics and governance in each state are the result of historical and contemporary differences in culture, economy, and environment.

Chapter 6

REPRESENTATION AND GERRYMANDERING

In Chapter 2, we identified the philosophy of particular representation as critical to the development of the system of democracy unique to the United States. A crucial aspect of the philosophy of particular representation is the division of space into territories for the purpose of electing representatives. States, counties, and cities have been divided into constituencies for electoral purposes since long before the American Revolution. Allegations that the districting process has been biased against the interests of particular parties, political factions, or ethnic groups are almost as old as districting procedures themselves. In recent years, biases associated with representation have been the subject of considerable popular, legal, and scholarly attention.

The Nature of Representation

What do we mean by representation? What is the purpose of representative democracy? We must first consider these fundamental questions in order to provide a context for the geographical analysis of electoral districting.

Direct and Representative Democracy

Procedures by which citizens' views on public questions are translated into public policy are central to the nature of democratic governance. There are two basic forms of democratic governance: direct democracy and representative democracy. Under direct democracy, people vote directly on public policies. Town meetings, which are part of the moralistic political culture of New England and are still held today in rural communities in that region, typify direct democracy. All residents of New England towns are entitled to participate in town meetings. New England town meetings are generally held once a year. At these meetings, residents discuss and vote on the town's budget, on local ordinances, and on other matters.

Another type of direct democracy is initiative and referendum elections, which are held frequently in many states and communities. Proposed constitutional amendments and statutes are voted on directly by the electorate. In recent years, voters in various states have expressed their opinions on such controversial topics as capital punishment, property tax limitations, gun control, and English as an official language.

Representative democracy is much more common than direct democracy in today's world. Representative democracy is a two-step process. Voters elect legislators, and legislators enact policy decisions. Under direct democracy, it is presumed that the outcome of a vote on a public question reflects the will of the majority. Under representative democracy, on the other hand, there is no guarantee that the preferences of a majority of voters will be translated into public policy. The fact that public views are not automatically translated into public policy decisions under representative democracy requires us to examine more thoroughly what is meant by representation itself.

The Functions of Representation in Representative Democracy

In examining representation, we must first ask what it is that a representative should do. Why should we be concerned about the right to vote and its meaning? We can identify three specific yet distinct meanings of the right to vote and its effect on representation (Karlan, 1993). The first is the right of participation, that is, "the formal ability of individuals to enter into the electoral process by casting a ballot" (Karlan, 1993, p. 1708). As we have seen, U.S. history has been characterized by a slow and steady increase in the right of participation, although expanding the right to participate has not always been associated with an expanded voter turnout.

The second meaning of the right to vote involves the process of aggregation. How are voter preferences translated into policy?

In most democratic societies, decisions are made by majority vote. Typically, Americans regard majority rule as "fair," and most would regard minority rule as inherently unfair and undemocratic. In some cases, more than a simple majority is used to make public decisions. For example, the Constitution specifies that treaties be ratified and impeached officials be removed from office by a two-thirds majority of the Senate. In some communities, the law requires that bond issues and other expenditures be approved by more than half of the electorate before taking effect.

Regardless of the actual decision rule, any successful democracy must come close to achieving two often incompatible goals. First, the will of the majority should prevail. At the same time, however, the rights of the minority should be respected, so that the "tyranny of the majority" can be avoided.

Achieving these objectives is somewhat more difficult under representative democracy, because there are two separate steps by which public opinion is translated into public policy. It is not uncommon for a legislature to enact policies that are supported by only a minority of the citizens or to refuse to enact laws supported by majorities. A frequently stated goal of representative democracy is the preservation of levels of support for particular parties or policies. If, for example, a given political party was supported by two-thirds of the electorate, then it should hold two-thirds of the seats in the legislature. As we shall see, however, such an objective can be achieved only at the expense of other equally desirable characteristics of representative government.

The third fundamental characteristic of the right to vote involves the right to govern. Elections are contested because citizens disagree about public policy. Members of parties or factions that win legislative majorities can determine public policy, while minorities may have little or no influence. That particular parties win certain seats cannot guarantee public input in the governance process itself.

The distinction between aggregation and governance was established in the case of *Presley v. Etowah County Commission* (112 S.Ct. 820 [1992]). *Presley* was initiated following the resolution of an earlier lawsuit claiming racial discrimination in Etowah County, Alabama. The earlier case required Etowah County to draw single-member districts to elect its county commissioners, and for the first time in the county's history an African-American was elected to a seat on the commission. Before the new commissioner could take office, however, the white holdovers passed a series of laws that transferred power from individual commissioners to the commission itself. Thus, the African-American community had no input on public policy decisions despite having elected a member to a commission seat. In effect, plaintiffs in *Presley* sued to ensure that governance, as well as aggregation, was undertaken in a racially unbiased manner.

Systems of Representation

Representative democracy is practiced in many parts of the world, but the specific procedures by which representatives are elected vary considerably from one country to another. Two frequently used systems of representation are single-member district representation, which is used most commonly in the United States, and proportional representation. Single-member district representation is practiced in the United States, Canada, Britain, Australia, and other English-speaking countries. Under single-member district representation, the country is divided into constituencies or districts on a territorial basis. Each district elects one or more representatives to the legislature.

Single-member district representation implies a direct geographical linkage between representatives and their constituents. Americans frequently talk about and communicate with "their" senators, members of the House of Representatives, and state legislators. Each representative is accountable primarily to the voters in the territorially defined constituency from which he or she has been elected. Many representatives concentrate on legislation that is of particular importance to the economies of the regions from which they have been elected. For example, representatives of oil-producing Oklahoma, Texas, and Louisiana pay close attention to government policy that affects petroleum prices, while those from the Corn Belt may specialize in legislation affecting agriculture and agribusiness.

Because representatives often concentrate on legislation of particular interest to their own districts, they may exchange votes with one another to ensure the passage of legislation benefiting their own constituencies. For example, a Wisconsin representative may agree to vote for a bill expanding funding for navy installations in Florida in exchange for the Floridian's support for legislation increasing dairy price supports. The process of exchanging votes in order to secure the passage of bills of particular interest to local constituencies is known as "logrolling." Critics of the U.S. House of Representatives have charged that logrolling is responsible for excessive federal spending and is associated with recent increases in the federal budget deficit.

In many non-English-speaking countries, proportional representation is used to elect legislators. Under proportional representation, legislative seats are allocated to political parties on the basis of vote percentages. Usually, legislative districts under proportional representation are larger than under single-member district representation, and each district elects several representatives to the legislature. Voters in proportional representation systems cast ballots for parties and party platforms rather than for individual candidates for office. Within each district, the percentage of seats in the legislature is proportional to the percentage of votes received by that party.

Whether a country uses single-member district representation or proportional representation can affect the nature of party organization and activity significantly. Generally, countries using single-member district representation have strong, stable, two-party systems. In the United States, for example, politics is dominated by the Democratic and Republican parties, which have remained the two major U.S. parties for more than one hundred years. Likewise, British politics is dominated by the Labour and Conservative parties. Because a majority of votes is needed to ensure the election of a candidate to a legislative seat, it is difficult for a third party to play a major role in elections under single-member district representation.

Under proportional representation, on the other hand, small parties need only small percentages of votes to ensure the election of at least a few members to the legislature. Many small parties compete for control of the government, and thus few countries that use proportional representation are characterized by stable, two-party politics. Moreover, the territorial linkage between representative and constituent characteristic of single-member district representation may be tenuous or lacking under most systems of proportional representation. On the other hand, the correlation between voter support among the electorate and party strength in the legislature, which is absent under single-member district representation, is preserved under proportional representation. Single-member district systems promote political stability, but often at the expense of full representation of distinctive minority interests within the country.

In single-member district systems, parties whose supporters are concentrated geographically may also find themselves at a disadvantage, creating spatial bias. As we shall see, it is easier to apply the methods of gerrymandering to areas containing large concentrations of supporters. Thus, a party whose members are concentrated in large cities may be at a disadvantage compared to its opponents whose members are spread more evenly throughout the region. Spatial and aspatial biases in electoral districting have been demonstrated empirically and theoretically in the United States and several other countries (Gudgin and Taylor, 1979; Johnston, 1979; Taylor and Johnston, 1979; Burnett and Taylor, 1981; Shelley, 1984; Johnston et al., 1990; Taylor, 1993a).

Gerrymandering

The explicitly territorial nature of particular representation implies that the location of district boundaries can have a critical impact on election outcomes. The deliberate distortion of boundaries for political purposes, or gerrymandering, is a U.S. tradition nearly as old as particular representation itself. Gerrymandering has been practiced by Democrats, Republicans, Federalists, and Whigs; in crowded cities and in the countryside; and in moralistic, individualistic, and traditionalistic political cultures.

The term "gerrymandering" derives from the use of partisan bias in district boundaries in the state of Massachusetts in 1812. Governor Elbridge Gerry, a Republican, approved a bill that created districts assuring a Republican majority over his Federalist opponents in the state legislature. A contemporary cartoonist noted a resemblance between one of the more grotesquely shaped districts and a mythical dragon or salamander. He drew a cartoon adding wings, claws, and a tail to the district map. A Federalist editor of the Boston *Gazette*, in order to ridicule Gerry, called it a "gerrymander" (Figure 6-1). Since that time, the term "gerrymandering" has been used to describe the deliberate distortion of constituency boundaries for political purposes.

Effective, Excess, and Wasted Votes

Under what circumstances can allegations of gerrymandering be sustained? This question can be addressed by considering that each vote in a legislative election can be placed into one of three categories: effective votes, excess votes, or wasted votes. Effective votes are those needed by a successful candidate to secure a legislative seat. In a two-candidate election, half plus one vote are effective, although an election can be won with less than a majority if more than two candidates are competing. Excess votes are those cast for successful candi-

FIGURE 6-1. "A creature of infernal origin: THE GERRY-MANDER," 1811. From Lossing (1872), p. 505.

dates above and beyond those needed to win. Wasted votes are those cast for losing candidates. For example, if in a given election a Republican defeats a Democrat by a margin of 60 percent to 40 percent, it follows that 50 percent (plus one vote) of the votes are effective, 10 percent are excess, and 40 percent are wasted. In areas where two parties are competing for a large number of seats, half of all the votes cast are effective, while the other half are not. In order to win as many seats as possible, each party attempts to ensure that as many of its votes as possible are effective rather than to excess or wasted.

Because the objective of each party is to force its opposition to cast as many excess and wasted votes as possible, there are two basic techniques of gerrymandering. Opponent-concentration gerrymandering, also known as excess-vote gerrymandering, forces opposition parties to cast large numbers of excess votes. Thus the opposition wins its seats with large majorities, but loses more seats elsewhere. Opponent-dispersion gerrymandering, or wasted-vote gerrymandering, on the other hand, disperses the opposition party's supporters between districts, forcing the opposition to waste its votes by losing large numbers of close elections. Districts are drawn so that the opposition loses most elections by narrow margins. Figure 6-2 illustrates the two methods for the 60 percent to 40 percent election already cited as an example.

In practice, both gerrymandering techniques are used (Morrill, 1981; Archer and Shelley, 1986). Whether opponent concentration or opponent dispersion is practiced depends on the geographic distribution of a party's supporters and its opponents. Moreover, geographers have discovered that biases are inherent in the districting process regardless of the extent to which gerrymandering is intended. In general, larger parties have an inherent advantage over smaller parties in electing legislative majorities. For example, a party commanding the loyalty of only a quarter of the electorate is unlikely to garner a majority in any individual district.

Typically, majorities among the electorate are magnified in legislatures. In two-party regions, a party holding even a slight majority of votes tends to command a substantial majority of legislative seats. The "cube law" (Kendall and Stuart, 1950) has been developed to explain the legislative advantages of majority parties. The cube law suggests that the ratio of legislative seats between two parties will be the cube of the ratio of votes cast for the parties. The general form of the "cube law" seats/votes relationship can be mathematically stated using the following formula:

$$S/(1 - S) = [V/(1 - V)]^E$$

where S and $(1 - S)$ are the proportions of seats held by the party of interest and the opposition party, V and $(1 - V)$ are the proportions of popular votes received by the two parties from all constituencies added together, and E is an

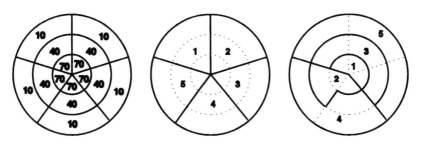

FIGURE 6-2. Hypothetical Gerrymanders. From Archer and Shelley (1986), p. 80.

exponent. According to the specific cube law seats–votes equation, the exponent is assumed to be 3.0, although some variation around this value has been observed in practice for single-member district elections (Tufte, 1973; Gudgin and Taylor, 1979; Taylor and Johnston, 1979; Brady, 1988). Exact "proportional representation," it may be noted, would involve a seats–votes equation with an exponent of 1.0, though this is rarely if ever achieved, even through multimember district list representation systems, which are common in continental Europe.

Numerous analyses of legislative bodies in the United States and other countries have illustrated the basic validity of the cube law (Tufte, 1973; Gudgin and Taylor, 1979; Taylor and Johnston, 1979; Brady, 1988). In the United States, it has been shown that the cube law explains changes in patterns of party affiliation in Congress quite effectively, although the statistical "best fit" exponent for the Democratic Congressional seats–votes equation for the U.S. House of Representatives from 1896 to 1992 is found to be 2.75, or slightly less than 3.0 (with an equation R^2 of 0.901, which indicates a very close empirical statistical fit) (Figure 6-3). The cube law has also been applied to state legislatures. In the South, for example, the cube law explains why most state legislatures continue to be dominated by Democrats

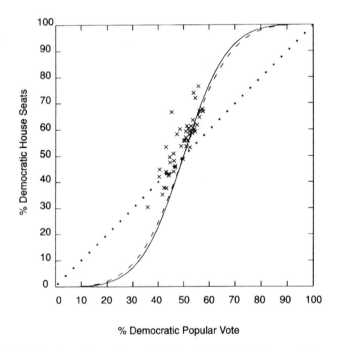

FIGURE 6-3. Cube Law Seats–Votes Relationship for U.S. House of Representatives, 1896–1992. —— Cube Law ($E = 3.00$); – – – Best Fit Seats/Votes Equation ($E = 2.75$); · · · Proportional Representation Law ($E = 1.00$); × Observed Seats/Votes Ratios.

despite a steady increase in Republican support for legislative candidates among voters.

The cube law applies primarily to circumstances in which one party enjoys clear majority support. When parties are of relatively equal strength, however, the party whose adherents are dispersed across space also enjoys advantages over the party whose supporters are clustered. The concentration of supporters in particular areas facilitates the strategy of opponent concentration when parties are equal in size. Spatial bias in electoral districting has been documented empirically in the United States and several other countries (Gudgin and Taylor, 1979; Taylor and Johnston, 1979).

In the United States, the concentration of Democrats in inner-city areas has afforded the Republicans an advantage in many states. On the other hand, spatial concentration may improve the chances that minority parties or ethnic groups will elect at least a few candidates to legislative seats. Spatial concentration can in fact facilitate the election of minority candidates to individual legislative seats but not to legislative majorities—a fact that has proven to be critical to the thorny issue of ethnic minority representation, as we shall see.

The Reapportionment Revolution

The U.S. Constitution requires that seats in the U.S. House of Representatives be apportioned among states on the basis of their relative population sizes, but it does not explicitly describe how this mandate is to be put into practice. Almost from the earliest, controversies have arisen over specific methods for apportioning representatives among the states, since different methods can apportion different numbers of representatives to a particular state (Box 6-1). The gain or loss of even one House seat can be politically important to the citizens and representatives of a state (Martis and Elmes, 1993). Rarely, however, have alternative apportionment methods differed by more than one seat for a particular state, so that the fractions of total U.S. population and of representatives assigned to each state have generally been brought relatively close together through reapportionment after each decennial census. In fact, the U.S. Constitution demands that a Census of Population be taken every ten years for this purpose.

However, a relative overall uniformity of ratios of population and congressional delegation size from one state to another does not necessarily preclude substantial variations in population numbers between congressional or other legislative constituencies within a state. Indeed, throughout the nineteenth and early twentieth centuries, the states had wide latitude to draw legislative district boundaries as they saw fit. During the 1960s, however, the federal judiciary began to deal explicitly with the constitutionality of post-census redistricting plans used to draw legislative districts within states. The resulting reapportionment revolution has had a profound impact on U.S. public life ever since.

Box 6-1. *Congressional Apportionment*

Article I, Section 2 of the U.S. Constitution stipulates that

> Representatives . . . shall be apportioned among the several States which may
> be included within this Union, according to their respective numbers. . . . The
> actual enumeration shall be made within three years after the first meeting of
> the Congress of the United States, and within every subsequent term of ten
> years, in such a manner as they shall by law direct. The number of representa-
> tives shall not exceed one for every thirty thousand, but each State shall have
> at least one Representative.

Since the actual populations of the states were unknown when the Constitution
was drafted, further language of Article I, Section 2 established the size of the
first House at sixty-five members and specified an initial apportionment among
the original thirteen states.

For Congresses thereafter, the Constitution explicitly required that an "actual enumeration shall be made," but it did not specifically establish how the
results of such an enumeration would be used to calculate the number of
House seats allocated to each state. It soon became apparent that this issue
would be politically troublesome. Debate on House apportionment lasted over
a year in the First Congress. Then, after Congress finally did manage to pass a
compromise bill on the issue, President George Washington, acting on the advice of Secretary of State Thomas Jefferson, cast the very first ever presidential
veto, sending the first House apportionment bill back to Congress for reconsideration (Zagarri, 1987, pp. 138–39; Martis and Elmes, 1993; Davis, 1981).
Since then, few other issues have been as continuously divisive and controversial as House apportionment.

During the nineteenth century, controversy over reapportionment was
softened by the practice of expanding the size of the U.S. House of Representatives after each census. Thus, changes in population rarely caused states to actually lose seats (Martis and Elmes, 1993). By 1910, however, many believed
that the House of Representatives was becoming too large to function effectively, and so Congress passed a law fixing the total number of seats at 435. This
law made reapportionment a zero-sum game, in which a gain in seats by one
state required a loss of seats by one or more other states. In the late 1980s, a
few representatives from Northeastern states, which were continuing to lose
population to the South and the West, introduced legislation to enlarge the
House, but their proposals were not enacted into law.

During the 1920s, forty-two reapportionment bills were introduced and
debated, but not one was passed after the 1920 census uncovered a sharp decline in the nation's rural population. Doubtless speaking for other members
from rural districts as well, Representative Ira G. Hersey, a Republican from
Maine, asserted that "one of the greatest dangers that confront the Republic
to-day is the tendency of the large cities to control the American Congress"
(Martis and Elmes, 1993, p. 154). Representatives of rural constituencies in the
East blocked any efforts that would have resulted in the transfer of representation to the South, the West, and the large cities. In the face of growing evidence

of a constitutional crisis, President Herbert Hoover finally managed to pressure Congress into passing a law in 1929 that called for automatic reapportionment after each census.

Except for requiring that each state receive at least one seat, however, the U.S. Constitution does not mandate a specific procedure for calculating the apportionment of House seats from state population counts. Historically, several different methods have been used (Martis and Elmes, 1993, pp. 16–24; Harvison et al., 1985). Jefferson's method of "fixed ratio with rejected fractions" was adopted after Washington's veto and was used from 1792 to 1832. A mathematically related method of "fixed ratio with major fractions" was used in 1842.

The "Vinton" method was embodied in reapportionment laws passed from 1850 to 1901, but the procedure was found to suffer from what came to be called the "Alabama Paradox" (Davis, 1981, p. 24): After the 1880 census, it was discovered that under certain circumstances an expansion in the size of the House might actually cause Alabama to lose a seat. After the 1890 census, it was found that Arkansas would gain a seat in a 359-member House, lose a seat in a 360-member House, but gain a seat in a 361-member House. After considerable debate, Congress embedded a divisor technique known as the "method of major fractions," which was not subject to the Alabama Paradox, in the 1911 reapportionment law.

A study of techniques immune to the Alabama Paradox was undertaken by the National Academy of Sciences at the request of Congress in 1929. The study gave its support to the method of "equal proportions," which was finally adopted in 1941 and is still in use (Martis and Elmes, 1993, p. 17). This procedure has the mathematical effect of minimizing the percent difference in the number of persons per representative (Harvison et al., 1985, p. 394). Because House districts cannot cross state boundaries, no apportionment procedure can make each state have an exactly equal ratio of representatives to population, but the equal proportions method causes the percent difference to be as small as possible.

The equal proportions apportionment method works as follows: First, give each state one House seat to start. Symbolically, set $S_i = 1$, for $i = 1$ to 50, where S_i is the number of House seats allocated to state i. The second step involves calculating a "multiplier" equal to the reciprocal of the square root of the product of the current number of seats times the current number of seats plus one for each state. Then, calculate a "priority value" equal to the multiplier times the apportionment population for each state. Finally, identify the state with the highest priority value, and allocate one additional seat in the House to that state. Symbolically, for $i = 1$ to 50, calculate

$$M_i = [1/(S_i^*[S_i + 1])]^{.5}$$

and

$$V_i = M_i^* P_i$$

where for each state i, M_i is the multiplier, V_i is the priority value, and P_i is the apportionment population. After all V_i have been newly calculated, find the state for which the value of V_i is greatest, and then add 1 to S_i for that state. This process is then repeated until all 435 House seats have been allocated to states.

After the total number of House seats allocated to each state has been determined, the focus of activity then shifts to the states, where the geographical boundaries of new House districts are established. Table 6-B1-1 illustrates how the 51st through 60th and the 431th through 435th House seats were assigned according to the equal proportions method after the 1990 census. Table 6-B1-2 shows the overall post-1990 apportionment of seats for the 103rd U.S. House of Representatives, whose members were elected in November 1992.

It can be noted that the 435th seat in the 103rd House would have gone to Massachusetts rather than to Washington, if Massachusetts's apportionment population had been about 12,600 greater while Washington's apportionment population stayed the same. This would have increased Massachusetts's House delegation from 10 to 11 seats, and reduced Washington's House delegation from 9 to 8 seats. Clearly, state power in the U.S. House of Representatives can be influenced by slight differences in population numbers. This coupled with the fact that the various methods that can be used to apportion seats yield different results continues to make the issue of apportionment controversial. In fact, Montana, which lost one of its two House seats after the 1990 census, unsuccessfully sued the federal government for restoration of its second seat on the grounds that an alternative allocation procedure would be more fair.

TABLE 6-B1-1. Sequence of Congressional Seat Allocation by Method of Equal Proportions after 1990 Census

Next seat	State	Apportionment population (P)	Multiplier (M)	Priority (V)	Total seats (S)
51	California	29,839,250	0.70711	21,099,536	2
52	New York	18,044,504	0.70711	12,759,391	2
53	California	29,839,250	0.40825	12,181,823	3
54	Texas	17,059,804	0.70711	12,063,103	2
55	Florida	13,003,362	0.70711	9,194,765	2
56	California	29,839,250	0.28868	8,613,850	4
57	Pennsylvania	11,924,710	0.70711	8,432,043	2
58	Illinois	11,466,682	0.70711	8,108,169	2
59	Ohio	10,887,325	0.70711	7,698,501	2
60	New York	18,044,504	0.40825	7,366,638	3
...	...	...	...	...	...
431	Wisconsin	4,906,745	0.11785	578,265	9
432	Florida	13,003,362	0.04446	578,070	23
433	Tennessee	4,896,641	0.11785	577,075	9
434	Oklahoma	3,157,604	0.18257	576,497	6
435	Washington	4,887,941	0.11785	576,049	9

Source: Computed using data from U.S. Bureau of the Census, 1992.

TABLE 6-B1-2. Apportionment Population and Number of Representatives, 1990, by State

State	Apportionment population	Number of representatives
Alabama	4,062,608	7
Alaska	551,947	1
Arizona	3,677,985	6
Arkansas	2,362,239	4
California	29,839,250	52
Colorado	3,307,912	6
Connecticut	3,295,669	6
Delaware	668,696	1
Florida	13,003,362	23
Georgia	6,508,419	11
Hawaii	1,115,274	2
Idaho	1,011,986	2
Illinois	11,466,682	20
Indiana	5,564,228	10
Iowa	2,787,424	5
Kansas	2,485,600	4
Kentucky	3,698,969	6
Louisiana	4,238,216	7
Maine	1,233,223	2
Maryland	4,798,622	8
Massachusetts	6,029,051	10
Michigan	9,328,784	16
Minnesota	4,387,029	8
Mississippi	2,586,443	5
Missouri	5,137,804	9
Montana	803,655	1
Nebraska	1,584,617	3
Nevada	1,206,152	2
New Hampshire	1,113,915	2
New Jersey	7,748,634	13
New Mexico	1,521,779	3
New York	18,044,504	31
North Carolina	6,657,630	12
North Dakota	641,364	1
Ohio	10,887,325	19
Oklahoma	3,157,604	6
Oregon	2,853,733	5
Pennsylvania	11,924,710	21
Rhode Island	1,005,984	2
South Carolina	3,505,707	6
South Dakota	699,999	1
Tennessee	4,896,641	9
Texas	17,059,804	30
Utah	1,727,784	3
Vermont	564,964	1
Virginia	6,216,568	11
Washington	4,887,941	9
West Virginia	1,801,625	3
Wisconsin	4,906,745	9
Wyoming	455,975	1
TOTAL	249,022,783	435

Source: U.S. Bureau of the Census, 1992.

Malapportionment and the Supreme Court

As we saw in Chapter 4, the twentieth century has been characterized by large-scale urbanization. Despite this urbanization, many of the states refused to redraw their congressional or legislative district boundaries. By the 1950s, the population of districts within states varied dramatically. The Atlanta-area congressional district had about seven times the population of the smallest district of Georgia, for example.

Inequalities between urban and rural areas were justified by arguments that legislators represent territories as well as people—an argument stemming from the British tradition of virtual representation (see Chapter 2). Others argued that rural residents have a greater stake in their communities than do city dwellers and thus are deserving of more representation than their urban counterparts. This argument is reminiscent of the property qualifications for voting of the eighteenth and nineteenth centuries.

The Supreme Court Addresses Malapportionment

Residents of large, malapportioned districts often sued to induce the courts to order that district populations be equalized. Prior to 1962, however, legal claims of malapportionment were dismissed by the courts as being political questions outside the purview of judicial scrutiny. In 1962, however, the Supreme Court ruled in *Baker v. Carr* (369 U.S. 186) that any state's failure to redraw malapportioned districts violated the equal protection clause of the Fourteenth Amendment to the Constitution.

Baker v. Carr meant that congressional districting was to be guided by the basic principle of "one person, one vote." The reapportionment revolution was under way. Over the next several years, a series of cases extended the "one person, one vote" principle to state and local legislative bodies.

By the 1970s, federal courts had generally required strict adherence to the equal population criterion in congressional districting. In 1982, New Jersey proposed a districting plan whose maximum population deviation between the largest and smallest district was only 0.7 percent. Nevertheless, the Supreme Court struck the plan down as malapportioned in *Karcher v. Daggett* (462 U.S. 725). Thus, *Karcher* asserted that equality of district population is the paramount criterion for constitutionality in congressional districts.

Courts usually require strict adherence to equal population in congressional districts, but even with modern Geographic Information System (GIS) technology, it can be difficult to achieve mathematical accuracy in determining district populations (Box 6-2). Those charged with drawing the districts must rely on data from the U.S. Census of Population, but there is widespread evidence that the population figures provided by the census are inaccurate. In fact, some demographers have argued that census population figures may be off by as much as 3 to 5 percent. Census figures are particularly inaccurate in large metropolitan areas, because immigrants, low-income ethnic minorities, transients, and the homeless are most likely to go uncounted.

After the 1980 census, in fact, several large cities, including New York, Philadelphia, and Detroit, sued the federal government in order to overturn the census results on the grounds that the census had underestimated their populations, reducing not only their congressional and legislative representation but also their eligibility for federal funds, whose levels are tied to population. The courts rejected these arguments in the early 1980s, but after the release of the 1990s census results, similar lawsuits were filed in several courts. In August 1994, the Second Circuit Court of Appeals ruled in favor of cities suing the Census Bureau and ordered that the results of the 1990 census be revised or thrown out. An appeal to the Supreme Court is pending, but if upheld the decision will have far-reaching implications. For example, it would involve the shift of two congressional districts, from Wisconsin and Pennsylvania to Arizona and California. Moreover, it would require most of the larger states to redraw their district boundaries, increasing the number of urban representatives and decreasing the power of suburban and rural areas.

Reliance on census data to draw legislative districts also ignores the impact of migration on district populations. The United States is a highly mobile society, and large numbers of Americans move between congressional districts each decade. Between 1980 and 1990, for example, some inner-city districts lost as many as 20 to 30 percent or more of their residents, while rapidly growing suburban and Sunbelt districts gained by as much as 50 percent. Thus, over the course of a decade, some districts may grow to twice the population of others despite initial population equality.

A third problem associated with reliance on census population data is that not all local residents are eligible to vote. U.S. courts have made clear that total population is to be the basis of apportionment, regardless of voter eligibility. Courts in some states have dealt with whether military personnel, students, prisoners, or other nonvoters should be counted for reapportionment purposes. In Hawaii, for example, the state attempted to base its reapportionment on numbers of registered voters rather than on actual population figures because the state's population included large numbers of military personnel who were registered to vote elsewhere.

The fact that birthrates vary among different ethnic groups has also generated controversy. Because Hispanic-Americans and African-Americans tend to have higher birthrates than do Americans of European or Asian ancestry, districts dominated by members of these minority groups contain fewer residents of voting age. During the 1970s, a lawsuit addressing this issue was filed by Jewish-American advocates in New York City, arguing that representation ought to be based on the number of eligible voters rather than on the total population. The Supreme Court rejected this argument, however, firmly establishing that representation is to be based on the total population.

Box 6-2. *GIS and TIGER*

Many federal, state, and local agencies are responsible for the timely and accurate compilation and publication of maps. The time constraints and production volume demands associated with government map making have encouraged a rapid transition to the use of Geographic Information Systems (GISs). A GIS is a computer-based hardware and software system for the entry, editing, updating, analysis, and graphic display of locational information. Thus, a GIS can be thought of as a set of interrelated and automated components for the creation and analysis of cartographic data, which in turn represent three-dimensional geographic patterns. A GIS is to a map what a word processor is to an essay.

After the 1980 census, several members of Congress became quite concerned when they found that budget restrictions were retarding the publication of 1980 census results, which were important for the reapportionment and redistricting of the House of Representatives. Moreover, it was becoming apparent that there were serious deficiencies in the data being reported for rural parts of the United States. Problems involving the geographic specificity of census population data threatened to prevent the achievement of federal equal population objectives. This, in turn, raised the specter of potentially unending legal challenges to newly drawn congressional districts outside of metropolitan regions.

A wave of alarm rose from state legislatures, which are responsible for drawing the boundaries for their own constituency districts as well as those for the U.S. House of Representatives, and quickly descended on Capitol Hill in Washington, DC. Census officials summoned to testify had to explain to irate representatives that although the reporting of official 1980 population counts might be expedited, there was little that could be done to refine the coverage of rural areas without wholesale changes in underlying census procedures. The basic problem was that, although automated methods could be used to tabulate and report data for metropolitan areas, there were no comparable methods in place for nonmetropolitan areas.

It soon became evident that existing technology, of direct and even personal relevance to the representatives themselves, was subject to severe limitations. When House members learned that their own districts might be subject to legal challenges because of these limitations, they usually become quite supportive of efforts to expand census use of GIS technology beyond the boundaries of metropolitan areas. The result was one of the largest domestic cartographic efforts in U.S. history, an effort that led to the creation of the Topologically Integrated Geographic Encoding and Referencing (TIGER) system.

In all, about $50 million was spent on the cooperative effort between the U.S. Bureau of the Census and the U.S. Geological Survey to develop the TIGER system and to geocode and correct TIGER locational data for the entire nation in time for the 1990 census. The outlay was perhaps modest compared to the cost of even one military reconnaissance satellite, but the impact on the extent and rate of adoption of GIS technology for domestic purposes has been enormous.

The census TIGER system includes proprietary GIS programs used by the U.S. Bureau of the Census in its own internal operations and a massive geographic database that is partly confidential and partly available for public use.

Some confusion arises because noncensus sources rarely mention the confidential or proprietary components of the overall TIGER system, and somewhat inaccurately use the acronym to refer to what census documents identify as the public "TIGER Extract" component.

The TIGER system comprises a vast geographic database for all of the United States, spanning nonmetropolitan as well as metropolitan areas, at a level of attribute detail and locational accuracy that corresponds to that of a U.S. Geological Survey topographic map at a scale of 1:100,000. TIGER contains topological details, latitude and longitude coordinates for many landmark point features, most transportation and hydrological line features, and virtually all jurisdictional area features for the entire United States. This means, for example, that railroads, highways, roads, streets, streams, rivers, lakes, National Parks, and Native American reservations, as well as township, school district, voting district, municipality, county, and state boundaries, can all be located with considerable accuracy using TIGER Extract data published on CD-ROMs (Figure 6-B2-1).

In addition, the unpublished proprietary portion of the TIGER system contains mailing addresses and geographic coordinates for nearly every occupied private or public dwelling unit or other structure in the entire United States, including over 100 million dwelling units in all. This detailed address information is needed for the fast and locationally accurate tabulation of returns from individuals, households, firms, institutions, and other entities that are surveyed by the U.S. Bureau of the Census. It was largely the lack of detailed geocoded address-matching information that had made it impossible for the census to quickly and accurately report rural population data for small areas in 1980. Confidentiality rules prevent the most detailed geocoded address information from being released even to other federal agencies, but published TIGER Extract files do indicate address ranges between street or road intersections.

In addition to its value in constructing electoral districts, the TIGER Extract address range information has proven to be quite useful for dispatching emergency vehicles, assigning school attendance, and managing public and private utilities. In each of these instances, a considerable economy of time and expense, a substantial reduction of risk, or an improvement of service can be achieved by quickly and accurately determining a geographic location to within a few tens or a few hundreds of yards or meters. Such positional accuracy is well within the capabilities of GIS using published TIGER Extract data.

The initial impetus to TIGER, of course, came from congressional concerns over the reapportionment and redistricting of the U.S. House of Representatives. Comparatively advanced GIS technology was used for House redistricting in virtually all states in 1991–1992, whereas much cruder methods had been used in the previous reapportionment and redistricting round in 1981–1982. In some cases, however, the new technology has led to previously unattainably refined levels of partisan or incumbent-protecting gerrymandering.

Moreover, local election officials in many jurisdictions across the country have adopted GIS technology for day-to-day purposes of correcting and maintaining voter registration and polling place records. In San Francisco, for example, GIS technology has made it possible for employees of the Office of the Registrar of Voters "to produce maps of precincts that need a polling place . . .

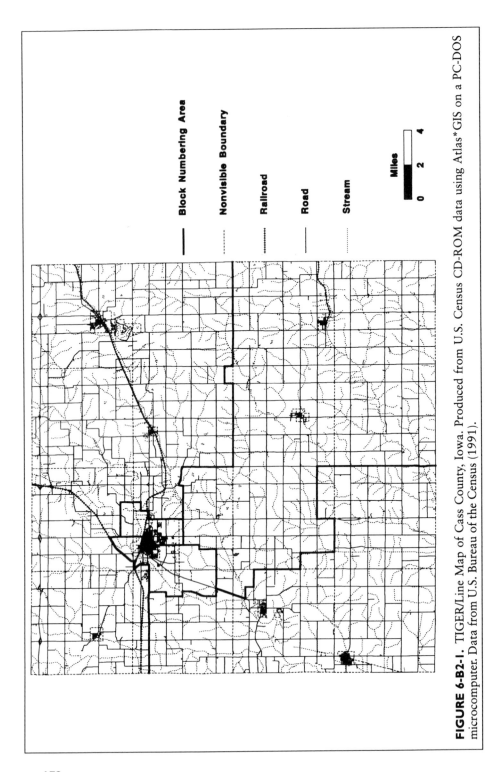

Block Numbering Area

Nonvisible Boundary

Railroad

Road

Stream

Miles

0   2   4

FIGURE 6-B2-1. TIGER/Line Map of Cass County, Iowa. Produced from U.S. Census CD-ROM data using Atlas*GIS on a PC-DOS microcomputer. Data from U.S. Bureau of the Census (1991).

[which] show all streets, color code steep slopes that might impede handicapped access and indicate previously used polling places and public facilities" (Borden and Wong, 1994, p. 24). The staff also uses GIS to create maps that show voter registration by age or ethnic groups at geographic scales as small as city blocks—or even smaller—for organizations planning voter-registration drives. "Such maps clearly indicate which buildings have no registered voters" (Borden and Wong, 1994, p. 24).

Although not originally so intended, GIS using TIGER data is coming to play an important role not just occasionally, at the start of a decade for legislative districting, but often, in frequently held election campaigns. After all, the members of public interest groups with civic-minded concerns for matters of voter registration and participation are not the only ones who find the technology potentially appealing. As one political campaign consultant remarked, "Imagine your voter list displayed in a snapshot with registered voters appearing as red icons, $1,000+ donors appearing as green icons, and independent voters appearing as grey icons on the map. . . . Groups of formerly untargeted or loosely targeted voters can be collected into powerful new subsets of the voter list in any given area to give a candidate or an issue a new boost, possibly even the winning boost" (Sachs, 1993, p. 59).

Microcomputer GIS technology actually was used in the 1992 presidential campaign by Clinton–Gore strategists to target voters, determine the timing and extent of TV ads in specific markets, and "chart trends, decide where to send their candidates and recruit volunteers. Even those now-famous bus trips were plotted in response to data from a GIS" (Bryan, 1993, p. 29). "In fact, based on geographical targeting that was enhanced using GIS, the [Clinton–Gore] campaign was successful in 30 of the 31 targeted states" (Bryan, 1993, p. 28). It seems likely that in the future, election campaign organizations that fail to exploit available GIS technology will handicap their own candidates in contests with candidates whose campaign organizations have adopted this important technology.

Despite these difficulties, strict adherence to the equal-population standard remains in force for congressional districts. On the other hand, the courts have generally permitted greater variation in districts for state legislatures and local governments. In general, deviations of less than 10 percent are considered consistent with the equal population standard at the state and local level. Larger deviations are permitted only if justified on the basis of additional criteria, such as those discussed below.

From Malapportionment to Gerrymandering

Once *Baker, Reynolds,* and the other cases comprising the "reapportionment revolution" of the 1960s had been decided, most of the states were required to redistrict themselves in order to eliminate malapportionment. While *Baker*

did not focus on gerrymandering per se, the fact that new districts were required focused attention on the districting process, generating public debate
about criteria in order to mitigate or eliminate gerrymandering.

Initially, this public debate focused on formal districting criteria. Formal
criteria include contiguity, compactness, and respect for the integrity of the
boundaries of subnational political units. Contiguity implies that a single,
contiguous line can be drawn around the district. For the most part, the contiguity criterion has been noncontroversial, although questions concerning
contiguity have been raised in some redistricting controversies in recent years.
For example, some proposed districts contain blocks of territory that meet
only at corners. Are such districts contiguous?

In other cases, critics have charged that proposed districts that appear to
be contiguous on maps are drawn in such a way that it is impossible to tra-
verse them without entering adjoining districts. For example, some proposed
districts have extended across rivers along stretches without bridges. Thus,
someone wishing to drive from one end of the district to the other would be
forced to enter another district in order to cross the river. Similarly, proposed
districts that are described as contiguous have been drawn across mountain
ranges or in other environments without passable roads enabling candidates
or voters to travel across the districts without leaving them.

Compactness has proven to be a much more controversial criterion. The
intent of requiring districts to be compact was to eliminate "obvious" gerrymanders such as that undertaken by Elbridge Gerry himself. Odd and
grotesquely shaped districts such as the original gerrymander of 1812 were
frequently used as evidence that gerrymandering had in fact occurred, and in
fact many people associate gerrymandering with the use of strangely shaped
districts regardless of their actual political consequences.

Geographers and other social scientists have devoted considerable effort
to measuring compactness (e.g., Morrill, 1981; Niemi et al., 1990; Horn et
al., 1993). These measures involve comparing characteristics of actual or proposed districts to those of squares, circles, or hexagons. Many state constitutions or legislatures have required that districts in their states be compact, although only Colorado and Michigan actually spell out how compactness of
their districts is to be measured (Grofman, 1985).

By the late 1960s, it had become clear that compactness was not necessarily associated with fairness in electoral districting. Districts can be equally
apportioned and compact yet gerrymandered. Moreover, a district that appears to be compact on a map may in fact contain territory isolated by mountains, rivers, or other natural features or by inadequate transportation and
communication facilities, even if the district is contiguous. Whether apparently compact districts are gerrymandered depends on the ethnic, demographic,
social, economic, and political characteristics of their inhabitants. As we will
see, the evaluation of compactness today has become linked with the idea that
districts should be associated with communities of interest.

In many states, law or custom recommends that congressional or legislative districts respect the integrity of existing boundaries between cities, counties, and other units of local government in electoral districting. Local governments are easily recognized units of administration with identifiable collective goals and needs, and drawing districts without splitting local government units tends to foster the sense of community that is essential to effective territorial representation. In response, many states have attempted to reduce or eliminate the number of times district boundaries cross existing county or municipal boundaries. Some state constitutions require that the integrity of existing county or municipal boundaries be maintained as much as possible, but these requirements must give way to federal equal protection criteria when conflicts between them occur.

Political Criteria

Three decades of redistricting experience have demonstrated that formal criteria such as contiguity, compactness, and respect for existing political boundaries cannot by themselves ensure fair and effective representation. In response to this awareness, social scientists have come to focus on the explicitly political and geographic aspects of districting. Political criteria include maximizing electoral competitiveness, protecting incumbent legislators, maintaining district stability by minimizing the frequency that an area is shifted between districts, and equalizing seat–vote ratios between parties, political factions, or ethnic and cultural groups.

While these and other overtly political criteria are often used in delineating electoral districts, their execution and evaluation must be based on extensive knowledge of local geographic and political circumstances. Few would disagree that "fairness" is a fundamental goal of any districting procedure, but the concept of fairness may prove to be ambiguous. In general, however, fairness implies that parties be treated symmetrically in the redistricting process, so that they are neither packed nor divided disproportionately—in other words, so that no party is forced to cast large numbers of excess or wasted votes compared to the others.

Why is this definition of fairness in representation important? Why should political parties, which are after all not mentioned in the Constitution, be entitled to such protection? To answer such a question cuts to the very core of the theory of representative democracy. This theory addresses two fundamental issues: respect for the will of the majority and respect for the rights of the minority. Fairness in representation implies that majority parties should win legislative majorities, but that minority parties should nevertheless win seats in proportion to their numbers. Yet the territorial nature of representation in U.S. society, which establishes close linkages between an elected official and the territory from which he or she is elected, is inconsistent with the idea of partisan proportional representation. The very idea of fairness insists that over the long run and across a substantial set of districts there should be a fair correspondence between the share of votes received and the number of seats won. Otherwise, members of the frustrated minority cannot but conclude that they are effectively disenfranchised.

One view of effective governance argues that maximizing the competitive responsiveness of elections to changes in voter sentiment is a priority. An alternative view posits that experience in office and a long-term relationship between representative and constituent is an important value, although those favoring term limits for legislators may disagree with this argument (see Chapter 2). To accommodate both views, an optimum balance between safe and competitive districts may be desirable. If too many seats are safe, as is the case today, then the overall set of seats will not be responsive to genuine shifts. On the other hand, if too many seats are balanced, there is a risk of severe electoral bias if one party wins all or most of these competitive seats with narrow margins.

The question of effective districting is complicated by the fact that it is impossible to satisfy all of these criteria simultaneously. One goal must be traded off against another. For example, the goal of establishing safe seats for political parties or ethnic and racial groups may be traded off against the goal of maximizing political competitiveness within each district. Whether these or other formal or political criteria can be satisfied often depends on who has the responsibility of determining district boundaries. Increasingly, the courts have recognized that the districting process may be as important in evaluating the possibility of gerrymandering as the pattern itself.

Who Draws the Boundaries?

Each state is charged with delineating its own congressional and state legislative district boundaries. Although each is required to satisfy the criterion of equal district population and to avoid conflict with federal equal protection guarantees, the federal government imposes few other constraints on the boundary delineation process. Each state has its own set of procedures, but the likelihood that gerrymandering will occur varies considerably from one procedure to another.

In many states, the legislature is charged with district boundary delineation. In such cases, the legislature must pass a bill outlining the proposed districts, and this bill must be signed into law by the governor. When both houses of the legislature and the governor belong to the same political party, the potential for gerrymandering is greatest. Not surprisingly, some of the most bitterly fought court cases in recent years have been pursued in states that permit such partisan districting.

Frequently, control of the legislature and the governorship is divided between the two parties. In such cases, neither party will allow a blatantly partisan gerrymandering bill to become law. Other states have laws that are intended to eliminate overt partisanship in district boundary delineation. This can be done in two ways: through nonpartisan districting and bipartisan districting. Nonpartisan districting is undertaken without reference to any information about the political preferences of voters, whereas bipartisan districting is that done by agreement or compromise among leaders of both parties.

Nonpartisan districting can be done by computers or by human beings working without reference to local political conditions. During the 1960s, considerable effort was devoted to developing computer programs and other procedures to draw districts "scientifically," that is, without the biases associated with human effort. Today, nonpartisan procedures are seldom used, in part because of the inherent biases described above. Iowa, however, has developed a nonpartisan procedure in which plans are drawn by a staff of professional appointees, although the initial plan was developed in the late 1970s by a Republican legislature that feared that it would be turned out of office in 1980.

Bipartisan compromises, on the other hand, have become increasingly prevalent. In fact, some states require bipartisan procedures in order to initiate the districting process. For example, Illinois law stipulates that the majority and minority leaders of each house of the state legislature each nominate one member of the state's five-member districting commission. Thus, the commission consists initially of two Democrats and two Republicans. These four individuals then must meet and agree upon a fifth member, who serves as the commission's chair. That Democrats and Republicans must agree on the identity of the chair is seen to reduce partisan bias in the districting process.

Communities of Interest

As it became clear that formal criteria could not eliminate gerrymandering and that political criteria could not be satisfied simultaneously, political geographers began to pay attention to perhaps the most explicitly geographic criterion of all. The idea of a community of interest, that is, a territorially defined group of people with common economic, social, political, or cultural interests, links the formal redistricting criteria such as contiguity, compactness, and respect for existing governmental units with the political implications of proposed or actual district boundaries. The idea that a legislator should represent a community of interest is fundamental to the philosophy of particular representation underlying U.S. representative democracy.

How can a community of interest be defined? A major concern of the discipline of geography is to identify, describe, and analyze how communities within societies develop over time. The concept of community overlaps with concepts of racial identity, political affiliation, and political unit identification, but it encompasses much more than these. Communities of interest can be identified through patterns of work, patterns of demography, patterns of residence and patterns of social, economic, religious, and cultural as well as political participation.

Communities of interest can be identified at all geographic scales. Within the United States as a whole, for example, distinct regions such as New England, the South, the Great Plains, or the Pacific Northwest can be identified as communities of interest. Distinct communities of interest exist within individual states. In many states, large metropolitan areas form communities of interest distinct from other parts of their states. New York, Illinois, Minnesota, Georgia, and several other states are dominated by major metropolitan centers, and the politics of these states often revolve around competition between the metropolitan center and outlying areas such as "upstate" New York and "downstate" Illinois. In other states, differing physical environments or economic bases create different communities of interest within them. As we have seen, distinct communities of interest can be found in northern and southern California, eastern and western Washington, northern and southern Louisiana, and eastern and western Colorado.

Communities of interest are also evident at smaller geographic scales. Perhaps the clearest example of a community of interest at a regional scale is a small city and its surrounding rural hinterland. Within the hinterland, people commute to the city in order to work, shop, and participate in recreational activities. People in the city and the hinterland read newspapers published in the city, watch city-based television stations, and listen to radio stations located in the city. The community of interest is maintained by the area's employment structure, communications media, and other social, economic, and political institutions that reinforce a sense of common interest among residents of the area. Areas such as these can be identified easily as communities of interest even when they are racially diverse or fairly evenly divided between political factions or parties.

With respect to electoral district boundary delineation, the importance of communities of interest is closely related to the fact that territory has been the major basis of representation in U.S. society throughout the country's history. Electoral districts should not be regarded as arbitrary aggregations of people for the sole purpose of conducting elections. Rather, districts should be meaningful entities with legitimate collective interests arising from the identity of citizens within real places and areas. If districting ignores the neighborhood or community within which most people carry out their daily lives, the district's representative may be faced with difficult conflicts of interest between people in disparate parts of the district, and citizens in isolated parts of the district may come to feel that their community is unrepresented.

In recent years, several courts have taken notice of the concept of community of interest in evaluating proposed districting plans. In Colorado, for example, a judge ruled that "communities of interest represent distinctive units which share common concerns with respect to one or more identifiable features such as geography, demography, ethnicity, culture, socio-economic status or trade. We are convinced that a plan which provides fair and effective representation for the people of Colorado must identify and respect the most important communities of interest within the state" (*Carstens v. Lamm,* 543 F. Supp. 68 [1982]).

The concept of a community of interest also enables us to assess more meaningfully the idea of compactness in legislative districting. Compactness can be viewed as facilitating effective representation because it restricts the possibility that some portions of a district are isolated physically or economically from others. Residents of isolated areas within districts are less likely to feel represented adequately. Also, it is more likely that a compact district will be composed of territory that includes people with shared interests. Thus, compactness can be regarded as a useful criterion to the extent that it facilitates the establishment of districts based on communities of interest.

This interpretation of compactness has also been recognized in recent court decisions. For example, a federal district judge in Alabama stated that "the degree of geographical symmetry or attractiveness is therefore a desirable consideration for districting, but only to the extent it aids or facilitates the political process. . . . [A] district would not be sufficiently compact if it was so spread out that there was no sense of community, that is if its members and its representatives could not easily tell who actually lived within the district" (*Dillard v. Baldwin County Board of Education,* 686 F. Supp. 1459 [1988]). Along the same lines, a federal district court in Louisiana stated succinctly that "a proposed district is sufficiently compact if it retains a natural sense of community" (*East Jefferson Coalition v. Jefferson Parish,* 691 F. Supp. 991 [1988]). The interface between compactness and community of interest has become increasingly important in evaluating districting proposals in recent years. During the 1990s, in fact, it has become the primary point of controversy in the electoral districting process.

Contemporary Controversies in Reapportionment

More than thirty years have passed since the reapportionment revolution was initiated by the Supreme Court. Clearly, much progress has been made: Excessive malapportionment has been eliminated, and blatant racial gerrymandering is disallowed. Yet gerrymandering and the manipulation of territory for political purposes is still widely practiced. Several Supreme Court cases decided during the late 1980s and early 1990s illustrate the continued controversy associated with district boundary delineation.

Race and Ethnicity in Districting

Thus far, our discussion of representation has focused, at least implicitly, on gerrymandering involving political parties. By no means, however, has gerrymandering been restricted to political parties. Among the most bitter controversies involving electoral districting in recent years has been that concerning bias against racial and ethnic groups.

The considerable body of litigation concerning electoral bias against racial and ethnic groups stems from the conjunction of the reapportionment revolution just described and the civil rights movement of the 1960s. Thus, law concerning racial and ethnic issues in districting derives from three main sources: the reapportionment cases, which were founded on the equal protection clause of the Fourteenth Amendment; the original Voting Rights Act of 1965, which was a landmark outcome of the civil rights movement; and, later, the extended Voting Rights Act of 1982.

In general, the law concerning the impacts of race, ethnicity, and culture in electoral districting recognizes racial and ethnic groups and the areas in which these persons live as explicit communities of interest. The fact that many minority group members are clustered in easily identifiable areas, especially in cities, adds an explicitly territorial dimension to such law. Frequently, clustering of racial minorities is the historical result of racial prejudice, often coupled with discrimination in housing, education, and employment.

Racial Bias in Electoral Districting

Most claims of discrimination against racial and ethnic minorities are based on evidence that minority groups are completely unrepresented or are less well represented than their actual numbers merit. The argument that such minorities are entitled to representation in proportion to their numbers implies that minority-dominated localities are communities with explicit interests that can clearly be differentiated from those of the larger polity.

Racial bias in electoral districting has been perpetuated in three ways: through at-large as opposed to district- based elections, through gerrymandering, and through selective annexation to distort population balances. While members of Congress and of state legislatures are elected from territorially defined districts, many local governments elect their legislators at large. In fact, more than half of all U.S. cities with populations of less than 50,000 elect their council members at large (Welch, 1990). In at-large elections, all representatives to the legislative body are elected by the entire voting population of the polity.

The use of at-large elections generally has had the effect of underrepresenting minority interests. The fact that minority groups win considerably greater representation in district elections than in at-large elections is well documented (O'Loughlin and Taylor, 1982; Engstrom and McDonald, 1986; Welch, 1990). For example, one study in the late 1970s found that only a minority of Southern cities with at least 15 percent African-American population, with at least 5,000 people, and using at-large representation had at least one African-American city council member. On the other hand, over 90 percent of those using territorial representation had at least one African-American on the city council (Barry and Dye, 1978). The degree to which underrepresentation of minorities has occurred with at-large elections decreased during the 1980s, but it has not disappeared entirely (Welch, 1990).

In 1965, the Supreme Court ruled that at-large elections were not unconstitutional per se in *Fortson v. Dorsey* (379 U.S. 433). Thus, allegations of racial discrimination associated with at-large elections became justiciable issues. The following year, *Burns v. Richardson* (384 U.S. 73) established that a charge that at-large elections discriminate against racial minorities is a fundamental challenge to minority civil rights.

Gradually, standards were developed for ascertaining the presence and impact of racial bias in at-large elections. Evidence of racial polarization in past elections was seen as an important indicator of discrimination. Polarization implies that many citizens were voting exclusively for members of their own race and, consequently, that minorities had little opportunity to elect candidates of their own ethnic backgrounds. This decreased opportunity to influence the outcome of the electoral process is known as "vote dilution." Vote dilution, which was generally identified through systematic geographic analysis of election returns, became recognized as an important precondition for proof of racial bias in election procedures.

During the 1960s and 1970s, courts articulated several factors that could be used as evidence that vote dilution constituted racial bias. Together, such factors were to be used in order to evaluate evidence of the discriminatory *effect* of at-large election systems. In 1980, however, the Supreme Court ruled that discriminatory *intent* must be proven in order to overturn at-large election systems.

Although its population is 35 percent African-American, the city of Mobile, Alabama, had never elected an African-American to its three-member city commission. African-American plaintiffs sued to overturn the city's at-large election system. In response to these charges, the city pointed out that its at-large election system had been established in 1911, when Jim Crow laws (see Chapter 4) had prohibited African-Americans from voting entirely. Thus, the election system used in Mobile had not been developed with the intention of discriminating against African-American voters, although the fact that no African-American had ever won a commission seat was clear evidence of its discriminatory effect.

The city's position was upheld by the Supreme Court. In *City of Mobile v. Bolden* (446 U.S. 55), the Court ruled that discriminatory *intent* as well as discriminatory effect must be established in order to prove vote dilution. Because it is much more difficult to prove discriminatory intent than discriminatory effect, *City of Mobile* was seen as a roadblock to supporters of African-American voting rights.

Two years later, Congress passed an extension of the Voting Rights Act. The revised act specified that courts could once again establish the existence of vote dilution through a combination of factual circumstances. These included (1) a history of official discrimination; (2) racial polarization in voting; (3) specific features of the election system, such as large districts or majority vote requirements; (4) minority access to the candidate slating process; (5) the degree of discrimination in education, health, employment, and other services; (6) the degree to which campaigning has been characterized by racial appeals; and (7) the extent to which minority group members have previously been elected to public office.

Although the discriminatory effects of at-large elections have been a prominent feature of much litigation, the identification and treatment of racially motivated gerrymandering has also commanded considerable attention. Deliberate distortion of electoral district boundaries against the interests of ethnic and racial minorities has occurred in congressional, state legislative, and local elections, and both opponent concentration and opponent dispersal strategies are used (O'Loughlin, 1982).

Racial issues in gerrymandering were addressed by the Supreme Court even before the reapportionment revolution of the 1960s began. In 1960, the Court ruled that racial gerrymandering was a justiciable issue in *Gomillion v. Lightfoot* (364 U.S. 339). In *Gomillion,* the Court found that the city of Tuskegee, Alabama, had been guilty of unconstitutionally gerrymandering against African-Americans by redrawing its boundaries and placing most of them outside the city limits. In 1964, *Wright v. Rockefeller* (376 U.S. 52), a case involving allegations of racially motivated gerrymandering in New York City's congressional districts, reached the Supreme Court. The Court declined, however, to rule that the districts in question were gerrymandered.

Political Gerrymandering in the 1980s and 1990s

By the end of the 1980s, political and racial gerrymandering had been placed on the same legal footing by the Supreme Court. This ruling stemmed from litigation in Indiana, where the Republicans had used both excess-vote and wasted-vote gerrymandering to minimize the political influence of areas of Democratic strength. In addition, they used multimember districts of varied size to minimize Democratic representation, and these multimember districts had the effect of disenfranchising residents of Indianapolis and other urban, Democratic areas in the state.

The Democrats sued on the grounds that the substantial disparity between votes for Democratic candidates and the number of Democratic seats represented gerrymandering. A federal district court ruled that the Republican-drawn districts were unconstitutional because they constituted an intentional partisan gerrymander. The Indiana case soon reached the Supreme Court. In *Bandemer v. Davis* (478 U.S. 109 [1986]), the Supreme Court ruled that political gerrymandering is indeed a justiciable issue. This implies that political as well as racial discrimination is grounds for potential legal action in the future. However, the Court was not impressed with the case made by Indiana Democrats, and so it declined to rule that gerrymandering characterized this particular situation. Ironically, by the end of the decade the Democrats had captured eight of Indiana's ten congressional districts, lending credence to the Court's arguments. Democratic success by the late 1980s can be traced to the effects of recession on the Rustbelt, which generated voter shift away from the Republicans. In California, meanwhile, Democrats placed several Republican incumbents in the same districts so they completed against each other, packed Republican voters into districts that were far too safe, and created Democratic majority districts in new seats and in seats opened up through the displacement of Republican incumbents, despite population shifts that had been thought to aid the Republicans. The result was an electoral bias of 11 percent, or five seats in 1982, although this bias dropped to 5 percent by 1986 (Morrill, 1987).

Karcher and *Bandemer* illustrate several substantive differences between the malapportionment cases of the 1960s and the racial and political gerrymandering cases in the courts today. During the reapportionment revolution of the 1960s, the courts focused on the voting rights of individuals. Malapportionment claims involve individual voting rights, whereas gerrymandering claims necessarily involve group rights. A claim of gerrymandering, in effect, is a claim made on behalf of a territorially defined community of interest.

Perhaps the key arguments summing up this debate were put forward by Justice John Paul Stevens in his concurring opinion in *Karcher*. This opinion, which cited the work of several prominent political geographers, began to lay the groundwork for determining the validity of allegations of political gerrymandering. Stevens argued first that plaintiffs must show that they are members of an identifiable political group whose voting strength has been diluted. He then argued that they must show that the proportional voting influence of the group has been diluted or otherwise adversely affected and that this adverse affect is the result of discrimination.

Stevens's argument formed the cornerstone of the *Bandemer* decision. The *Bandemer* ruling requires that, in order for plaintiffs' claim of partisan gerrymandering to be upheld, the instance of gerrymandering must result in long-term dilution of votes, with the effect of excluding the plaintiffs from the political process. *Bandemer* set a precedent for future rulings. To what extent have the distinctions between racial, partisan, and other forms of gerrymandering been clarified since *Bandemer* was decided? Shortly after the *Bandemer* decision was announced, prominent political scientists and political geographers ventured to predict the eventual impact of *Bandemer* on districting in the United States (Grofman, 1990).

Several issues arose in the prediction process. First, why did the Court rule that political gerrymandering per se was a justiciable issue, while failing to conclude that the Indiana case represented an instance of impermissible partisan gerrymandering? The district court's opinion, which was overturned by the Supreme Court, had identified several circumstances that led to its conclusion that gerrymandering *had* taken place (Grofman, 1990, pp. 32–35). For example, there were no public hearings on the proposed plans, which had been made available for inspection to the Legislature only a few days before being voted upon. Democratic leaders in the Legislature were not consulted about the proposal, and, in fact, they were specifically informed that their opinions would have no weight in the eventual plan. No effort was made to preserve communities of interest, and in several cases two or more strong Democratic incumbents were placed in the same district. Moreover, there was clear evidence that the seat–vote ratio favored the Republicans. The Republicans all but admitted that they had gerrymandered the districts.

Two additional questions emerge from this discussion. If the Indiana circumstances do not allow the conclusion that gerrymandering has occurred, under what circumstances could such a conclusion be drawn? In other words, what are the practical limitations and implications of *Bandemer*? And second, how does *Bandemer* affect the relationship between partisan gerrymandering, racially motivated gerrymandering, and other forms of electoral bias? As of the mid-1990s, federal courts have provided us with little guidance toward the resolution of these questions. In several cases, plaintiffs have claimed that they have been victimized by partisan gerrymandering, but in no case has the court accepted their claims. In short, the post-*Bandemer* plaintiffs have failed to demonstrate that their own claims, in contrast to those in Indiana, met the conditions set forth by *Bandemer* as associated with long-term partisan gerrymandering.

Minority Vote Dilution and Influence Districts

The revised Voting Rights Act of 1982 established the standards for evaluating claims of racial discrimination in representation during the 1980s. These provisions of the revised Voting Rights Act were challenged in court, and in 1986 the Supreme Court clarified its interpretation of them in *Thornburg v. Gingles* (478 U.S. 30). The *Thornburg* decision identified three factors required to establish vote dilution claims: Plaintiffs had to establish that the minority in question was sufficiently large and geographically compact to constitute a majority in a single-member district. In addition, the minority had to show that it was a politically cohesive group and that "a bloc voting majority must *usually* be able to defeat candidates supported by a politically cohesive, geographically insular minority group" (*Thornburg v. Gingles*). Once these preconditions are established, the factors associated with the Voting Rights Act of 1982 are applied in order to determine whether vote dilution has indeed taken place.

Of course, the *Thornburg* conditions are not free from ambiguity. In particular, the definition of a "politically cohesive group" could be fraught with controversy. Under what circumstances can one conclude that the minority community is politically cohesive in a manner distinct from the larger polity? Typically, courts have examined this issue by comparing the performance of minority and European-American candidates across different precincts, but differences in voter behavior between places may not constitute conclusive proof of political cohesion that is consistent with the concept of the community of interest described earlier.

Even if political cohesiveness could be demonstrated, how large a majority is needed to ensure that a minority group is adequately "large and geographically compact"? Many minority communities are neither large nor sufficiently concentrated geographically to meet this requirement. In such cases, some have argued for the creation of "influence districts." Influence districts contain substantial numbers of minority group members, although minority group members remain minorities within influence districts. The creation of an influence district concentrates nonminority populations into other districts, implying that representatives elected from the latter constituencies can ignore minority-group interests.

The Arkansas Litigation and Influence Districts

Whether influence districts help or hinder minority interests is a controversial question. This question was addressed in litigation involving the redistricting of Arkansas following the 1990 census. The Arkansas litigation also illustrates several of the other major controversies involving electoral districting in the United States.

Following the 1990 census, the Arkansas legislature began the process of redrawing the boundaries of its four House districts. The plan adopted by the legislature involved only minor changes from the plan that had been used during the 1980s (Figure 6-4). A few counties were shifted between districts in order to meet equal population standards, but only a small percentage of state residents were shifted between districts in the post-1990 redistricting (Figure 6-5).

The legislature's plan was opposed by some African-American citizens and interest groups who advocated that the state create an African-American influence district. Because only 16 percent of Arkansas residents are African-American and because the state is entitled to only four seats in the House of Representatives, it is not possible to construct a district with a majority African-American population. Nevertheless, opponents of the legislature's plan demonstrated that a district with over 42 percent African-American population could be constructed. Clearly, the proposed district would be considered an influence district. Yet the proposed influence district would have extended from the northeast corner to the southwest corner of the state. The plan would also have split several counties and several cities between districts.

After the legislature's plan was signed into law by then-Governor Bill Clinton, the National Association for the Advancement of Colored People (NAACP) filed suit in federal court. The suit alleged that African-Americans were being denied representation by the legislature's plan, which split the state's African-American population among the First, Second, and Fourth House Districts. Instead, the NAACP supported the creation of an influence district.

The legal debate that ensued involved two issues of direct relevance to U.S. political geography: First, would the long-run interests of the African-

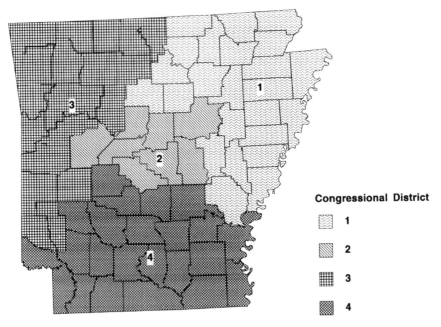

FIGURE 6-4. Congressional Districts: Arkansas, 1982. Data from U.S. Bureau of the Census (1983a), p. 5.16.

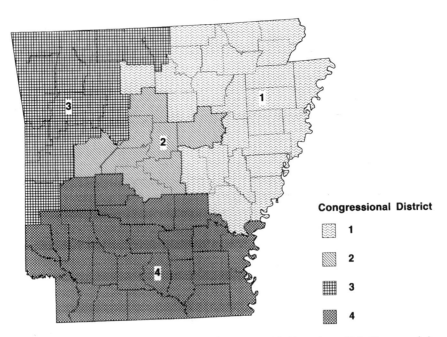

FIGURE 6-5. Congressional Districts: Arkansas, 1992. Data from U.S. Bureau of the Census (1993b), p. Arkansas-1.

Americans of Arkansas be served by concentrating them into a single district? Supporters of the legislature's plan pointed out that the First, Second, and Fourth Districts were all represented by moderate to liberal Democrats. The voting records of these representatives indicated their support for most bills of interest to the NAACP, and all had enjoyed substantial support among African-American constituents in previous elections. Concentrating most of the state's African-Americans into a single district would perhaps assure the election of a candidate sensitive to African-American concerns from that district. On the other hand, it might increase the possibility that candidates elected from other districts would vote against bills of interest to the NAACP and its membership.

More fundamentally, the Arkansas litigation highlighted the critical question of whether race—or for that matter, any of the other cultural divisions described in Chapter 2—is an appropriate basis upon which to determine the existence of a community of interest. The judges who ruled in the Arkansas case pointed out that the plaintiffs' plan to establish an influence district cut across well-defined communities of interest, fragmenting cities and counties and in general violating general standards of compactness in districting. On this basis, it was rejected by a federal district court (*Turner v. State of Arkansas*, 784 F. Supp. 553 [1991]).

In establishing this argument, the court noted that Arkansas, like many other states, contains clear regional divisions. The Delta region has historical and economic ties to neighboring Mississippi and Tennessee. Southern and southwestern Arkansas, on the other hand, is a community of interest that has close economic ties with northern Louisiana and northeastern Texas. These regions, of course, are culturally, politically, and economically distinct from the Ozark and Ouachita Mountain regions of northwestern Arkansas— an area with historic and contemporary ties not only to neighboring Missouri but to the metropolitan centers of Kansas City, St. Louis, and Chicago.

The Little Rock area, as the state's primary metropolitan region, represents a distinct community of interest. Employees commute to work in Little Rock from several counties surrounding the city. These economic ties are reinforced by communications media centered in Little Rock, and many people in surrounding counties commute into Little Rock to shop and attend cultural or recreational activities as well as to work. For many decades, Little Rock has been the center of a House district in Arkansas. The districting plan ultimately approved by the court in *Turner* preserved a district based on each of these long-standing communities of interest, with communities of interest defined on the basis of the state's traditional regional geography.

Shaw v. Reno

Although the concept of community of interests proved to be crucial to the decisions rendered by federal courts in *Jordan* and *Turner,* the relationship between community of interest, geography, and nongeographic criteria for defining communities of interest remains unresolved. While Arkansas drew its districts by identifying communities of interest on a geographic basis, other states paid less direct attention to geography in identifying communities of interest. Instead, communities of interest were defined on the basis of ethnicity alone.

The latter circumstance is illustrated by the district lines drawn in North Carolina in the 1980s (Figure 6-6) and then the early 1990s (Figure 6-7). After the 1990 census, districts were drawn with the specific intention of concentrating African-American strength. As a result, some of the districts were far from compact, but the state justified these boundaries as promoting minority-group representation. Controversy erupted because the two African-American districts had highly irregular boundaries. The First District, which extends across much of eastern North Carolina from the Virginia border to just north of the South Carolina boundary, has been described as a "Rorschach ink-blot test" and a "bug splattered on a windshield" (*Shaw v. Reno,* 125 L. Ed. 511 [1993] at p. 521). The Twelfth District was approximately 190 miles long, but for much of its length it was only as wide as the corridor containing Interstate Highway 85. Essentially, the district was created by combining the African-American neighborhoods of Charlotte, Greensboro, and Durham, using little more than the highway between them to complete the district to comply with federal mandates that districts be equal in population. In November 1992, Democrats Eva Clayton and Melvin Watt were elected to Congress from the First and Twelfth Districts, respectively. Clayton and Watt became the first two African-Americans elected to Congress from North Carolina since the nineteenth century.

Opponents of the districting plan sued in federal court on the grounds that the North Carolina districts had been drawn with the sole intention of promoting minority representation. The Supreme Court accepted this argument. Plaintiffs claimed that the General Assembly had "created two Congressional Districts in which a majority of black voters was concentrated arbitrarily—without regard to any other considerations, such as compactness, contiguousness, geographical boundaries or political subdivisions with the purpose to create Congressional Districts along racial lines" (*Shaw v. Reno,* p. 522).

On June 28, 1993, in *Shaw v. Reno,* the U.S. Supreme Court declared North Carolina's congressional districting plan to be unconstitutional. The majority opinion declared that North Carolina's reapportionment plan was "so irrational on its face that it can be understood only as an effort to segregate voters into separate voting districts because of their race, and that the separation lacks sufficient justification" (*Shaw v. Reno,* p. 536).

On these grounds, the Court ordered North Carolina to justify its districting plan on alternative grounds. If such justification could not be provided, the plan would be considered unconstitutional. In 1994, a federal court upheld the state's claim that the two unusually shaped districts could indeed be justified on other grounds. The court made specific reference to the concept of community

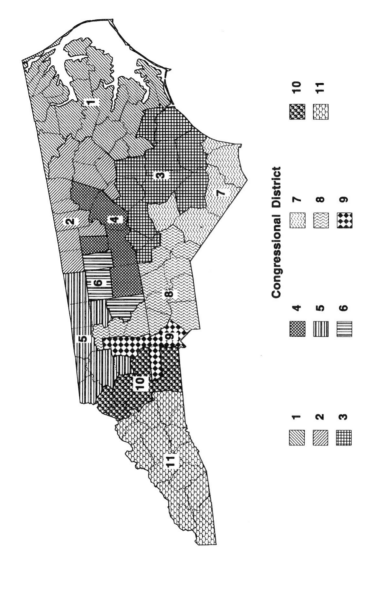

FIGURE 6-6. Congressional Districts: North Carolina, 1982. Data from U.S. Bureau of the Census (1983b), pp. 35.27–35.29.

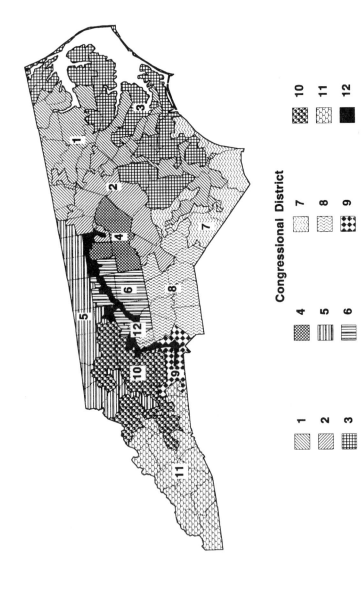

FIGURE 6-7. Congressional Districts: North Carolina, 1992. Data from U.S. Bureau of the Census (1993b), pp. North Carolina-1–North Carolina-55.

of interest in rendering its decision. The First District, which contained a majority of the state's productive agricultural counties, was justified as containing a "rural" community of interest. The Twelfth District was recognized as an "urban" community of interest. Thus, the court concluded that "within each of the districts [there was] substantial, relatively high degrees of homogeneity of shared socio-economic—hence political—interests and needs among the citizens" (*Shaw v. Hunt,* 861 F. Supp. 408 [1994], p. 470).

The North Carolina court's use of the concept of community of interest was strikingly different from that of Arkansas. While Arkansas associated communities of interest with well-defined geographic regions, North Carolina did not do so. "There is no convincing evidence in the record that the irregularities and lack of geographical compactness of these two districts have had or are having any significant adverse effects upon their citizens' interests in fair and effective representation" (*Shaw v. Hunt,* 861 F. Supp. 408 [1994], p. 471). The court went on to assert that "the districts' configurations in relation to transportation facilities, media markets, commuting patterns and volumes certainly do not support any finding that their irregularities of shape necessarily will make their representatives less accessible and responsive than those of other districts" (*Shaw v. Hunt,* p. 472).

At the same time, similar analyses were undertaken in other states. Other lower courts did not share the North Carolina court's view that their states' oddly shaped districts could be justified on grounds other than race. In Texas, for example, the oddly shaped Thirtieth District in the Dallas area was "carefully gerrymandered on a racial basis to achieve a certain number of African-American voters" (*Vera v. Richards,* 861 F. Supp. 1304 [1994], p. 1335). Likewise, a Georgia court concluded, after a review of relevant evidence, that "it [is] exceedingly clear that there are no tangible 'communities of interest' spanning the hundreds of miles of the Eleventh District" (*Johnson v. Miller,* 864 F. Supp. 1354 [1994], pp. 1389–1390). In June, 1995, this view was upheld by the Supreme Court, further narrowing the range of acceptable minority-majority districting schemes and procedures.

These and other decisions handed down since the 1990 census illustrate a fundamental dilemma associated with contemporary electoral districting. Should districts be drawn on the basis of race and ethnicity, on the basis of geography alone, or on some combination of the two? The very nature of U.S. democracy is such that successful candidates for public office must build coalitions of disparate groups of voters. Any successful candidate for the House of Representatives must appeal to voters representing a wide variety of occupations, income levels, political and religious affiliations, racial and ethnic identifications, and many other factors. Candidates whose appeals are too narrow for the district are unlikely to be elected. Yet the very nature of this appeal to the voters, of course, depends on the political characteristics of district residents.

Each voter in a district has a variety of personal characteristics that could influence his or her voting decision. A particular voter, for example, might be an African-American, a woman, a teacher, a resident of a particular city or county, a union member, a Baptist, and a member of various organizations advocating particular policy initiatives. Thus ethnicity, gender, occupation, state and community of residence, social class, religious affiliation, and organizational membership are but a few of the many factors that influence voting decisions and electoral outcomes.

Is it right to single out only one characteristic—race—as the sole basis for district composition? Aside from the fact that race has historically been a significant basis of discrimination, race may be a convenient surrogate for other characteristics for two reasons: The race of a person is easily identified, and neighborhoods and communities dominated by particular races or ethnic groups are similarly easy to identify and map. That it is impossible to delineate territorially based districts on the basis of gender, on the other hand, may explain why we have never seen a gender-based politics in U.S. history.

A related problem that several courts have addressed involves communities inhabited by two or more minority groups. In some communities, efforts have been made to establish minority-dominated districts even if the district population consists of two or more distinct minority groups, such as African-Americans and Hispanics. Should minority groups be counted jointly for representational purposes? This has become a potentially explosive issue in many areas where three or more ethnic groups are struggling for political power, as, for example, in southern California and south Florida.

Conclusion

The U.S. system of representation is based on territorial linkages between legislators and their constituencies. At no time in the nation's history have alternatives such as virtual or proportional representation been sanctioned in electing the members of the House of Representatives or the legislatures of the several states. The Constitution provides for a system of congressional representation that is explicitly territorial yet preserves majority and minority rights.

In recent years, a series of cases has established and upheld two important constitutional guarantees concerning representation: Representation must be undertaken according to the principle of "one person, one vote," and representation must safeguard the legitimate political interests of racial and ethnic minorities. Gerrymandering continues to be practiced, but the fact that territoriality in itself is a critical component of representation in U.S. society provides a basis for considering, comparing, and evaluating the multitude of criteria for electoral district boundary delineation. In particular, techniques of gerrymandering can be demonstrated to have a high probability of long-term over- or underrepresentation of certain areas or population groups. To the extent that gerrymandering influences the effectiveness of such representation, it must be seen to frustrate the intent of the Constitution—an intent that is explicitly territorial and yet preserves both majority and minority rights.

Chapter 7

THE UNITED STATES
AND THE WORLD

s the twentieth century draws to a close, many Americans are ques-
tioning whether the United States will retain its pre-eminence in the
international arena. Throughout U.S. history, foreign affairs have often influenced domestic politics and vice versa. Interaction between the domestic and foreign spheres has resulted in interesting and significant conflicts
at the ballot box, in the halls of Congress, and, occasionally, on the battle-
field.

In this chapter, we trace the political geography of relationships between
the United States and the outside world, focusing particularly on the geographic consequences, within the United States and elsewhere, of American
foreign policy. We begin this chapter by examining fundamental concepts of
geopolitics. Discussion of geopolitics is followed by an analysis of the historical geography of U.S. foreign policy in the United States. Next, we turn to discussion of changes in the U.S. role in the world political economy and how
this role is affected by changes in the overarching geopolitical order. The final
section addresses the development of a post–Cold War world order and con-
cludes with a discussion of possible scenarios concerning the U.S. position
within that new world order.

U.S. Geopolitics

For decades, geographers have analyzed conflicts between states. The study of
geographic impacts on international relations and international political conflicts is known as "geopolitics."

Concepts of geopolitics can be found in the writings of prominent ancient and medieval scholars, including Aristotle, Confucius, and Machiavelli.
Yet geopolitics as an explicit field of inquiry did not emerge until the late
nineteenth century. By that time, the Age of Exploration had come to an end.
The habitable portions of the earth's surface had been divided by the Euro-

pean powers into colonies. The European powers continued to compete among themselves for political and economic influence, but a country could no longer expect to further its influence through colonial activity.

Once the process of colonialism was complete, leaders within each of the competing European powers began to examine the geographic strengths and weaknesses of each country more systematically. How could a country take advantage of its location, resources, and economic base to improve its position within the world economy? During the late nineteenth and twentieth centuries, several distinct geopolitical concepts arose in various countries. In each case, these geopolitical concepts were closely linked to the development of foreign policies in their respective countries.

European Geopolitics

As we saw in Chapter 2, Great Britain became established as the world's strongest country following the Seven Years' War. It maintained its dominant position throughout the nineteenth century. By 1900, nearly a quarter of the world's population lived in the British Empire. Yet many in Great Britain were uneasy about the prospect of continued British domination of the world economy. The British geographer Sir Halford Mackinder viewed history as an ongoing conflict between sea-based and land-based powers. During the nineteenth century, the Industrial Revolution and improvements in the technology of land transportation had allowed land-based powers to gain strength at the expense of sea-based powers such as Great Britain. Thus, Mackinder argued that any power that could unite the population, resources, and industrial strength of continental Europe would become a major threat to the security of the British Empire.

Mackinder summarized these views by stating, "Who rules East Europe commands the Heartland; who rules the Heartland commands the World Island; who commands the World Island commands the World." For Mackinder, the "Heartland" consisted of the great continental landmass of Eurasia. He believed that any country able to control eastern Europe would be in a strong position to assert control over the world, and he used effective cartographic techniques to convey his message. (Cartography, which involves the making and use of maps, continues to be of importance in the conduct and analysis of foreign policy; see Box 7-1).

British foreign policy was strongly influenced by Mackinder's views. The British took pains to ensure that central and eastern Europe remained divided and to assert British domination of the seas. British apprehensions of geopolitically ascendant "Heartland" power prompted Britain to ally against and to militarily oppose Germany in both World Wars. Later, Mackinder's "Heartland" theory served as an underlying rationale for U.S. foreign policy maker's adoption of the Cold War containment policy stance against the Soviet Union and its Eastern bloc allies (Walters, 1974; Taylor, 1993b).

Box 7-1. *Cartography and Foreign Policy*

Throughout U.S. history, cartography has had and important role to play in the development of U.S. foreign relations. The essential relevance of cartography to the analysis and conduct of foreign policy can be seen by examining the geography of foreign policy mapping within the Washington, DC, metropolitan region. The Office of the Geographer, U.S. Department of State, is found in the main office building of the U.S. Department of State. Cartographers in the Office of the Geographer are charged with maintaining maps of the sometimes rapidly shifting international boundaries throughout the world. The office adapted geographic information systems (GIS) technology (see Box 6-2) in order to improve the accuracy and speed of map making.

Just eight miles to the west is located the main entrance to the U.S. Central Intelligence Agency (CIA) in Langley, Virginia. "The CIA creates maps of practically every place on earth, from Aden to Zimbabwe" (Makower, 1986, p. 42). Other, less well-known foreign-policy-related mapping units also are located in the Washington area, including the National Reconnaissance Office (NRO), which manages and interprets U.S. spaceborne and airborne reconnaissance from around the world. Hundreds of thousands, perhaps millions, of high-resolution satellite images have been collected by CORONA and other classified intelligence satellites. While LANDSAT and other nonmilitary satellites usually have yielded coarse-grained images with resolutions of 20 meters or more, intelligence satellites have provided finely detailed images with resolutions of 2 meters or less since the mid-1960s (McDonald, 1995). In 1995, more than 2.1 million square feet of secret reconnaissance images obtained from 1960 to 1972 were declassified for use in historical and environmental research (Asker, 1995) (Figure 7-B1-1). The three-decades-old NRO once was so super-secret that its existence was not even mentioned in public debate in Congress until 1987, when Representative George E. Brown was forced to resign his seat on the House Intelligence Committee because of this lapse. The NRO employs nearly 3,000 workers in its new $310 million headquarters in suburban Virginia (*USA Today,* September 30, 1994).

Diplomats and trade representatives also need to use maps in order to gain a synoptic view of U.S. interests in relation to the rest of the world. Whereas the intelligence community often requires large-scale maps that provide detailed information about small areas, persons involved in diplomacy and international trade tend to prefer small-scale maps, which are useful for comprehending more abstract and generalized cultural, demographic, economic, and political patterns for large areas.

Maps are often regarded as faithful, objective depictions of areas. But like any other communications medium, maps are subject to omissions and biases, intended as well as unintended. Speier (1941, pp. 310–11) pointed out that "maps are not confined to the representation of a given state of affairs. . . . Instead of unknown relationships of facts they may reveal policies or illustrate doctrines. They may give information, but they may also plead. Maps can be symbols of conquest or tokens of revenge, instruments for airing grievances or expressions of pride."

Such problems are exacerbated by the fact that it is impossible to preserve

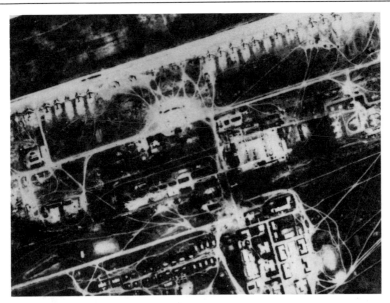

FIGURE 7-B1-1. Declassified CORONA Intelligence Reconnaissance Satellite Image of Soviet Strategic Bomber Base Located near Dolon, Kazakhstan, August 20, 1966. Data via Internet from U.S. Geological Survey's Earth Resources Observation Systems (EROS) Data Center, Sioux Falls, South Dakota.

all important geometrical properties of the earth's spherical surface during *map projection,* which is the process of depicting the three-dimensional surface of the earth on a two-dimensional flat surface (Muehrcke, 1986; Monmonier, 1991). Map projections can show correct distances or directions from one or a few locations, correct areas for all locations, or correct shapes for most areas, but correct distances, directions, areas, and shapes cannot all be shown at once on one map (Monmonier, 1995).

Because it is impossible to project a three-dimensional sphere onto a flat surface with complete accuracy, the resulting distortion may serve to perpetuate inaccurate images of the earth's surface in the minds of the public. A distinguished geographer and State Department cartographer, S. Whittemore Boggs, stated that "illusion may occur when people use world maps instead of globes in seeking to understand some of the world relationships of our times" (Boggs, 1946, p. 1120). Because projection errors increase with the size of the area being mapped, special caution must be taken by map readers who study geopolitical maps of large areas.

Sir Halford Mackinder regarded world history in terms of ongoing conflict between land-based and sea-based powers. Mackinder used cartography quite effectively in order to demonstrate his views. Figure 7-B1-2 shows the Eurasian Pivot Area as demarcated by Mackinder (1904). The Pivot Area is given visual strength by shading and by textual notations that curve around it in a manner

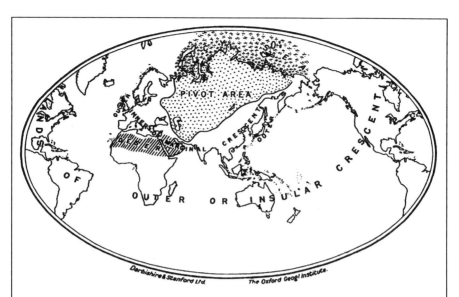

FIGURE 7-B1-2. Mackinder's "Pivot Area" or "Heartland" on Mercator Cylindrical Projection. From Mackinder (1904), p. 435.

which suggests a sequence of zones of diminishing importance with increasing distances. The oval neat-line reinforces this perception.

But another, more subtle form of visual persuasion was also employed. The map is based upon an equatorial aspect Mercator conformal cylindrical projection. The Mercator projection was developed by the famous Flemish cartographer, Gerhardus Mercator, in 1568 to aid sailors in navigation, because any straight line on the projection represents a rhumb line of constant direction on the earth's surface. Although a rhumb line route can be much longer than a great-circle route over a long voyage, it is often convenient for navigators to plot a course of constant bearing or direction. Unfortunately, projections that preserve direction sacrifice accurate representations of areas. Thus, the equatorial aspect Mercator cylindrical conformal projection increasingly misrepresents areas at increasing distances from the equator. Places distant from the equator are depicted as considerably larger than they really are. Because Mackinder's Heartland was centered on the northerly countries of Germany and Russia, his map makes these countries appear larger and thus more threatening than was the case in reality.

During and after World War II, cartography again played a role in the articulation of U.S. foreign policy. The "old" rectangular equatorial aspect cylindrical projections, such as the one used by Mackinder, yielded an image of the United States comfortably isolated from the "Old World" on the east by the Atlantic Ocean and on the west by the Pacific Ocean. Instead, a modernized "Air Age geography" was to be better depicted by circular projections from the zenithal class (Ristow, 1944), such as the pole-centered azimuthal equidistant projection shown in Figure 7-B1-3. Zenithal class projections were hardly novel in a technical sense, since some were actually developed by the ancient Greeks while others were invented about the time of the American Revolution, but they had rarely been used to show areas of global or hemispherical proportions before (Thrower, 1972). The "new" polar or oblique aspect azimuthal projections visually implied that U.S. isolation was "a geographical myth. In terms of air-geography the Heartland and North America appear in destiny-laden proximity. As viewed over the top of the world, the Heartland assumes a location different from that which Mackinder assigned to it, plotting it from Britain, with the destinies of Britain foremost in his mind. . . . [T]he skyways of the Arctic Mediterranean give validity to a new way of regarding the geographical relations of North America and the U.S.S.R." (Weigert et al., 1957, p. 217). Revised cartography thus contributed to renewed U.S. emphasis on the Arctic region during the Cold War.

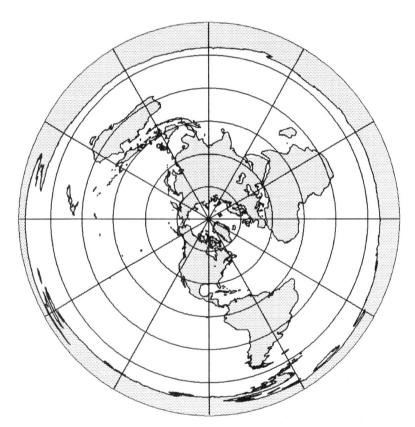

FIGURE 7-B1-3. "Air Age" Azimuthal Equidistant Projection Centered on North Pole at 90 North. Produced using *MicroCAM* software on a PC-DOS microcomputer; see Loomer (1993).

Distinctive geopolitical views emerged in the major countries of continental Europe (Parker, 1985). French geopolitics, for example, recognizes France's unique position as both a maritime and a continental power. The geopolitics of Germany is centered on the fact that the German-speaking areas of central Europe were fragmented politically until well into the nineteenth century. Once German unification had been achieved, Germany became one of the world's major economic and political powers. Yet many Germans believed that Germany was sandwiched between hostile powers, with France to the west and Russia to the east. Both of these geopolitical problems could be resolved by expanding the German state to include all of the German-speaking people of central and eastern Europe.

After World War I, German geopolitical views encompassed the concepts of *Lebensraum* and *pan-regions*. Karl Haushofer argued that *Lebensraum*, or room in which to expand, was needed for a state to achieve political and economic self-sufficiency. Some extended this view further, arguing that German interests would also be served by overland expansion into the Middle East and Africa. It was argued that the world should be divided into *pan-regions*, each consisting of a large area of the world under the domination of a single country.

The foreign policy of Russia and the Soviet Union has been based on several consistent themes since the days of the czars. The cornerstones of Russian foreign policy include securing Russia's borders, territorial expansion, development of trade and access to warm-water ports. Both the czars and the Soviet leaders worked to establish buffer states in eastern Europe to help secure Russia's borders against foreign threats or invasions. The significance of such threats was devastatingly underscored by the extent of Soviet casualties in World War II, which exceeded 13 million military and 7 million civilian deaths, by far the greatest losses of any country in that conflict. In comparison, Germany's war casualties totaled about 8 million, and Great Britain and the United States suffered losses of one-half million or fewer war casualties. The vivid memory of war devastation heightened Russian policy makers' fears of foreign threats. From the Russian perspective, Western Cold War containment policies threatened Russian security, as is illustrated by a Soviet cartographic representation of Western strategic forces deployment in the early 1980s (Figure 7-1). Under Cold War circumstances, increased military security for one side implied increased military risks for the other side.

Geopolitics in the United States

The transformation of the United States from colony to world power has been one of the most significant developments in international geopolitics over the past two centuries. Since the early nineteenth century, U.S. geopolitics has emphasized domination of the Western Hemisphere. In the twentieth century, two additional themes emerged: domination of the air and control of the Arc-

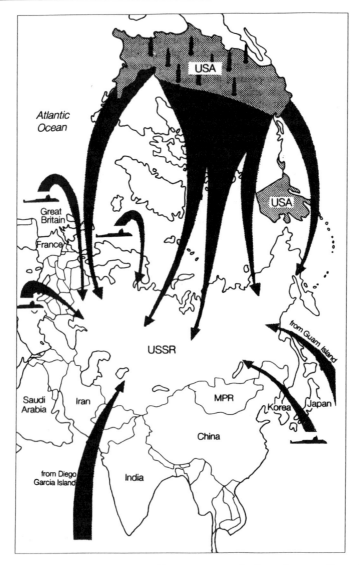

FIGURE 7-1. Soviet View of U.S. Cold War Strategic Defense Posture. From U.S.S.R. Ministry of Defense (1982), p. 68.

tic. A fourth underlying theme of U.S. geopolitics, which we discuss in detail in the next section of this chapter, is ongoing tension between isolationism and interventionism.

Less than half a century after the American Revolution, the United States emerged as the strongest power in the Western Hemisphere. In the early nineteenth century, revolutionary movements arose throughout Latin America. Many of the leaders of the Latin American independence movements were in fact influenced by the American Revolution. The government of the United States strongly supported efforts of the various Latin American countries to achieve political independence from Spain and Portugal.

In 1823, President James Monroe announced what has become known as the Monroe Doctrine. The Monroe Doctrine asserted that the United States would actively oppose any attempt on the part of the European powers to re-assert control over their former colonies in the Americas. Opposition to European interference in the Western Hemisphere has remained a cornerstone of U.S. geopolitics ever since.

In the twentieth century, U.S. geopolitical thinkers began to emphasize the importance of aviation and air power. Prior to the invention of aviation, the three thousand miles separating the United States from Europe allowed the United States to develop without becoming actively involved in European conflicts. Airplanes drew the United States much closer to Europe, however. "Our country lives next door to the world. Our former vacuum of insulating space has been filled, literally, by air and airplanes" (Hurd, 1944, p. 109).

In response to this perception, many U.S. geopolitical thinkers began to emphasize U.S. domination of the world's airspace. Aviation had been invented in the United States, and U.S. air superiority had already proven to be of major importance in World War I. Since that time, Americans have paid considerable attention to the development of military and civilian superiority in the skies. During World War II, the editors of *Fortune* commented that "whoever controls the main strategic postwar air bases, together with the technical facilities to keep them manned, will unquestionably be the world's strongest power" (Weigert and Stefansson, 1944, p. 121). Dominance of the air was seen as consistent with U.S. efforts to promote free trade throughout the world, in opposition to German and Japanese efforts to establish more isolated pan-regions.

The shortest air distance between two places is along the great-circle route, which is determined by connecting the two places by a straight line along the surface of the globe. Since great-circle routes are accurately represented as curved lines on most map projections, they were challenging for navigators to plot using older technology. Modern navigational computers solve the necessary equations quite quickly, however. Great-circle routes between many international airports in the United States and Europe in fact extend across the Arctic. For example, air travelers flying from London or Moscow to Los Angeles or from Moscow to Washington, DC, usually fly directly over Greenland and the Arctic Ocean (Figure 7-2).

Because important international great-circle routes extend across the Arctic Ocean, U.S. geopolitical thought has also emphasized control of the Arctic region. The Arctic Ocean has been called the "American Mediterranean," a sea located between Europe and North America much as the Mediterranean itself is located between Europe, the Middle East, and Africa (Stefansson, 1922). The development of modern aviation has made it easier to overcome the often harsh climatic conditions of the Arctic region. The main-

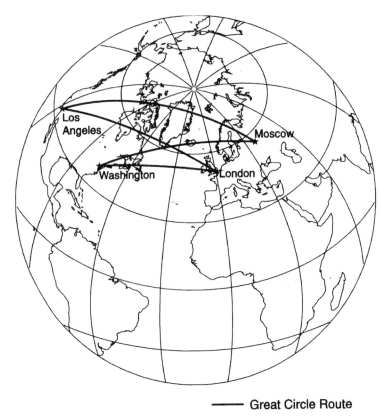

—— Great Circle Route

FIGURE 7-2. Great-Circle Routes on Azimuthal Equal-Area Projection, Centered at 40 North, 15 West. Produced using *MicroCAM* software on a PC-DOS microcomputer; see Loomer (1993).

tenance of friendly relations with Canada and the establishment of military bases in Iceland, Greenland, Canada, and Alaska are testimony to the importance of this objective in twentieth-century U.S. foreign policy.

Isolationism and Internationalism in U.S. Foreign Policy

The U.S. position within the international community has evolved continuously over the two centuries since the ratification of the Constitution. The first century and a half of independence were characterized by a steady increase in U.S. influence in the world political economy. In 1800, the newly independent Thirteen Colonies were struggling against the possibility of renewed European colonialism. A century later, the United States had become the world's leading industrial power, and by the end of World War II, it had become the leading actor on the global geopolitical stage as well.

The United States enjoyed several substantial geographic advantages in its rise to international prominence. In contrast to the powers of Western Europe, the United States has always enjoyed an abundance of natural resources, a large land area, and secure borders. Its great distance from Europe enabled the United States to remain neutral in most European conflicts. Free from the need to defend its borders against hostile attack, the United States expended a far smaller percentage of its resources on its armed forces than did the nations of Europe during the nineteenth and early twentieth centuries. This, in turn, freed a greater proportion of governmental resources for civilian purposes, expediting the pace of U.S. industrialization and economic development. America's isolation from European conflicts helped the United States to become the world's leading industrial power by 1900.

During the course of its rise to world prominence, the United States has experienced ongoing tension between proponents of isolationism and of internationalism. Proponents of isolationism have argued that the primary goal of U.S. foreign policy should be to protect the borders of the United States and that the United States should not take an active role in foreign affairs. Proponents of internationalism, on the other hand, have argued that the United States should take a more active and assertive role in international affairs.

The relative importance of isolationism and internationalism within the United States has oscillated in cycles of approximately twenty to thirty years throughout the course of U.S. history (Klingberg, 1983; Schlesinger, 1986; Goldstein, 1988; Berry, 1991). Cycles dominated by the isolationist perspective are called "introvert cycles," while those in which an internationalist perspective has been dominant are known as "extrovert cycles." Four extrovert cycles, each followed by an introvert cycle, can be identified (Table 7-1).

TABLE 7-1. American Foreign Policy Mood Phases

Introvert phase	Extrovert phase	Major challenges	Major conflicts
1776–1798	1799–1825	Independence Trans-Appalachian frontier	American Revolution War of 1812
1825–1844	1845–1867	Manifest destiny Slavery	Mexican War U.S. Civil War
1868–1897	1898–1919	Closing western frontier Industrialization	Spanish–American War World War I
1920–1939	1940–1969	Hegemonic rivalry Globalizing world economy	World War II Korean War
1970–??		Post-hegemonic trauma Post-Fordist global economy Global ecological limits?	Vietnam War Persian Gulf War

Source: Expanded from Klingberg (1983), p. 2 and passim; Schlesinger (1986), p. 44 and passim.

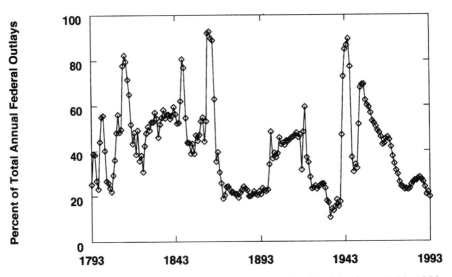

FIGURE 7-3. Defense Outlays as a Proportion of Total Federal Outlays, 1793–1993. Data from U.S. Bureau of the Census (1975), pp. 1114–15; U.S. Office of Management and Budget (various years).

The periods 1799–1825, 1845–1867, 1898–1920, and 1941–1968 are recognized as extrovert cycles, with the intervening periods recognized as introvert cycles. The relative importance of U.S. government defense and nondefense spending represents a useful indicator of introvert and extrovert cycles (Figure 7-3). Note how the percentage of total federal outlays devoted to defense spending has risen and fallen over time in conjunction with shifts between the extrovert and introvert cycles.

Introversion and Extroversion in the Nineteenth Century

The newly independent Thirteen Colonies entered the first extrovert cycle after the ratification of the Constitution. After the Revolutionary War, the new nation's main foreign policy concerns included ensuring sovereignty over its territory and removing European influence from the New World. Achievement of these objectives brought the newly independent United States into periodic conflict with Britain and France, including the War of 1812. The Louisiana Purchase of 1803 helped to secure U.S. sovereignty over eastern and central North America, while the purchase of Florida from Spain in 1819 eliminated Spanish colonization of the southeastern United States. The crowning point of the first extrovert cycle, however, was the announcement of the Monroe Doctrine in 1823.

The second extrovert cycle began in the mid-1840s. As we saw in Chapter 3, it was during this period that the United States expanded to the Pacific Ocean. Texas was annexed, the Mexican War was fought, and a treaty resolving the disputed Oregon Territory was negotiated with the British. By 1853, all of what would become the forty-eight contiguous states had been acquired by the United States. This second extrovert cycle culminated with the Civil War and the purchase of Alaska from Russia in 1867.

Foreign Policy in the Late Nineteenth and Early Twentieth Centuries

After Appomattox, in the latter half of the nineteenth century, the United States devoted itself primarily to the expansion of settlement across these new territories and the development of industry. At the end of the nineteenth century, however, the United States entered its third extrovert cycle. For the first time, the United States became a colonial power. The previously independent kingdom of Hawaii was annexed, and the territories of Cuba, Puerto Rico, and the Philippines were acquired from Spain after the Spanish–American War.

During this period, many Americans came to believe that nineteenth-century isolationism was no longer a feasible policy. The world was shrinking, and the United States was strong enough to play a major role in preserving the balance of power between the countries of Europe. Theodore Roosevelt, who served as president from 1901 to 1909, stated that the United States was to "speak softly and carry a big stick." Roosevelt enlarged the scope of the Monroe Doctrine, using it to justify direct U.S. involvement throughout the Western Hemisphere (LaFeber, 1986, p. 130). During Roosevelt's presidency, the size of the Navy was doubled and the Panama Canal was constructed. Between 1900 and 1920, the Monroe Doctrine was invoked to justify the deployment of U.S. troops or warships in several Central and South American countries.

The third extrovert cycle culminated in U.S. entry into World War I. The United States was initially neutral in the European conflict. In 1916, the slogan "He kept us out of war" was critical to the narrow reelection victory of Woodrow Wilson. Despite this slogan, Wilson's concern for a continued balance of power in Europe tilted U.S. foreign policy toward Great Britain. Late in 1917, Congress declared war on Germany. Congress approved the declaration of war by a vote of 82 to 6 in the Senate and 373 to 50 in the House of Representatives. Most of the opposition votes were cast by senators and representatives from the Middle West, the Plains, and the Rocky Mountain states, and many represented areas with large populations of German ancestry. Once the United States entered the war, U.S. industrial, military, and air power soon tipped the balance of power in favor of the Allies. World War I ended with the armistice of November 11, 1918.

Isolationism in the 1920s and 1930s

Woodrow Wilson's vision of the world "emphasized the force of American ideals—including peace, progress, brotherhood, liberty, democracy, self-determination, free enterprise, and free trade—in the construction of a world based upon a community of interests rather than conflicting national interests" (Powaski, 1991, p. 5). Wilson began to express his vision of a "just peace" to the world as World War I wound down. A cornerstone of Wilson's "just peace" was the establishment of a League of Nations. The entangling alliances and national subjugation of prewar Europe would be replaced by the principles of national self-determination and the resolution of disputes through open discussion (Powaski, 1991, p. 12). <u>Wilson, in fact, viewed the League of Nations as a logical extension of the Monroe Doctrine.</u> In a speech to Congress on January 22, 1917, Wilson stated that all nations "should with one accord adopt the doctrine of President Monroe as the doctrine of the world: that no nation should seek to extend its polity over any other nation or people" (LaFeber, 1989, p. 277).

Wilson spent most of January and February 1919 in France at the Versailles Peace Conference. Although the Treaty of Versailles fell short of Wilson's vision, he gave the treaty enthusiastic support. After returning to the United States, Wilson began to campaign for public support for the Treaty of Versailles and for the League of Nations. Despite Wilson's efforts, the United States renounced the internationalism of the two previous decades and, instead, swiftly moved into an introvert cycle. <u>The U.S. Senate refused to ratify the League of Nations Covenant, voting against the treaty by a margin of 55 to 39 in November 1919.</u>

Wilson's foreign policy activism was repudiated by the electorate in the election of 1920. Republican Warren Gamaliel Harding won a landslide victory by calling for a return to "normalcy," a philosophy that many interpreted as implying a return to nineteenth-century isolationism. Isolationism dominated U.S. politics throughout the 1920s and 1930s. As we saw in Chapter 4, restrictive immigration laws were enacted in the early 1920s. Meanwhile, high tariffs restricted U.S. trade with other parts of the world.

The debate between isolationists and interventionists increased in intensity during the 1930s, following the rise to power of Hitler in Germany, Tojo in Japan, and Mussolini in Italy. Many influential Americans argued that the United States had moral or practical obligations to support Great Britain and her allies, while others argued for continued neutrality. Between 1939 and 1941, several foreign policy issues commanded considerable attention in Congress. For example, the Lend-Lease program, which provided ships to Great Britain and her allies, passed Congress by a narrow margin, while President Franklin D. Roosevelt's proposal to extend the first peacetime military draft in history passed the House of Representatives by a single vote in August 1941.

The Cold War Extrovert Cycle

U.S. isolationism came to an abrupt end on December 7, 1941. The Japanese attack on Pearl Harbor in Hawaii prompted a nearly unanimous U.S. declaration of war against Japan, Germany, and Italy. By 1945, the United States fielded over 15 million troops and suffered nearly 300,000 of a million battle deaths. The end of the war in 1945 left the United States the world's strongest military and economic power. However, the United States did not retreat into isolationism as it had done following World War I. Most Americans embraced the idea of maintaining a strong U.S. presence overseas. The United Nations Charter was ratified by the Senate by a vote of 89 to 2 in September 1945.

By the late 1940s, many U.S. leaders had become concerned that the Soviet Union would continue to extend its influence beyond Eastern Europe. Many U.S. officials advocated a policy of containment, that is, of preventing the expansion of Soviet influence throughout the world. Associated with the containment policy was the so-called domino theory, which suggested that adjoining nations were likely to fall victim to Communist takeover one after another in analogy to a row of toppling dominoes. Only by containment, according to advocates of the domino theory, could the United States hope to stop the spread of communism. Advocates of containment policy supported U.S. military action in places threatened by Communist takeover. U.S. foreign policy commitments thus extended well beyond the Western Hemisphere, raising the possibility that U.S. military, diplomatic, or commercial interests might be challenged virtually anywhere in the world (Figure 7-4).

Sam's responsibilities

FIGURE 7-4. "Sam's Responsibilities." Oliphant in *Denver Post*, 1967, from Ferrell (1969), p. 892.

Responding to the philosophy of containment, President Harry Truman established the Truman Doctrine in 1947. The Truman Doctrine provided that U.S. military and economic assistance would be offered to European countries threatened by Communist takeover. Soon afterward, aid was provided to fight Communist insurgency in Greece and Turkey. In Germany, the United States supported an airlift to counteract an Eastern blockade of West Berlin. The philosophy of the Truman Doctrine was reinforced by the Marshall Plan and the establishment of the North Atlantic Treaty Organization, which coordinated military activities between the United States and Western Europe.

By no means was the increasing hostility and competition between the United States and the Soviet Union confined to Europe. In Asia, Americans were concerned about the Communist takeover of China and North Korea. In 1950, North Korean forces invaded South Korea. Led by the United States, the United Nations dispatched thousands of troops to Korea. The Korean War lasted three years and resulted in the deaths of 53,000 U.S. soldiers.

By the middle of the 1950s, the Cold War was in full swing. U.S. troops were stationed at numerous bases along the perimeter of the Sino-Soviet sphere of influence in a geographic counterpoint to the Eurasian Heartland defined by Mackinder, who has been described as the "intellectual father of U.S. containment policy" (Gray, 1988, p. 5). The containment policy led to the large-scale foreign deployment of U.S. forces to counter Communist domination of the Heartland and surrounding areas; this deployment of troops would be maintained for several decades into the future (Figure 7-5). About half a million U.S. servicemen and women, with about 250,000 accompanying dependents, were stationed continuously at overseas bases until the end of the Cold War. Even as late as the early 1990s, there were still over 200,000 U.S. military personnel in Europe, especially in Germany and England, and over 100,000 in Asia, especially in Japan and South Korea.

The United States and the Soviet Union also became locked in an escalating arms race. In 1957, the Soviet Union announced the launching of its first orbiting satellite, Sputnik. The launch of Sputnik sparked Western fears that the Soviet Union was prepared to outdistance the United States in technological development. "Gaps" in U.S. military technology compared to the purported capability of the Soviet Union were reported in the press, and the so-called missile gap became an important issue in U.S. election campaigns during the late 1950s and early 1960s. The launch of Sputnik not only raised fears that Soviet technology was outstripping U.S. performance, but in the minds of many Americans it represented a direct challenge to U.S. domination of the air, which, as we have seen, represented a fundamental component of the nation's geopolitical worldview.

In the early 1960s, a series of confrontations brought the United States to the brink of armed conflict with the Soviet Union. In 1961, Soviet Premier Nikita Khrushchev demanded that Western troops be withdrawn from West Berlin. In August of that year, the East German government constructed a

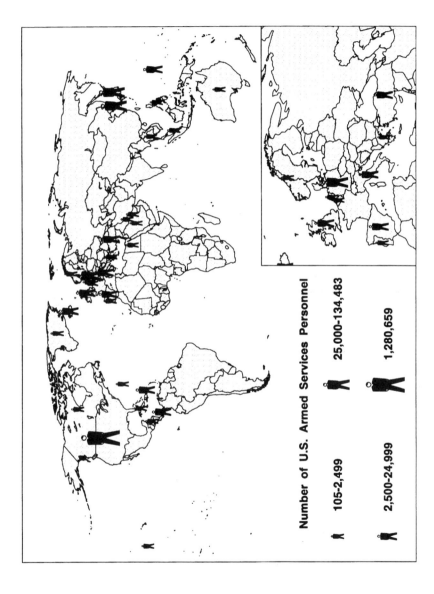

FIGURE 7-5. Worldwide Deployment of Active Duty U.S. Military Personnel, 1992. Data from Famighetti (1993), p. 705.

Number of U.S. Armed Services Personnel

105-2,499

2,500-24,999

25,000-134,483

1,280,659

wall across Berlin to prevent East German citizens from fleeing to the western sector. For a while, U.S. and Soviet tanks faced each other across the wall. The tension was broken only when the West agreed to let its personnel be inspected before they entered Berlin. The Berlin Wall remained in place until 1989 as a symbol of the Cold War.

A year later, another crisis developed over Cuba. During the summer of 1962, the Soviet Union deployed missiles in Cuba. On October 22, President John F. Kennedy gave a televised speech in which he announced that the United States would establish a naval blockade of Cuba. Long-range strategic bombers were placed on continuous airborne alert so that they could not be destroyed at airfields on the ground, and ICBMs were fueled and readied for launching. The crisis receded when Kennedy told Khrushchev that the United States would not invade Cuba if the missiles were withdrawn, and the Soviet Union agreed.

The sobering implications of hair-trigger strategic readiness prompted military policy reassessments on both sides, with the result that the years following 1962 were characterized by a significant lessening of tension between the United States and the Soviet Union. For example, some forward-based U.S. missiles, which had greatly worried Khrushchev because of their close proximity to key Soviet naval bases along the Black Sea, were quietly withdrawn from Turkey. In 1963, the two countries signed a partial test ban treaty that outlawed atmospheric testing of nuclear weapons. Additional treaties were signed in 1966 and 1968. These banned the introduction of nuclear weapons into outer space and limited the spread of nuclear technology to non-nuclear nations.

During the 1950s, President Dwight D. Eisenhower began to commit military advisers to aid the government of South Vietnam in resisting Communist North Vietnam. Eisenhower's policy of backing the anti-Communist South Vietnamese government was supported by his Democratic successors, John F. Kennedy and Lyndon B. Johnson. By the late 1960s, over half a million U.S. troops were stationed in Vietnam.

As U.S. involvement in Vietnam increased, the U.S. role in the Vietnam conflict came under increasing criticism by prominent political leaders as well as by the public. By the end of the decade, policy toward Vietnam was questioned with increasing stridency in many parts of the United States. Public opinion polls showed that fewer and fewer Americans supported continued U.S. activity in Vietnam.

As opposition to U.S. Vietnam policy mounted, the fourth extrovert cycle, which had lasted since the end of World War II, came to an end. The 1970s and 1980s were decades of introversion in foreign policy. Leaders of both parties took pains to distinguish foreign policy initiatives from the Vietnam quagmire of the 1960s. Yet the United States continued to supply large quantities of armaments throughout the world (Figure 7-6). Many were shipped to Western European allies, but large numbers of arms were also sent to Latin America, Asia, Africa, and, especially, the Middle East. However,

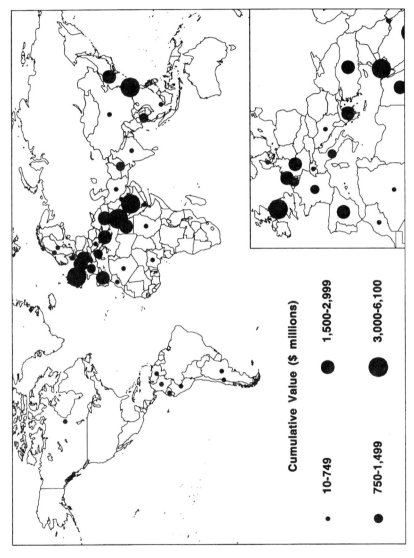

Cumulative Value ($ millions)

- ·   10-749
- ●   1,500-2,999
- ●   750-1,499
- ⬤   3,000-6,100

FIGURE 7-6. Value of U.S. Arms Sales and Transfers to Foreign Nations, 1985–1989. Data from U.S. Bureau of the Census, *Statistical Abstract of the United States, 1993*, p. 353.

most of U.S. foreign policy encounters during the 1970s and 1980s, including crises in Lebanon, Panama, and Grenada, involved only short-term involvement with no large-scale commitment of resources.

Has this fourth introvert cycle ended? Nearly a quarter of a century has passed since it began, and if history repeats itself we should be near its end. During the fall and winter of 1990–91, U.S. involvement in Kuwait suggested the likelihood that a new extrovert cycle was underway. Yet, as we have seen, Republican George Bush was soundly defeated in his reelection bid less than two years later, despite his foreign policy successes, in an election decided largely on domestic policy grounds. Subsequent debates concerning the North American Free Trade Agreement (NAFTA) and other important foreign policy issues underscore the deep-seated ambivalence concerning foreign involvement characteristic of the contemporary United States.

The Geography of Foreign Policy before the Cold War

Conflict between isolationism and internationalism has long been characterized by geographic as well as temporal dimensions. Domestic sectionalism has been characteristic of foreign policy debate throughout the history of the United States (Bensel, 1984; Trubowitz, 1992).

In earlier chapters, we noted the role of sectionalism in disputes over such issues as the Louisiana Purchase, the War of 1812, and the Mexican War. The Louisiana Purchase was supported in the South and the West and opposed in the Northeast. The Mexican War was, likewise, more popular in the South than in the North. In each case, sectional support or opposition to these foreign policy initiatives depended on a variety of cultural and economic factors.

The Cultural and Economic Basis of Foreign Policy Sectionalism

Conflict within the domestic political arena concerning the U.S. role in the world economy had both economic and cultural overtones. Regional differences in attitude toward foreign policy are related to the very forces that helped to create regional political cultures. The South, for example, had depended since colonial days on export markets overseas to sell its cotton and other agricultural products. Indeed, it has been argued that the international cotton trade linked the United States most directly with the world economy during the nineteenth century (Agnew, 1993a). Regional specialization created three separate regional economies within the economy as a whole, mirroring the sectional divisions characteristic of U.S. politics in general. "The cotton-exporting South imported increasing amounts of food from the West, and with the income received the West bought manufactured goods from the Northeast" (Agnew, 1993a, p. 212).

By 1900, transition from an agricultural to an industrial economy was

well underway. As the twentieth century dawned, the annual value of manufacturing in the United States was twice that of agriculture (Agnew, 1993a, p.
213). Increased industrialization generated increased overseas demand for
U.S. manufactured goods, and Northeastern industrial interests began to pay
more and more attention to foreign developments in order to promote U.S.
business interests abroad. While the Northeast and the South became increasingly concerned with the establishment and maintenance of overseas economic connections, most Middle Western agricultural products were consumed
within the United States. Hence, many Middle Westerners were skeptical
about foreign involvement, and many tended to adopt an isolationist position, whereas contemporaries in the East and the South were more prone to
international activism.

By the close of the twentieth century, however, a large proportion of U.S.
production was destined for export, including agricultural, forest, mineral,
and manufactured products. Domestically, production for export has become
especially important to the economies of many states along the Atlantic or Pacific Coasts of the United States, although export production is also important to several states along the shores of the Great Lakes as well (Figure 7-7).
Even the traditional isolationism of interior rural communities has begun to
erode, to the extent that the governors of several agricultural states, including
those of Iowa and Nebraska, have traveled internationally as commercial ambassadors to promote their states' agricultural products in Europe and Asia.

Immigration and ethnicity have also played a major role in the distribution of foreign policy attitudes. Throughout U.S. history, many immigrant
Americans and their descendants have continued to pay close attention to developments in their countries of origin, where, indeed, many maintained relationships with relatives and friends. Thus, for example, the isolationism of the
upper Middle West was reinforced by the presence of large numbers of German-Americans who resented U.S. alliance with Great Britain and France
against Germany before and during the World Wars. Anti-British sentiment
was also strong among Irish-Americans, who were concentrated in many
large Eastern cities. Boston, with a very large Irish-American population, was
a center of isolationist sentiment before both World Wars.

Sectional Conflict over Foreign Policy in the Early Twentieth Century

By the early twentieth century, ongoing debate over the merits of isolationism
and intervention had come to pit the East and South against the interior sections of the country. Residents of the interior regions were most critical of the
internationalist foreign policies of Theodore Roosevelt and Woodrow Wilson.

After the war ended, Wilson's advocacy of the League of Nations was
most strongly supported in the South and the East. In 1920, the *Literary Digest* commissioned a poll of newspaper editors throughout the United States.
Newspaper editors in the South were most likely to support U.S. membership

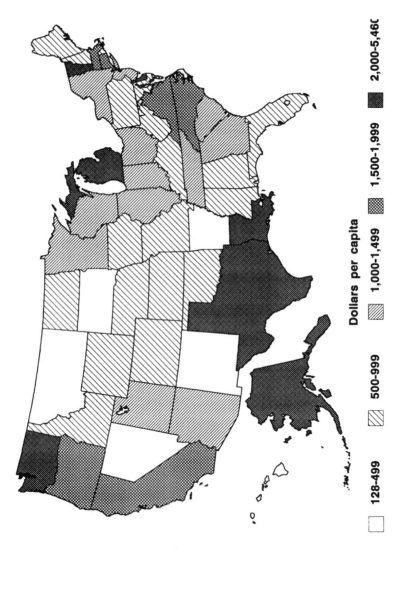

FIGURE 7-7. Value of U.S. Foreign Exports by State of Origin, 1992. Data from U.S. Bureau of the Census, *Statistical Abstract of the United States*, 1993, p. 808.

Dollars per capita

128-499   500-999   1,000-1,499   1,500-1,999   2,000-5,46(

in the league, whereas those in New England, the Plains states, and the Rocky Mountain states were most likely to oppose the idea (Figure 7-8).

Throughout the 1920s and 1930s, isolationism remained predominant in the interior, whereas interventionist sentiment was concentrated in the South and the Northeast. "The Midwest and West clashed with states from the Atlantic seaboard, the Gulf Coast and the Pacific Rim over the White House's efforts to centralize foreign policy-making power and to stimulate and regulate American involvement in the world economy" (Trubowitz, 1992, p. 175).

Why were the South and the East generally in favor of intervention, whereas the Middle West was isolationist? To answer these questions, we need to consider the relationships between foreign policy issues and the cultures and economic bases of these sections. The Northeast was geographically closest to Europe, and the Northeastern commercial and industrial economy were becoming more and more closely linked with the European-centered global economy. The South, meanwhile, continued to depend on export markets for its products. Moreover, the nation's military establishment was dominated by Southerners—a trend that would intensify after World War II.

The isolationism of the Middle West was the result of several important processes: Many Middle Western isolationists were themselves of German ancestry or represented states or districts containing large German-American populations. During and shortly after World War I, German-Americans were victims of substantial ethnic discrimination. Many anglicized their names, while other words of German origin were also changed. Sauerkraut, for example, became known as "liberty cabbage." In fact, more than half of the states passed laws banning publishing or teaching in German until the Supreme Court declared these laws unconstitutional in 1921.

Many German-Americans opposed anti-German efforts in U.S. policy. Yet ethnicity was by no means the only basis of Middle Western isolationism during the years before World War II. Middle Western isolationism has also been associated with the legacy of populism. As we have seen, Middle Western Populists argued against the concentration of wealth in the hands of Northeastern industrial interests. "Thousands of westerners came to believe that intervention was only another tool of the trusts in their battle against the people" (Billington, 1944, p. 51).

Many Middle Western isolationists were farmers and small business owners who felt that interventionism would continue the erosion of the Jeffersonian agrarian ethic. Moreover, isolationists representing farming areas "realized that war would bring few military contracts to their home districts, while draining both manpower and political strength to the city" (Doenecke, 1979, p. 22). In fact, few industrial war facilities projects constructed during World War II were sited in the Great Plains or in nonindustrialized subsections of the Middle West (see Figure 4-2). For many, "fiscal solvency, clean and limited government, rural and small-town values, economic individualism, a self-determined foreign policy—all appeared interconnected and all appeared beyond recall" (Doenecke, 1979, p. 24).

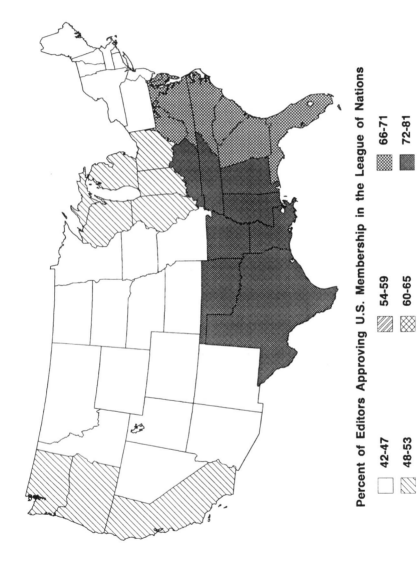

Percent of Editors Approving U.S. Membership in the League of Nations

	42-47		54-59		66-71
	48-53		60-65		72-81

FIGURE 7-8. *Literary Digest* Poll of Newspaper Editors on Proposed U.S. Joining of League of Nations, 1919. Data from Chester (1975), p. 180.

The Preparedness Movement and World War II

While the United States grappled with the longest and most severe economic depression in its history during the 1930s, the threat of warfare deepened across the Atlantic. Dictators such as Hitler in Germany, Mussolini in Italy, and Franco in Spain seized power, allying against the democracies of Western Europe. Meanwhile, a militaristic Japanese government had seized Korea and China and was expanding into southeastern Asia.

After Hitler took power in 1933, Germany entered a sustained period of aggression and belligerence in its foreign policy. The Nazi government rearmed the Rhineland region, annexed Austria, and took over the Sudetenland. In 1939, Germany invaded Poland. Great Britain and France declared war on Germany, and World War II began.

After the war in Europe began, Americans remained deeply divided over the appropriate response of the United States. Interventionists advocated active support of Great Britain, France, and their allies, while isolationists preferred that the United States remain neutral. It was the fate of the Seventy-Sixth Congress, which historians have often called the "Neutrality Congress," to determine U.S. foreign policy during this critical period (Porter, 1979). The Neutrality Congress debated and enacted several critical measures that would affect U.S. policy during the war years and beyond.

Both houses of Congress were relatively evenly divided between interventionists and isolationists. Most of the internationalists came from the Northeast or the South, whereas the isolationists tended to represent the western half of the country. Although the debate between interventionists and isolationists cut across party lines, a majority of interventionists were Democrats; isolationists were more likely to be Republicans. Many interventionist Democrats were Roman Catholics—a fact contrary to the stereotype of isolationism among Catholics of Irish or German extraction (Porter, 1979, p. 17).

During the 1930s, several Congresses had passed laws mandating U.S. neutrality. The Johnson Act of 1934, for example, prohibited the United States government from loaning money to any foreign country that had defaulted on its debts. The Neutrality Act of 1935 prohibited loans to any country on either side of a war, and the renewed Neutrality Act of 1937 prohibited U.S. ships from carrying arms to belligerent powers. Most Americans during this period approved the principles of neutrality embodied in these laws (Barone, 1990, p. 127).

As the Seventy-Sixth Congress convened, President Roosevelt supported U.S. aid to Great Britain and France. Yet Roosevelt moved cautiously in light of public and congressional opposition to abandoning the principle of neutrality. After World War II actually began, interventionists in both houses of Congress began to press for legislation to give the president more authority to deal with the worsening European crisis. Roosevelt called Congress, which had already adjourned, into special session on September 21 and urged its members to repeal the Neutrality Act. Senator Key Pittman, a Nevada Democrat, drafted a bill permitting the sale of arms to belligerents.

The Pittman bill passed both houses despite a lengthy filibuster by Senate isolationists. Members from the Plains states, the Great Lakes region, and the West Coast tended to oppose the bill, which was supported by large margins in the East and South. The pattern of congressional support for the Pittman plan reflected broader divisions of support and opposition to foreign policy activism during this time. For example, a *Fortune* poll of Americans taken in early 1939 indicated that 39.6 percent of all Americans believed that the United States should sell no arms to foreign countries. In the northern Plains states, 53.7 percent took this position, but only 29.7 percent of Southwesterners did so. Similar geographic divisions characterized other important foreign policy issues during this period, including the establishment of the first peacetime military draft in U.S. history and the development of the Lend-Lease program (Porter, 1979).

Foreign Policy Debates during the Cold War

The sectional debate between isolationists and interventionists came to a sudden end, of course, with the bombing of Pearl Harbor. As we have seen, the United States refused to reject internationalism after World War II as it had done after World War I. The Truman Doctrine, the Marshall Plan, and the North Atlantic Treaty Organization formed the basis for an internationalist foreign policy that would remain in effect for more than two decades. Yet the strength of commitment to this policy varied sectionally. During this period, foreign policy debates within the United States centered on the issues of foreign aid and economic development assistance to both Europe and Asia and the creation and preservation of military alliances in association with the containment philosophy. Such policies were more strongly supported in the traditionally internationalist East and South than in the traditionally isolationist Middle West.

Whether by coincidence or by design, the domestic geographic pattern of major defense installations tends to mirror the geographic pattern of foreign policy opinion. With some exceptions, most military bases and other major defense installations are concentrated along the southeastern and southwestern coasts of the United States (Figure 7-9). No doubt, this siting is partly pragmatic or policy based, since the mild climates of these areas facilitate year-round training exercises, and the United States happily no longer faces military threats along its borders with Canada or Mexico. There are some notable exceptions, however, including several long-range strategic bomber and land-based ICBM bases, which are concentrated in the northern Great Plains, near the geographic center of North America.

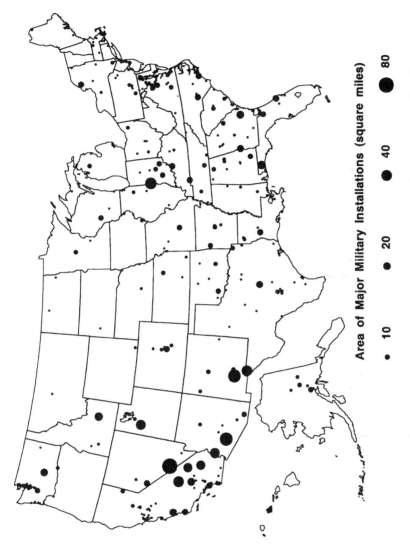

Area of Major Military Installations (square miles)

● 10   ● 20   ● 40   ● 80

FIGURE 7-9. Location and Land-Area of Major Defense Installations. Data from U.S. Department of Defense (1988); Bureau of Transportation Statistics, U.S. Department of Transportation (1955).

Cold War Internationalism

Trubowitz (1992, p. 177) has shown that support for what he terms "Cold War internationalism"—that is, support for bills "designed to promote an open, interdependent world economy and isolate or 'contain' the Soviet bloc"—was greatest in the South and the Northeast during the early part of the Cold War. Opposition to Cold War internationalism, on the other hand, was most pronounced in those areas that had been isolationist prior to Pearl Harbor (Huntington, 1961; Doenecke, 1979). The Republican Party divided over this debate, with many conservative Middle Western Republicans opposed to the internationalism espoused by their Eastern counterparts during the Truman and Eisenhower administrations.

The geography of foreign policy began to change during the late 1960s. During that decade, the United States became more and more heavily involved in an undeclared war in Vietnam. Americans became more and more deeply divided over the desirability of continued involvement in Vietnam. The traditional internationalist alliance between the Northeast and the South collapsed. "The coastal-interior axis of conflict underlying debates over American foreign policy during the height of the Cold War in the late 1940s and early 1950s [had become] a thing of the past" (Trubowitz, 1992, p. 183). By the 1970s, a new cleavage separating the Sunbelt from the older, manufacturing-oriented North had emerged to replace the previous pattern of conflict between coastal and interior regions. This new pattern remained intact until the Cold War ended.

The Sunbelt and the Gunbelt

Why did the geography of foreign policy support change during the Vietnam period? By the 1960s, the Sunbelt had emerged as the most rapidly growing region of the United States. As we have seen, industrial growth outside the Northeastern industrial core outpaced that within the core during the period of post–World War II economic expansion. This industrial growth in the Sunbelt was reinforced by expansion in the military and defense-related sectors associated with the Cold War itself (Bluestone and Harrison, 1982; Markusen et al., 1991). Meanwhile, it had become increasingly apparent to many in the now-declining Rustbelt that the nation's traditional manufacturing core had lost its competitive position compared to the Sunbelt.

At the same time, the declining competitiveness of the Rustbelt also made this region increasingly vulnerable to foreign competition. Large numbers of jobs in automobile manufacturing, steel, electronics, and other heavy industries moved to the Sunbelt and overseas (see Chapter 8). In response, calls for increased protectionism became stronger and stronger in the Rustbelt, while the booming Sunbelt focused on free trade and a strong national defense, whose benefits were concentrated in the Sunbelt.

By no means, however, can we regard the locational consequences of industrial restructuring as independent of the Cold War itself. The Sunbelt, along with the East and West Coasts, were the primary economic beneficiaries of the Cold War. A preponderance of military bases were located in the Sunbelt, as were many corporations that specialized in the production of military hardware and other items purchased by the U.S. government and those of her allies during the Cold War.

The region consisting of communities whose economies benefited substantially from Cold War spending has been called the "Gunbelt" (Markusen et al., 1991). Community leaders often took great pains to attract and maintain defense-related industry. Several such urban areas, including Seattle, Colorado Springs, and the Los Angeles area, deliberately and systematically cultivated economic bases oriented to the U.S. military–industrial complex during the Cold War (Markusen et al., 1991).

Because the profit base for military-related firms relies on government contracts, these companies rely on alliances with community leaders and key figures in Congress and the Pentagon to ensure a steady flow of business. Many produce weapons systems or other products that have short product cycles, in some cases becoming outmoded before finally being produced and sold to the government (Markusen, 1986). As a result, many military–industrial firms are inefficient, dependent on governmental funding, and reliant on research and development funds provided by the Department of Defense and other federal agencies.

The Sunbelt proved to be the primary beneficiary of federal Cold War–related spending for several reasons. For one thing, military contractors seeking to reduce production costs found the same advantages in the South as had their civilian counterparts. Labor costs and wages were low, and the Southern labor force was much less unionized than that in the North. Moreover, many of the products manufactured by military contractors were consumed at military bases, which themselves tended to be located south of the Mason–Dixon Line. The concentration of military bases in the southern United States has occurred in part because of the efforts of powerful Southern congressional committee chairs, who used their political power to direct vast sums of federal dollars to their home districts. The political clout of powerful members of Congress helps to explain the concentration of military bases in such communities as Charleston, South Carolina, and Pensacola, Florida. Moreover, federal defense expenditures were geographically stable during the Cold War. Communities that received the largest sums of federal defense dollars early in the Cold War generally continued to do so throughout the period (Crump and Archer, 1993).

The Geography of Congressional Foreign Policy Support

The rise of the Gunbelt coincided with changes in the geography of congressional foreign policy votes during the 1970s and 1980s. This was particularly

evident during the administration of Ronald Reagan. During the Ninety-
Eighth Congress (1983–84), for example, support for Reagan's generally
hawkish approaches to foreign and military policy was greatest in the South
and West, which tended to benefit most directly from increased military
spending. On the other hand, support was considerably less in the Northeast,
the upper Middle West, and the Pacific Northwest (Trubowitz and Roberts,
1992).

Of course, this transition is not independent of broader changes in partisan support within the national electorate that occurred in conjunction with
the shift to the Conservative Normal Vote during the 1970s and 1980s (see
Chapter 9). Ronald Reagan's administration was most popular in rapidly
growing regions of the United States, in particular the Sunbelt and the West.
His popularity was weakest in the Northeast and upper Middle West, and in
particular among residents of areas dependent on declining primary- and sec-
ondary-sector economic activities (Archer et al., 1985). In part because of increased dispossession in the Rustbelt and economic growth in the Sunbelt, national politics since the mid-1970s have been considerably influenced by
conflict between Republican strength in the Sunbelt and Democratic strength
in the Rustbelt (Shelley and Archer, 1994).

Both location and partisanship affected support and opposition to the
political agenda of the Reagan and Bush agendas of the 1980s. During this
period, Republicans were far more likely than Democrats to support Reagan
on foreign policy, although a regional cleavage is also evident in analyzing
foreign policy votes during the Reagan administration. This is illustrated by
the vote on aid to the Nicaraguan Contras, (guerrillas fighting against the
Communist-dominated Sandinista government of Nicaragua). A Reagan-sup-
ported proposal to expand aid to the Contras was voted down by the House
of Representatives in 1986. A large majority of House members voted along
party lines. Nevertheless, eleven Republican representatives voted against
Contra aid, while thirty-five Democrats supported it. All eleven anti-Contra
Republicans came from the Rustbelt, while thirty-two of the thirty-five pro-
Contra Democrats represented the Sunbelt. Throughout the Reagan and Bush
administrations, a combination of partisanship and location determined the
geography of support and opposition to the administrations' foreign and domestic policy agendas.

NAFTA, Free Trade, and Foreign Policy

All of these considerations came under public scrutiny during the fall of 1993,
when Congress and the public intensely debated the value of the NAFTA bill.
After weeks of intense controversy, the NAFTA bill was passed by the House
of Representatives by a margin of 234 to 200. The NAFTA debate had several significant geographic overtones.

Protectionism and Free Trade in U.S. History

Analogous to the ongoing debate between isolationism and interventionism is a long-standing conflict between supporters and opponents of free trade between the United States and other countries. At many junctures in U.S. history the over tariffs (taxes levied on the import of goods from other countries) has played a critical role in domestic policies. During the late nineteenth century, Northeastern industrial interests usually advocated high tariffs in order to protect nascent U.S. industry from foreign competition. On the other hand, Southerners, who were dependent on the sale of cotton and other agricultural products overseas, preferred lower tariffs and supported free trade. The tariff debate also influenced the issue positions of the two major political parties. Typically, the Republicans advocated protectionism, while Democrats, especially in the South and West, opposed it (Kenkel, 1983).

The traditional geography of protectionism is evident from the distribution of votes in the House of Representatives on various protective tariffs between the 1920s and the 1950s (Smith and Hart, 1955). High protective tariffs were strongly supported in the Northeast, with only a few big-city Democrats bucking the general trend. A large majority of Western representatives also voted for high tariffs. Most Southerners, in contrast, voted against high tariffs. For the most part, however, large majorities within Congress voted on tariff bills along party lines. For example, only 21 of 160 House Democrats voted for the highly protectionist Smoot-Hawley Tariff of 1929, while only 12 of 270 Republicans opposed it.

Many blamed high tariffs for the Great Depression, and as a result public support for protective tariffs waned in association with the increasing popularity of the Democrats during the 1930s and 1940s. Yet the general regional pattern of support and opposition to protective tariffs continued throughout the 1930s, 1940s, and early 1950s (Smith and Hart, 1955). Typically, fewer than 10 percent of House members crossed party lines on tariff votes.

Since the 1960s, the historical positions of the two major parties on free trade have for the most part reversed themselves. Democrats have increasingly embraced protectionism, and Republicans are increasingly associated with support for free trade. The reversal of the historical positions of the two parties may be associated with voter and politician perceptions of the achievement and subsequent decline of U.S. hegemony in the world economy since World War II (Wade and Gates, 1990). The once extremely protectionist position of the Republicans had been discredited by the depression. Meanwhile, many Eastern Republicans came to support a bipartisan, internationalist approach to foreign policy after World War II. Support for free trade became increasingly associated with the "Cold War internationalism" described by Trubowitz (1992). A broad, bipartisan consensus in favor of free trade characterized the period of rapid economic growth in the 1950s and 1960s. With the recession and restructuring of the 1970s, however, came the reversal of the traditional party positions on free trade.

The Gephardt Amendment

During the boom years of the 1950s and 1960s, trade-related issues received little attention from either Congress or the public. After the economy began to experience recession in the 1970s, however, trade policy again became controversial.

In 1987, the House narrowly passed the Gephardt Amendment to the Omnibus Trade Act of 1988. The Gephardt Amendment would have required countries with large trade surplus to cut surpluses voluntarily or be assigned quotas or tariffs to rectify trade imbalances (Wade and Gates, 1990). The House vote on the Gephardt Amendment was dominated by partisan considerations. Only 18 of 159 Republicans supported it, and all but two of these Republicans represented districts in the Northeast. On the other hand, only 55 of 255 Democrats, 45 of whom came from the South or the West, voted against the Gephardt Amendment.

The Gephardt Amendment vote illustrates the changes in the geography of protectionism that occurred over the course of the Cold War. Protectionist sentiment had become strongest among Northern Democrats, while support for free trade was greatest in the South and West and among Republicans. The West had emerged as the most ardently free trade region, whereas the historical antagonism between the North and the South over trade and tariff policy had become muted.

The Gephardt Amendment vote also illustrated the increased convergence of foreign policy and tariff voting. To an increasing extent, patterns of support on both issues had coalesced around conflict between the booming Sunbelt and the stagnating Rustbelt.

The NAFTA Debate

This coalescence was even more evident in the distribution of support for the NAFTA bill of 1993 (Figure 7-10). The possibility of a free trade agreement among the United States, Canada, and Mexico had been raised several years before the actual NAFTA bill was drafted. During the 1980s, NAFTA had been proposed by Republican President Ronald Reagan. Formal agreement among the three countries to implement a free trade agreement was initiated by Reagan's successor, George Bush, shortly before Bush left office in January 1993.

Although NAFTA was originally a Republican initiative, President Bill Clinton, a Democrat, emerged as a strong supporter of the bill. Many congressional Democrats argued against NAFTA, while some Republican leaders

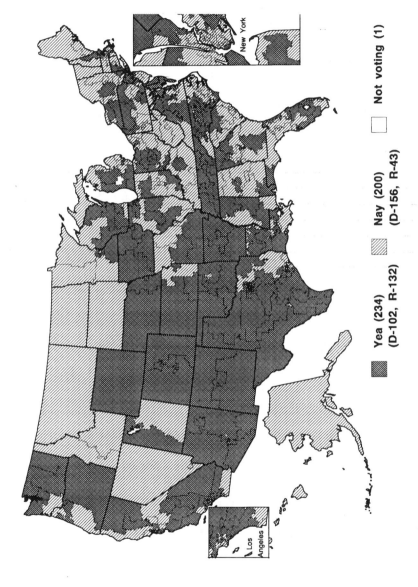

FIGURE 7-10. North American Free Trade Agreement (NAFTA) Implementation Vote (HR 3450) in U.S. House of Representatives, November 17, 1993. Data from *Congressional Quarterly Weekly Report* (1993), pp. 3494–95.

Legend:
- Yea (234) (D-102, R-132)
- Nay (200) (D-156, R-43)
- Not voting (1)

emerged as key supporters. For the most part, NAFTA was strongly opposed by Democrats from the Northeast and Midwest but supported by Southwestern and Western Democrats. Republicans throughout the country were more prone to support NAFTA, although Republican support for the initiative was especially strong in the West and Middle West.

Overall, support for NAFTA was considerable among members of both parties from the South. Fifty-four of eighty-six southern Democrats supported NAFTA, as did thirty-six of the region's fifty-four Republicans. Support was weakest in the Deep South, in part because a large majority of African-American Democrats from this region and elsewhere voted against it. Democrats in the Southwest (Louisiana, Texas, Arkansas, and Oklahoma) supported NAFTA by a 23 to 8 margin, and only one of the Southwest's sixteen Republicans voted against the bill. States such as Kentucky, Tennessee, North Carolina, and Virginia were intermediate between these extremes.

In contrast, representatives from outside the South were sharply divided along partisan lines. In the Northeast, large majorities of Democratic members of the House voted no on NAFTA. All eleven of Pennsylvania's Democrats and all but two of the seventeen-member Democratic delegation from New York voted against the bill. Likewise, only nine of fifty-six Democrats from the eight Great Lakes and Middle West states supported the bill. In the Northeast region as a whole, Democratic opponents of NAFTA outnumbered supporters by a margin of 85 to 17.

While Northeastern Democrats strongly opposed NAFTA, Northeastern Republicans gave the bill strong support. Republican support for NAFTA was especially strong in the Midwest, where thirty-four of thirty-nine Republican representatives voted for the bill. NAFTA was as popular among Republicans in the Northeast and Middle West as it was unpopular among Democrats in the Rustbelt. All five Michigan Republicans supported the measure, while all ten of the state's Democrats opposed it. Nearly two-thirds of the Republicans from New England and the Middle Atlantic states also supported the bill.

Among Western Democrats, NAFTA was supported by a narrow majority. Fourteen of thirty California Democrats voted for NAFTA, although seven of Washington's eight Democrats, perhaps influenced by the Pacific Northwest's increasing involvement with the Pacific Rim, also did so. Meanwhile, a large majority of Republicans from all three subregions within the West voted for the NAFTA bill. Eighteen of California's twenty-three Republicans supported NAFTA, as did all Republicans from Washington, Oregon, Arizona, and New Mexico. Thus, the West can be regarded as intermediate between the Northeast, where representatives were divided primarily on a partisan basis, and the South, whose representatives were generally divided locationally.

Certainly, the geographic outcome of the NAFTA debate is consistent with the commonly held belief that a post–Cold War world order is likely to integrate geopolitics with domestic politics and economics more directly than in the past. How might these changes be symbolic of the future politics of for-

eign policy within the United States? We turn to this question in the final section of this chapter.

The Changing Geography of the U.S. Role in the Contemporary World

The transition to the post–Cold War world order is certain to have significant
disruptive consequences for the United States itself. As we have seen, many
U.S. communities became active in promoting the expansion of Cold War–related industry during the Cold War itself. Malecki (1991) has pointed out that
well over half of the government's research and development funds during
1985, when the Cold War was in full swing, was allocated to military purposes. The concentration of such funds on defense-related industries made these
far more lucrative targets for local officials than nonmilitary industries.

As Markusen and Yudken (1992, p. 1) put it, "Ever since the Depression,
preparing for warfare has been a permanent and potent American preoccupa-
tion. Consuming considerable human, financial and public-sector resources, a
military-oriented economy is and has been the industrial policy of the United
States." With the end of the Cold War, however, many of these military expenditures will no longer be justified by government officials. In addition, increased political pressure to convert military spending to spending on infrastructure, public works, and social services will probably result in a
significant decline in military budgets during the next several years.

During the Cold War, high levels of government expenditure on research
and development for military purposes were justified on the grounds that the
research would spin off products of value to civilians. By the 1980s, however,
it had become clear that these linkages between military and civilian production were tenuous (Malecki, 1991). Little of the expensive and sophisticated
military hardware designed and built during the Cold War is of much use to
civilians. As a result, government spending on military production contributes
less to a domestic economy than does nonmilitary spending. This suggests
that government expenditures on civilian items such as social services, infrastructure, and economic development will have greater long-term impacts on
the domestic economy than will military expenditures—a phenomenon
known as the "peace dividend."

Reduced military spending may benefit the economy in the long run.
Crump and Archer (1993) have pointed out that post–Cold War federal expenditures are likely to be distributed more evenly than in the past, since domestic outlays tend to be allocated on a more geographically uniform basis
than defense outlays. Communities once heavily dependent on the
military–industrial complex, including many within the southern and western
Gunbelt, however, are likely to suffer adverse effects from a downsized military.

The extent of military downsizing can be partly gauged in terms of numbers of personnel. In 1988, on the eve of the disintegration of the Soviet empire, U.S. armed forces totaled 2.2 million active duty military personnel worldwide, with 1.7 million U.S. servicemen and women stationed either within the United States or on board ships sailing from U.S. naval ports (Hoffman, 1989, p. 754). Five years later, in 1993, U.S. active duty military personnel stood at 1.7 million worldwide, with 1.4 million domestically based (Famighetti, 1994, p. 160). The greatest reductions took place in Europe, where U.S. forces declined from 343,000 to 166,000, a 50 percent reduction in the first years after the end of the Cold War. In the absence of major international conflicts, further planned reductions may diminish the total number of U.S. active duty military personnel to barely more than one million worldwide, though this issue remains contentious, in part for domestic economic and political reasons.

While the need for military conversion and industrial restructuring received some attention during the first post–Cold War presidential election campaign, in 1992, it is apparent that politicians have tried to avoid public controversy as much as possible. One very important and disquietingly long-range set of issues involve the risks and disposition of nuclear weapons materials and the necessary cleanup of nuclear weapons production and storage facilities (Box 7-2). Additional political complexities surround the problem of decommissioning military bases rendered redundant by military downsizing. Community leaders are rarely willing to acquiesce to government-mandated cuts in local military facilities without attempting to fight back. Military personnel and their adult dependents, townsfolk who offer shopping opportunities near military bases, the employees of defense contractors, and many other concerned citizens are likely to be directly affected and to vote accordingly in congressional and presidential elections.

The considerable potential for political deadlock in the face of opposing national and local interests led to the adoption of the Defense Base Closure and Realignment Act of 1990. The elaborate and complex base-closing procedure established by the act can be regarded either as a meritorious effort to elevate nationwide interests above parochial interests or as an odious evasion of the obligations of senators and representatives to their own constituents. Upon reflection, the political philosophy underlying the act seems more akin to the discredited notion of virtual representation than to the ideal of particular territorial representation fought for by patriots in the American Revolution (see Chapter 2).

According to the act, the chief responsibility for choosing specific military facilities to be closed is delegated to the appointed members of a blue-ribbon Defense Base Closure and Realignment Commission. Members of the commission are collectively charged with preparing and presenting a list of bases slated for closure to the secretary of defense, who in turn is expected to transmit the list to the president. The president is permitted only to either return the list to the commission for reconsideration or to submit the entire list

Box 7-2. *The Nuclear Legacy*

The first atomic bomb was exploded in a secret test near Alamogordo, New Mexico, on Monday, July 16, 1945. Three weeks later, at 9:15 A.M. on Monday, August 6, 1945, the first atomic weapon to be used in war was dropped on the Japanese city of Hiroshima from the U.S. B-29 *Enola Gay*. The Hiroshima nuclear fission weapon detonated with an explosive force equivalent to more than 20,000 tons of conventional explosives, and it caused more than 60,000 deaths. Reconnaissance photographs reportedly showed that the destruction extended over more than four square miles, spanning 60 percent of the area of a city with a prewar population of 340,000 persons (Daniel, 1987, p. 597). The third atomic bomb destroyed the Japanese city of Nagasaki on August 9, 1945. Japan surrendered unconditionally one day later, on August 10, 1945, to end hostilities in World War II.

The atomic devices exploded at Alamogordo, Hiroshima, and Nagasaki were developed under the Manhattan Project, begun in August 1942. This was a super-secret effort (which cost over two billion 1940s dollars) to design nuclear bombs and to obtain and refine sufficient weapons-grade uranium and plutonium to build the devices. The work was conducted at Oak Ridge, Tennessee, Hanford, Washington, and Los Alamos, New Mexico, where nuclear research, production, and testing facilities, as well as entire new towns to house scientists, workers, and their dependents, were built in strict secrecy (U.S. Congress, Office of Technology Assessment, 1991; U.S. Congress, Office of Technology Assessment, 1993).

The facilities at Oak Ridge, Hanford, and Los Alamos were transferred to the Atomic Energy Commission in 1946, and then to the Department of Energy (DOE) in 1977. With the onset and persistence of the Cold War during the decades following the close of World War II, these successors to the Manhattan Project oversaw the expansion of what became a sprawling nuclear weapons development and production complex that eventually included some fifteen major facilities spread over twelve states. There are also thousands of other, smaller facilities that are or were involved in nuclear weaponry as well.

U.S. nuclear weapons production facilities were used to build a cumulative total of perhaps as many as 70,000 nuclear warheads. At any one time, the U.S. arsenal contained perhaps 20,000 to 25,000 nuclear warheads, about half of which were large enough to be regarded as "strategic" warheads. Current terminology, it may be noted, classes the Hiroshima device toward the upper end of smaller "tactical" warheads. By the mid-1980s, the U.S. strategic nuclear arsenal totaled 10,398 warheads with an overall yield of 2,649 megatons (U.S. Bureau of Census, *Statistical Abstract of the United States 1986*, p. 339). Soviet strategic weaponry at the time was estimated to total 9,544 warheads with an overall yield of 5,790 megatons (U.S. Bureau of the Census, *Statistical Abstract of the United States 1986*, p. 339). These amounts correspond to over ten tons of TNT-equivalent U.S. nuclear strategic firepower for each resident of the Soviet Union, and over twenty tons of TNT-equivalent Soviet strategic firepower for each resident of the United States at the time. However, contemporary estimates of Soviet nuclear weaponry fell well short of a later report, attributed to Viktor N. Mikhailov, head of Russia's Ministry of Atomic Energy, that at the peak in the mid-1980s, the Soviet nuclear arsenal held as many as 45,000 warheads (*Lincoln Journal*, September 26, 1993, p. 2B).

Even before the collapse of the Soviet Union, it was becoming apparent that the nuclear arsenals of the two nations and their allies were far larger than any conceivable military threat warranted. A nuclear exchange of as few as 3,000 warheads could cause 70 to 130 million U.S. casualties (Van Voorst, 1990, p. 19). According to some estimates, larger "countersocietal" nuclear conflicts could destroy about 40 percent of the Soviet population and about 90 percent of the more metropolitanized U.S. population due to blast effects alone, and even more from nuclear fallout (Pry, 1990, pp. 220–21).

Treaty agreements have promised substantial reductions in nuclear weaponry by both sides (Blechman, et al., 1993). Tactical and short-range strategic nuclear weapons have been withdrawn from Europe. Long-range strategic nuclear weapons are also being reduced. According to the terms of the second Strategic Arms Reduction Treaty (START-II), signed in January 1993, each side will eliminate all multiple warhead (MIRVed) ICBM and will, moreover, be limited to between 3,000 and 3,500 nuclear warheads by the year 2004. This means that each side must destroy half or more of its strategic nuclear arsenal.

The very same facilities that originally were built to produce nuclear weapons are now being used to dismantle those weapons (Figure 7-B2-1). Since 1991, thousands of nuclear weapons, from nuclear artillery shells to missile warheads and bombs, have been shipped to the Department of Energy's Pantex plant near Amarillo, Texas. "The 3,300 people there labor to reduce the nuclear arsenal from 21,000 weapons to 3,500 by 2003" (Potok, 1994, p. 7A).

But the U.S. nuclear weapons facilities complex is not likely to go out of business even if the dismantlement process is carried out as intended under START-II and other existing treaties. For one thing, the United States has not adopted a policy of full nuclear disarmament (U.S. Congress, Office of Technology Assessment, 1993, p. 5). It has been announced that the United States "will no longer produce weapons-grade plutonium or highly enriched uranium for warheads.... [T]he United States plans to store some of the materials extracted from disassembled warheads for possible future military use" (U.S. Congress, Office of Technology Assessment, 1993, pp. 5–6). Although the "exact numbers are classified," several hundreds, perhaps several thousands, of tons of weapons-grade plutonium and uranium now exist, with half-lives of at least 24,000 years (U.S. Congress, Office of Technology Assessment, 1993, p. 10).

The costs of dismantling nuclear weapons appear to be running about one billion dollars per year (U.S. Congress, Office of Technology Assessment, 1993, p. 7). However, the costs of dismantling nuclear weapons pale by comparison with the projected costs of dealing with the long-term storage of nuclear materials and of undertaking the cleanup of nuclear weapons production facilities. By one estimate, the various sites in the Department of Energy's nuclear weapons facilities "complex holds in storage over 100 million gallons of highly radioactive waste, 66 million gallons of waste contaminated with plutonium, and even larger volumes of waste with lower levels of radioactivity. In addition, radioactive and other hazardous substances have contaminated soil and

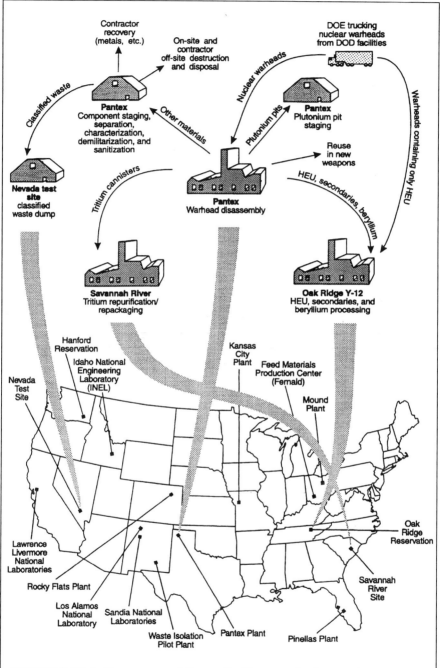

FIGURE 7-B2-1. Department of Energy Facilities Involved in Nuclear Weapons Dismantlement. Data from U.S. Congress, Office of Technology Assessment (1993), p. 34.

groundwater at DOE's installations" (U.S. Congress, Congressional Budget Office, 1994, p. ix). Annual clean-up funding is expected to rise above $7 billion per year by 2000, with total costs estimated to accumulate to "from $400 billion to $1 trillion" (U.S. Congress, Congressional Budget Office, 1994, p. ix).

To note a specific example, DOE's Hanford, Washington, plant was established in 1943 to produce weapons-grade plutonium as one of the original facilities of the Manhattan Project. The plutonium used in the "Fat Man" that was dropped on Nagasaki was produced at Hanford. The total cost of the Manhattan Project, as noted above, was about two billion current dollars. A half-century later, the projected cleanup budget for the Hanford site is $1.5 billion per year "for the foreseeable future" (U.S. Congress, Congressional Budget Office, 1994, p. 63). If the two other Manhattan Project sites at Oak Ridge and Los Alamos are included, it is found that over $11.5 billion was spent from 1990 to 1995 on environmental cleanup at these three sites alone. All told, there are over 7,000 DOE weapons facilities sites. The nuclear legacy will have a very long half-life.

to Congress as a presidentially approved measure. The act further stipulates that Congress can only approve or disapprove of the list in its entirety, without floor amendments to add or subtract bases from the list. This all-or-nothing approach was clearly designed to insulate members of Congress from their constituents in affected areas, who were likely to be angered.

Interestingly, one of thirty-five major and ninety-five minor bases slated for closure during the 1993 base-closure selection round was the Philadelphia Naval Shipyard. After failing to gain Senate approval of his resolution to reject the entire list, as required under the 1990 Base Closure Act, Senator Arlen Spector of Pennsylvania challenged the whole procedure as unconstitutional. Spector argued that federal courts should have the authority to stay specific base closings. To his dismay, on May 23, 1994, the Supreme Court ruled that base-closure decisions are legislative and administrative matters not subject to judicial review.

Despite this decision, the Defense Base Closure and Realignment Act of 1990 has not entirely banished electoral politics from the calculus of base-closure selection, as illustrated by President Clinton's predicament during the 1995 base-closure selection round. On the one hand, California's fifty-four electoral votes added attention-getting emphasis to California Senator Dianne Feinstein's assertion that proposed cuts would "have a devastating effect on California's already fragile economy" (Komarow, 1995, p. 5A). But on the other hand, the remaining states could view rejection of the Base Closing Commission's recommendations as a signal of softness in dealing with the federal budget deficit. Clearly, the dilemmas presented by post–Cold War military downsizing underscore the impossibility of separating international geopolitics from domestic political geography.

Like other communities, present or former military–industrial complex communities maintain urban growth machines (Logan and Molotch, 1976). Local government and business leaders cooperate in order to promote industrial expansion and urban growth, and they can only be expected to continue to do so despite transition in the world order itself. To be sure, communities will have to adjust in response to the new world order. No longer are communities likely to identify dependence on the military–industrial complex as a means to growth and development. Rather, the development of stronger parallels between the world economy and the global political system suggests that the activities of an urban growth machine may focus more directly on those activities that promote international trade and circulation. Cities such as Miami, Los Angeles, and Seattle are apt to benefit from their locations near the geographically broad-scale trading horizons of the Caribbean and the Pacific Rim. Communities such as Buffalo, San Antonio, El Paso, and San Diego are likely to profit from the implementation of NAFTA, which will link the geographically adjacent U.S., Canadian, and Mexican economies more closely together. For example, Representative Ron Packard of California stated in a congressional debate that "NAFTA is key to San Diego's vision of the future. Because of the city's unique resources and position, it will become a gateway to emerging international markets" (*Congressional Record,* November 10, 1993, p. E2815). Thus, these communities recognize their positions as gateways between the United States and its major trade partners.

The debate over the merits of NAFTA highlighted the common belief that the post–Cold War world will emphasize an accelerated level of international trade. Many NAFTA advocates suggested that the development of a free trade zone within North America would be critical to U.S. efforts to compete with the growing economies of Japan and Western Europe. Indeed, NAFTA advocates frequently cited the European Community as a model for international cooperation supported by free trade. On this view, failure to enact NAFTA would seriously hinder U.S. efforts to compete in a post–Cold War global economy.

At the same time, many on both sides of the NAFTA debate expressed specific concern about particular communities within the United States. The underlying ambivalence is evident from a brief examination of the debates within the House during the several days before the passage of the NAFTA bill. Both sides recognized that the costs associated with the implementation of NAFTA were likely to be concentrated geographically, while potential benefits were distributed more evenly over larger areas.

During congressional debate over the merits of the NAFTA bill, many opponents of NAFTA pointed out the bill's impacts on particular communities or constituencies. These concerns were voiced particularly vigorously by Northeastern Democrats, many of whom represent manufacturing-oriented Rustbelt districts, whose residents feared the possibility of unemployment as a result of NAFTA. Some supporters of NAFTA, on the other hand, responded by calling attention to the argument that economic dislocation as a process is independent of the NAFTA agreement. Republican Doug Bereuter of Nebraska stated this position by saying, "The biggest myth surrounding debate over the North American Free Trade Agreement is that Congress or the President can stop the loss of U.S. jobs to the developing world" (*Congressional Record,* November 10, 1993, p. H9064). A Washington Democrat, Al Swift, stated, "Defeating NAFTA does absolutely nothing whatever to change the conditions that have led us to our unsatisfactory status quo" (*Congressional Record,* November 10, 1993, p. E2814).

The vote in the House of Representatives on the NAFTA bill can be regarded as the first major expression of U.S. foreign policy beyond the Cold War, to the extent that the United States is now entering an era in which international geopolitics will be structured by the forces of global economic competition. Thus, the NAFTA vote represents the beginning of the next phase of a trend in both tariff-related and foreign policy votes that has persisted since before the Great Depression.

Three trends coalesced into the geography of the NAFTA vote: the shift from a coastal–interior cleavage to a Sunbelt–Rustbelt cleavage in the foreign policy debate; the shift of the historical positions of the two political parties on protectionism in the ongoing struggle over tariff policy, and the gradual linkage between tariff policy and foreign policy. At the beginning of the Cold War, the geography of tariff support and the geography of foreign policy support were very different; today, at the end of the Cold War, these geographies have become quite similar.

In another sense, the anti-NAFTA rhetoric is reminiscent of the isolationist rhetoric of the World War II period. Central to the anti-NAFTA arguments is concern for the decline of U.S. values, as represented by the farmer, the small businessperson, and the worker. Much of the opposition to NAFTA involved concern that such individuals would be swallowed up by the forces of bigness and bureaucracy: large multinational corporations, agribusiness, large retail corporations, and so on.

Rural opposition to bigness and bureaucracy may also be evident in other contemporary foreign policy debates. In mid-1994, for example, the Clinton administration proposed to send troops to Haiti to restore to power the government of that country's elected president, Jean-Bertrand Aristide. Clinton's proposal was most strongly opposed in the interior regions and was supported along the eastern seaboard. Support for foreign policy activism may increasingly be related to attitudes toward immigration. A successful U.S. invasion of Haiti was seen to reduce the flow of Haitian immigrants to the United States, the large majority of whom settle in Florida and in the large cities of the eastern seaboard. Similarly, NAFTA supporters in California and Texas pointed to the possibility that improved economic conditions in Mexico would discourage Mexicans from moving to their states. Undoubtedly, the geography of positions on U.S. foreign policy will come into sharper focus with the passage of time and the march of international events.

Chapter 8

AFTER THE COLD WAR

Many historians have described the twentieth century as the "American Century." After World War I and certainly since World War II, the United States has emerged as the world's dominant economic and political power. While U.S. political influence was countered to a greater or lesser extent by the Soviet Union, as the largest and wealthiest unified market in the world, the United States was the unchallenged leader in the global economy. During this era, the domestic economy underwent an unprecedented expansion, and the majority of Americans came to enjoy a standard of living unmatched in world history.

As the twentieth century draws to a close, however, the U.S. position in the global economy is changing in reaction to dramatic and fundamental changes in the world political economy. These changes have included an unprecedented expansion of international trade, a tremendous increase in the complexity of global financial and investment markets, and major changes in the organization of production. In addition, the Cold War, which provided a focus for U.S. foreign policy, came to an abrupt end with the collapse of communism in eastern Europe and the Soviet Union. All of these changes have affected the U.S. government's ability to influence both external and internal economic events.

These and other recent events have had a substantial impact on U.S. political geography. In this chapter, we first review current industrial restructuring in the United States. This discussion is followed by an examination of the potential impacts of the end of the Cold War on U.S. politics. Finally, we discuss the presidential election of 1992—an election that has been variously called the last Cold War election and the first post–Cold War election.

Industrial Restructuring

In recent years, the world economy has begun to undergo profound economic restructuring—a development with significant consequences for the future of

U.S. political geography. In earlier chapters, we have seen the close interaction between political geography and economics throughout the nation's history. In this chapter, we address explicitly the nature of economic restructuring in the global economy and its potential impacts on the geography of U.S. politics in the future.

The U.S. economy has gone through a number of rounds of restructuring since the beginning of the Industrial Revolution. As we have seen, periods of restructuring occurred after the War of 1812, after the Civil War, and in the 1920s. The restructuring of the 1970s differs from previous restructuring periods, however. For the first time, the country's competitive position compared to the rest of the world began to decline. The current shift has produced an overall change in the U.S. economy, reducing the country's dependence upon manufacturing employment and greatly increasing the importance of service industries. This shift produced a relative decline in the importance of the manufacturing core, those states dependent on employment in declining sectors. In contrast, the states of the South and West, which are more dependent on the growing service sector of the economy, have become more influential.

The trigger for the end of the post–World War II expansion was the oil crisis of 1973. The oil crisis started when major Middle Eastern oil producing countries, including Iraq, Kuwait, and Saudi Arabia, declared an embargo against the United States and the other Western nations that supported Israel during the Yom Kippur Arab–Israeli War, which broke out on October 6, 1973. Although a cease-fire was arranged by the United Nations on October 22, the oil embargo was not lifted until March 1974, by which time long lines at filling stations in the United States and Western Europe had placed a large exclamation point behind the growing political–economic power of the Organization of Petroleum Exporting Countries (OPEC). Long before that crisis, however, the U.S. economy had been undergoing increasing stress as foreign competition, market saturation, and an aging fixed capital inventory began to cut into the ability to increase corporate profits. The tripling of oil prices in 1973 did not *cause* the end of the boom. Rather, the oil price increase was the last of a series of external shocks that brought to the surface a series of structural weaknesses in the economy.

The End of the Postwar Boom

By 1973, U.S. corporations were faced with several major problems that threatened to severely erode the profitability of their operations. In the first place, the oil crisis had triggered a worldwide recession that resulted in a drop in global demand and declining markets for U.S. products. At the same time, corporations found their markets saturated. Market saturation occurred both as U.S. companies reached the limits of penetration in the global marketplace and as European, Japanese, and Third World nations began to catch up with

U.S. industrialization. Competition was particularly damaging to U.S. companies because foreign competitors utilized newer technology and paid lower
wages (Storper and Walker, 1984).

As Germany, Japan, and Third-World nations began to industrialize,
they employed the most recent technology. Reliance on recent technology
helped these countries to overtake U.S. plants, which were still operating with
earlier-generation technologies. This problem could have been avoided had
U.S. firms continually invested in current technology. However, during the
boom years of the 1950s and 1960s, corporate strategy frequently favored
short-term profit over long-term growth, with the result that both research
and development and investment in new technology were often neglected
(Bluestone and Harrison, 1982).

In addition to the internal problems of the U.S. economy, there were a
number of endogenous events that weakened the U.S. hegemony on world
markets. Since the Bretton Woods agreement of 1944, the majority of the
world's convertible currencies had been tied to the U.S. dollar. This kept exchange rates stable and at levels generally favorable for U.S. exports. In 1971,
the Bretton Woods agreement was abandoned. Subsequently, U.S. currency
was allowed to fluctuate in value relative to foreign currencies. Floating currency created a far greater level of economic uncertainty in the global economy than had existed during the 1950s and 1960s. Moreover, by the 1970s improvements in global communication technology were beginning to lead to
the breakdown of captive national markets, ushering in an era of true global
capitalism—a situation that both hurt U.S. corporations and provided them
with their initial incentive to restructure.

None of these problems alone reduced profit potential sufficiently to create the need for restructuring until the oil crisis. As the world economy
plunged into recession, U.S. companies found themselves at a distinct competitive disadvantage in a global market that was no longer expanding. Faced
with this crisis, U.S. corporations responded in a variety of ways in their
search to maintain profitability in an increasingly unfriendly global economy.
One of the first responses was to increase competitiveness by cutting costs.

At first, many corporations attempted to cut labor costs. By the 1970s,
labor costs had come to comprise a very large proportion of the overall costs
associated with manufacturing plants located throughout the United States
(Figure 8-1). During the boom years, management had been content to submit to annual rounds of collective bargaining with labor unions that covered
everything from annual wage increases and benefit packages to shopfloor
control of work practices (Bluestone and Harrison, 1982). This bargaining
process was advantageous to management because it minimized worker-relat-
ed disruptions in the production process. The high rates of economic growth
that were being achieved justified the high wages and benefits paid by management to employees.

The tradition of trading wage and other benefits for industrial harmony
is an old one in the United States (Gordon, 1977; Storper and Walker, 1984).

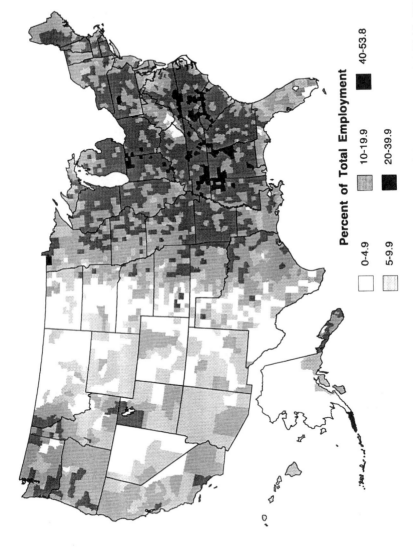

FIGURE 8-1. Manufacturing Employment, 1990. Data from U.S. Bureau of the Census (1993a), Table P77.

As economic growth slowed, however, the high wages and benefits that had been awarded during the boom could no longer be sustained if corporations were to continue to extract the same levels of profit that they had previously. Management was no longer prepared to continue the annual process of increasing wages and benefits and, in fact, began to use the annual bargaining process as a forum for negotiating wage and benefit cuts (Box 8-1).

The power to force declining wage and benefit standards on labor was derived from management's discovery of a "spatial fix" (Hudson, 1992) for the problem of increasing competition and decreasing market share. This spatial fix involved shifting production processes away from the old industrial heartland of the Northeast, where labor was expensive and had a history of militancy, to peripheral areas with lower wage rates (Massey and Meegan, 1982; Trachte and Ross, 1985). Such movement was especially pronounced in those industries whose products had reached the end of the product cycle (Box 8-2). Those aspects of firm activity that require highly skilled labor, such as research and development and higher-level management, are separated geographically from the actual manufacturing process, which is in turn established in regions of cheap, low-skilled labor.

This decentralization had begun as early as the 1930s, and the process continued slowly throughout the postwar expansion. Through the 1960s, however, profit rates remained high enough that there was no apparent need to overcome the inertia of a location in the industrial core. The labor cost savings to be gained from operating in many potential low-wage sites were not yet sufficient to outweigh the increased communications, transportation, and facility construction costs (Bluestone and Harrison, 1982). After 1973, however, it became increasingly profitable for U.S. firms to shift production outside the United States, where wage rates were generally much lower. Firms could simply abandon the previously dominant sites and seek out new sites with lower costs, thus achieving international competitiveness through spatial relocation rather than technical or organizational change. Many companies did so, and large numbers of U.S. jobs were lost to Mexico, Latin America, East Asia, and other parts of the world.

Dealing with the crisis through spatial relocation was such a popular strategy for U.S. corporations that it became known as "capital flight" (Bluestone and Harrison, 1982). Capital flight led to a major economic crisis in many of the old industrial regions of the United States, a crisis that was known as "deindustrialization." Deindustrialization was in many ways the most visible manifestation of post-1973 industrial restructuring, especially because capital was withdrawn from specific regions and reinvested in others.

Roots of Deindustrialization

Although deindustrialization became evident in the U.S. economy after the oil shocks of the 1970s, its roots go back to the economic situation that was

Box 8-1. *Unionization in the 1990s: Caterpillar versus the UAW*

Unionization has always been a very contentious issue in the U.S. economy. Until the Great Depression, labor unions were small and generally ineffective. The power of labor unions increased, however, during the depression. Labor unions formed a crucial component of Franklin D. Roosevelt's coalition of supporters, and Roosevelt and his supporters in Congress gave unions government backing.

Throughout the postwar boom years, unionization grew as the pool of blue-collar workers grew, reaching a peak during the mid-1960s. However, just as the increase in manufacturing (particularly traditional heavy manufacturing) employment created the pool of unionizable workers, so too the decline in that employment shrank the pool. By the mid-1980s, unionization in the United States was less than it had been in 1950.

While the sharp decline in heavy manufacturing contributed greatly to the decline in unionization, the political climate of the 1980s further weakened the union movement. It became very clear during the air traffic controllers' strike of 1981 that not only was the incumbent Republican administration hostile to unions, it was also prepared to act upon that hostility to further weaken the union movement. As companies began the process of rationalization, intensification, and overall cost cutting, management had the active support of the government in subsequent battles with labor unions.

By 1990, the extent of union retrenchment was clear from the greatly reduced number of strikes. In 1980, there were 187 strikes involving a thousand or more workers, but by 1990 there were only 44. The United Auto Workers (UAW), traditionally one of the most powerful unions, had suffered a number of setbacks, particularly with the retrenchment of employment in the auto industry. However, the UAW remained strong in the highly unionized agricultural and heavy machinery industries.

Overall, industrial unionization continues to be strong in the manufacturing sectors that remain concentrated in the traditional manufacturing core. While nationally less than a quarter of all manufacturing workers belong to labor unions, the proportions are much greater in Indiana, Michigan, New York, Ohio, and Pennsylvania, states that are all located in the Middle Atlantic or Middle Western regions of the country (Figure 8-B1-1). The lowest rates of industrial unionization are found in the Southeast and interior West.

In 1991, the UAW negotiated a contract between its members and the John Deere tractor plant in Moline, Illinois. The UAW then attempted to transfer that contract, in a system traditionally known as "pattern bargaining," to Caterpillar. Caterpillar's management was not prepared to accept this contract, however. Caterpillar leaders argued that the era of pattern bargaining was over. The technique had been used by the unions to ensure constant wages and benefits throughout an industry (and to prevent companies from undercutting union wage and benefit standards by negotiating with individual workforces). With increased global competition, they argued, companies needed the flexibility of individual contracts with their own workforce. Caterpillar argued that its greater overseas market and a higher level of foreign competition in the heavy equipment industry meant that it could not offer the same contract as had John Deere, a largely domestically oriented farm machinery maker.

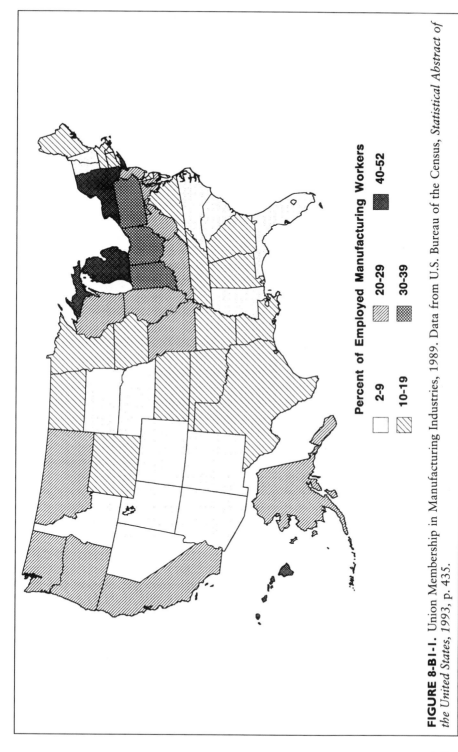

FIGURE 8-B1-1. Union Membership in Manufacturing Industries, 1989. Data from U.S. Bureau of the Census, *Statistical Abstract of the United States, 1993*, p. 435.

Caterpillar's refusal to accept the UAW contract led to the beginning of a three-year (and continuing) battle with the UAW. Initially, the union struck at Caterpillar's East Peoria and Decatur, Illinois, plants. On November 4, 1991, 2,400 workers struck. Ten days later, Caterpillar retaliated by locking out an additional 5,600 workers and it began laying off workers in other plants to avoid building up excess inventory. By December, 10,000 people were either on strike or laid off.

In April 1992, the strike ended after Caterpillar threatened to replace the striking workers permanently. Caterpillar workers went back to work without a contract, agreeing to abide by management's new terms, including a "flexible" work schedule that required workers to work either four ten-hour shifts a week or three twelve-hour shifts, removed premium pay for work on weekends and holidays, required workers to accept a share of the costs of their medical care, and introduced a two-tier wage system that allowed the company to hire new workers at below union rates.

Just as this strike was ending, Congress passed a bill making the permanent replacement of striking workers illegal. However, this new law applies only if workers are striking over unfair work practices, not wages or benefits. Thus, while there have been a number of wildcat strikes throughout the Caterpillar organization over the past two years, the union, in an attempt to protect its workers from losing both jobs and pay (since strikers during the 1991–1992 strike were forced to subsist on $100-a-week strike pay), has resorted to a new "negotiating" technique. At Caterpillar plants throughout the country, but particularly in Illinois, the UAW has encouraged the workers to adopt a "work-to-rule" strategy; that is, the workers literally work to the rules laid down by the company, even if the rules are inefficient and slow down production. Workers do not contribute suggestions for improvements in production and, in general, withhold their cooperation and initiative from the production process.

Management both denies that there is a work-to-rule strategy in place or that it is having any effect on production; however, internal memos clearly demonstrate that efficiency and productivity gains decreased. The union calls working to rule an "in-plant" strategy. It enables workers to express their displeasure at working arrangements without risking their jobs. This has become increasingly important as companies have first used the threat of foreign competition to demand givebacks and then threatened job losses if the workers strike.

There has been considerable debate among economists about the impact of weakened union organization on the economy. It has been argued that lessening union influence will increase productivity and profits by reducing labor costs and allowing more flexible work practices. In an era of increased foreign competition from countries with sub-U.S. wages, this argument goes, we cannot afford to pay union rates any longer. However, it is also argued that the marginalization of blue-collar workers not only weakens the economy by reducing the size of the domestic market, but also transforms industrial (usually skilled) workers from valued, highly trained employees to low-wage, low-skill commodities. Unable to strike and faced with increasing demands for givebacks from companies that may not even be in any financial trouble (Caterpillar awarded its chief executive officer a 25.4 percent pay increase between

1990 and 1993), workers are withholding their cooperation, initiative, and loyalty, which has serious potential consequences for the industrial economy. The carefully crafted and maintained management–union relationship that was in force throughout the 1960s and into the 1970s and that permitted the tremendous economic growth of the period has been seriously damaged by the last two decades of job losses and union busting.

---

created at the end of World War II. At that time, the United States became the financier and supplier of economic reconstruction for the rest of the world. It was this economic strength that allowed U.S. capital to penetrate European and Japanese economies, both through the direct establishment of production capacity in those countries and by entering into productive partnerships with foreign companies. These developments would eventually lead to the wholesale transfer of U.S. technology into the hands of foreign competitors.

In the rush to realize rapid profits, U.S. corporations sold or licensed production of thousands of patents to foreign firms, frequently setting up turnkey operations in which the jointly financed production facilities were eventually turned over to the host economy. These ventures have been extremely profitable for U.S. corporations because they have become major stockholders in the companies to which the patents were granted. Yet this indiscriminate transfer of U.S. technology to foreign companies contributed to structural problems in the domestic economy after 1973 (Bluestone and Harrison, 1982).

The establishment of U.S.-owned production facilities outside the United States has also contributed to deindustrialization in the domestic economy. Companies began investing abroad before the turn of the century, but the lure of uncontested markets and cheap productive capacity accelerated this process after 1945. Initially, most overseas investment was confined to Western Europe and Japan. The impact on the domestic economy of overseas investment was minimal during the 1950s and 1960s, when there was sufficient global demand to provide adequate and increasing economic growth for the United States and to allow offshore production to cope with external markets.

Not until after 1973 did this particular corporate strategy begin to have a negative impact on the U.S. worker. As global markets shrank and the costs of domestic production soared, corporations faced with the decision of where to cut capacity were much more inclined to cut domestic capacity, with its older technology and highly paid, militant labor force. Thus, during the 1970s, much of the increase in foreign competition was in fact competition from U.S.-owned offshore plants (Trachte and Ross, 1985).

The common misconception of deindustrialization is of the "runaway shop," that is, a situation in which a corporation accomplishes spatial relocation by shutting a plant in one location, transferring the capital equipment,

Box 8-2. *Product, Process, and Profit Cycles*

When it became clear in the 1970s that restructuring was taking place, a variety of theories developed to explain how corporations were dealing with restructuring and the spatial consequences of their actions.

The product cycle explains restructuring as a consequence of the changing life cycle of a particular product. In the first stage, the product is new and still being modified. Thus, production takes place close to the headquarters and research and development divisions, where design changes can be easily incorporated into the product. In the second stage, the product is perfected, and the task is to develop a market for it. Initially, at least, the price of the product will be high, but geographic expansion of the market through advertising encourages increased production and reduced price. In this stage, production may decentralize, but only to further accommodate market expansion. For example, the expansion of U.S. auto manufacturing into Europe in the 1920s was not an attempt to escape high costs in the United States but, rather, a method of gaining access to European markets.

It is only in the third stage of the product cycle model that decentralization becomes widespread. At this stage, the product is fully standardized, it is a "mature" product with a wide market, and market expansion depends upon reducing price enough to make the product affordable to the mass of consumers. In addition, at this stage the product is being produced by a number of companies, and price competition becomes the method of contesting market share. With a standardized product, it is possible to apply a spatial solution to the problems of high wages and labor militancy by moving production to new labor sites, often offshore.

The product cycle theory has been used to explain much of the spatial decentralization of production that has taken place both within the United States and overseas since the 1950s. The process began in the automobile and textile industries and has grown to encompass consumer electronics, semiconductors, and a host of other products. The spatial impact was greatest in those areas that specialized in products that had reached the mature stage by the time the restructuring crisis began in the 1970s, primarily the products of the old industrial core.

The process cycle model is a modification of the product cycle theory that was developed in the early 1980s (Malecki, 1991). The process cycle model adds the idea that it is not just the maturity of the product that determines the industry's ability to decentralize, but also the maturity of the process technology. In the first stage, the product is new, and it is manufactured in small batches as design changes are made. In the second stage, the product is being marketed; however, to expand the market, price reductions become increasingly important, driving the search to develop a standardized production process that will allow mass production. The technological requirements of developing and refining this new process therefore tend to limit decentralization and to keep production close to research and development and to headquarters functions.

It is in the third stage with a fully developed standardized production process that decentralization is possible. The standardized process, traditionally some form of assembly line, requires only low-skilled labor and little supervision from technical or executive personnel. Thus, production can be moved to peripheral locations with cost advantages such as low wages, tax incentives, and antilabor regulations. It is this third stage of the process cycle that enables the third stage of the product cycle to take place.

During the 1980s, Markusen (1986) developed the profit cycle theory as a third explanation for the spatial behavior of corporations in the 1970s and 1980s. In essence, this theory suggests that each product goes through a life cycle of profitability, and each of these stages has specific spatial requirements. The first stage, "zero profit," is the initial development and design stage of the product. At this stage, research and design are important, but there is no commercial production of the product. The only companies involved in this stage are those that are pioneering the product, and so there is a high degree of spatial concentration in a few research and development centers. In the second stage, the product goes into commercial production, and, with at most only a few companies involved in production, this is the stage of "super profit." In this stage, production is confined to the few areas in which the product first developed. These are the areas with the skilled labor, specialized suppliers, and entrepreneurs necessary to continue the development of the product. New firms do enter the market at this stage, to capitalize on the high rate of profit, but, again, they are drawn to the existing centers of production, where the necessary agglomeration economies are in place.

By the third stage, the successful firms are beginning to increase in size and develop into multiplant operations. This is the stage of "normal profit," and in spatial terms it corresponds to the second stage of the product cycle model, with dispersion taking place to further market penetration. In stage four—"normal plus" or "normal minus" profit—competition increases between large firms and retention of market shares becomes important; cost-cutting measures lead to increased dispersion, this time in search of low-wage, docile labor.

Finally, as a product reaches obsolescence and markets decline, it enters a stage of "negative profit." In this stage, corporations attempt to shut down capacity as fast as possible. Capacity shedding may take place long before negative profits are involved, if a conglomerate is operating the plant. Here, a division that is in the third or fourth stage of the profit cycle may be prematurely shut down to transfer capital into a division that is operating in an earlier stage.

Again, the profit cycle demonstrates that different stages of a product's life cycle have different spatial requirements. And again it was the core, with the highest concentration of mature products in the country, that experienced a wave of products simultaneously reaching the third, fourth, and, ultimately, fifth stages of the profit cycle and that therefore suffered the most severe employment shocks of restructuring.

and opening up the same production facility elsewhere. In fact, the runaway shop accounts for only a small percentage of the recent deindustrialization of U.S. industry, although Bluestone and Harrison estimate that some 450,000–650,000 private sector jobs in the United States were destroyed through runaway shops during the 1970s. Other types of disinvestment—including systematically reducing investment in one location and increasing investment in one or more other locations, siphoning off profit from one location to provide investment in another, and even contracting or shutting down plants in specific locations and using the savings to diversify into completely unrelated activities—affected far more jobs. In all of these processes, some locations are persistently deprived of new investment, whereas others persistently expand. When all these methods of deindustrialization are included, the estimate of jobs lost in the United States between 1970 and 1980 increases to 38 million (Bluestone and Harrison, 1982), with even more jobs affected after 1980.

Many of those jobs reappeared elsewhere in the United States or overseas. For example, General Electric increased its worldwide employment by 5,000 during the 1970s, but its workforce within the United States fell by 25,000. Other major corporations all followed similar strategies. Disinvestment in certain regions of the United States accompanied significant new investment and job creation elsewhere.

Although deindustrialization affected employment patterns throughout the United States, job losses were especially heavy in the Northeast during the 1970s. Every state in New England, along with New York, New Jersey, and Pennsylvania, experienced net losses of jobs in private manufacturing establishments over the course of the decade (Bluestone and Harrison, 1982). During the 1980s, Illinois, Indiana, Ohio, Michigan, and Wisconsin joined the ranks of net losers in manufacturing jobs. In fact, the rate of capital flight increased nationwide through the late 1970s and early 1980s, as the disinvestment of previous years began to catch up with the plants now deprived of adequate investment capital. For those plants chosen for disinvestment, the problem of obsolete technology was merely exacerbated during the 1970s, which made their final shutdown inevitable.

Other Causes of Restructuring after 1973

In addition to deindustrialization, several other processes contributed to the restructuring of U.S. industry after 1973. Massey and Meegan (1982) have proposed a three-stage topology of restructuring strategies: rationalization, intensification, and technological change. Each of these strategies has affected the geography of the economy dramatically during the past two decades.

Rationalization is the permanent shutdown of particular plants, product lines, or divisions of a corporation in order to reduce the production of an unprofitable (or insufficiently profitable) product. Thus, rationalization is a deliberate strategy on the part of management to shed unprofitable capacity in an attempt to maintain the viability of the entire corporation. Rationalization often occurs when industries are faced with excess capacity. This was a common situation during the 1970s, when demand for U.S. products declined in the face of stagnant global markets. Under such circumstances, there will eventually be excess supply, and companies attempt to shut down less profitable facilities or product lines. The spatial consequences of rationalization vary depending on circumstances, but the loss of jobs in those locations dependent on less profitable operations is an inevitable consequence of rationalization.

A second restructuring technique is intensification, that is, increasing output per worker with little change in technology or the organization of production. This strategy does not necessarily lead to increased unemployment as long as product demand is increasing. Intensification enables a firm to increase output without increasing labor costs, thereby cutting unit costs without relocating or reinvesting in new technology. When demand is steady or falling, however, intensification permits the company to maintain output levels with fewer employees, thus increasing competitiveness and slowing any potential loss of market share. For small firms, intensification is a survival strategy used to hold off bankruptcy. Even in larger firms, the ability to increase output per worker with minimal new investment may be a precursor to rationalization in a particular plant. In fact, a combination of the two strategies may take place in horizontally integrated firms, with rationalization in one plant leading to intensification in another (Peck and Townsend, 1984).

The final strategy in restructuring is the use of technological change to reduce unit production costs. As we have seen, during the expansion of the 1950s and 1960s, investment in updating process technology in domestic industries was generally neglected in favor of expanding production capacity and presenting large annual dividends to shareholders. Even after it became clear that new production technology was necessary to remain competitive in the global economy, changes came slowly to domestic industry. As late as 1980, the average age of domestic capital stock predated the oil shocks, with obvious implications for its energy efficiency. However, technological change is also another way to cut labor costs and, as such, has been employed both in industries that are unable to use the spatial fix to deal with their labor problems and in industries in which decentralization was possible and where technological change has accompanied the spatial relocation of production (Rees et al., 1985).

Technological change allows both for a reduction in the size of the labor force and for a reduction in the skill levels required to produce a product. Consequently, labor costs can be reduced both by labor shedding and by deskilling (with a subsequent reduction in wages). The advent of robotics, numerically controlled machine tooling, and computer controlled flow processes has meant that even traditionally labor-intensive industries were able to undertake labor shedding through the application of new technology (Schoenberger, 1987).

Post-Fordism

One of the effects of the most recent round of industrial restructuring has been the decline of Fordism as the dominant model of goods production (Hudson, 1992). There are a variety of reasons for the eclipse of Fordism, including a need for shorter product runs and more rapid design changes resulting from increasingly fragmented and volatile markets, the continued search to increase productivity through technological change, and the cost reductions to be gained from vertical disintegration, to mention only a few. As Fordism has declined, however, new models of production have developed. While it is yet unclear whether any one of these will achieve the dominance that Fordism once held, each provides a new framework for the relations between capital, labor, and space with significant implications for the U.S. political economy.

The two primary alternatives to Fordism are flexible specialization and just-in-time production systems (Hudson, 1992). In contrast to Fordism, which is based on the efficiency advantages associated with production by large corporations, flexible specialization is based on agglomeration economies associated with small, independent producers. Flexible specialization entails the creation of a local division of labor based on a small core of highly skilled permanent employees and a mass of less-skilled temporary workers. Even highly skilled workers are marginalized in this system, because the extensive use of subcontracting creates a large number of very small employers, many of whom rely on part-time or temporary employees (Donaghu and Barff, 1990).

Today, the markets for many consumer goods are becoming increasingly fragmented and volatile. Keeping up with market volatility requires rapid design and product innovation, resulting in a considerable decrease in the length of the product cycle. Flexible specialization is particularly suited to those industries that must respond to rapidly changing consumer tastes, such as the garment industry, or that depend on continuous technological innovation, such as the microcomputer industry (Milne and Tufts, 1993).

The rapidity of design innovation and the small size of firms require a great deal of worker flexibility and ingenuity, breaking down the much more rigidly demarcated job divisions typical of Fordist production strategies. High rates of innovation and flexibility, in turn, require a higher level of managerial control and also lead to high levels of inter- and intrafirm interaction. Consequently, spatial reconcentration takes place to reduce transportation and communication costs and to enable firms to take advantage of the creation of specialized labor pools.

While flexible specialization has been recognized as one of the successors to Fordism, it is limited to a relative few industries, including the garment and microcomputer industries. Thus the geographic effects of flexible specialization tend to be concentrated in those areas whose economies are dominated by these industries, such as the "Silicon Valley" region of northern California. Outside of this type of area, it is unlikely that flexible specialization will be the next dominant mode of production for the U.S. economy as a whole.

The just-in-time (JIT) system of production has developed as an alternative to Fordism in the automobile industry (Box 8-3). This system is based on the smooth and continuous flow of components and materials from suppliers to the production site. Under Fordism, other divisions of a corporation (often located in another state or, more recently, another country) supply component parts to the corporation's assembly plants. The great distances involved require assembly plants to maintain large component inventories.

Under JIT, in contrast, independent suppliers are responsible for providing a continuous supply of high-quality materials to the assembly plant. This not only frees the company from the cost of maintaining inventory, but the vertical disintegration also reduces cost by encouraging competition between suppliers. In addition, the automobile manufacturer is freed from the costs associated with providing benefits and services for the component-production workforce. Unlike the large, highly organized workforce of a traditional auto company, that of the vertically disintegrated components suppliers tends to be smaller and nonunionized. Consequently, labor forces under JIT are lower paid, less well provided with benefits, and much more vulnerable to layoffs and reduction from full-time to part-time work (Schoenberger, 1987; Mair et al., 1988; Mair, 1993).

The rapid and continuous contact between suppliers and assembly plants again requires that there be a degree of spatial concentration in the industry. Initial studies of JIT in Japan indicated a very high degree of concentration, with parts suppliers located in very close proximity to assemblers.

Japanese automobile manufacturers who maintain assembly plants in the United States in contrast, must balance the Japanese preference for sites in relatively "business friendly" states with the need to remain close to U.S. parts suppliers. Japanese automakers have a particular preference for rural sites, often in "right to work" states, that is, states in which unionization is discouraged. Most Japanese auto companies can be found within a ten-hour driving radius around the southern Michigan auto production core. New sites have developed that are independent of this traditional auto production area, however. In these cases, networks of component suppliers have begun to develop within a day's drive of the assembly locations. Thus, in the United States, the JIT system implies regional rather than local concentration.

As with flexible specialization, whether JIT will take the place of Fordism is open to debate. It cannot be argued that it is the direct successor to Fordism in the auto industry—the birthplace of both modes of production. However, it remains to be seen whether JIT can be applied to the wide variety

Box 8-3. *Fordism versus Toyotism—The Challenge of JIT*

The automobile industry has been one of the main battlegrounds of restructuring. In the United States, automobiles have traditionally been produced in assembly line operations, which involve routinized, low-skill labor. These operations are amenable to the spatial fix of decentralization when wages rise or workers become militant. Consequently, transportation equipment has been one of the main areas of employment loss in the industrial core, as U.S. automakers progressively decentralized their operations over the last forty years.

On April 1, 1913, Henry Ford introduced a makeshift production line to speed the production of flywheel magnetos, and Fordism was born. Prior to 1913, autos had been assembled individually by a team of skilled workers. Ford abandoned this system in a search for cheaper more efficient ways to produce cars. He built a product that was made up of standardized components and could be assembled in a short time by unskilled workers who remained at one workstation and performed one routine task as the chassis moved past them on a system of mechanized belts and conveyors.

Fordism was quickly diffused to a variety of other industries, and the assembly line became the standard form of production for everything from consumer electronics to food processing. In addition to the obvious advantages of speed and efficiency, the assembly line also returned control of the production process to management. No longer reliant on skilled labor and able to control the speed of production, management could not be seriously threatened by labor unrest, because unskilled employees could be replaced much more easily than more highly skilled workers. Thus, when the restructuring crisis unfolded in the 1970s, U.S. manufacturers were able to pick up their standardized product and assembly line production systems and move them to regions with cheaper, less militant labor.

At the same time, the automakers of Japan were demonstrating that Fordism was not the only way to produce a cheap, high-quality vehicle. The Japanese system, perfected by Toyota and therefore often known as "Toyotism," allows for a much greater degree of production flexibility, so that product lines can be changed rapidly or tailored to different markets in different places. This flexibility has given rise to the term "just-in-time manufacturing," which refers to the supply system of frequent, often daily, deliveries of components. With this system, it is no longer necessary to maintain a large inventory of parts and, more important, improvements in design can be implemented much more rapidly. JIT tends to lead to vertical disintegration, with Japanese automakers much more dependent upon small, independent parts suppliers than on supplies from other divisions of the company (Schoenberger, 1987; Mair 1993). Thus, there tends to be a spatial concentration of suppliers around the major auto plants. As JIT has diffused to the United States with the establishment of Japanese auto production plants, a debate has begun as to whether this will lead to a reconcentration of the U.S. auto industry. JIT requires a skilled labor force, and, more important, access to existing auto parts suppliers. In the United States, that implies a location somewhere in or close to the core. In fact, most of the Japanese plants are in this region—Diamond Star (Mitsubishi) in Bloomington, Illinois; Mazda in Battle Creek, Michigan; Honda in Marysville, Ohio; and Toyota in Georgetown, Kentucky—and there has been a wave of Japanese investment in auto parts manufacturing in the core in the early 1990s.

Even GM's grand experiment, the Saturn, has followed the same strategy, locating in Spring Hill, Tennessee, within a day's drive of parts suppliers in Ohio and Michigan. GM is the first major U.S. auto manufacturer to attempt to compete with the Japanese on this new basis. JIT production implies competition based on quality control, flexibility in design, and rapid response to changes in consumer desires. The traditional form of competition between auto companies, based solely on price, is no longer effective. U.S. automakers have all employed the spatial fix to bring down labor costs, the only avenue for cost reduction under Fordism, so that no one company has a cost advantage. In the process, quality and consumer satisfaction have been neglected. By focusing on these neglected issues, the Japanese have changed the forum for competition, and by capturing increasing shares of the U.S. auto market in the 1970s and 1980s, they have forced United States companies into considering a new mode of production.

The operation of JIT production in the United States presents the auto companies with something of a dilemma. While they can, as GM did, import skilled workers into a region that has no previous tradition of auto manufacturing, it is much harder to re-create the network of small independent parts suppliers that exists in the traditional auto regions. Thus, to take full advantage of the flexibility of JIT production, they are tied to locations within ten hours of the Ohio–Michigan auto production core. If U.S. automakers increasingly move toward the JIT strategy, the decentralization process of the past twenty years will have to be reconsidered, and restructuring will begin to take yet another form as production becomes tied to competitive strategy and forces for reconcentration develop (Mair, 1993).

of industries that eventually adopted Fordism as their primary mode of production (Gertler, 1988, 1992).

Restructuring the manufacturing sector has affected the political geography of the United States in a variety of ways. The decline of Fordism with its full-time, well-paid, unionized jobs and the emergence of flexible specialization, JIT, and "right to work" states has resulted in a significant erosion of the blue-collar, middle-class population. This erosion has contributed to the increased division of the working population into an expanding group of those with relatively secure, highly paid, and full-time jobs and an equally expanding group who are increasingly marginalized in poorly paid, part-time and tenuous employment.

The Employment Impacts of Industrial Restructuring

As we have seen, a variety of processes have been responsible for the restructuring of U.S. industry and economic activity since the early 1970s. These shifts have been so significant that some authors have described the period since 1973 as the beginning of the postindustrial era (Bell, 1973). Such discussion emphasizes the fact that the traditional manufacturing basis of the U.S. economy has been bypassed as the primary engine of employment growth and has been overtaken by services. This transition has had profound consequences for the economic and political geography of the United States.

An examination of employment data indicates the extent to which this shift has affected the employment structure of the United States (Figure 8-2). In 1970, 35 percent of the total employment in the United States was in manufacturing, but by 1990 that percentage had fallen to 20 percent. During the same period, employment in services had increased from 57 percent to 72 percent. Within the service sector, the most significant gains were made by the general services category, which includes everything from lodging and entertainment through business and professional services to health and education services. Between 1970 and 1980, employment in this group of activities grew by 155 percent, while employment in financial services grew by 90 percent. At the same time, the United States experienced a 19 percent decline in manu-

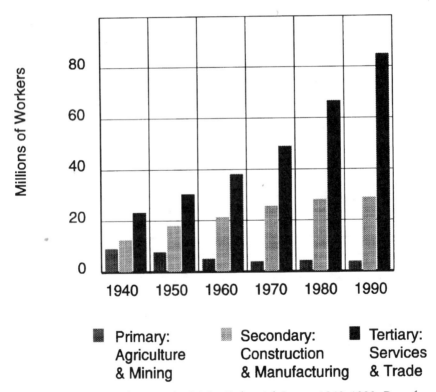

FIGURE 8-2. U.S. Employment by Major Industrial Sector, 1940–1990. Data from U.S. Bureau of the Census (decennial).

facturing employment. During the twenty-year period, the United States economy created over 36 million new jobs, but it experienced a net loss of half a million manufacturing jobs.

Employment Changes during the 1970s

During the 1970s employment grew in all sectors of the U.S. economy. While manufacturing experienced relatively small gains, there were much larger gains in the service industries, particularly in the general services group. However, in the following decade employment growth remained high in all sectors except manufacturing, in which there was a 9 percent employment decline. Clearly, the process of industrial restructuring, which is generally said to have begun in the 1970s, accelerated through the 1980s with the much wider divergence of growth rates for manufacturing and nonmanufacturing sectors. The 1980s saw manufacturing employment decline by 1.9 million jobs, a decline that not only wiped out all the gains in manufacturing employment in the previous decade but left the country with 500,000 fewer manufacturing jobs than had existed in 1970.

The overall figures only begin to tell the story of the regional effects of economic restructuring in the United States. By no means did this employment shift occur in the same way and with the same effects in all parts of the country. In 1970, the east north central states (Illinois, Indiana, Michigan, Ohio, and Wisconsin) and the Middle Atlantic states (New York, New Jersey, and Pennsylvania) each accounted for about 21 percent of all jobs in the United States. Nearly 40 percent of jobs in these regions, as in New England, were in manufacturing, whereas less than a third of all jobs elsewhere were in the manufacturing sector.

The primary region of manufacturing job loss was the region traditionally defined as the U.S. manufacturing core, a region that, by 1950, stretched from the New England states to Illinois (Figure 8-3). Between 1970 and 1990, the core experienced a 25 percent decline in manufacturing employment, with a net loss of 2.7 million jobs. The rest of the country picked up 2.1 million manufacturing jobs, bringing both regions to a much closer level of dependence on manufacturing. The core now had 22 percent of its employment in manufacturing, with the rest of the country reporting 19 percent.

Despite the net gains in manufacturing employment outside the core, this region still saw the importance of manufacturing employment diminish during the 1970s and, especially, the 1980s. This resulted from a very rapid growth in service industries. Between 1970 and 1990, the five categories of service industries (transportation and utilities, wholesale, retail, finance insurance and real estate, and general services) grew by between 71 and 212 percent. This growth, coupled with an absolute decline in manufacturing and shifts in the geographic origins of U.S. exports, resulted in the tremendous decline in the importance of manufacturing in the core.

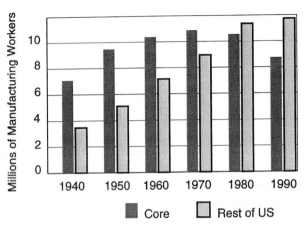

FIGURE 8-3. Manufacturing Employment in the Traditional Manufacturing Core versus the Rest of United States, 1940–1990. Data from U.S. Bureau of the Census (decennial).

It is this decline in manufacturing in the core that is most commonly associated with the term "industrial restructuring," and a brief examination of the employment consequences of this decline is in order here. Certain industries have become particularly prone to restructuring over the past two decades. These include textiles, metals industries, electrical and nonelectrical machinery, and transportation equipment.

The Textile Industry

The first indication that U.S. manufacturing was in trouble came in the textile industry. A key component of manufacturing throughout the country prior to

World War II, employment in the textile industry has declined in every decade since them. In 1950, textiles accounted for 7 percent of all U.S. employment and 16 percent of the employment in manufacturing. In the New England states (Connecticut, Maine, Massachusetts, New Hampshire, Rhode Island, and Vermont), textile employment accounted for as much as 23 percent of all employment. The textile industry had also achieved a significant degree of national dispersion by World War II, with slightly more textile jobs located outside the core than within it.

The pre-1970 spatial dispersion of the textile industry presents a vivid contrast with the concentration of many other important industries within the Northeastern industrial core. Textiles were the first mass-produced product of the Industrial Revolution. Textile production formed the economic base of the nation's first major industrial region in southern New England. By the early twentieth century, however, the textile industry began to move away from New England. New technology freed the textile industry from dependence on water-powered machinery, and as a result textile mill owners moved away from New England and its relatively high labor costs. Many moved to rural areas in the South, with a particularly large concentration found in the Piedmont area of North Carolina and South Carolina. Large numbers of textile mills were established within a hundred-mile radius of Charlotte, North Carolina, with profound consequences for politics in the Tar Heel State and its neighbors.

During the period between 1970 and 1990, the textile industry suffered a net loss of 219,746 jobs nationwide. These losses were felt disproportionately in the core, which lost 496,312 jobs, or 41 percent of its textile employment. In the New England states, losses were as high as 63 percent (in Rhode Island), and New York state lost over 190,000 jobs in textile mills and apparel factories. Conversely, there was a gain of 276,566 textile jobs outside the core, indicating a continuation of the prewar pattern of dispersion of the labor-intensive textile industry away from the core.

What happened to the textile jobs that had been lost between 1970 and 1990? Although some may be accounted for by technological change, foreign competition accounts for a large share. By the late 1960s, foreign-produced textiles were accounting for an increasingly large share of the U.S. textile market. Throughout the 1960s, the passage of tariff provisions and other federal subsidy programs encouraged U.S. corporations to undertake overseas investment, creating offshore "production platforms" in which goods were assembled to be reimported to the United States (Bluestone and Harrison, 1982). The textile and apparel industries were the first to make major use of these export platforms. Textile production, requiring simple technology and unskilled labor, was easily located overseas, thereby saving corporations labor costs and the cost of retooling obsolete factories in the United States.

By the 1970s, the textile industry in the core was in severe decline, and the following decades served only to further that decline. A further 28 percent decline in textile jobs occurred during the 1970s, followed by another 36 percent decline in the 1980s. By 1990, the core had lost 73 percent of the textile jobs that had existed in 1950. Some states, such as Connecticut and Rhode Island, had lost over 80 percent of their textile employment, the region as whole had lost almost 700,000 jobs, and New York state had lost almost 400,000.

By the 1980s, the states outside the core had also begun to lose employment in textiles, with over 250,000 jobs lost during the decade. In fact, the loss of textile employment outside the core eradicated all the gains of the previous three decades and left the region with only 1.3 percent more jobs in textiles than it had in 1950. These losses suggest that by the 1980s the states outside the core were experiencing the same problems of plant obsolescence and relatively high wage costs that had prompted the initial relocation of the textile industry from New England. The advantages of cheap land, low wages, and low taxes that had been offered by the South and West were no longer a sufficient incentive to keep U.S. textile firms producing in the United States. More and more textile production was shifted to offshore sites.

While the textile industry was the first sector in the United States to experience major restructuring, a number of other industries were to follow a similar path in the 1970s and 1980s. In contrast to textiles, these had continued to thrive nationwide throughout the postwar expansion. In the core this growth was slow, averaging only 3 percent, with a net gain of 283,000 manufacturing jobs during the two decades.

Despite this gain, indications of future problems were appearing in a few states. The core experienced an overall decline in employment in transportation equipment, which was created by a large employment decline in Michigan. This decline was partly a consequence of the shifting of military procurement contracts away from ground transportation equipment toward aerospace and electronics during the 1950s and 1960s (Crump, 1989). There was also a decline of employment in metals industries (primary metal industries and fabricated metal products) in a few states, including a large loss in Connecticut and slightly smaller declines in New York, Ohio, and Pennsylvania. Outside the core, again there was substantial growth in manufacturing (48 percent), particularly growth in many of the traditional heavy industries: nonelectrical machinery grew by 90 percent, electrical machinery by 264 percent, transportation by 84 percent; there was even a 28 percent growth in metals industries employment.

By the 1970s, the trickle of job losses in the traditional manufacturing industries of the core had become a river. Between 1970 and 1980, the region lost over 567,000 manufacturing jobs, 311,486 of them in metals industries, electrical machinery, and transportation equipment. The states worst affected—Michigan, New Jersey, New York, Ohio, and Pennsylvania—lost employment in every major manufacturing sector. However, even with a loss of half a million jobs, the real impact of restructuring was yet to be felt. During the 1980s, the river became a flood: The core lost 1.6 million manufacturing jobs, 1.35 million of them in the five traditional sectors. During this period, employment in every major industrial sector in the core declined, and every state in the core lost jobs in every one of the major manufacturing sectors.

The states outside the core made tremendous employment gains between 1950 and 1990 and by the end of the 1980s had 4.9 million more manufacturing jobs than in 1950, in contrast to the core, which had lost 1.9 million. Nonetheless, the impact of restructuring began to be felt in this region, too, during the 1980s. Only in transportation equipment did employment grow in this decade, and then by only 8 percent. Overall manufacturing declined by 3 percent outside the core, and there was a loss of almost 20 percent of jobs in metals industries in this region. Apparently, the same spatial pattern that characterized restructuring in the textile industry was unfolding in the remaining traditional industries.

The divergent rates and directions of employment change for the same industries inside and outside the core indicate an intranational spatial fix at work during the late 1960s and 1970s. The initial shift away from the decaying infrastructure, obsolete plants, and militant labor of the core proved to be only a temporary fix, however. By the 1980s, the traditional heavy manufacturing industries were following the path of textiles and either seeking another temporary spatial fix in international relocation or applying the more permanent solutions of restructuring—technological change, rationalization, and intensification—with all their employment consequences.

Political Consequences of Restructuring

The U.S. economy experienced a net gain of 36 million jobs between 1950 and 1990, despite the huge employment losses in manufacturing. Even in the core, employment grew by 77 percent; outside the core, employment growth reached 210 percent, nearly three times the rate of job growth in the traditional industrial region. One of the long-term consequences of the relative regional pattern of growth and decline in job availability has been a significant redistribution of the U.S. population, which can be discerned both from differing rates of population growth in the various regions and from net migration rates between regions.

In 1950, the core contained seven of the ten most populous states in the Union; the region was home to 47 percent of the nation, with the Middle Atlantic and east north central regions each containing 20 percent of the population. By 1990, only Massachusetts had dropped from the list of highly populated states (it was replaced by Florida), but the core as a whole contained only 37 percent of the population, and the south Atlantic had become the most populous region, with the middle Atlantic and east north central regions appearing as fourth and second, respectively.

Population change figures between 1950 and 1990 indicate that the most rapidly growing regions were all in the South and West. Nationally, there was a 64 percent increase in population, and, with the exception of the east south central region, all the Southern and Western regions exceeded that growth rate. Fourteen states achieved growth rates in excess of 100 percent over the forty-year period; thirteen of these states were in the South and West (Figure 8-4). This population change was driven by a variety of factors. Increasingly affluent and mobile retirees sought warmer climates, and, with the wide-spread adoption of air conditioning, the South was increasingly comfortable. However, the phenomenal population growth of the noncore regions would not have been possible without the economic growth of the region (and the si-multaneous economic decline of the core, which provided the labor force for the growth). As the redistribution of population and jobs to the South and West became more marked in the 1970s the terms "Sunbelt" and "Frostbelt" (or "Snowbelt" or "Rustbelt") became associated with the diverging fortunes of the two very different regions. There has been a great deal of debate about the exact composition of the Sunbelt, but for the purposes of the rest of this chapter, the term will be used with reference to the noncore states (excluding the west north central region, which shares the population trends of the core).

Economic growth in the Sunbelt came from two sources, the first being the already mentioned intranational spatial fix. In 1950, 8.93 percent of the workforce in the South and West were engaged in traditional manufacturing activities, in contrast to 14.4 percent of the workforce in the core. During the next 20 years, the Sunbelt increased its share of traditional manufacturing employment (a gain of 56 percent), while there was a marked decline in the core (a loss of 3 percent). In the following two decades, the intranational spa-tial fix began to break down as international production sites became more cost-effective; however, the Sunbelt still achieved a 7 percent growth of em-ployment in traditional manufacturing industries, with the core posting a loss in excess of 30 percent. Thus, much of the initial impetus for Sunbelt growth came from the traditional heavy manufacturing sector.

However, that growth was fueled by even greater growth rates in em-ployment in what can be termed "nontraditional" manufacturing industries, which include petrochemicals, food processing, printing and publishing, in-struments and related products, and miscellaneous manufacturing. In particu-lar, growth in the petroleum and chemical industries created substantial (if not always permanent) employment booms in many parts of the South and Southwest. The Sunbelt was also the primary beneficiary of job-producing federal spending. Spending on western water projects benefited the construc-tion, agriculture, and food processing sectors; shifting military priorities, which were moving away from conventional weapons tied to the traditional transportation sectors toward high-technology weaponry, boosted employ-ment in aeronautics and other high-tech activities in California, Arizona, Utah, and Washington (Crump, 1989; Rees, 1981).

The most obvious political consequence of restructuring follows from the population shifts associated with job shifts. As indicated in Chapter 6, after each census the process of reapportionment reallocates the 435 congressional seats according to the new population figures for each state. As might be

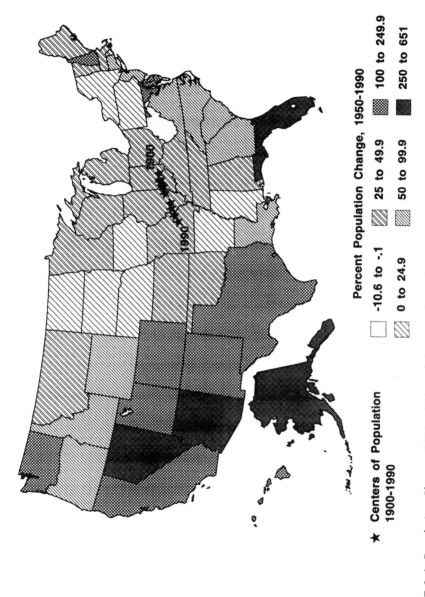

FIGURE 8-4. Population Change, 1950–1990, and Centers of Population 1900–1990. Data from U.S. Bureau of the Census, *Statistical Abstract of the United States*, 1963, pp. 8, 10; U.S. Bureau of the Census, *Statistical Abstract of the United States*, 1993, p. 28.

expected, the core's relative decline in population has led to a commensurate decline in its political representation in the House (Figure 8-5). In 1950, the core controlled 202 of the 435 seats. By 1970 they had lost 12 seats, and in 1990 a further loss of 28 seats reduced the representation of the core to just 162 seats. At the same time, the Sunbelt states' representation increased from 193 to 242 seats. The most rapid growth in representation was in the Pacific region, which saw its congressional representation jump from 41 seats in 1952 to 69 in 1992 (Martis and Elmes, 1993).

Although the redistribution of political power through reapportionment changes the political power of the regions, the primary importance of redistribution lies not in the numerical weight of votes in the House but, rather, in the ability of these new representatives to extract federal monies for their districts, a process known as "pork-barreling." As we have seen, among the most important areas in which elected representative are judged by their electorate is their ability to secure and maintain employment in their district. Nothing is more damaging to a politician's reelection hopes than a declining local economy. Thus, congressional representatives tend to fight hard to gain new federally funded projects, and they fight equally hard to retain them in the face of federal budget cuts (Archer and Shelley, 1986).

Consequently, increased representation in Congress means an increased flow of federal funds to the Sunbelt and a decrease in funds to the core. Each additional Californian representative to Congress increases the lobbying power for federally funded water projects in California. Each new representative for Florida increases the chances that the state will retain all its military bases in an era of cutbacks.

Throughout the postwar period, the South and West have indeed received an appreciable share of federal funds (Johnston, 1980; Archer, 1983; Crump and Archer, 1993). However, the Southern and Western relative advantage in federal spending generally has been greater for defense outlays (Figure 8-6) than for nondefense outlays (Figure 8-7). Although these regions have also contributed an increasing share of federal revenues as their population and economies have grown, research has shown that they consistently receive a much higher share of expenditures than they contribute in revenues; whereas states of the core are equally consistently in a deficit situation, contributing more than they receive. This situation exists largely because of the nature of federal spending in the West, in particular, because of funding for the large areas of federal land that have to be maintained and federal funding for new highways and new water projects. However, increased representation ensures that even where these projects are deemed to be inefficient and unnecessary, they will continue to be funded. At the same time, the Sunbelt states have become more successful at blocking legislation to increase revenues from their districts; witness the successful combined efforts of the Republican and Democratic members from the West to block attempts to increase rangeland fees in 1993.

While the increased political power of the South and West is a direct

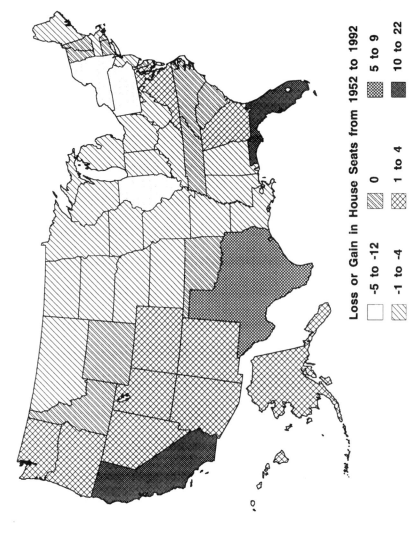

FIGURE 8-5. U.S. House of Representatives Apportionment Changes, 1952–1992. Data from U.S. Bureau of the Census, *Statistical Abstract of the United States, 1993*, p. 268.

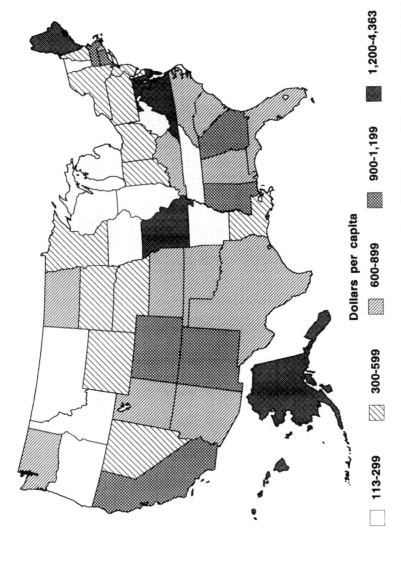

FIGURE 8-6. Federal Defense Outlays, Fiscal Year 1993. Data from U.S. Bureau of the Census (1994a), Table 8.

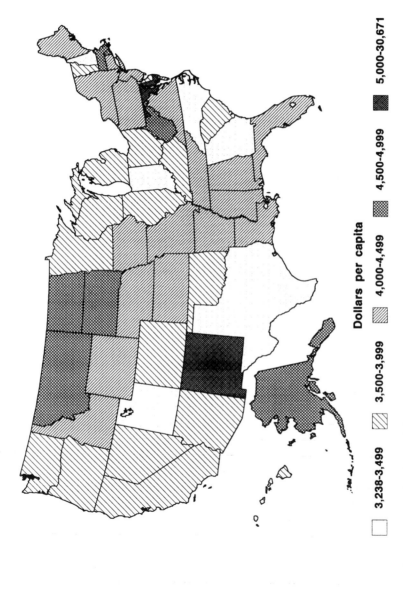

FIGURE 8-7. Federal Nondefense Outlays, Fiscal Year 1993. Data from U.S. Bureau of the Census (1994a), Table 8.

result of their growing economies and populations, it in turn promotes future economic growth by directing and maintaining federal funds to these regions. Thus, while the core suffers from declining infrastructure, with collapsing bridges, disintegrating sewer systems, and deteriorating roads, federal money provides a 90 percent subsidy to California farmers to grow rice and cotton in a desert and underwrites construction of an improved Interstate Highway 70 through Glenwood Canyon, Colorado, which costs over a million dollars per mile.

External Impacts of Restructuring

As has already been mentioned, one of the "solutions" that U.S. corporations applied to their profitability problems in the 1970s was the rapid expansion of operations to overseas production sites. Throughout the 1950s and into the 1960s, the United States was the primary source of foreign direct investment (FDI). However, by the later 1960s and into the 1970s, the volume of international investment rapidly expanded. FDI was driven by a variety of different factors, including the search for low-cost production sites, the quest for new markets, and the desire to circumvent import barriers. In addition, the increased tendency for diversification and the formation of conglomerates led to an explosion of acquisition-based FDI, in particular during the 1980s.

As the volume of FDI expanded, the system also increased in complexity, different motivations for FDI led to a variety of new host sites, and FDI expanded into the less-developed economies, in particular in Latin America and Asia. Simultaneously, the sources of FDI expanded, and European, Japanese, and, by the 1980s, even Third World firms gained the technological sophistication of U.S. firms and followed the U.S. lead in establishing production sites in foreign markets.

By the late 1970s, the United States itself was becoming one of the most popular host economies for FDI. In the manufacturing sector, FDI was becoming especially conspicuous in the Southeast and, to a lesser extent, in the West, so that FDI appears to have contributed to the decentralization of manufacturing employment away from the traditional industrial core (Figure 8-8). Nationally, 10.4 percent of all manufacturing workers, or slightly more than one out of every ten, was employed in a foreign-owned industrial plant within the United States in 1990. In Alaska and West Virginia, the corresponding proportions were more than one in five. All told, 15 percent or more of manufacturing workers were employed in foreign-owned plants in a dozen states in 1990.

By 1982, the United States had emerged as both the primary source and the primary recipient of global FDI. As FDI has expanded, the investors, primarily transnational corporations (TNCs), have become increasingly important players in the global economy. By 1990, TNCs comprised fifty of the hundred largest economic units in the world (Dicken, 1989). While TNCs

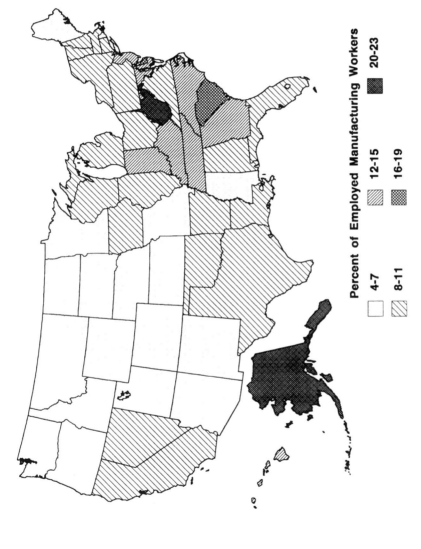

FIGURE 8-8. Manufacturing Workers Employed by Affiliates of Foreign-Owned Companies, 1990. Data from U.S. Bureau of the Census, *Statistical Abstract of the United States, 1993,* p. 799.

Percent of Employed Manufacturing Workers

4-7   12-15   20-23

8-11   16-19

generally have a home country affiliation, management's loyalty is to the corporation, not to the home nation. Thus, these firms are not only indifferent to the economic plans of the host countries in which they operate, but they are equally indifferent to the economic policies and fortunes of their home country. As the global economy has fallen increasingly under the control of TNCs, the influence of the U.S. government has waned not only on external economic events but even on internal economic events.

The complexity of the global economy has also been enhanced by the growth of the global capital market. Expansion in portfolio investment, currency speculation, and international debt financing has created a global financial structure in which the performance of the U.S. economy is subject to the actions of individuals, corporations, and governments around the globe. The ability of the U.S. government to manage the economy, in particular in times of recession, is now compromised by a global financial structure in which national policies and national borders have little meaning.

Economic restructuring has not been the only major global change to affect U.S. political geography in the last decade. While the end of U.S. dominance of the world economy has affected both the internal and external political geographies of the United States, the end of the Cold War has had a profound and far-reaching impact on the way the United States relates to the rest of the world. The ideological basis on which U.S. foreign policy was based during the Cold War has crumbled, leaving the administration with a far more complex world in which foreign policy must be shaped by increasingly interlinked political and economic factors.

The End of the Cold War and the New World Order

For more than forty years, the U.S. position within the world was dictated by the Cold War. By the early 1990s, however, the Cold War had come to an abrupt and surprising end. Structural weaknesses and inefficiencies within the planned economies of the Soviet Union and its satellites became increasingly evident during the 1980s, and standards of living suffered in comparison to those of the West. During the late 1980s, the Soviet Union's Eastern European satellites ousted their Communist governments. Free elections were held in Poland, Hungary, Czechoslovakia, and other former Soviet satellites. The Warsaw Pact was dissolved, and Eastern Europe looked increasingly to the West for foreign investment (Murphy, 1992). Meanwhile, the former Communist state of East Germany was integrated into the Federal Republic of Germany.

Soon the dissolution of the Cold War spread to the Soviet Union itself. In 1989, the Baltic republics of Latvia, Lithuania, and Estonia declared their independence from the Soviet Union. Although the Soviet government sent troops to quell uprisings along the Baltic, many within the international community supported the independence movement. The independent governments of Latvia, Lithuania, and Estonia were recognized by the European

Community a year later. In August 1991, Communist hard-liners attempted to oust Soviet premier Mikhail Gorbachev from power. After several days of confrontation, the coup effort failed, and the Communist government of the Soviet Union collapsed. Several of the former Soviet republics became independent states, and the others joined with Russia to form a new Commonwealth of Independent States, in which political dictatorship and central economic planning were supposedly replaced by multiparty democracy and a market economy.

With the collapse of Soviet communism, the Cold War ended. With the end of the Cold War has come an end to an international geopolitics dominated by military and political competition between the Soviet Union and the United States. No longer are international crises dominated by or interpreted in terms of the Cold War. Yet, thus far, we have no clear idea what new paradigm might replace the Cold War as the focus of geopolitics in the years ahead. What might this "new world order"—a phrase used by former President George Bush during Operation Desert Storm—look like? What might its consequences be for the political geography of the United States?

New World Orders

Geopolitical analysis has suggested that the history of world politics over the past two centuries has been characterized by relatively long periods of stable world orders followed by shorter transition periods (Dalby, 1990; Agnew and Corbridge, 1989). The Cold War world order dominated world politics from the late 1940s to the collapse of Soviet communism in the early 1990s. Currently, we are in a period of transition.

In order to examine and predict what new world order may emerge during the next several years, it may be fruitful to examine previous geopolitical transition periods. For example, the period between the end of World War II and the emergence of the Cold War is recognized as a transition between the Eurocentric world order of the interwar years and the Cold War itself. Taylor (1990) has examined this transition period. Why did the Cold War emerge as the dominant world order of the post–World War II period, rather than some alternative?

In order to answer this question, Taylor noted that the defeat of Germany and Japan and the devastation of Europe at the end of World War II left the world with three powerful countries: the United States, the United Kingdom, and the Soviet Union. He identified five possible patterns of more or less permanent alliances among these three countries and their allies. The five possibilities included a continued alliance among all three countries, perhaps under the auspices of the United Nations; the separate and hostile development of blocs consisting of each individual power and its allies; or alliances of two of the three superpowers against the third. Thus, an alliance of European-centered Great Britain and Russia against the non-European United States was a plausible scenario, as was an alliance of the United States and the Soviet Union against British imperialism. (This alternative was favored by some prominent U.S. politicians, notably Henry Wallace, who ran as a third-party candidate against Truman in 1948.) The final scenario—an alliance of the capitalist, democratic United States and Great Britain against the Communist Soviet Union—was, of course, the alternative that actually emerged.

Since the Cold War ended, some political geographers have been actively trying to identify and evaluate those "new world orders" that could conceivably emerge during the next several years (i.e., Agnew, 1992; Cohen, 1992; de Blij, 1992; O'Loughlin, 1992; Taylor, 1992; Thrift, 1992; van der Wusten, 1992; Taylor, 1993b; Williams, 1993; Demko and Wood, 1994). For example, O'Loughlin (1992), identified ten potential scenarios and evaluated them in order of their likelihood. He argued that the most likely scenario was what he termed "unilateralism by the United States." Under this world order, the United States would remain the only state with sufficient capability to deploy forces to direct international events. Such had been the case during the Persian Gulf crisis of 1990–1991. This scenario suggests that the United States will remain committed to high levels of military spending and to a worldview emphasizing democracy and free enterprise. The validity of this scenario may be questioned, however, in light of the election of 1992, in which the campaign was dominated by domestic political considerations.

A second scenario discussed by O'Loughlin (1992) and also by de Blij (1992) questions whether the Cold War is really over. Conservative opposition to Boris Yeltsin's government in Russia, fueled by poor economic conditions and shortages of basic goods, may eventually reconstruct a hard-line government in the former Soviet Union. Indeed, a right-wing party dedicated to the reconstruction of the Soviet Union scored impressive gains in Russian elections in December 1993. Third most likely, according to O'Loughlin, is a world order dominated by three large trading blocs, or pan-regions. The passage of the NAFTA by Congress in November 1993, along with parallel developments in Europe and East Asia, suggests the creation of pan-regions centered on the United States, Germany, and Japan, respectively.

The New World Order and Contemporary Foreign Policy

Regardless of which potential new world order actually develops, the development of U.S. foreign policy will be linked closely to the establishment of that new world order. Moreover, its development is likely to have profound consequences for national, state, and local politics within the United States. The 1992 presidential election was decided primarily upon domestic policy concerns. Republican President George Bush received high marks from the U.S. electorate for his foreign policy initiatives after he decisively defeated his Democratic opponent, Michael Dukakis, in 1988 (Figure 8-9). His popular Presidential Approval Rating ballooned to over 80 percent following the Al-

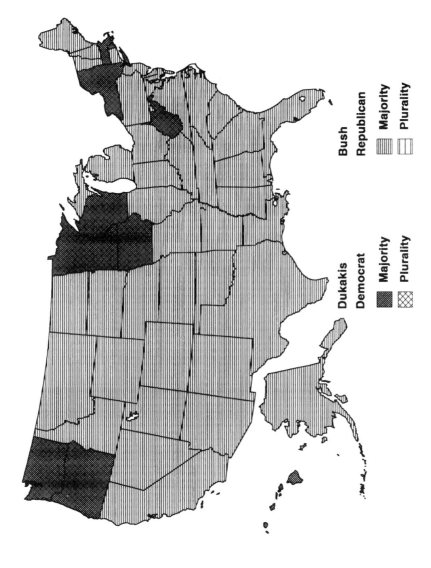

FIGURE 8-9. U.S. Presidential Election, 1988. Data from U.S. Bureau of the Census, *Statistical Abstract of the United States, 1992*, p. 253.

lied victory in the Persian Gulf War in 1991. But as the reelection campaign unfolded, many voters turned their attention to domestic matters, including a weakening economy. In 1992, Bush was defeated in a three-way race by Democratic challenger Bill Clinton, whose campaign focused on the administration's failure to implement effective domestic policies (Figure 8-10). Only a small minority of voters based their decisions on foreign policy considerations, and Clinton articulated few differences with Bush concerning international affairs.

Yet Clinton's election placed the development of the nation's post–Cold War foreign policy into sharp focus. During and after the election, several of Clinton's advisers suggested that U.S. foreign policy during the previous administration had lacked a specific ideological focus and, instead, concentrated on reacting to specific international events (Sigal, 1993). Several of Clinton's advisers have suggested that the new administration will attempt to develop a more coherent foreign policy based on four key issues: a more explicit recognition of global economic interdependence, commitment to democratic governance and national self-determination, concern for collective security through international organizations such as the United Nations, and concern for the global environment and resource base (Madison, 1993).

Most informed predictions concerning the future of U.S. foreign policy are based on a recognition that the global economy and the world political map have become increasingly interdependent. Today's global economy is far more complex and sophisticated than that of the late 1940s, when the Cold War began. As we have seen, manufacturing and communications have become increasingly globalized. Production is increasingly financed by an expanding global network of capital, whose circulation is largely unregulated by individual state policies. Global production networks have been enhanced by the expansion of multinational corporations, the rapid increase in the availability and liquidity of international finance capital ("global money"), and improvements in computers, communications, and other technologies that have expedited the flow of capital across international boundaries (Thrift, 1992). Thus, many regard the development of a post–Cold War world order as bound inextricably to the transition from Fordism to post-Fordism in the global economy.

The increased globalization of the international economy has resulted in a much closer linkage between international politics and international economic policies. At the same time, the collapse of the Soviet system has discredited efforts by states to manage production; numerous countries in addition to the former Soviet Union and her satellites have undergone transition from centrally planned to market-oriented economies during the past decade. The economic health and the political strength of the United States is likely to depend more and more on its interaction with the world economy. Clinton's emphasis on righting the domestic economy in order to strengthen the U.S. position overseas is consistent with this view.

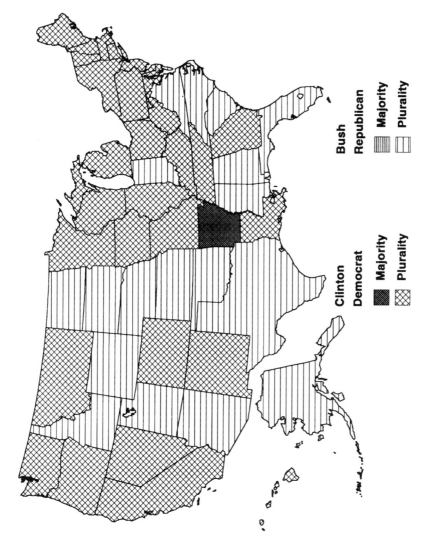

FIGURE 8-10. U.S. Presidential Election, 1992. Data from U.S. Bureau of the Census, *Statistical Abstract of the United States, 1993,* p. 265.

Chapter 9

PRESIDENTIAL POLITICS IN HISTORICAL AND GEOGRAPHIC PERSPECTIVE

Over the course of this text, we have discussed the interaction among major economic, cultural, and political trends affecting the geography of U.S. politics. All of these trends, individually and collectively, have profoundly influenced the outcomes of national and local election campaigns. Our purpose in this chapter is to discuss this influence as it affects the historical sequence of recent presidential elections in the United States. Following this discussion, we present and interpret the results of quantitative analyses of presidential election data at state and county levels from throughout the United States.

U.S. Politics in the Post–Cold War Era

The major transitions that have occurred within the global economy over the past two decades have had a dramatic impact on U.S. politics. The presidential elections of 1976, 1980, 1984, 1988, and 1992 form an interesting and important historical sequence and are likely to provide a backdrop for twenty-first-century elections.

The Electoral Geography of the Late Twentieth Century

The Democratic Party's nomination of Jimmy Carter of Georgia for the presidency in 1976 reestablished the core South as a major political battleground. In the general election, Carter combined a near-sweep of the core and rim South with substantial strength in the Northeast to oust Republican Gerald Ford by a narrow margin, although Texas and Hawaii were the only states in the western half of the country to support the Georgian. Thus, the Democratic Party combined strength in the Northeast and the South to win the 1976 election—an election that set an interesting precedent for the elections of the 1980s and the 1990s.

Four years later, the Republican Party nominated former California Governor Ronald Reagan to challenge Carter. Carter's reelection prospects were dimmed by deteriorating economic conditions and dashed by a disastrously failed effort to rescue Americans being held hostage in Iran. In the end, Carter was unable to maintain his grip on his Southern base, and he was trounced by Reagan, who swept the West and the South and won all of the large Northeastern states as well.

Reagan's enormous popularity in the West and South provided the foundation for his easy reelection over former Vice President Walter Mondale in 1984. During Reagan's two terms, Republican support was strongest in the country's most affluent and rapidly growing areas, including the Sunbelt and suburban areas. On the other hand, Democratic vote percentages were considerably higher in declining or depressed areas. Mondale won majorities in only about 10 percent of the approximately 3,000 counties in the United States. Most were central cities, minority-dominated communities, Native American reservations, and areas dominated by declining Rustbelt heavy industry (Archer et al., 1985). Bush, who was vice president under Reagan, also enjoyed considerable Southern and Western support in his 1988 defeat of Democratic challenger Michael Dukakis (see Figure 8-9). Thus, the electoral geography that began with Carter's 1976 defeat of Ford continued through the 1980s.

In 1992, however, Bush was defeated by his Democratic challenger, Governor Bill Clinton of Arkansas. Clinton's victory was the culmination of a highly successful, geographically based campaign strategy. Whether Clinton's election represents a continuation of recent trends or a new direction in the geography of presidential politics remains to be seen, however (Shelley and Archer, 1994).

The 1992 Election Results

As the popular votes were counted on November 3, 1992, it became apparent that Clinton would win a substantial victory in the Electoral College. The final tally was 370 electoral votes each for Bill Clinton and Al Gore, to 168 electoral votes each for George Bush and Dan Quayle. Perot received no electoral votes, despite his strong popular showing.

Only two previous Democratic candidates in the twentieth century, Franklin D. Roosevelt and Lyndon Johnson, have won as many electoral votes as Clinton received in 1992. He swept the recession-weary Northeast, winning ordinarily Republican bastions such as Vermont, New Hampshire, and Maine. He won the entire Middle Atlantic region and the Great Lakes states, except for Vice President Quayle's home state of Indiana. He won several Southern states that had not voted Democratic since 1976. He also won seven Western states—the best Democratic showing west of the 100th meridian since 1964.

Clinton's success contrasts sharply with the Republican landslides of the 1980s. Analysis of the distribution of Clinton's support indicates that he succeeded where his predecessors had failed by maintaining the traditional Democratic base while cutting into areas that had been dominated by the Republicans in 1980, 1984, and 1988.

The Geography of Clinton's Support at County Scale

In 1992, Clinton ran strongly in those counties carried by Mondale and Dukakis (Figure 9-1). Unlike his predecessors, however, Clinton also cut into Republican strength in suburban areas, the Sunbelt, and the West. Clinton's success in the suburbs proved to be an important key to his successful campaign. He carried suburban-dominated states, such as Maryland, New Jersey, and Connecticut, that had gone Republican in recent presidential elections, as well as Southern and Western states, including California, Colorado, Georgia, Tennessee, Kentucky, Louisiana, Arkansas, Montana, New Mexico, and Nevada, that had been reliably Republican in the 1980s. By holding onto the Democratic voting base and cutting into that of Reagan's Republicans, Clinton was successful in returning control of the White House to the Democrats.

Clinton ran strongly in areas of traditional Democratic strength in the central cities, among minority-dominated communities, and in areas with sagging and troubled economies. In fact, his county-level percentages in many of these counties were roughly equivalent to those won by Mondale eight years earlier despite the fact that Clinton had two major opponents.

The most important shift toward Clinton and the Democrats occurred in suburban areas throughout the United States. The importance of suburbia to the outcome of presidential elections was underscored by the census of 1990, which revealed that nearly half of all Americans now live in suburban rather than central-city or rural communities. Since World War II, the rapidly growing suburbs have been an important source of Republican votes. As suburban populations grew at the expense of central cities, Republican influence on the nation's metropolitan areas continued to increase. In 1992, however, Clinton succeeded in cutting into the traditional Republican base in the suburbs, largely on the basis of his emphasis on economic policy.

The Geography of Bush's Support at County Scale

Clinton's success in wrestling the presidency from his Republican opponent hinged on his holding onto the traditional Democratic base and cutting into Republican dominance of the suburbs, the South, and the West. Conversely, Bush's failure to execute his electoral strategy cost him the election. Bush was

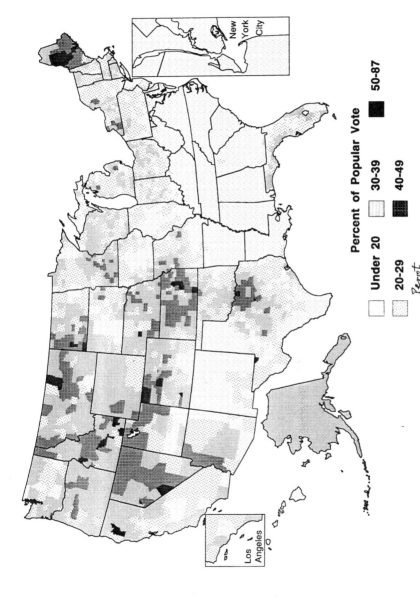

Percent of Popular Vote

Under 20	30-39	50-87
20-29	40-49	

Perot

FIGURE 9-1. Popular Vote for Democratic Presidential Candidate ~~Clinton~~ at County Level, 1992. Data from state secretaries of state (various states); Hoffman (1992), pp. 74–101; Scammon and McGillivray (1993), pp. 73–530.

only partially successful in holding onto the traditional Republican base, and he had no success at all in taking votes away from Clinton in Democratic strongholds.

Despite this failure, Bush ran very well in many parts of the country (Figure 9-2). By no means was the successful Republican coalition of the 1980s confined to the rapidly growing Sunbelt, the West, and suburban areas. The Republican heartland in the 1980s also included several peripheral areas of long-term Republican strength, including parts of the Great Plains and the traditionally Republican Appalachians (with the exception of those mining-dominated communities described earlier, which have been Democratic since the New Deal). In addition, it included parts of the rural South and West that had turned Republican since the 1960s in response to the Democrats' emphasis on civil rights and isolationism in foreign policy. In general, it was these areas in which Bush received his strongest support. Unfortunately for the Republicans, most of these communities are relatively small, are growing slowly, and do not have an impact on overall state and national electoral totals.

Military-dominated counties—those containing major military installations—also strongly supported President Bush. The military community's support for Bush can be attributed to support for its Commander in Chief during Operation Desert Storm, along with apprehension that a new Democratic administration would carry out its promise to restructure and scale back the military. Several military-dominated counties gave Bush an absolute majority of their votes. He won 55 percent of the vote in Dale County, Alabama (Fort Rucker), 54 percent in Santa Rosa County, Florida (Eglin Air Force Base) and 54 percent in Harrison County, Mississippi (Keesler Air Force Base). These totals, though, were far below Reagan's percentages: Reagan had won 77 percent in Dale, 82 percent in Santa Rosa, and 72 percent in Harrison.

Bush also scored comfortable victories in the suburbs of many Southern cities. In general, the gap between central-city and suburban Republican percentages was greater in the South than elsewhere, although the impact of suburban voters on overall electoral totals is somewhat less in that region than in other parts of the country. Overall, Bush's strongest areas were those in which the Republicans had done best in the 1980s. Yet, while Clinton's three-party percentages approached Mondale's two-party strength, Bush fell well below the Republican percentages he himself had won in 1988 and Reagan had won in 1980 and 1984. Bush was much less successful in holding onto the Republican base in 1992 than in 1988, in part because of dissension in the Republican ranks, in part because of Perot's presence on the ballot, and in part because of Clinton's strengths in areas whose support was critical to Bush's reelection effort.

The Geography of Perot's Support at County Scale

Although he won no electoral votes, Perot achieved the best popular showing by a third-party candidate since 1912. While many third-party candidates

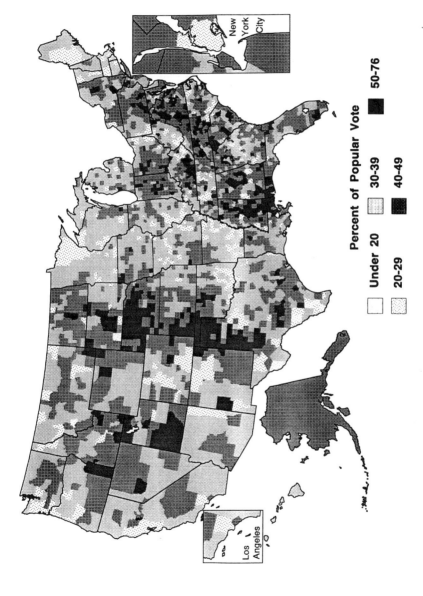

Percent of Popular Vote

Under 20   30-39   50-76

20-29   40-49

FIGURE 9-2. Popular Vote for Republican Presidential Candidate Bush at County Level, 1992. Data from state secretaries of state (various states); Hoffman (1992), pp. 74–101; Scammon and McGillivray (1993), pp. 73–530.

have highly regionalized bases of support, Perot did reasonably well throughout most of the country, although his support was noticeably weaker in the South than elsewhere (Figure 9-3). Only in Mississippi did Perot fail to win more than 10 percent of the total popular vote. Perot's strongest performance occurred in the Rocky Mountain and Plains states, especially outside metropolitan areas. He received over a quarter of the popular vote in Alaska, Idaho, Kansas, Maine, Montana, Nevada, Oregon, Utah, and Wyoming.

How did Perot's presence in the race affect the outcome of the general election? Exit poll responses suggest that Perot took away at least some support from each of his two major-party opponents. Perot voters who were asked whom they might have supported if Perot had not received their support were divided roughly evenly between Bush and Clinton as second choice candidates (Schneider, 1992). But among 1992 Perot supporters who reported that they had voted in 1988, however, former Bush voters were about twice as numerous as former Dukakis voters. Indeed, exit poll data indicate that although more than eight out of ten 1988 Dukakis supporters voted for Clinton in 1992, fewer than six out of ten 1988 Bush voters also supported the Republican ticket in 1992.

Most Perot supporters described themselves as moderates or conservatives, and an overwhelming majority were white. Yet Perot's emphasis on the need to reform economic policy was much closer to Clinton's platform that to that of President Bush. He strongly defended the pro-choice position on abortion and was highly critical of religious conservatives' impact on the Republican Party. Thus, Perot's supporters included people who were opposed to the Democratic Party's recent liberal tradition (dividing this support with Bush) and voters who expressed concern about the state of the economy (dividing this support with Clinton). Overall, though, it is doubtful that Bush could have won even without Perot's name on the ballot (Shelley and Archer, 1994). Perot was relatively weak in those states that Bush had to carry to win, especially in the Great Lakes states and the South. On the other hand, Clinton won several key states despite a strong showing by Perot.

The Perot's strength was concentrated in areas of relatively minor importance in the Electoral College underscores the small-town, nonmetropolitan core of his support. In some ways, the Perot vote can be interpreted as a reaction against the ongoing metropolitanization of U.S. society. The census of 1990 showed that, for the first time in history, more than half of Americans live in metropolitan settlements whose population exceeds one million, yet Perot's appeal was reduced in these settings. Nationwide, Perot received 18.1 percent of the popular vote in heavily metropolitanized Consolidated Metropolitan Statistical Area (CMSA) counties, 19.0 percent in smaller Metropolitan Statistical Area (MSA) counties, and 20.5 percent in nonmetropolitan counties.

Although Perot was stronger in less-urbanized areas, his strength was greatest in those nonmetropolitan counties within commuting range of cities or urban retail opportunities. In the Great Plains states of Nebraska and

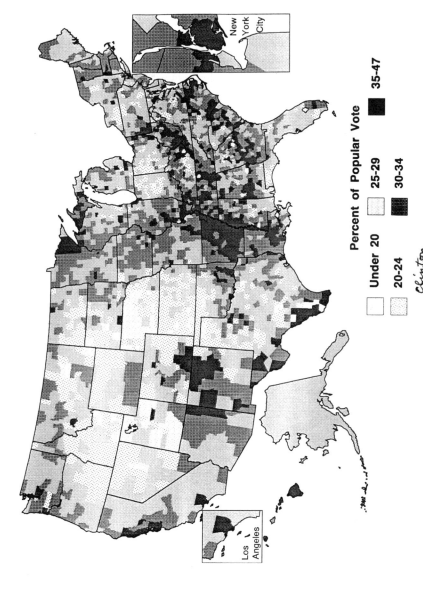

New
York
City

Clinton
Clinton:Perot

Percent of Popular Vote

Under 20   25-29   35-47

20-24   30-34

Los
Angeles

FIGURE 9-3. Popular Vote for Independent Presidential Candidate Perot at County Level, 1992. Data from state secretaries of state (various states); Hoffman (1992), pp. 74–101; Scammon and McGillivray (1993), pp. 73–530.

Kansas, for example, the very smallest and most isolated counties were less apt to support Perot than those whose populations were between 5,000 and 20,000 people in 1990. For example, Perot won over 30 percent of the vote in twenty-eight of the forty-nine Kansas counties in this population range, while he achieved this level of support in none of the eight counties with fewer than 3,000 people and in only one of the state's eight counties with more than 50,000 residents. Similarly, he won over 27 percent of the vote in twenty-six of Nebraska's forty-eight mid-range counties, but in only eight of the Cornhusker State's nineteen very small counties and in none of its three metropolitan counties. This phenomenon suggests that support for Perot was highest in nonmetropolitan communities whose residents nevertheless recognized linkages between their communities and the national economy, and who felt they have a high stake in preserving the viability of their communities.

Overall, it is clear that Clinton's electoral success hinged on his exploitation of the economic issue, on his ability to hold the areas of traditional Democratic strength, and on his success in areas of traditional Republican support. Clinton appeared strongest among those voters who were attuned to the metropolitanization of American culture but who were eager to see government work more effectively. Bush failed to hold the Republican coalition of the 1980s together, with particularly disappointing performance in the South and among blue-collar "Reagan Democrats" elsewhere. Bush did well among voters who tended to view economic trends as being favorable, but this group was a decided minority of the electorate as a whole in the fall of 1992. Finally, Perot proved strongest among those voters who question or regret the transition of the United States to a fully metropolitanized culture.

Analyzing Election Sequences

The simultaneous analysis of elections in sequence provides valuable insight into the underlying forces influencing the political geography of the United States. American politics are characterized by relative stability over time (Turner, 1932; Wright, 1932; Merriam and Gosnell, 1940; Converse, 1966; Burnham, 1970; Archer and Taylor, 1981; Bensel, 1984; Archer, 1988; Polsby and Wildavsky, 1991). For the most part, states or regions that were dominated by the Democrats or Republicans at a given election have tended to remain Democratic or Republican over successive elections (Turner, 1932; Key and Munger, 1959; Shelley and Archer, 1989; Black and Black, 1992).

Critical, Maintaining, and Deviating Elections

Occasionally, however, an election or sequence of elections occurs that precipitates or signals a long-term geographic realignment. Such elections are known as "critical elections" (Key, 1955; Pomper, 1967; Burnham, 1970).

Most elections, however, are "maintaining elections," in which prevailing sectional cleavages continue. A "deviating election" is one in which a distinctive but short-lived electoral configuration is later succeeded by the resurgence of an earlier pattern. Examining the history of U.S. elections collectively, we can identify those critical elections whose geographic impacts are especially notable.

The theory of critical realignment has become well developed in political science over the past several decades. Recently, some scholars have criticized the theory by pointing to the impacts of financing general election campaigns with public funds, the apparent orchestration of campaigns by consultants seeking "free media sound bites," and the seeming attenuation of party loyalties among citizens who split their ballots between candidates of opposing parties or who register as independent voters (e.g., Ladd, 1982; Shafer, 1991; Wayne, 1992). These and other arguments raised by "dealignment" theorists are not easily dismissed, especially for the modern political era. Yet critical realignment theory provides an important basis for geographic analysis of presidential and subnational elections over time.

Moreover, electoral change seldom occurs uniformly throughout the United States. Thus, any particular election conceivably might show features of realigning, maintaining, deviating, or even dealigning processes in different regions of the country. In 1992, for example, the nomination by the Democratic Party of Southerners as both the presidential candidate and the vice presidential candidate may have served to kindle traditional party feelings more in that region than in others. Through comparative analysis of elections in different regions of the United States, we will illustrate that elections that are critical in some areas of the country may be maintaining elections elsewhere.

Identifying Critical Elections

Geographers, political scientists, and historians have used a variety of cartographic and statistical techniques to study election sequences. The simplest is the comparison of maps between pairs of elections. Visual or quantitative map comparison can highlight temporal discontinuities in the patterns of popular election outcomes among states, counties, or other places. The extent to which some areas have become relatively more Democratic or Republican than others is evident from comparing maps of elections in earlier chapters. For example, even casual comparison of the election maps for 1880 (see Figure 3-9) and 1964 (see Figure 4-10) indicates the decline of the Solid South along with the rise of democratic strength in traditionally Republican areas north of the Mason–Dixon Line.

Visual map comparison has frequently been supplemented by the calculation of areal correlation coefficients. Correlation coefficients measure the strength of association between two variables. The correlation coefficient, r, ranges from 1 to −1. A high positive value represents strong direct association between two variables. A negative value indicates an inverse relationship, while a value near zero implies little or no association between the variables.

How can correlation coefficients be used to identify critical elections? High correlations between pairs of successive elections usually implies that both are maintaining elections. States that are heavily Democratic at the first election remain Democratic at the later election. The relative Democratic (or Republican) strength of the states varies little, and hence the election is a maintaining election. On the other hand, a low or negative correlation coefficient indicates the likelihood of realigning or deviating elections.

Unfortunately, simple bivariate correlations may fail to differentiate deviating from realigning elections adequately. These difficulties are even more likely when large numbers of elections are being considered simultaneously. Visual comparison between large numbers of maps is difficult, if not impossible, and reliance on simple correlations is likely to obscure long-term patterns or trends in the data. In response to the problems of simultaneous visual or statistical comparison of many election pairs, political geographers have in recent years undertaken extensive research on historical election sequences using factor analysis. Some of this research has focused on the United States as a whole (Archer and Taylor, 1981; Archer et al., 1985; Archer and Shelley, 1986; Archer et al., 1988; Shelley and Archer, 1994). Other studies have focused on subregions within the United States (Arnold, 1985; Webster, 1988; Shelley and Archer, 1989; Watrel, 1993).

Factor Analysis of Election Data

Factor analysis provides an effective tool for identifying long-term maintaining sequences, which otherwise might be obscured by occasional deviating elections or by the deceptively slow pace of some kinds of realignment processes (Archer and Taylor, 1981, pp. 213–33). The technique permits an entire matrix of correlations to be examined simultaneously (Taylor, 1981; Archer et al., 1988). Thus, it is possible to computationally reduce an unwieldy large correlation matrix between many elections to a smaller and more manageable matrix of similarities between each observed election and a more limited number of mathematically derived factors or dimensions. The factors, or dimensions, can then be interpreted as identifying the most distinctive and representative separate election patterns discernable for the study period as a whole (Archer and Taylor, 1981).

Two types of factor analysis have been applied to electoral research (Figure 9-4). T-mode factor analysis reduces a large number of elections to electoral epochs by analyzing matrices of correlations among elections over areas. Each epoch includes elections whose geographic patterns are similar to one another but distinct from those of earlier or later epochs. Thus, each epoch describes what has been termed a "geographical normal vote" (Archer and Taylor, 1981; Archer et al., 1988). S-mode analysis, on the other hand, groups

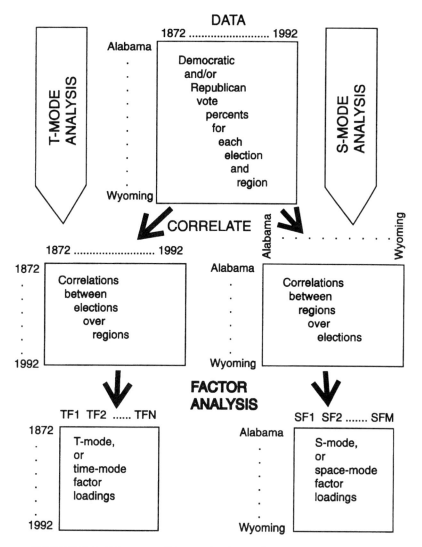

FIGURE 9-4. Schemata of Factor Analyses of Popular Election Returns.

areas under investigation into electoral regions by analyzing matrices of cor-relations among areas over elections. Each region consists of places with sim-ilar electoral trajectories over time.

S-Mode Analysis of U.S. Presidential Elections

Throughout U.S. history, sectional conflicts have pitted Northeastern, South-ern, and Western interests against one another. The tripartite division of the political economy is reinforced by an S-mode factor analysis involving state-level Democratic and Republican percentages of the total popular presidential vote between 1872 and 1992. The analysis yielded three significant factors, which together explained 87.4 percent of the variance. The loading for each state on each factor can thus be regarded as a coefficient representing correlation between that state's electoral trajectory and the trajectory typical of the section in question.

The three factors clearly identified the Northeast, the South, and the West, respectively (Table 9-1 and Figure 9-5). Most of the Northeastern states reported loadings of greater than 0.66 on the Northern factor, Factor 1, as did the Pacific Coast states of Washington, Oregon, and California. In contrast, the states of the Deep South reported zero or negative loadings. Moderate loadings characterized the Great Plains and the Border states.

Factor 2 represents association with the West. The states in the Great Plains and Rocky Mountain regions loaded highly on this factor, as did Indiana. The lowest loadings were associated with the South. Factor 3 represents the South. High loadings throughout the old Confederacy in combination with low or negative loadings in New England and the upper Middle West are evident. The regional pattern is reinforced by a map of the highest factor loading in each state. With few exceptions (the Pacific Coast states and Indiana), each state reported the highest loading for the factor associated with its region.

National T-Mode Analysis of Presidential Elections

In several studies, presidential election returns at a state level have been analyzed using T-mode factor analysis. Here, we describe research involving Democratic vote percentages by state from the elections between 1872 and 1992. (These results are described in detail in Shelley and Archer, 1994.)

T-mode factor analysis extends the scrutiny of correlations involving individual pairs of elections to a statistically simultaneous examination of the entire matrix of all correlations among all elections examined. The factor model employed in previous studies was a T-mode principal axis common factor model with oblique direct oblimin rotation to simple structure (Rummel, 1970; Archer and Taylor, 1981, esp. Appendix A; Norusis, 1988). The appropriate number of factors to be rotated was determined using the strategy of over-factoring advanced by Cattell (1958) and encouraged by Rummel (1970, p. 365). This meant extracting a successively larger number of factors until the last rotated factor exhibited unmeaningfully small loadings, and then choosing the solution with the next lower number of factors for interpretation. Because of difficulties with missing data in factor analysis (Rummel, 1970; Norusis, 1988), it also should be mentioned that the real but analytically awkward increase in the number of states admitted to the Union and

TABLE 9-1. S-Mode Factor Analysis of State-Level Popular Presidential Democratic and Republican Vote Proportions: United States, 1872–1992

State	Factor Loadings[*] Factor 1	Factor 2	Factor 3
Alabama	−.247	.028	.845
Alaska	.438	.847	.387
Arizona	.290	.777	.606
Arkansas	.040	.051	.952
California	.717	.548	.152
Colorado	.165	.840	.187
Connecticut	.873	.332	−.043
Delaware	.717	.361	.261
Florida	−.071	.173	.921
Georgia	−.072	−.081	.953
Hawaii	.966	−.020	.256
Idaho	.141	.964	.121
Illinois	.822	.484	−.013
Indiana	.491	.704	.225
Iowa	.714	.567	−.191
Kansas	.331	.876	−.198
Kentucky	.457	.275	.729
Louisiana	−.189	−.029	.924
Maine	.774	.408	−.298
Maryland	.718	.180	.573
Massachusetts	.877	.034	−.202
Michigan	.797	.488	−.196
Minnesota	.793	.379	−.128
Mississippi	−.358	−.034	.874
Missouri	.490	.359	.647
Montana	.290	.728	.419
Nebraska	.235	.919	−.039
Nevada	.179	.805	.406
New Hampshire	.642	.516	−.085
New Jersey	.824	.444	.041
New Mexico	.541	.663	.546
New York	.910	.246	.093
North Carolina	.203	.173	.900
North Dakota	.458	.805	−.088
Ohio	.723	.601	.096
Oklahoma	.248	.662	.642
Oregon	.664	.634	−.014
Pennsylvania	.877	.378	−.179
Rhode Island	.861	−.020	−.094
South Carolina	−.290	−.053	.887
South Dakota	.480	.772	−.110
Tennessee	.245	.219	.884
Texas	−.017	.064	.982
Utah	.105	.846	.339
Vermont	.662	.412	−.520
Virginia	.033	.226	.915
Washington	.692	.586	.115
West Virginia	.793	.140	.438
Wisconsin	.762	.429	−.032
Wyoming	.362	.896	−.006

[*]Principal axis factors with varimax rotation.

285

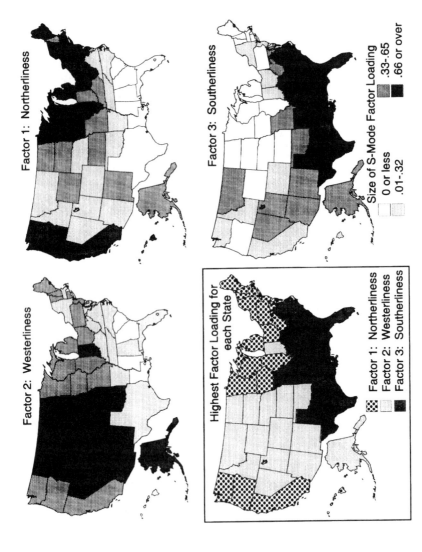

FIGURE 9-5. S-Mode Factor Loadings from Factor Analysis of State-Level Democratic and Republican Popular Presidential Election Returns, 1872–1992 (a cartographic representation of Table 9-1).

participating in presidential elections, from thirty-seven in 1872 to fifty in 1960, was dealt with by pairwise deletion of missing cases (Norusis, 1988).

The Sectional Normal Vote

The results of the analysis yielded seven factors, each of which identified an important period of U.S. electoral history (Table 9-2 and Figure 9-6). The 1870s were a period of transition between the sectionalism of the Civil War and that of the late nineteenth century. During the Reconstruction era, restrictions on voting in the Confederate states were lifted slowly, but Reconstruction was more rigorous in some states than in others.

By 1880, Reconstruction had ended and the Sectional Normal Vote pattern had emerged. During this period, the North was dominated by Republicans, but Democratic presidential candidates scored most heavily in the Solid South. Recently settled and politically volatile areas of the West and industrial sections of the Northeast, including New York, New Jersey, Ohio, Indiana, and Illinois, were the major electoral battlegrounds.

This Sectional Normal Vote pattern was interrupted by the election of 1896, in which Republican William McKinley was opposed by Democrat William Jennings Bryan. Bryan was also the nominee of the Populist Party, which had arisen in the West in response to intense dissatisfaction among farmers who felt that their interests were overshadowed by Northeastern industrial interests that had come to dominate the Republican Party. As we have seen, Bryan's efforts to unite the Populist West and the Democratic South against the Northeast was unsuccessful. Thus, the Populist Normal Vote is associated only with Bryan's campaigns in 1896 and 1900.

After the turn of the century, the Sectional Normal Vote pattern reemerged. It continued to dominate the geography of U.S. politics until after World War II. Although the Great Depression and the New Deal made the Democrats the nation's majority party, the Democratic resurgence during the 1930s had little impact on the relative strengths of the parties over major regions of the United States. Republicans remained strongest in the North, while Democratic strength remained greatest in the South.

Not until after World War II did the Sectional Normal Vote pattern begin to disintegrate during the important but deviating 1948 election, in which Democrat Harry Truman narrowly edged out Republican Thomas Dewey for the U.S. presidency. After 1948, Democratic candidates won substantial majorities among racial and ethnic minorities and in central cities, while Republican candidates showed growing support in the suburbs and started to make inroads into the once solidly Democratic South. The interior and far West became dependably Republican. With the exception of Lyndon Johnson's 1964 landslide victory, the Western states cast only a handful of electoral votes for Democratic nominees between 1952 and 1988.

TABLE 9-2. T-Mode Factor Analysis of State-Level Popular Presidential Democratic Vote Proportions: United States, 1872–1992

	Factor Pattern Loadings*						
Election	Factor 1	Factor 2	Factor 3	Factor 4	Factor 5	Factor 6	Factor 7
1872	−.215	.004	.999	.012	.006	−.000	.001
1876	.175	.031	.758	−.178	−.055	.102	.046
1880	.572	−.128	.540	.008	−.089	.138	−.062
1884	.685	−.051	.380	−.021	−.051	.062	.039
1888	.758	−.080	.196	−.082	−.126	.181	−.049
1892	.577	.338	.269	.205	−.416	.113	−.011
1896	.588	−.230	.276	−.139	.379	−.178	−.331
1900	.939	−.054	.040	−.059	.143	−.104	−.061
1904	.895	.040	.076	.019	−.181	.020	.063
1908	.962	.047	.022	−.025	−.048	−.187	−.014
1912	.904	.056	.024	−.051	−.098	−.064	.094
1916	.910	−.143	−.051	−.114	.072	−.002	−.047
1920	.852	−.108	−.026	−.088	−.121	.033	.222
1924	.853	−.008	.014	−.033	−.144	.025	.268
1928	.999	.098	−.208	.087	.003	.132	−.155
1932	.829	.059	−.005	−.240	.261	−.079	.017
1936	.761	−.020	.106	−.252	.208	.046	−.132
1940	.783	−.039	.017	−.193	−.018	.203	.013
1944	.736	−.026	−.017	−.241	−.053	.269	−.029
1948	−.110	−.011	.230	.491	.592	.060	.466
1952	.232	.161	.243	−.424	−.084	.442	.126
1956	.053	.270	.220	−.729	.260	.224	.132
1960	.001	−.008	.002	.024	.066	.964	−.003
1964	−.151	.147	−.017	.770	.241	.114	.197
1968	−.255	.253	−.139	.563	.059	.330	−.149
1972	−.352	.448	−.101	.346	.111	.236	−.265
1976	.297	.654	.134	−.162	.051	.163	.247
1980	.264	.737	.163	−.126	−.210	.080	.158
1984	−.113	.935	−.082	−.034	−.040	.074	−.058
1988	−.177	.902	−.184	.080	.199	−.064	−.097
1992	.048	.867	.124	.029	−.107	.038	.028

Factor Correlations

Election	Factor 1	Factor 2	Factor 3	Factor 4	Factor 5	Factor 6	Factor 7
Factor 1	1.000						
Factor 2	−.068	1.000					
Factor 3	.405	.006	1.000				
Factor 4	−.583	.134	−.260	1.000			
Factor 5	−.212	−.105	.007	.065	1.000		
Factor 6	.168	.506	.225	−.006	−.019	1.000	
Factor 7	.064	.129	.307	.016	−.064	−.140	1.000

*Principal axis factors with direct oblimin rotation.

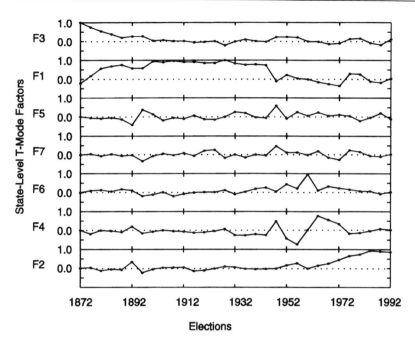

FIGURE 9-6. T-Mode Factor Loadings from Factor Analysis of State-Level Democratic Popular Presidential Election Returns, 1872–1992 (a graphical representation of Table 9-2).

The Liberal and Conservative Normal Votes

In 1952 and in 1956, Republican Dwight Eisenhower's victory over Democrat Adlai Stevenson was due in part to a strong Republican performance in the Southern border states. The "core South," which includes the Deep South states of Georgia, Alabama, Mississippi, Louisiana, and South Carolina, supported Stevenson despite his moderate to liberal leanings. Yet Eisenhower ran well in the Southern border states.

By 1960, the Republicans had begun to make inroads in the Deep South as well. During the 1960s, a "liberal normal vote" configuration emerged, in which the Democrats were strongest in the Northeast, weak in the West, and weakest in the core South. As we have seen, Johnson lost only the Deep South when he trounced the conservative Goldwater in the election of 1964. During this period, support for the Democrats among white Southerners eroded as the national Democratic Party became identified with civil rights, labor unions, and isolationism in foreign policy in response to the Vietnam War (Barone, 1990; Black and Black, 1992).

As we indicated at the outset of this chapter, the election of 1976 ushered in a Conservative Normal Vote period, which has been associated with presidential elections ever since. The Conservative Normal Vote, which highlights Democratic strength in the Northeast, Republican dominance in the West, and a volatile electorate in the South, may reflect the domestic geography of Cold War politics, during which the South was cut loose from its traditional moorings to the Democratic Party. Since 1976, in fact, the Democrats have won only in 1976 and 1992, when their ticket was headed by a Southerner.

T-Mode Analysis by Region

The national T-mode analysis has enabled the identification of electoral epochs, each characterized by a distinctive electoral geography. Surprisingly, however, few have attempted to compare election sequences from one section to another. Here, we present the results of recent research extending the T-mode analysis described above to county-level data within the three major sections (Shelley and Archer, 1994).

As we have seen, T-mode analysis of the country as a whole has identified the Populist era and the elections of 1948, 1960, and 1976 as critical elections. Somewhat different patterns emerge, however, when correlations are analyzed within each of the three major regions. Within each of the regions, we gathered county-level electoral data and subjected the data to T-mode factor analysis using the procedures described above.

In the present study, we applied correlation and T-mode factor analysis to county-level Democratic vote percentages from 1872 through 1992. Before these analyses could be undertaken, however, it was necessary to use GIS procedures to bring earlier historical election data into congruence with modern county boundaries. In older portions of the nation, county boundaries have changed little since before the Civil War. In several of the newer states west of the Mississippi River, however, county boundaries did not stabilize in near modern configuration until the second decade of the twentieth century. Moreover, the number of states participating in presidential elections during the study period increased from thirty-seven in 1872 to fifty-one with Washington, DC in 1964. For the United States as a whole, the number of modern county equivalents included in the analysis rose from 2,359 in 1872 to 3,079 in 1964.

Roughly half of the county boundary adjustments encountered involved simple subdivisions of older, larger units. In these cases, the same Democratic voting proportions were given to each of the resulting modern county equivalents up to the time of partition. In instances in which county boundaries were repositioned, vote numbers were reallocated according to areal correspondence with modern county boundaries before the vote proportions used in the analyses were computed.

The Historical Electoral Geography of the Northeast

In the Northeast, the election of 1928 stands out as a critical election, initiating realignment of the electorate *within* the Northeastern states. Thus, the period of the Great Depression had a substantial effect on the geography of elections in the Northeastern region, although its effect on the geography of elections nationwide was minimal.

Ethnicity and Northeastern Politics

Before 1928, the electoral geography of the Northeast had been influenced primarily by ethnic identity and settlement history (Key and Munger, 1959; Fenton, 1966; Phillips, 1969; Kleppner, 1970; Shelley and Archer, 1989). For example, German Catholic immigrants and their descendants usually voted Democratic, whereas immigrants from the Netherlands usually supported Republicans. This distinction helps to explain the long-standing Democratic loyalties of German Catholic communities such as Dubuque County, Iowa, Stearns County, Minnesota, and Dubois County, Indiana, as well as the heavy Republican majorities in Dutch-settled areas such as Sioux County, Iowa, and Holland County, Michigan. Areas dominated by Anglo-Saxon New England "Yankees" and their descendants were heavily Republican as well, whereas those settled initially by Southerners moving from Virginia or Kentucky, as in much of southern Indiana, were Democratic.

The Great Depression and the New Deal transformed the politics of the Northeast from one dominated by rivalry between ethnic and settlement groups to one dominated by urban–rural competition. The fast-growing industrial cities of the Northeast, populated by large immigrant communities, supported the 1928 candidacy of Al Smith, the Democratic governor of New York who became the first Roman Catholic nominated for the presidency by a major political party. During and after the New Deal, major cities became dependably Democratic while rural areas—and after World War II, the rapidly growing suburbs—gravitated to the Republican party, regardless of the ethnic identity of their residents.

The importance of the 1920s and 1930s to the political geography of the Northeastern states is evident from several studies. For example, the thirteen counties of northwestern Ohio were evenly split in partisan loyalty between 1860 and 1916. Seven gave Democratic candidates majorities in at least eleven of the fifteen presidential elections during this period. Five of these seven contained substantial German Catholic populations, and the Republicans won only two of the seventy-five contests. On the other hand, Republicans won twelve or more of the fifteen elections in the remaining six counties. After 1920, the political geography of the thirteen-county region changed dramatically. Between 1920 and 1980, only Lucas County (Toledo) went Democratic more than half of the time. Eleven of the twelve rural counties supported Republican nominees in at least thirteen of the sixteen counties (Sternsher, 1987).

The shift by rural Northeasterners away from ancestral Democratic loyalties has been attributed to the Democratic Party's increasing orientation to urban interests, organized labor, immigrants, and racial minorities during and after the New Deal and, in the specific case of German-Americans, to Democratic support for U.S. involvement in conflict against Germany before and during World Wars I and II, in contrast to the isolationist positions espoused by many Middle Western Republicans. Comparable results have been presented in studies of Illinois (MacRae and Meldrum, 1960) and New Hampshire (McCarthy and Tukey, 1978).

The importance of the New Deal period was also evident. Factor analysis of presidential election returns for Illinois, Indiana, and Ohio, for example, led to the identification of two factors representing distinctive regions. The Corn Belt factor identified agriculturally oriented counties, generally outside metropolitan areas, that had gravitated to the Republicans. Corn Belt farmers, residing in the most prosperous and productive agricultural region of the United States, resented the New Deal's agricultural policy once the immediate impact of the Great Depression had been eased, and they began to associate the Democrats with high taxes and production controls (Fenton, 1966). The second factor identified the Rustbelt, which consists of heavily industrial areas and large cities such as Chicago, Gary, Cleveland, and Akron. Ancestral Republican loyalties in the Rustbelt gave way to firm Democratic support during and after the New Deal (Shelley and Archer, 1989).

The importance of the New Deal to the electoral geography of the Northeast was underscored in the factor analysis of data from throughout the region. The six factors identified for the Northeast region together accounted for 89.9 percent of the variance in the county-level electoral data (Table 9-3 and Figure 9-7). The factors are numbered in order of extraction, but discussed in order of historical significance.

Factor 1 accounts for the elections of the late nineteenth century, or the early part of the state-level Sectional Normal Vote period. During this period, the two major parties were highly competitive. The larger industrial states, especially New York, New Jersey, Ohio, Indiana, and Illinois, were the key battlegrounds in most elections.

The next factor (Factor 5) identifies the elections between 1896 and 1924. The unsuccessful fusion of the Democrats and the Western-oriented Populists turned the Northeast strongly against the Democrats. Many Northeasterners were offended by Bryan's Protestant pietism and by his attacks on Northeastern financial interests. During the 1890s, strong Republican shifts occurred throughout the Northeast (Phillips, 1969; Burnham, 1970; Kleppner, 1987). Many Northeastern cities that a generation later formed the backbone of Democratic strength shifted to the Republicans during this period. Local Democratic organizations were dominated by Irish-Americans, but many other ethnic groups, including Jewish-Americans and Italian-Americans, tended to support Republican nominees, in part because they resented Irish control of local political machines (Kleppner, 1987).

TABLE 9-3. T-Mode Factor Analysis of County-Level Popular Presidential Democratic Vote Proportions: North Section, 1872–1992

| Election | Factor Pattern Loadings* | | | | | |
	Factor 1	Factor 2	Factor 3	Factor 4	Factor 5	Factor 6
1872	.820	.023	.012	.014	.141	−.128
1876	.999	.048	−.065	.085	−.039	−.087
1880	.921	.002	−.038	.123	.051	−.031
1884	.806	.041	.017	−.123	.175	−.034
1888	.857	−.028	.110	−.078	.083	.066
1892	.911	−.054	.077	−.067	−.011	.159
1896	.109	.029	.344	−.183	.643	−.263
1900	.267	−.016	.131	−.145	.702	−.018
1904	.342	−.004	−.122	−.090	.722	.057
1908	.184	−.069	.098	−.174	.786	.070
1912	.214	−.064	.061	−.190	.740	.185
1916	−.007	−.056	.122	.065	.828	.229
1920	.037	−.035	−.105	.264	.922	−.046
1924	.085	.029	−.160	.149	.884	−.162
1928	.224	.122	.467	−.237	.173	.363
1932	.036	.045	.849	−.372	.154	.007
1936	.213	.008	.849	.201	−.184	.077
1940	.047	.090	.494	.555	.127	.165
1944	.016	.190	.456	.507	.102	.215
1948	−.072	.248	.663	.231	.218	.036
1952	.187	.329	.357	.486	.157	−.040
1956	−.081	.398	.605	.249	.210	−.178
1960	.154	.394	.310	.267	−.034	.331
1964	.050	.529	−.117	.282	.124	.485
1968	−.002	.567	.032	.253	−.040	.430
1972	−.111	.690	.152	−.097	−.092	.367
1976	−.040	.773	.212	.118	.158	−.072
1980	.145	.815	.015	.185	.014	−.031
1984	−.050	.918	.090	−.029	−.110	.041
1988	−.106	.974	.043	−.169	−.046	.056
1992	.118	.999	−.156	−.026	−.034	−.100

Factor Correlations

Election	Factor 1	Factor 2	Factor 3	Factor 4	Factor 5	Factor 6
Factor 1	1.000					
Factor 2	.104	1.000				
Factor 3	.258	.450	1.000			
Factor 4	.022	.386	.153	1.000		
Factor 5	.721	.035	.322	.061	1.000	
Factor 6	.084	.351	.285	.131	−.016	1.000

*Principal axis factors with direct oblimin rotation. Historical data adjusted to modern county boundary equivalents.

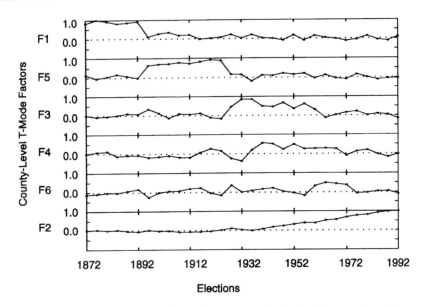

FIGURE 9-7. T-Mode Factor Loadings from Factor Analysis of County-Level Democratic Popular Presidential Election Returns in the North Section, 1872–1992 (a graphical representation of Table 9-3).

Twentieth-Century Realignment in the Northeast

Overall, the early twentieth century represented the apex of sectional politics, with Republican strength concentrated in the nation's core area, the rapidly growing industrial areas of the Northeast. In rural areas, political preferences continued to be determined by ethnicity and Civil War ancestry, but the Northeast as a whole became the nation's most strongly Republican section. The breakdown of this pattern occurred during the Great Depression, resulting in electoral realignment.

The third factor (Factor 3) describes the New Deal period through World War II, a period that marked the development of the modern Democratic Party coalition—including labor union members, racial minorities, European immigrants, and ideological liberals—as forged by Franklin D. Roosevelt. Urban areas gravitated to the Democrats, while Republicans gained strength in rural areas especially after 1940. Political conflict between cities and rural areas remains considerable in many Northeastern states today.

The next factor (Factor 4) identifies the 1940s and 1950s as an additional transition period. These decades, of course, were the period of maximum prosperity within those communities dominated by automobile manufacturing, steelmaking, and other heavy industries. Northeastern politics were often dominated by conflict between labor and management as well as among city, suburb, and countryside. The next factor (Factor 6) chronicles the upheavals of the 1960s, while the contemporary Northeastern electoral pattern (Factor 5) begins to emerge in the 1950s and becomes dominant by 1972. Indeed, the 1992 pattern is most representative of the contemporary period in the Northeast.

The Historical Electoral Geography of the West

The Northeastern factor analyses are very much consistent with the electoral patterns identified as "party-systems" in the political science literature (i.e., Chambers and Burnham, 1967; Kleppner, 1970, 1987). Yet the Northeast factor pattern proved to be quite different from the factor patterns of the West and the South at a county level, complicating the nationwide historical geography of presidential elections and rendering questionable the standard assumption within the political science literature of geographic uniformity.

Volatility and the Western Periphery

During the nineteenth century, the Western periphery was an extremely volatile region. Its economy depended on agriculture and resource-extractive industry dominated by Northeastern capital and financial interests. Even the entry of the Western states into the Union depended on political considerations. Thus, the Republican administration of Benjamin Harrison expedited the admission of six thinly populated Western states—North Dakota, South Dakota, Wyoming, Montana, Idaho, and Washington—into the Union in order to increase Republican electoral strength between 1889 and 1893. Arizona, New Mexico, and Oklahoma, on the other hand, were dominated by Democrats and were not admitted to the Union until after the turn of the century.

The uneasy alliance between conservative Northeastern business interests and Western settlers was tested on several occasions during the late nineteenth century. Objections to economic dominance by Wall Street and major industrial corporations led many Westerners to espouse a variety of third-party movements—the Grange, the Greenback movement, the Farmers' Alliance, and the Populist Party—throughout the last three decades of the twentieth century. Following the failure of populism nationwide, local populist-oriented movements such as the Non-Partisan League of North Dakota, arose in several states, achieving considerable success in electing candidates to state and local office. Moreover, national third-party candidates—Populist James Weaver in 1892 and Progressives Theodore Roosevelt in 1912 and Robert LaFollette in 1924—got their highest levels of support in the West.

The volatility of the West is evident from the low correlations between successive pairs of elections during the late nineteenth and early twentieth centuries. Throughout the West, sharp swings in voter attitude occurred between individual pairs of elections, in part because Western farmers and settlers tended to blame the party in power for their economic woes and vote for the opposition. This tendency remains characteristic of the Great Plains and other primarily agrarian areas even today (Shelley, 1993), but the declining importance of the agricultural sector in Western and other states has dampened the impacts of this tendency on election outcomes at state or national levels. As the West has become urbanized and fully integrated into the U.S. political economy, its politics have stabilized.

During the late nineteenth and early twentieth centuries, the Western states were known as hotbeds of progressive, even radical, thought and political activity. Over the course of the twentieth century, the once radical and volatile West became a conservative and stable region. For example, Rogin (1967) and Gunther (1947) described North Dakota of the early twentieth century as among the most radical of states. Today, the Peace Garden State is one of the more dependably Republican states of the Union, although liberal Democrats continue to enjoy success at the polls in elections to Congress and to state and local offices.

Twentieth-Century Growth and Conservatism

The increasing conservatism of the West has occurred in conjunction with its integration into the U.S. mainstream. In 1930, only 13 million Americans lived west of the 100th meridian (Barone, 1990, p. 17). Many Western communities were only marginally integrated into the U.S. and global economies, and most Westerners lived outside urban areas. Since 1930, of course, the West has been the fastest-growing section of the country. The importance of agriculture and resource extraction to Western economies has declined, while nearly all of the West's growth has occurred in and near metropolitan areas. Los Angeles, Denver, Phoenix, Seattle, San Diego, and the San Francisco Bay area are but a few of the major cities and urban areas whose growth has occurred largely since World War II.

After 1940, all of the correlation coefficients between successive pairs of elections in the West are very high, with each accounting for well over half of the variance. The once volatile West had become quite stable politically, with the Republicans dominating most elections. Yet pockets of Democratic strength can be found throughout the region. In particular, the Pacific Coast region from San Francisco north to Seattle—the area identified by Joel Garreau (1982) as "Ecotopia"—stands out as a Democratic stronghold compared to the remainder of the West. Furthermore, counties with Native American and Hispanic majorities and those containing mining communities have been dependably Democratic since the New Deal. On the other hand, Republicans have dominated most other areas, including the cities, since World War II. The sharp distinction between central cities and suburbs characteristic of other regions of the country is largely lacking in the West, with the possible exception of Denver and the large cities of California.

The Western Factors

The volatility of the past and the relative stability of the present in the West are also evident from the results of the factor analysis of this region (Table 9-4 and Figure 9-8). Nine salient factors were identified, accounting for 89.9 percent of the variance. Seven are associated with the first half of our study period, prior to the Great Depression, whereas the elections since the New Deal are accounted for by only two factors.

The first five factors (Factors 3, 6, 8, 2, and 9) account for the elections between 1872 and 1916. During this period, the Western states were only marginally integrated into the mainstream of the economy, and Western voters frequently shifted their loyalties in opposition to entrenched political interests and economic domination by the Northeast. The elections of 1896, in which William Jennings Bryan won the combined nominations of the Populist and Democratic Parties, represented an attempt to unite the peripheral South and West against the Northeastern industrial core. As we have seen, the nationwide failure of populism resulted in the continuance of the old Sectional Normal Vote for another generation.

After the failure of populism, Democratic strength in the West faded dramatically. In some states, in fact, the Democrats were essentially reduced to third-party status while elections were contested between progressive and conservative factions within the Republican Party or between the Republicans and various state-level third parties such as North Dakota's Non-Partisan League and Minnesota's Farmer-Labor Party. The elections of 1912 and 1924 marked the apex of progressive Republican strength, and Progressive Party candidates Roosevelt and LaFollette ran especially well west of the 100th meridian.

Since the New Deal, only two factors account for most of the electoral variance in the West. Factor 4 is a transitional factor between the New Deal and the modern period, and Factor 1 accounts for the emergence of modern, Republican-dominated Western politics. For several reasons, 1952 was an interesting watershed year. It was the first presidential election after the census of 1950, which marked the emergence of the West as the fastest-growing area of the nation. It also marked the election of Barry Goldwater to the United States Senate from Arizona. A dozen years later, of course, Goldwater became the Republican nominee for president, initiating a conservative movement within the Republican Party that culminated in the election of Ronald Reagan in 1980 and 1984. All of the elections since 1952 load highly on Factor 1, indicating the considerable stability of Western politics since World War II. Yet, as Clinton demonstrated in 1992, the Western states may not remain depend-

TABLE 9-4. T-Mode Factor Analysis of County-Level Popular Presidential Democratic Vote Proportions: West Section, 1872–1992

Factor Pattern Loadings[*]

Election	Factor 1	Factor 2	Factor 3	Factor 4	Factor 5	Factor 6	Factor 7	Factor 8	Factor 9
1872	−.001	.097	.965	.084	−.085	−.111	−.037	−.094	−.080
1876	−.108	.012	.837	.154	.053	.115	−.112	−.030	−.040
1880	.052	−.001	.823	−.022	.133	.116	−.010	.150	.113
1884	.110	−.058	.678	−.106	.242	.267	.040	.082	.209
1888	.121	.174	.371	.007	.305	.492	−.143	.096	.183
1892	.057	−.049	.113	.322	−.147	.784	−.072	−.076	−.083
1896	−.084	.461	−.058	.103	.000	−.161	.109	.622	.160
1900	−.047	.802	.007	.108	−.051	−.068	.070	.113	.090
1904	.030	.773	.375	−.036	−.008	.023	.137	.040	−.045
1908	−.075	.630	−.187	−.115	.039	−.015	.162	−.160	.354
1912	.084	.623	−.137	−.083	.183	.233	.110	−.469	.159
1916	−.154	.076	.023	.057	−.070	−.043	.113	.012	.825
1920	.036	.124	.164	.153	−.056	−.070	.777	.065	.167
1924	−.004	.075	−.226	.070	.111	−.015	.857	−.032	.024
1928	.094	.118	−.061	.142	.889	.010	−.001	.168	−.122
1932	−.091	−.144	.137	.015	.904	−.096	.061	−.194	.073
1936	−.128	.088	.027	.887	.198	.084	−.005	−.075	−.037
1940	.044	.004	.125	.830	−.015	.131	.133	.044	.042
1944	.136	−.079	.084	.767	.043	.131	.090	.104	.082
1948	.193	−.062	.013	.633	.075	−.051	.143	.056	.322
1952	.426	−.011	.125	.547	−.029	.065	.134	.135	.106
1956	.474	−.119	.151	.413	.080	.010	−.157	−.006	.251
1960	.473	.114	.159	.417	.199	−.127	−.120	.157	.022
1964	.724	.106	.007	.268	.032	−.116	−.167	.015	.133
1968	.793	.056	−.021	.267	.022	.003	−.170	.026	.039
1972	.858	.023	−.004	−.040	.145	.112	−.205	−.053	.035
1976	.790	−.032	.112	.094	.065	−.302	−.065	−.324	−.038
1980	.921	−.036	.082	.081	−.132	.011	.212	−.055	−.086
1984	.958	−.059	−.020	−.020	.018	.122	.035	.055	−.064
1988	.999	−.026	−.110	−.093	.032	.017	−.012	.029	−.003
1992	.962	.000	.047	−.107	−.020	.100	.138	.077	−.082

Factor Correlations

Election	Factor 1	Factor 2	Factor 3	Factor 4	Factor 5	Factor 6	Factor 7	Factor 8	Factor 9
Factor 1	1.000								
Factor 2	−.043	1.000							
Factor 3	−.236	−.081	1.000						
Factor 4	.433	.078	.400	1.000					
Factor 5	.223	.147	.247	.262	1.000				
Factor 6	.130	.012	.309	.128	−.136	1.000			
Factor 7	−.092	.397	−.142	.080	.056	−.070	1.000		
Factor 8	−.006	.098	.102	.192	.087	−.034	.072	1.000	
Factor 9	.017	.406	.120	.285	−.245	.024	.329	.059	1.000

[*]Principal axis factors with direct oblimin rotation. Historical data adjusted to modern county boundary equivalents.

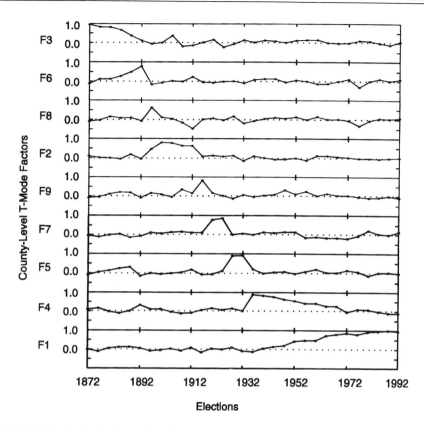

FIGURE 9-8. T-Mode Factor Loadings from Factor Analysis of County-Level Democratic Popular Presidential Election Returns in the West Section, 1872–1992 (a graphical representation of Table 9-4).

ably Republican, especially if the Grand Old Party remains internally split between its ideological and economic conservatives, as has been the case for the past decade.

The Historical Electoral Geography of the South

The post–Civil War electoral structure of the Solid South characterized Southern elections prior to and during World War II. Prior to 1948, in fact, the Democrats won 2,194 electoral votes in the thirteen Southern states, compared to 132 electoral votes for the Republicans. In all but four of the seventeen presidential elections during this period, in fact, all thirteen Southern states went Democratic, although a few areas within some Southern states tended to support Republican candidates.

The sectional cleavages within the South continued partisan divisions

that had been established during and after the Civil War nearly a century earlier. The Deep South from the Carolinas to East Texas, was almost uniformly
Democratic, while Republican strength was marginally greater in the rim
South, including the Southern border states. The major repository of Republican strength in the South was in the Appalachian region, extending through
western Virginia, western North Carolina, eastern Kentucky, eastern Tennessee, and northern Georgia. Here local inhabitants' Republican loyalties
stemmed from their ancestors' opposition to slavery and secession prior to the
Civil War (Key, 1949). Smaller but politically similar pockets of mountain Republicanism were found in the Ozarks of Arkansas and Missouri and other
Appalachian outliers in Tennessee, Kentucky, and Alabama.

The Decline of the Solid South

The 1948 election had a cataclysmic effect on Southern electoral politics, as
already noted. The decline of Democratic influence on the South stemmed
from several factors. The national Democratic Party's strong pro–civil rights
policies, articulated with particular force in 1948 and again in the 1960s, disappointed many white Southerners who opposed the integration of minorities
into U.S. culture and the integration of the Southern economy into the national economy. Democratic strength in the region was further weakened by the
Democratic Party's abandonment of internationalism in foreign policy during
and after the Vietnam War in the 1960s (Barone, 1990; Black and Black,
1992). The Republicans, meanwhile, seized the opportunity to make the
South a competitive, two-party region, especially in the region's fast-growing
urban areas and their suburbs.

The once Solid South has passed into history. Since 1948, the Republicans have won well over half of the electoral votes of the South. The Republicans have won 1,048 electoral votes in the South since 1948, with 640 for the
Democrats and 102 for third-party candidates. During the same period, no
president has failed to win at least several Southern states en route to the
White House. Clearly, the once predictable Solid South has become highly
volatile and competitive in national elections, and critical to national election
outcomes.

By 1964, the geographic positions of the two parties had reversed in the
South. The Deep South gave its electoral support to Republican Barry Goldwater, who opposed the pace of the civil rights movement, in his unsuccessful
effort against Lyndon Johnson. Four years later, independent George Wallace
swept the Deep South (Shelley et al., 1984) despite the opposition of African-
Americans, who had been enfranchised following the enactment and enforcement of the Voting Rights Act. Democratic weakness in the South continued
in 1972, when George McGovern's candidacy, identified with opposition to
the Vietnam War and support for civil rights and affirmative action, was
soundly rejected by white Southerners. Since then, the Democrats have fared

well in the South only in 1976 and 1992, when Southerners headed the Democratic ticket.

The Southern Factors

The Southern factor analysis revealed six factors that accounted for 85.8 percent of the variance (Table 9-5 and Figure 9-9). Factor 3 accounts for the post-Reconstruction elections of 1872, 1876, 1880, and 1884. At this time, the Democratic Party was reasserting its dominance over the former Confederate states. Factor 6 accounts for the Populist era (elections of 1892, 1896, and 1900). The amalgamation of the Democratic and Populist Parties nationally was anathema to wealthy white Southerners, who were anxious to preserve control over the Southern regional economy and who abhorred the threat of a coalition between low-income whites and African-Americans (who at that time overwhelmingly supported the Republicans, the party of Lincoln and the Emancipation Proclamation). In some Southern states, in fact, the Populists had been allied with the Republicans.

In response to the Populist threat, Southern leaders took steps after 1900 to prevent a recurrence. Jim Crow laws institutionalizing racial segregation and restricting African-American access to the political process were enacted throughout the South in the first decade of the twentieth century. As a result, the Deep South came to be dominated by one-party politics (Key, 1949). Although the Republicans made inroads into the border states and the rim South in 1920 and 1928, the Deep South remained overwhelmingly Democratic until after the Dixiecrat revolt of 1948. Thus, Factor 1 identifies the traditional Southern partisan structure, with lopsided Democratic majorities in the Deep South and smaller majorities in the rim South and with Republican strength being confined to the Appalachians and other mountain areas.

Factor 5 represents the Southern revolts of 1948 and 1964, when opposition to Democratic emphasis on civil rights resulted in widespread defection from the Democratic Party. Factor 4 identified the elections of 1952, 1956, and 1960, a period when the Democrats, under Adlai Stevenson and John F. Kennedy, muted their support for civil rights. Meanwhile, Southern legislatures and congressional delegations continued to be dominated by rural interests, lending support to the moderate approach to racial integration taken by the popular Eisenhower administration while frustrating the goals of more liberal activists. Indeed, it has been suggested that the Supreme Court's refusal to address the reapportionment issue in earnest until *Baker v. Carr* was decided in 1962 may have retarded the success of the civil rights movement and its consequent impacts on the geography of Southern politics (Barone, 1990). Hence, the Voting Rights Act and its effects on minority and white political activity have proven to be pivotal to the geography of recent electoral change in the South (Webster, 1992).

TABLE 9-5. T-Mode Factor Analysis of County-Level Popular Presidential Democratic Vote Proportions: South Section, 1872–1992

| | Factor Pattern Loadings[*] | | | | | |
Election	Factor 1	Factor 2	Factor 3	Factor 4	Factor 5	Factor 6
1872	−.102	−.113	.819	.109	.170	−.141
1876	−.017	−.007	.949	−.019	.010	−.121
1880	−.015	.023	.868	−.020	−.069	.164
1884	.128	.028	.868	−.109	−.010	.126
1888	.194	.068	.627	−.018	−.135	.326
1892	−.030	−.024	.029	.033	.108	.935
1896	.189	.077	.181	.035	−.176	.661
1900	.462	.008	.036	−.041	.012	.585
1904	.774	−.036	−.026	−.200	.010	.279
1908	.792	−.007	−.021	−.297	.027	.240
1912	.950	−.045	.035	−.074	−.055	−.009
1916	.945	−.037	.095	−.052	−.054	.002
1920	.849	.040	.002	.026	−.125	.045
1924	.951	.020	.068	.034	−.061	−.090
1928	.572	.263	−.144	.170	−.220	.160
1932	.818	−.018	.098	.177	.092	.036
1936	.912	−.029	−.016	.140	.083	.009
1940	.875	.008	.017	.201	.012	−.006
1944	.787	.033	−.038	.315	.018	.052
1948	−.053	−.133	.053	.238	.908	.064
1952	.248	.166	.054	.758	.087	−.028
1956	.176	.090	.096	.795	.128	.072
1960	.288	.120	.017	.639	.375	−.126
1964	−.175	.134	.054	−.018	.861	−.048
1968	.214	.525	−.052	−.459	.558	−.094
1972	.016	.803	−.091	−.327	.279	−.060
1976	−.026	.562	.189	.552	.138	.037
1980	.137	.760	.132	.381	−.111	−.091
1984	.034	.965	−.028	.076	−.078	−.043
1988	.012	.915	.009	−.090	.138	.037
1992	−.143	.966	−.069	.145	−.156	.103

| | Factor Pattern Loadings[*] | | | | | |
Election	Factor 1	Factor 2	Factor 3	Factor 4	Factor 5	Factor 6
Factor 1	1.000					
Factor 2	.253	1.000				
Factor 3	.217	−.047	1.000			
Factor 4	.245	.180	.240	1.000		
Factor 5	−.066	.241	.109	.037	1.000	
Factor 6	.534	.028	.263	.055	−.224	1.000

[*]Principal axis factors with direct oblimin rotation. Historical data adjusted to modern county boundary equivalents.

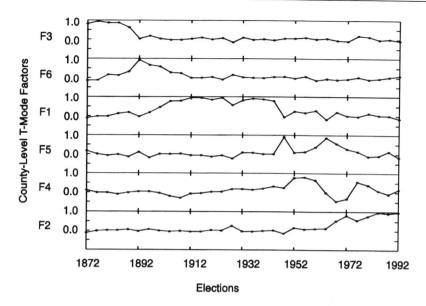

FIGURE 9-9. T-Mode Factor Loadings from Factor Analysis of County-Level Democratic Popular Presidential Election Returns in the South Section, 1872–1992 (a graphical representation of Table 9-5).

The Second Reconstruction

Modern Southern partisan cleavages emerged in earnest after 1968, as indicated by Factor 2. The 1960s had a cataclysmic effect on the politics of the South; indeed, the period has been called the "Second Reconstruction" by some commentators who have noted the collective impacts of the civil rights movement, the Voting Rights Act, and the Supreme Court's desegregation and reapportionment decisions on the economic and political structure of the Southern states (Bartley and Graham, 1976; Cotter, 1981). Today, Southern Democratic strength is greatest among minorities and in central cities. Republican strength is concentrated in suburbs and in highland areas whose early Republican loyalties have remained unchanged. The growth of Republican strength in Southern urban areas was noted as early as the 1960s (Parks, 1966). Factor analyses of electoral returns in the South have underscored the importance of urban Republicanism to the growth of Republican strength in the region (Brunn and Ingalls, 1972; Webster, 1992; Shelley and Archer, 1995).

Factor 2, the Second Reconstruction factor, accounts for all of the elections since 1968, when the Second Reconstruction was completed. The election of 1992 typifies the sectional cleavages within the South represented by this factor. African-Americans supported Clinton with large majorities, and African-American-dominated counties, such as those in the Mississippi Delta, the Black Belt of Alabama and Georgia, and parts of the Tidewater regions of Virginia and North Carolina, supported him with large majorities. Heavily Hispanic south Texas and the Cajun country of southern Louisiana also went strongly for Clinton, as did some traditional Democratic strongholds, such as middle Tennessee and the coal-mining communities of eastern Kentucky, which had also supported Johnson in 1964. Bush, on the other hand, was strongest in suburban areas, in military-dominated communities, such as Charleston and Pensacola, and in rural areas of the Southwest, although Perot cut heavily into President Bush's strength in rural Oklahoma and Texas. Clinton's strength in cities, among minority voters, and among Southern populists was sufficient to enable him to split the region with Bush and win the election nationwide.

Clearly, Clinton's 1992 victory put to rest any premature notion of a solid Republican South, and it indicates the continuing willingness of many working-class white voters to support Democratic candidates. Clinton's coalition of African-Americans, urban residents, and working-class white voters was strong enough to make him competitive across the South, guaranteeing a nationwide victory. Will future elections in the South be determined on the basis of race, class, or other factors? Since the Populist era, Southern populists have dreamed of a coalition between "rednecks and blacknecks," that is, low-income whites and African-Americans. The extent to which political cleavages in the South will be drawn primarily on the basis of race or class remains uncertain, but it is evident that Arkansas native Clinton succeeded in blunting the impact of race on the internal politics of this volatile region. That Clinton's strongest successes occurred in peripheral Southern states with relatively low African-American populations, including Arkansas, Louisiana, Tennessee, and Kentucky, adds credence to this observation.

National County-Level T-Mode Analysis

We have already seen that county-level analysis of the three regions has shown electoral epochs distinctive from those identified within state-level national analysis. To what extent can these differences be attributed to the fact that data had been collected at the state rather than the national level? In order to address this question, we undertook an analysis of all of the counties and county equivalents throughout the fifty states.

The national county-level factor analysis (Table 9-6 and Figure 9-10) can be regarded as an amalgamation of the three regional factor analyses. Nine salient factors were extracted, together explaining 92.8 percent of the variance in the county-level data. Several interesting differences emerged between the state-level and the national-level analyses.

The Sectional Normal Vote period, which forms a single factor in state-level analysis (Archer and Taylor, 1981; Shelley and Archer, 1994), is divided into several key periods at the county level. Factors 3, 8, and 6 account for

TABLE 9-6. T-Mode Factor Analysis of County-Level Popular Presidential Democratic Vote Proportions: United States, 1872–1992

	Factor Pattern Loadings[*]								
Election	Factor 1	Factor 2	Factor 3	Factor 4	Factor 5	Factor 6	Factor 7	Factor 8	Factor 9
1872	.048	−.063	.916	.119	−.044	−.042	−.193	−.073	.120
1876	.022	.025	.918	.008	−.038	−.007	−.001	.025	.002
1880	−.055	.025	.851	−.051	.027	.096	.117	.116	−.054
1884	.044	.024	.797	−.009	.080	.133	.125	.113	−.094
1888	−.021	.011	.554	−.135	.110	.216	.189	.297	.041
1892	.099	.009	.133	−.003	.043	−.062	−.032	.882	.001
1896	.040	.001	.105	−.012	.002	.941	−.027	−.068	.013
1900	.514	−.017	.022	.024	.042	.510	−.066	.123	.064
1904	.722	.026	.071	−.025	.011	.069	−.011	.241	.043
1908	.800	−.023	−.001	.020	.122	.202	.017	.095	−.029
1912	.784	.008	.101	−.044	.026	−.008	.122	.050	.078
1916	.615	−.002	.079	.019	.011	.185	.308	−.054	.013
1920	.667	.100	−.004	.044	−.176	.150	.120	.131	−.004
1924	.742	.082	.101	.029	−.182	−.014	.076	.108	.031
1928	.329	.035	−.002	−.329	.276	.081	.135	.063	.583
1932	.386	−.012	.201	−.038	.073	.019	.505	−.105	.212
1936	.242	−.005	.031	.064	.044	.100	.612	.080	.175
1940	.253	.069	.005	.093	−.090	.083	.505	.219	.146
1944	.171	.077	−.042	.078	−.077	.106	.481	.252	.250
1948	.053	−.079	.047	.938	−.073	.044	.123	−.001	.033
1952	.011	.210	.040	.162	−.295	.116	.117	.218	.496
1956	−.125	.186	.082	.150	−.288	.204	.196	.048	.554
1960	−.048	.059	.071	.226	.021	−.007	.062	.035	.789
1964	−.004	.088	.042	.739	.283	−.141	−.233	−.027	.109
1968	−.104	.372	−.111	.392	.562	−.057	.064	.055	−.051
1972	−.169	.600	−.104	.115	.522	−.023	−.052	−.034	.085
1976	.141	.610	.256	.105	−.216	−.069	.120	−.083	.237
1980	.206	.714	.152	−.010	−.205	−.114	.043	.137	.144
1984	−.040	.928	−.052	−.030	.059	−.016	.030	.069	.059
1988	−.026	.917	−.025	.070	.189	.032	.062	−.115	−.065
1992	.057	.957	−.019	−.077	−.078	.056	−.096	.109	.015

Factor Correlations

Election	Factor 1	Factor 2	Factor 3	Factor 4	Factor 5	Factor 6	Factor 7	Factor 8	Factor 9
Factor 1	1.000								
Factor 2	.107	1.000							
Factor 3	.450	.060	1.000						
Factor 4	−.112	.297	.124	1.000					
Factor 5	−.149	.221	−.224	.125	1.000				
Factor 6	.559	−.002	.422	−.147	−.058	1.000			
Factor 7	.549	.195	.268	.020	−.136	.440	1.000		
Factor 8	.550	.276	.475	−.070	−.085	.333	.340	1.000	
Factor 9	.397	.449	.355	.279	−.142	.226	.472	.290	1.000

[*]Principal axis factors with direct oblimin rotation. Historical data adjusted to modern county boundary equivalents.

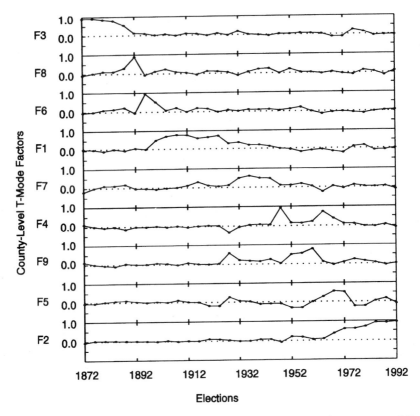

FIGURE 9-10. T-Mode Factor Loadings from Factor Analysis of County-Level Democratic Popular Presidential Election Returns in the United States as a Whole, 1872–1992 (a graphical representation of Table 9-6).

the 1870s and 1880s, the election of 1892, and the Populist era respectively. Factor 1 then emerges, accounting for the elections of 1900 through 1924, the height of the Sectional Normal Vote period.

The New Deal transition is represented by Factors 9 and 7. The latter accounts for Franklin Roosevelt's Democratic coalition (1932 through 1944), while the former combines Al Smith's candidacy in 1928 with the elections of 1952, 1956, and 1960. Factor 4 (1948 and 1964), emerges, followed by the elections of 1968 and 1972 in Factor 5 and the contemporary Conservative Normal Vote since 1972 in Factor 2. Three recent elections—1984, 1988, and 1992—load very highly on this factor. That the three elections are highly correlated shows the extent to which support for Republican nominees has declined uniformly throughout the country. Eight short years after Ronald Reagan's "morning in America" landslide, the Republicans were unceremoniously evicted from the White House.

Examining the election from the perspective of 1992, we can see from the regional and national T-mode analyses that the 1992 election was a maintaining election—essentially an unsuccessful referendum on the economic policies of Reagan and Bush. To be sure, state-level factor analysis of Republican votes showed somewhat less continuity between the 1992 election and its immediate predecessors (Shelley and Archer, 1994), in part because of Perot's candidacy and perhaps also because of the disarray of a Republican Party deeply divided between supporters of Republican economic initiatives and advocates of conservative positions on social issues, or "family values." Whether the results of the 1992 election imply relatively uniform shifts in favor of one party or the other or whether it involves a deeper and more lasting realignment of the electorate remains to be seen.

Chapter 10

POLITICAL GEOGRAPHY OF THE TWENTY-FIRST CENTURY

Over the past four centuries, the U.S. polity has reached levels of cultural and geographic inclusiveness, as well as power and influence, unimagined by the English colonists who founded Jamestown in 1607. The twenty-first century—the fifth in the history of European settlement of North America—is now only a few years away. With the dawn of each new century has come a wealth of literature predicting the future of various aspects of U.S. society.

During the 1880s and 1890s, for example, there arose a large literature that was intended both to predict the future and to propose social reform. Much of this literature was inspired by Edward Bellamy's classic novel *Looking Backward* (Bellamy, 1888). *Looking Backward* was the leading bestseller of the late nineteenth century. For several years, in fact, sales of *Looking Backward* were second only to those of the Bible in the United States.

In *Looking Backward*, a young Boston gentleman, Julian West, underwent hypnosis as a cure for chronic insomnia. One night, West hypnotized himself into a deep sleep. During the night, his house burned down, leaving him undisturbed and undiscovered in his underground bedroom. He remained asleep until awakening in the year 2000.

The remainder of *Looking Backward* is an account of West's reactions to the Boston of the then-distant future. In describing West's reactions to changes in Boston, Bellamy tried to predict the future while criticizing contemporary conditions. Many of Bellamy's predictions—including credit cards, shopping malls, computers, and cable television—proved surprisingly accurate. He was notably less successful, however, in predicting some of the social revolutions of the twentieth century, such as the rise and fall of communism, the demise of colonialism, and the improved status of women.

As the twentieth century draws to a close, experts have already begun to make predictions about the twenty-first. As Bellamy did a century ago, contemporary journalists, social scientists, and other experts are hard at work in reviewing the century past, evaluating the state of society today, and providing educated guesses about the future. Our purpose in this chapter is to venture some predictions about possible changes in the structure of U.S. political geography in the twenty-first century. In doing so, we hope to anticipate those changes in political geography that future students of political geography will describe from the standpoint of history. Our discussion will relate to major issues addressed in previous chapters, including culture, representation, elections, and relationships among individuals, government, and the world economy.

Changes in political organization do not occur in isolation. Rather, they occur in response to combinations of technological innovations, changes in values and belief systems, changes in the global economy, and political events in the United States and elsewhere. In the United States and other democracies, the structure of government and politics encourages the development, import, and exchange of new ideas. Ideas can emerge from a variety of sources: from the genius of individuals within and outside the United States, from other cultures, through new technologies, and in many other ways. Through a variety of media, these new ideas are disseminated to people in other places. Over time, these new ideas influence attitudes, cultures, policies, and legislation. Such is the evolution of new ideas that those considered visionary or impractical in the past may be commonplace in the present, and indeed may come to be regarded as archaic or obsolete in the future.

Revising the Constitution

We begin our gaze into the crystal ball of the future of the U.S. polity by considering the possibility of changes in the Constitution of the United States. As we saw in Chapter 2, the Constitution provides the general framework of U.S. governance. It defines the duties, responsibilities, and privileges of the executive, legislative, and judicial branches of government, the rights of citizens, the qualifications required of those seeking or holding public office, the process of enacting legislation, and many other aspects of governance.

That the Constitution, which is the oldest such document in the world today, has survived more than two centuries of extraordinary economic, cultural, social, demographic, and environmental change is testimony to its vitality. Yet the Constitution, like all constitutions, is inevitably a product of the place and time in which it was written. We saw in Chapter 5 the extent to which the constitutions of the fifty states can be categorized according to where and when they were written. For example, the constitution of Oklahoma, a product of the Populist era written by natives of the South and the lower Middle West, differs markedly from the constitution of Vermont, a document written more than a century earlier and closely associated with New England's moralistic political culture.

The Worldview of the Framers

The framers of the Constitution believed that the initial document would underlie the structure of U.S. governance for many generations. Yet they recognized the likelihood—indeed the inevitability—of social, economic, and political changes that would necessitate constitutional revision. The twenty-seven amendments that have been added to the Constitution are testimony to the process of constitutional change. As we have seen in earlier chapters, many of these amendments have had the effect of democratizing the polity. At the time the Constitution was written, U.S. public life was dominated by a small elite of white males. The framers represented this elite: All were Caucasian males, and most had achieved wealth and high social status in business or the professions. Most were of English descent, although a few had immigrated from elsewhere.

By comparison with contemporary Americans, the framers were a homogeneous lot. They came from similar backgrounds, spoke the same language, and shared similar views on politics, religion, the rights of citizens, and the responsibilities of those in charge of government. These first citizens, legislators, and politicians had rather limited worldviews. Their travels were restricted to places close by, in part because of poor transportation and communication. Although some had close or direct experience with England and limited parts of continental Europe, their main concern was establishing some political order to the newly independent Thirteen Colonies.

As we saw in Chapters 2 and 3, the United States at the time the Constitution was written was a collection of largely rural settlements along the Atlantic seaboard. Well over 90 percent of Americans lived in rural areas. When we view the Constitution as a document written by a small group of elite white males in an isolated rural society, it is not difficult to understand problems that have arisen since in regard to issues of citizenship, rights, representation, governmental responsibilities, elections, and the separation of powers. The Constitution does not include many of the words and phrases that are currently used in political dialogue, proposed legislation, enacted laws, or court decisions, such as "urbanization," "suburbanization," "minorities," "women," "environment," "gender," and "technology"—all of which, as we have seen, have influenced U.S. political geography dramatically during the more than two centuries of independence. Also not mentioned in the Constitution are lobbies and special interest groups, telecommunications, the elderly, children, health care, and computers. The Framers could not anticipate many of the controversies characteristic of modern U.S. society, notably over guaranteeing the rights of women and minorities, protecting society from environmental polluters, providing security and health care for children and elderly, and ensuring fairness in representation.

Will the Constitution Be Amended?

As we saw in Chapter 2, amending the Constitution requires a proposed amendment to be approved by a two-thirds majority of each house of Congress and then approved by three-fourths of the state legislatures. The states have seven years in which to adopt the amendment. If, after that time, the necessary three-quarters have not ratified it, the proposal is defeated. Such was the case of the failure of the proposed Equal Rights Amendment during the 1970s.

Should the necessary states fail to adopt the amendment, then supporters of the proposal will look to subsequent congressional legislation or the courts to support their proposal. Thus, for example, proponents of the Equal Rights Amendment have subsequently promoted their views through legislative and judicial activity, while the constitutions of several states now include equal rights amendments.

It is not easy, nor was it meant to be easy, to amend the Constitution. Constitutional change requires a broad consensus within the polity. Yet the requirement that the legislatures of three-quarters of the states must support any amendment means that small states, with a small percentage of the total U.S. population, have veto power over many crucial constitutional issues. There are few very large states—a presidential candidate winning the electoral votes of the country's twelve largest states is assured the presidency—and while they hold the sizable majority of the U.S. population, they are not numerous enough, even if their legislatures voted alike on an amendment, to see amendments added. Even if one counted the states with dominant traditionalist, moralistic, and individualistic political cultures, no one group in itself would be able to muster the three-quarters of the states necessary to ensure ratification of an amendment. The result is that those amendments that are proposed must be general enough to garner support across a wide range of political cultures and across both large and small states.

Those supporting constitutional changes or wishing the document to be contemporary rather than dated in its language and interpretation see flaws in the present procedures. And these criticisms are voiced not only by traditionalists but by reformers (if we can use those labels) as well. From time to time, especially when crucial problems seem to go unaddressed for reasons of political in-fighting or archaic language or interpretation of the Constitution, there are calls for a new constitutional convention. These calls are generally citizen-based; it is unusual for elected public officials to generate such calls.

Article V of the Constitution provides that a Convention for proposing amendments can be called at the request of two-thirds of the state legislatures.

Such a convention has never been called, and thus the ramifications of Article V are uncertain. The major question is on what basis such a convention can be called. One position is that a convention can only be called to address a specific issue. The other position, with equal weight in legal arguments, is that once a convention is called, the conclave can address any topic delegates wish to consider. In view of these differences of opinion, it is not difficult to understand why there has been no such convention called in recent years. If one opened up discussion among delegates and committees to discuss a variety of neglected or thorny political issues, one could easily envision weeks or months devoted to issues unrelated to the original goals of those promoting the convention in the first place.

Aside from calling a constitutional convention and specifying whether its agenda was to be limited or catholic, there would be several other issues to be resolved. Who would issue the call? Where would the convention take place? To what extent would ordinary Americans participate in selecting delegates? Would the convention's membership be representative of the demographics of U.S. society? Or, on the other hand, would it be representative of those elected to Congress, in which case women, minorities, and certain citizen interest groups would be seriously underrepresented? Who would issue the charges to the committees and the convention, and what role would Congress and state legislators play in any proposed amendments or an entire new document? Perhaps it is because of these legal difficulties that there has been no second constitutional convention, why there have been so few amendments during the past two centuries, and why members of legislatures and courts continue to wrestle with the existing document to interpret it for contemporary U.S. society.

Identity, Territory, and Representation

As our discussion in Chapter 6 has implied, one of the most fundamental issues that any constitutional convention would need to address is that of the relationship between cultural identity, territory, and representation. Americans are not different from other cultures in their strong attachment to place. Ties to place were especially strong among early agrarian societies, in which people worked in some of the same fields as had their ancestors and often lived in the same houses and small towns. Being born, being raised, and living one's working and retiring years in the same place contributed to a sense of permanence and tradition. Crude and expensive systems of communication and transportation discouraged long-distance travel, reinforcing individual loyalty to place. Many people did not venture far from their home towns. Travels to distant markets may have been a rarity, and few Americans undertook trips that required several days travel.

At the same time, millions of Americans participated actively in the settlement of the western frontier. Many of the original settlers of the Pacific

Northwest, for example, journeyed overland along the Oregon Trail, which extended for nearly two thousand miles between Council Bluffs, Iowa, and Portland, Oregon. The cross-country journey required six months, and few parties survived the trip without the tragic loss of one or more persons to cholera and other diseases, accidents, or food shortages—causes that killed far more westward travelers than did Native American attacks. Anxious friends and relatives "back home" were often obliged to wait a year or more for news that loved ones had completed the trip successfully. By today's standards, westward settlers were venturing into an unknown and potentially hostile environment with little or no opportunity to preserve ties with familiar places.

Tension between newcomers and residents has often influenced the political organization of U.S. communities. Those already in residence would often seek to preserve their own traditions, whether it be ways of defining groups within society (as equals or inferiors), ways of determining eligibility to participate in the political processes of the place or territory, or assigning responsibility to the government to preserve the status quo or provide public goods. Those who sought to retain their position would adopt new and creative ways to solidify their positions in power and governance. Any change coming from new groups moving into the community or newcomers wishing to participate in the processes of governance would be unwelcome, just as any efforts by a central government, socially and spatially separated from the supporters of traditionalism, would be challenged.

The framers of the Constitution were very mindful of the importance of place in the evolving nation. They were living and writing at a time when there was little mobility for large numbers of voters and little diversity among the nation's initial settlers, and when methods of communication between places were crude, at best. As was mentioned in Chapter 2, one of the thorny questions that arose in the formative years of the democracy was the issue of representation in government: What criteria should be used to define how individuals and groups would be represented in government? Since there was already a strong attachment of people to places, in part because of land ownership, territory became the major criterion used to define representation. Where one lived was important in defining one's rights and one's representation. Territory seemed to be the most reasonable criterion to early framers of the constitution, for it could be clearly defined using surveying methods and the defined spaces could be depicted on maps. Since there was little mobility or communication with places long distances away, the most appealing way to apportion representation was according to places of residence or places of common interest among homogeneous populations living in relatively close proximity.

The fact that territory was used to define political identity and representation was one of the most important decisions to affect the identity of the nation's residents. How else might the early decision makers have addressed representation? Leaders could have been elected at large and without any territorial home or base, much as had been done in England. But the decision makers, who had fresh memories of the flaws in the English system thought this method of selecting representatives unfair. That is, while a system of selecting representatives without territory was possible, it was not considered politically prudent; leaders wanted to ensure that they came from some definable political base or territory, and voters subsequently also wanted to elect those who had a home locally or who were familiar with their local problems, economies, and social constituents.

In the historical context, it is not difficult to understand the importance of identity with territory or the association of territory with representation: This was a time of limited geographic mobility and of little transportation between or communication with distant people and places. Since the late eighteenth century, however, this has changed as the nation's political and social spaces have expanded. Nevertheless, U.S. democracy is strongly defined by and associated with delimited spaces, including not only the states themselves but also the counties, cities, and other bounded spaces within states or regions. Critics of the primacy of territory in representation point to the fact that boundaries drawn decades or centuries ago continue to influence national decision making.

Over the more than two centuries since the Constitution was originally written and ratified, four fundamental changes have occurred that are very important in addressing the meaning of identity, territory, and representation in the U.S. polity. First, the nation's population continues to increase, although rates of population growth are uneven and some states and some metropolitan areas are experiencing only very slow growth, or even decline.

Second, there are new mixes of ethnic and racial groups that comprise the nation's population. Whereas "We the People" meant white Europeans in the late 1700s, today it includes people who have roots on all continents and among most of the world's cultures and ethnic groups. In short, a rich tapestry of ethnicity and nations best depicts those who live within the U.S. political spaces and who are its citizens.

Third, while ties to place and region remain strong, Americans' awareness of distant peoples and places is substantially greater than was the case in the late eighteenth century. This knowledge also extends to information about current events and problems, political controversies, and the personalities, achievements, and opinions of candidates for public office and other political leaders. Radio, television, and national newspapers and magazines promote an extraregional consciousness.

Fourth, the mobility of Americans continues to increase with each generation. Improved transportation and communication, especially during the past half-century, have brought distant places closer together. What was considered a long distance during the covered-wagon or rail days is nothing in the face of the ease of traveling across the continent by air, using the interstate highways for rapid coast-to-coast travel by car, or making phone calls or electronic mail connections instantly to places, large and small, that were impossible to reach this way even fifty years ago.

As a result of these changes, the U.S. social and cultural scene is much different than it was two hundred years ago. Today, the nation is more densely populated, highly urbanized, and characterized by much greater cultural diversity and heterogeneity than was the world of the framers of the Constitution. Transport and communication networks reinforce awareness of national issues. Yet some have argued that these dynamic changes in population and technological advances in the ways we move about and communicate are constrained by a political system that reflects the agrarian part of our heritage. That is, the case can be made that Americans are living under a system of politically organized spaces that still represents the relatively immobile and parochial population of two centuries ago.

The debate concerning the constitutionality of North Carolina's congressional districts as addressed by the Supreme Court in *Shaw v. Reno* (see Chapter 6) highlights the question of whether the same relationships between identity, territory, and representation used to elect government officials in the past will continue to be useful in the future. Many have argued that territoriality is no longer an accurate or effective way of defining communities of interest (Guinier, 1994). While few people dispute the general contention that representative districts should be based on communities of interest, many people may no longer identify with communities of interest based on contiguous territory. Rather, their community includes individuals and groups and special interests in other locations, which might be close by but which might be long distances from where they reside. What we are witnessing in this definition of a community is a place-spanning network, not a physically bounded space.

Most contemporary Americans identify themselves with many different communities of interest. Many belong to a large range of organizations representing such communities, which might include communities promoting cultural or ethnic awareness, regional identity, religion, occupational goals, political agendas, and many others. An African-American high school science teacher in Little Rock, Arkansas, for example, might belong to the NAACP, a neighborhood historic preservation society, the Methodist church, the American Federation of Teachers, the National Organization for Women, the National Audubon Society, and many other organizations. Each of these organizations, in effect, can be regarded as representing a particular community of interest. Some of these communities of interest are comprised mainly of local residents, while others include people from across the United States. Thus, a local historic preservation society, which is devoted primarily to issues involving the quality of life in an urban neighborhood, draws mostly from the local community. On the other hand, our teacher would share cultural and political interests with other African-American science teachers in Los Angeles, Miami, or Cleveland through association with the educational, scientific, and African-American communities that transcend existing city, county, or state boundaries. In light of such considerations, that fixed boundaries continue to determine representation in the U.S. polity has been questioned frequently in recent years.

Regionalism and Political Reorganization

Keeping in mind the changes in population mobility and advances in transportation and communication that have occurred during the twentieth century and the persistence of state boundaries and states as major political units, it is useful to examine the meaning of the state as a frame of identity and political reference. All Americans are defined politically by the spaces that surround them, be they precincts, wards, townships, counties, or states. These spaces also include politically defined districts to elect school board members, justices, city council members, and state senators and House members. Thus, the political map is a mesh of multilayered units.

States under the Federal System

Under the federal system, however, the states enjoy a privileged role. In Chapter 5, we noted that local governments owe their existence and powers to the states in which they are located, whereas the Tenth Amendment reserves to the states all governmental powers not mentioned specifically in the Constitution itself. Despite the critical importance of states to the federal system, their boundaries were determined in many cases either arbitrarily or as a result of political expediency. The historical political geography of the United States includes numerous cases of states carved out as charters, states that were once part of other states, and states that were once included in larger territories (such as the Old Northwest and the Louisiana Purchase). Some territories and states were defined, named, and delimited before politicians knew who was there and what their cultures were or would be.

Later, what determined whether a territory would become a state was whether it had the requisite number of residents to apply for statehood. Even this requirement was often overlooked on the grounds of political expediency. Nevada, for example, was admitted to the Union in 1864 despite a sparse and scattered population and a weak, mining-dominated economy in order to bolster Abraham Lincoln's reelection chances against his Democratic opponent, General George McClellan. Likewise, the decision to admit Republican-leaning North Dakota and South Dakota as separate states in 1889 was based on politics, as the Republican administration of Benjamin Harrison wanted to increase Republican strength in Congress. Oklahoma, with a much larger population but a history of Democratic voting, was not admitted until nearly twenty years later.

If we look carefully at the state boundaries and the political cultures within them, we observe that many states in reality contain "other states." Distinct differences in political culture, economic circumstances, demography, levels of urbanization, and other important characteristics are found within many states. Many large states have regions with different political cultures; witness upstate and downstate Illinois, southern and northern California, peninsular and panhandle Florida, and coastal and interior areas of Virginia and North Carolina. Many of those differences can be traced to contrasts in historical migrations, religious preferences, economic productivity, and the perception and responsibility of government. In some places, the migration streams overlapped, leaving varying cultural influences, such as in the areas north and south of the Ohio River, east Texas, and southern California.

The mix of cultures within states has also varied over time. The nation's racial and ethnic mixing reflects streams of new groups replacing old ones in some locations or adding to the ethnic diversity in other locations. During the last two decades, new immigrant groups from a dozen Asian and Latin American countries have provided new ethnic dimensions to many cities from California to Florida. At the same time as these new ethnic groups were arriving, other demographic shifts have been occurring nationwide. These include retirees moving from the Northeast and Middle West to the Florida peninsula and panhandle, from the Great Plains to Texas, and from California itself into Colorado, New Mexico, and the Pacific Northwest. Along another dimension, the migration is toward major metropolitan areas and away from the small towns and rural areas of much of the nation's interior. The growth of large and medium-sized metropolitan areas, especially the suburbs, represents another major residential shift.

Should State Boundaries Be Redrawn?

These changes in mobility and awareness lead one to question whether the states themselves, as major administrative units, are appropriate to the solution of pressing problems or to the representation of Americans in Congress. Citizen groups and politicians alike have expressed major concerns about the high costs of government services, the duplication of services, and the inability of either states or the national government to address a broad range of problems, including health care, consumer and environmental protection, education reform, and job retraining.

If there are too many government units, a point raised earlier in Chapter 5, the question that is raised is, what alternative political units might be proposed? Political units are important, for they define voters, consumers, special interests, and power brokers within them. While there may be reasons to explore the meaning of "communities of interest" and "interest districts," any long-lasting change in the American political system will probably still be tied to some spatial organization.

In recent years, this point has been raised by activists in a variety of places who have responded to frustration with the governments of their states by proposing to secede from these states or to create new ones. During the past two decades, secessionist movements have arisen, with varying degrees of seriousness, in New York City, on the islands of Martha's Vineyard and Nantucket in Massachusetts, in the Upper Peninsula of Michigan, in western Nebraska and Kansas, and in northern California. In each of these cases, local residents proposed to create new states or to join different existing states. For example, residents of the Upper Peninsula have proposed to create a new state, Superior. Some argued that Superior should contain not only the Upper Peninsula but also neighboring areas in Wisconsin and northeastern Minnesota. Residents of the Nebraska Panhandle have occasionally expressed a desire to join neighboring Wyoming, whose capital, Cheyenne, is much closer geographically than is Nebraska's capital, Lincoln, which is more than four hundred miles away.

Some have taken such arguments a step further and have proposed to redraw state boundaries entirely. How might state boundaries be redrawn? One possibility for change on the political map is to identify a set of macrolevel administrative districts that are based on some sense of residents' identities. What are the major regions that we can identify on a map? Elazar has identified and mapped the major political cultures of the United States (Elazar, 1984; Brunn, 1974). Although much has changed since Elazar first undertook to map U.S. political cultures, the concept of cartographically representing the "mixes" of political cultures is a step in the direction of considering alternatives. If we accept the notion that there are many "states within existing states," then we can attempt to delimit relatively homogeneous districts on the basis of prevailing political cultures.

One such proposal defines a series of macrolevel administrative units, drawn on the basis of strong regional identity rather than following existing state boundaries (Figure 10-1). The proposed units reflect areas whose residents express strong regional loyalties. Three examples illustrate the growing importance of regionalism among residents, voters, and legislators. Residents of New York City sometimes complain that the city is poorly served by a state legislature whose members neither understand nor care about the city's problems. Similar divisions between large metropolitan areas and rural areas are evident in other states, including Illinois, Minnesota, Michigan, and Georgia. Other states are characterized by strong traditional rivalries, for example, between east and west Texas and northern and southern California. And regional rivalries also exist within states that have marked contrasts between rural and urban areas; consider Appalachian Kentucky versus the bluegrass region, northern rural Michigan versus the southern metropolitan areas, or Denver's dominance of Colorado's economy and politics.

Today, many metropolitan areas, including New York, Philadelphia, Chicago, Memphis, Cincinnati, St. Louis, Kansas City, and Portland, extend across two or more states. Residents of these metropolitan areas share common communities of interest, which are reinforced by television and radio

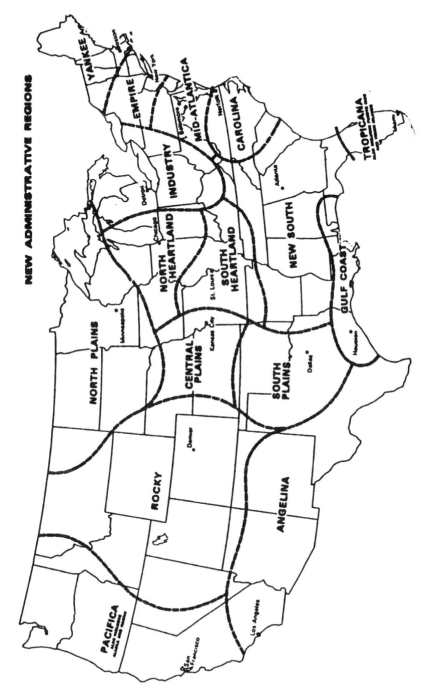

FIGURE 10-1. Macrolevel Administrative Units. • Capitals of Administrative Units.

319

news programs, commuting patterns, professional sports and cultural activities, and circulation of major newspapers. But because representation is limited by state boundaries, it is often difficult, if not impossible, for representatives to fully articulate policy positions associated with the metropolitan-wide community of interest in which they live. Thus, it has been argued that redrawn boundaries should be based on the location of metropolitan areas.

This proposal is for administrative districts, not for representation. The intent was not to define districts with the same number of residents; rather, the center of each newly created district would be responsible for addressing the concerns of its residents and the problems within its spaces. Very few districts on the map follow existing state lines because most political cultures do not. That several states are divided among two or more new districts reflects the varying regional sentiments within them; such states include Kentucky, Virginia, Maryland, and Michigan, all states that historically had strong regional identities. In fact, as we have seen, most states contain more than one political culture. State boundaries are not the best limits to use in seeking cultural homogeneity, measures of economic activity, or metropolitan hinterlands.

In Chapter 6, we noted that the Supreme Court has in recent years mandated that districts delineated to elect members of the House of Representatives be as equal in population as possible. Such decisions, as we have seen, were motivated by the principle of "one person, one vote," on the grounds that fairness in political decision making requires that each person's vote in the process count the same as all others. Yet this ideal cannot be achieved among states. Seats are allocated among the states in integral rather than fractional units, and the Constitution requires that each state be allocated at least one seat regardless of population (see Box 6-1).

Using figures from the 1990 census, we find that, nationwide, there is on the average one member of the House of Representatives for every 572,466 Americans. The populations of the country's smallest states, Wyoming and Alaska, are well below this national average. Meanwhile, although Arizona, Colorado, Kentucky, Oklahoma, and South Carolina all have six congressional seats, the average number of constituents per representative varies among these states from 526,267 for Oklahoma to 616,495 for Kentucky, based upon official 1990 apportionment populations for these states (see Table 6-B1-2). Thus, compared to the nation as a whole, Kentucky is underrepresented and Oklahoma, with half a million fewer residents, is overrepresented.

Because the "one person, one vote" principle first articulated in *Baker v. Carr* was subsequently applied to state legislatures and most state and local governments, the U.S. Senate is the only major legislative body in the contemporary United States whose members are not elected from districts with substantially equal populations. During the 1990s, both Wyoming, with less than half a million residents, and California, with nearly 30 million, or sixty times as many people, sent two senators to Washington. Why not draw Senate districts based on the principle of equal population? Using the 1990 apportion-

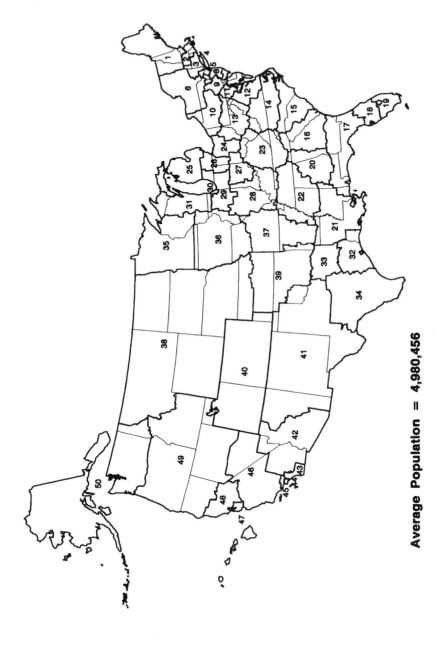

Average Population = 4,980,456

FIGURE 10-2. A New United States: Proposed U.S. Senate Districts Based on Equal Population Apportionment, 1990. Produced from U.S. Census Bureau data using Atlas*GIS on a Gateway 2000 microcomputer. Data from U.S. Bureau of the Census (1993a). See Strategic Mapping 1992.

ment population for the United States as a whole, each of fifty equally populated Senate districts should contain a population of 4,980,456 persons each.

There are many possible ways to divide the United States into fifty equally populated districts. Which of the millions of possible district plans would actually be chosen would undoubtedly be a matter of prolonged controversy. Nevertheless, we present one possible proposal here in Figure 10-2. How might the implementation of this plan affect the Senate? For one thing, several senators would be elected from districts almost entirely contained within large metropolitan areas, such as New York City (Districts 4, 5 and 7), Chicago (District 30) or Los Angeles (Districts 43, 44, and 45). On the other hand, the number of senators from the sparsely populated Great Plains and Rocky Mountains would diminish greatly. For example, the five states of Montana, Wyoming, Nebraska, and North and South Dakota, which now have a total of ten Senators, are combined, along with part of northern Kansas, to reach the needed population threshold in proposed District 38. Under an equal population criterion, these states' U.S. Senate representation would diminish by over 80 percent. In the long run, it is quite likely that issues of concern to large-city residents might be given an even higher priority in the federal legislative process than is the case today.

Of course, residents of the Great Plains and other areas whose legislative clout would be diminished by such a proposal would object vehemently. For example, Kansas is divided among Districts 38, 39, and 40, and nearby Arkansas is split among Districts 21, 22, 37, and 39. It is unlikely that any residents of what is now Arkansas would be elected to the Senate, since they might face tough opponents from areas such as Kansas City, St. Louis, Oklahoma City, Memphis, or New Orleans. Likewise, Alaskans might complain that their voice in the Senate will be overwhelmed by the more populous Seattle area, although the common interest of Seattle and Anchorage in the Pacific Rim might make such a prospect more attractive. Hawaiians would probably also object to being placed in District 47, along with San Francisco, California. Yet it is important to realize that any plan will meet with objections from those who fear disenfranchisement. A plan more favorable to residents of contemporary Arkansas, for example, might work against the interests of those living in Texas, Oklahoma, or Missouri.

To be sure, it is unlikely that the plan proposed in Figure 10-2 or any similar proposal will be enacted in the near future. The U.S. Constitution prevents states from being divided or joined with others without "the consent of the legislatures of the States concerned as well as of the Congress" (Article IV, Section 3). Yet it is unlikely that the political map of the United States at the dawn of the twenty-first century will be identical to that of a century or two in the future. For one thing, the United States contains two large populations—residents of the District of Columbia and of Puerto Rico—who remain unrepresented in the Senate and represented only by nonvoting delegates in the House of Representatives. Many residents of Puerto Rico and the District of Columbia have argued for their admissions as states. It is conceivable, although perhaps less likely, that other areas—for example, Cuba or some of the current Canadian provinces—may eventually seek to join the Union as well. The admission of new states would not only force reconsideration of patterns such as that depicted in Figure 10-2, but it would also reopen the more fundamental questions of identity, territory, and representation articulated earlier in this chapter.

Moreover, the continued globalization of the U.S. economy, urbanization of the U.S. population, and development of sophisticated transport and communication systems may render territorially based representation increasingly anachronistic, perhaps prompting the enactment of constitutional amendments restructuring the procedures by which members of the Senate are elected to office. In general, it is unlikely that the political map of the future will be static. One is reminded of the statement by the late Senator Everett Dirksen of Illinois: "In the future, the only people concerned about state boundaries will be Rand McNally."

Presidential Electoral Reforms

In previous sections, we addressed questions about the election of members to the House of Representatives and to the Senate. We also raised questions about whether "communities of interest" or "influence districts" might be valid ways to identify special interests and overlapping networks of citizens, either in proximate or widely separated locations. An important element of this earlier discussion was to demonstrate the overlapping of political cultures across state lines, the sprawl of metropolitan hinterlands over one or more state boundaries, and the utility of measuring representation based on territorial units.

Similar questions might be raised about presidential elections. Many critics have charged that the process of electing presidents is confusing and unfair. As we have seen, the winner-take-all system may discourage some from voting. "Why vote if one's vote doesn't count?" is the sentiment. The result of the present system is not only that millions of popular votes mean nothing, but also that the campaign strategy encourages targeting key states and ignoring others. In 1992, for example, the successful Clinton campaign wrote off eighteen of the fifty states and invested no campaign resources in them. Clinton won only Montana among those eighteen states (Shelley and Archer, 1994).

When voters go to the polls on election day, they are not actually voting for a president and vice president. Rather, they are voting for electors, that is, for those who meet after the election day to cast votes for the next president. Most voters have no idea who these individuals are; they are literally faceless and nameless. But they are those entrusted by the Constitution with officially electing the next president. And since these slates of electors are identified by party, most vote for their party's candidate. How these electors are selected is another of the mysteries to the voting public.

It is the appearance of strong third parties that raise questions about the present system of electing presidents. Since most third parties in the United States have a strong regional base (Shelley et al., 1984), the questions leading party candidates must consider is whether third-party candidates will win any states. In 1992, for example, Ross Perot won no electoral votes despite garnering nearly 20 percent of the popular vote—the best third-party showing in eighty years. Those who support these third-party candidates for president also see their votes wasted in the current system of electing presidents. "Why," they ask, "should I waste my vote on a losing candidate?" One result is that some decide to support a candidate who has a chance to win the state. Another result is that these disillusioned voters do not vote.

Even though third-party candidates have not been successful enough to see a popular winner different from the Electoral College winner, the potential exists for such a situation. The dilemma would unfold if the winner of the popular vote did not receive a majority of votes in the Electoral College, mainly because the third-party candidate had won sufficient electoral votes to guarantee that no one had the necessary majority. Of course, the electors of the third party could vote for the party that had the first or second most popular or electoral votes. Nothing would preclude this possibility, although it has not happened in practice.

The confusion and unfairness in the system increase when we consider the next step. Should no candidate have a majority of Electoral College votes, the election of the president is decided by the House of Representatives. This situation has happened twice before (in 1800 and 1824), but not in over 170 years, and not since the voting franchise has been extended to more Americans. In the House, each state gets one vote in the election. That is, very large states receive one vote, as do the smallest. The vote that each state would cast would depend on which party had the most delegates, in current context, Republicans and Democrats. If the delegation was tied, the state would cast no votes. States that would be likely to have delegations with potentially equal numbers of Democrats and Republicans are those with large populations and mixes of political cultures, specifically, California, New York, Illinois, Florida, Ohio, Pennsylvania, and Texas, all states with large numbers of voters, electoral votes, and members in the House of Representative.

Various scenarios could be presented that would delay the final decision on the election of a president, result in confusion among the populous, and alienate voters and politicians of both winning and losing parties. At least three scenarios could occur: In one, the popular vote winner failed to achieve the majority Electoral College vote, but when the vote went to the House, she or he won because her or his party had the majority of state delegations. Another possibility is that the second-place winner in the popular vote also failed to achieve the college majority, primarily because of a strong third-party candidate who won one or more large states, but when the vote went to the House, this candidate won because her or his party had more majority delegations than anyone else. In a third scenario, the third party played the spoiler role, that is, the third-party candidate used his or her political strength in the electoral college to support either the popular vote winner or the second-place finisher. The questions that need to be raised in these scenarios, and others that can be painted, is whether the electorate and political parties will accept this amount of delay, confusion, unfairness, and arm-twisting. If the vote went to the House and there were large states with delegations tied between the major parties, the selection of the president could be made by a large number of small states that have only a small percentage of the total population and only a few members in the House.

Should We Reform the Electoral College?

Solutions to this above confusion are immediately available. One is to eliminate the Electoral College and all its unfairness. Public opinion polls during the past couple of decades have indicated that there is some support for this position. Eliminating the College would eliminate the unit rule or any separate body selecting the president. Replacing the College would be a direct popular election of the president. Whoever won the most popular votes would be the winner; this is plain and simple. It would remove political parties and another arm of government from the decision.

If the selection was based on popular votes, then the campaigns might assume different strategies. Candidates would seek to increase registration levels and voter turnout. Both are variables that have reflected geographic variation. As was pointed out in previous chapters, the participation of citizens in the political (voting) process is one that varies with the political culture. Even though there are party and independent voter registration drives before each election, there remain many eligible citizens of voting age who do not register. Innovative efforts to increase the registration have been tied to "voter-motor" legislation; that is, once someone obtains a drivers license, he or she also is eligible to vote. But there are many adults who do not drive or own cars. One might argue that the reason the major political parties are not in favor of any kind of mandatory registration to vote is that they do not know how the expanded electorate would vote. That almost half of eligible voters do not vote for presidents reveals some flaws in the registration system, the difficulties in actually voting, acknowledged unfairness in the process, and disillusionment with politicians and political parties.

Turnout will likely become the crucial issue should a direct popular election decide presidents. Candidates would seek to increase turnout by their supporters, especially in states with close races. In many presidential elections, the parties are usually competitive in the largest states, where most voters live and where most votes would be. Voter turnout currently is highest in the Northeast, New England, and the Great Plains and lowest in the South, especially rural portions of the South. Turnout is also lower in the inner cities than in the suburbs. If the voters elected presidents directly, then everyone's vote would count the same as all other votes. There would not be the disappointment that many voters now face when they realize that, in the winner-take-all Electoral College process, their votes meant nothing.

Perhaps voter turnout would increase if there was computer voting—that is, if one could "vote" from any number of computer bases within a town or city—or if one could vote from home or from one's place of employment using a television monitor or push-button phone. The problems of standing in long lines, waiting outdoors in inclement weather, and missing work, family obligations, and even meals would be avoided. It is also possible that if the voting occurred over a two-day period, the number of voters would increase. Also, should the dates be scheduled in the spring or early autumn, the turnout might be better. These are questions that also call for agreement among the political parties and the utilization of current telecommunications technology in the voting process.

These questions about electoral reform for the presidency go to the heart of a participatory democracy. Whether a separate group will make that crucial decision or whether the people will is the major question. The likelihood of a political quagmire is real, especially if there is a very successful third regional party movement or a strong party movement in one or two large, heavily populated states.

Legislation, Special Interests, and the Electronic Age

In all democratic regimes, more or less organized groups or communities of interest compete for power and influence in the legislative process. Agricultural, industrial, financial, military, environmental, and gender-related interest groups are just a few of the many special interests dedicated to securing the passage of desired legislation. The identity and influence of these special interests have changed, of course, over the course of U.S. history. In recent years, for example, the influence of labor unions and agricultural organizations has declined as the economy continues to be dominated by growth in the tertiary and quaternary sectors. Likewise, the influence of the health and education sectors has increased. Over the past several decades, more and more physicians and teachers have served in legislatures, while the number of farmers and blue-collar workers has declined accordingly.

Special Interests and Political Parties

Over the course of U.S. history, political parties have coalesced around major interests that were important to the nation's economy and society. But parties also emerged because leaders themselves perceived the duties and responsibilities of government differently, as our discussion of geographic differences in political culture implies. Because there was also strength in party organization, leaders with similar views and interests put forward programs or agendas they wished to see enacted in state and national legislative bodies. Thus, one party might adopt programs that favored strong centralized government and another might favor decentralization and more responsibilities for decisions by the states. As we noted in previous chapters, the nation's political history is also marked by parties taking contrasting positions on foreign policy, civil rights, monetary programs, business incentives, and resource conservation.

Those elected to political office receive the support of others. These may be members of ethnic groups or religious bodies, bankers, industrialists, or professionals (physicians, teachers, attorneys). The financial support provided those running for office may be minuscule or grandiose, but the intent is that, should the candidate be successful, he or she will support the positions or programs endorsed by those who provided financial backing.

The concept of special interests being important in the election of members of Congress or the presidency is not a late-twentieth-century phenomenon. Nominees for the presidency and vice presidency of major and minor political parties in the last century and early in this century had their campaigns supported by specific individuals and specific interests, be they industrialists, those in railroad and highway construction business, coal mining, agriculture, or banking. Some candidates openly courted the votes of new immigrant groups, specific religious bodies, labor unions, and farmers, each of which was considered crucial in building a successful statewide or national campaign. Putting together a successful national campaign requires piecing together a complex array of special interests, often with distinct regional foci. The traditional New Deal coalition, which includes ideological liberals, intellectuals, Southerners, African-Americans and other minorities, and labor unions, was critical, for example, to the electoral success of the Democratic Party for the three decades following the initial election of Franklin D. Roosevelt in 1932.

During the past several decades, the backgrounds of political actors have become more diversified, and the special interests have become more numerous. Part of this diversification is attributed to participation by groups that had previously been excluded from the political process, such as African-Americans, Hispanics, and women. There are also others who were not earlier considered numerous enough to be important, specifically, new immigrant groups from Latin America and Asia and retirees, who continue to increase in numbers rapidly. Legislation encouraging the registration of new voters contributed to their growing role in political parties, but also the social climate has also changed. Although the number of women currently serving in Congress remains small, an increasing number have run successfully for state legislatures and local offices such as mayor and city council member. Other new interest groups that have emerged in recent years include environmentalists, Christian fundamentalists, and gay and lesbian activists.

New special interests have their own agendas, some of which may be at odds with the agendas of those who have been in leadership positions for long periods. African-Americans and Hispanics elected to national office are interested in questions about fairness in representation, quality housing and education, and job training and retraining. These representatives are also interested in U.S. foreign policy issues affecting Africa and Latin America. Many women identify with organizations that support programs dealing with pay equity, estate settlement, abortion and reproductive rights, children and nutrition programs, and environmental and consumer protection. These and other issues have emerged in recent years as increasingly important components of the political agenda.

The emergence of new topics for political discussion reflects in part the opening up of the democratic process to groups formerly excluded, but it also represents key features of a postindustrial society in which information and communication are key attributes. The presentation, packaging, selling, and promotion of information by many sources is a major feature of postindustrial society. What this means is that there are many more groups, associations, and organizations who are interested in seeing that their positions are disseminated and heard. The plethora of new groups interested in women's issues, environmental preservation, consumer protection, children, domestic and television violence, drug rehabilitation, and health care reflect the diversity of groups interested in participating in the political process. A check of the registered lobbyists who support or oppose specific legislation would reveal the extent of democratization. During the early 1990s, for example, numerous special interest groups were active in support of or opposition to the Clinton administration's health care proposals.

In recent years, the democratization of the political agenda has been accelerated by improved communications. Special interest groups and lobbying organizations regularly publish information for their supporters and others, not only through regular newsletters and magazines but also through various electronic services, including electronic mail, electronic bulletin boards, and Internet nodes. There are groups whose members can be alerted, via electronic mail, about specific pieces of legislation that are pending or decisions that have been made. Citizens can either phone the offices of their members in Congress, they can fax a message, or they can send an electronic mail message. A growing number of senators and representatives are providing electronic mail addresses to constituents who may wish to convey their views to or receive policy-relevant information from their delegates in Washington. An ever growing number of individual Americans have personal computers in their places of work and residence and are able to utilize the electronic information provided by the groups they support to influence local, state, or national decision makers. The White House itself has an electronic mail address that citizens can use to send messages to the nation's chief administrator, as well as an Internet "Home-Page" that presents trendy textual and audiovisual bulletins from the president or other members of the incumbent administration. During the Clinton administration, the White House Internet Home-Page even featured a downloadable photo of the president's cat, Socks.

Electronic Democracy

Contemporary electronic communication can have profound effects on U.S. democracy. For one thing, the volume of communication coming into representatives' offices is likely to increase dramatically. In particular, the volume of communications from outside the representative's constituency is likely to expand. Electronic information may come from members of special interest groups elsewhere inside the U.S. or even outside the United States. Highly organized special interest groups will ask their supporters to target specific legislators about individual pieces of legislation that they agree or disagree with. Again, the result is that the decision made by the representative may be influenced not only by those "folks back home whom I represent" within a territorially defined constituency, but by groups of supporters and constituents nationwide and even outside the United States.

Characteristics of this evolving "electronic state" raise a series of questions about human rights and welfare, protection, regulation, and state power that were not envisioned even thirty years ago, let alone by those who drafted the Constitution. Words were not even invented in 1787 to describe many of the current issues confronting city councils, state governments, Congress, and the Supreme Court. And issues about rights, welfare, regulation, power, citizenship, and identity, which have always been issues important to citizens, legislators, and courts, are at the heart of concerns of the state, the spaces it governs, and the protection of people within its boundaries. Those who make laws are influenced by many of the political actors and special interest groups discussed above. These do not operate in a vacuum; rather, they are influenced by demographic changes, technological advances, the content of information flows, changes in morality and social behavior, and aspiring groups seeking entry into the political process.

Human rights issues in an electronic state include concerns about civil liberties, protection, privacy, the rights of new and old minorities, the rights of individuals and groups, and the role of the national government as a provider of necessary goods and services to all residents within its borders. The electronic state would have to address questions about fairness and equity in a way that considers race and gender; questions about the regulation and limitation of power and control by information; questions about communication, about access to information services (libraries, health centers, employment offices), and about computer corporations engaged in interstate and international commerce.

Much of what the state produces is information, which it in turn communicates with its citizens and with other governments. The state also supports many other businesses and enterprises that are also in the information economies, whether financially or through favorable legislation and regulation. The U.S. government has been a major promoter of companies in the information, communication, and computer industries, as well as of mechanisms and an infrastructure to deliver services and products. Telephone, telegraph, television, and computer communication industries have been the recipients of state support at one time or another, whether it was legislation to set rates, to finance infrastructures, or to encourage competition or guarantee consumer and producer protection. Another part of the picture includes those government offices and private companies collecting massive amounts of data about individuals. Health, employment, and banking records are only part of this information; it also includes data on consumer purchases, travels, and investments.

Rapid technological and scientific developments in information, communication, and computers have not been matched by equal gains in the areas of human rights and welfare. It is almost as if one part of society is being exposed to vast amounts of information and a host of new ways to communicate, calculate, produce, and consume, while another part of the same society is struggling to cope with what all this new information means. The fast pace of these developments, and the thorny legal and ethical issues that have subsequently arisen, suggest that the legislative and judicial branches at the state and federal level themselves have difficulties coping.

Human Rights and Welfare Issues in Electronic Democracy

There are four crucial human rights and welfare issues that await legislation and judicial decisions. First are questions about what is public and what is private. How is privacy defined when all one's purchases are tabulated by marketers interested in regional social behavior and "consumer communities"? Is there anything about one's electronic mail, work, leisure, travels, hobbies, purchases, reading and television preferences, and political party registration that is private and protected from unwarranted government and corporate invasion?

Second are questions about the "right" to have a computer, modem, and videophone and to be connected to the information superhighway. Is the computer a "public good" much like phone and mail service? Does someone not having access to the superhighway or unable to purchase a computer have a legal recourse to file a geographic discrimination suit? Can a parent file a social discrimination suit because her or his children are in a school without certain educational programs that help in preparing for standardized college entrance exams? Is this a form of "cultural determinism" based on available information and technology?

Third are questions about the protection one is entitled to against a state or corporation that conducts unauthorized inquiries into one's mail, credit card purchases, checking accounts, casual and professional phone conversations. "Knowledge vandals" and "computer hackers" are among those who snoop into the information one receives and sends.

Finally, there are legal questions about perpetrators of electronic and information crimes, which run the gamut from blatant plagiarism of a copyrighted journal article to stealing logos of little-known foreign businesses to intellectual property issues. Judicial issues also surface: For example, can someone charged with a copyright violation of a video, musical score, or even a map charge the judicial system is unfair that does not permit an attorney to question prospective jurors about their uses and fears of computers, their cellular phone usage, or their credit card holdings?

Answers to these questions are fuzzy, not clear-cut. They represent a tangled web of social and legal issues relating to the rights of producers, the protection of consumers, and the role of government and different levels of government. It is because information technologies are advancing so rapidly and because the demands on society for many kinds of information increase each year that governments lag behind in establishing regulations on industries and protection of consumers.

In resolving these issues, the state faces three challenges. First, how can the U.S. government protect citizens and ensure their privacy while, at the same time, individual and group data are being gathered, used, and sold by the private sector? Second, will the state be able to take the lead in defining human rights for the new and old majorities and minorities, or must the state continue to lag behind technological advances? And, third, will these patterns of "electronic human rights" be defined unevenly across the United States, resulting in another messy patchwork of state and local laws in which some residents (and states) will have better protection than others? Or will there be congressional legislation and landmark Supreme Court decisions that ensure equal protection for citizens regardless of economic station, social class, ideology, gender, or location?

The Evolving Sphere of International Influence

As we observed in previous chapters, the United States has a history of both participation in international affairs and relations and of attempted withdrawal from what was going on elsewhere. The establishment of colonies and later the Declaration of Independence from England represented early examples of those extraterritorial linkages. The colonies could not divorce themselves from their European ties, with which they maintained family linkages, obtained assistance for fledgling businesses, defended themselves from other nations, or fashioned trade contacts.

While the colonists and early Americans may have felt isolated from events in Europe or elsewhere in eastern North America, they were not. They were dependent on friends, traders, and governments in England, France, Germany, Holland, and, later, other countries. Early triangular trade assured that those networks and contacts among companies and states would continue. Treaties with European governments (France, Spain, and England) over newly acquired territory not only continued this new North American state's role in the evolving global commercial, military, and political spheres during the eighteenth and nineteenth centuries, but they also convinced the leaders and the citizenry that isolation was impossible and impractical.

Additional evidence of those international linkages appeared during the nineteenth century, when territorial acquisition and boundaries had to be negotiated with Canada and Mexico. International treaties reflect a state's position in hemispheric or world affairs. U.S. involvement in Latin American affairs, especially in the nineteenth and twentieth centuries, in part because of the interpretation of the Monroe Doctrine, reflected a policy that this specific region was in the evolving democracy's sphere of interest. This doctrine marked a turning point in U.S. foreign policy. The government retained its strong ties to Europe, in large part because of the many immigrants coming from northern, central, and, later, southern Europe. The largest volume of trade was with those countries that supplied immigrants as well as investment capital and trading contracts. Thus, it was only natural that the English-speaking United States would have its strongest ties with Europe. But the Monroe Doctrine represented two changes in U.S. foreign policy. First, it told Europeans and others that the countries and territories to the south were "off-limits" to intervention by Europeans and others. Second, and perhaps indirectly, it reflected a wish on the part of political parties and commercial interests to see this part of the world as in the U.S. sphere of interest. In part, this U.S. influence in the Caribbean and Central America came as a result of acquiring Florida from Spain, the Louisiana Purchase from France, and large sections of the Southwest and West from Mexico. During the nineteenth century, the United States was very jealous of its territorial acquisitions and wished to signal to outsiders that its legislators and military supported the spaces it had acquired and its diplomatic and military successes in the region.

During the late nineteenth and early twentieth centuries, the United States found itself again a part of global political changes. The country could not isolate or insulate itself from what was occurring in Europe or in Asia. U.S. military presence was desired where U.S. business interests were developing in Latin America and Asia, not only to protect those Americans living there and their enterprises but to support governments of countries where Americans lived or had interests. Military involvement was expected when Americans and their property were threatened. The United States found itself embroiled in Asian interests, even if feelings of noninvolvement and isolation were strong. Protection of property and support for friendly governments in Europe, Latin America, and Asia contributed to the United States being drawn into wars and conflicts of varying magnitude and in widely varying locations. Some of those wars were waged against former friends, including countries that had large immigrant populations in the United States.

Thus, by the mid-twentieth century, the United States had become a global power with strong international interests in what was going on in all parts of the world. That power position was not simply because of population size or economic and military strength, but because many Americans, and therefore the government, felt a responsibility to support democracies and democratic governments regardless of location. But the United States also was strategically well positioned to become a world power: The extra-European and global commercial ties that developed during the past several centuries have been in North and South America, East Asia, and, to a lesser extent, Africa.

During the past several decades, three major changes have occurred in U.S. foreign policy, and each is significant in what it portends for the next twenty-five years. During the Cold War, the United States was engaged in superpower rivalry with the Soviet Union. The military and diplomatic energies expended were immense, and they were also global in scope. The United States was identified as a global power because of its involvement in wars to stop the threat of Soviet and Chinese communism, the treaties it formed with various countries in Europe, Asia, and the Pacific, the economic and military support it provided friendly governments opposed to Soviet and Chinese expansionism, and its sales of arms to a wide variety of friendly Third World states and paramilitary groups. In all these efforts, the United States was seeking to define its spheres of influence around the world. But those efforts were designed not only to defeat and contain the enemy (the Soviet Union) but also to stake out territories and regions where the United States held superiority (by itself or with allies) and where it was competitive with the perceived enemy.

Since the Cold War ended, the United States has emerged as the world's only major superpower. Since then, U.S. presidents, legislators, and military leaders have sought to define what the role of a single superpower is in Europe, Africa, Asia, and Latin America. Not having an easily identified enemy makes the task of defining spheres of interest much more difficult. Assuming the role of a peacekeeper or working with international forces is a different responsibility, but so is deciding what and where those regions, countries, and places of U.S. interest are. Are they in Bosnia, Somalia, Iraq, and Afghanistan, which all seem so far away, or are they in Cuba, Haiti, and Nicaragua? It is not clear where we ought to become involved, unilaterally or multilaterally, and until there is further debate, legislation, and clarification of the U.S. role, its spheres of influence will remain undecided.

A third change in U.S. foreign policy came to center stage in 1993 with the passage of NAFTA. This agreement marked a sea change in U.S. relations with its neighbors. As we pointed out in Chapter 7, congressional passage of this bill facilitated trade between the United States, Mexico, and Canada. It was supported by many legislators from the Sunbelt states, especially, who saw their recent economic growth continuing with additional efforts to expand plants and sales in Mexico. The importance of this vote was that it demonstrated the nation's commitment to solidifying hemispheric economic and political ties. But it also can be seen as a commitment to pursue stronger ties with Latin America than with Europe.

This new political "shift" toward the Caribbean and Central and South America and away from Europe is a major departure from more than two centuries of foreign policy decisions that tied the United States to Europe. This "south" perspective did not begin with the NAFTA vote, for the past two decades have demonstrated the economic and political importance of the Sunbelt states. Electoral votes, candidates for presidents, illegal Central American immigrants, and foreign policy decisions—including on military actions—directed toward Nicaragua, Honduras, Cuba, the Canal Zone, Colombia, and Panama are further evidence of this shift. Congressional debate on U.S. interests in establishing democracy in Haiti (including votes on participation and withdrawal of troops), on the elections and assassinations in Mexico, and on negotiations with Castro over Cuban immigrant quotas are further indications of this shift toward seeing Central and South America as a major sphere of national interest.

It is too early to determine how successful NAFTA will be in achieving its objective of stimulating the North American economies. If NAFTA does succeed, however, it may well be expanded to other countries. Some legislators in Argentina, Chile, and Brazil have already discussed the possibility of joining NAFTA, extending this agreement from the North American continent to the entire Western Hemisphere. Moreover, the possibility exists that NAFTA's members will seek closer political as well as economic cooperation. This has already happened in western Europe, where the European Economic Community, that is, the "Common Market," has expanded in both membership and levels of cooperation over the past four decades. Is it possible that NAFTA will be expanded to an "American Union"? If so, how will delegates from member countries resolve issues concerning not only representation but also cultural identity, language, and many other issues inevitably associated with even a partial merger of countries whose sovereignty has been unquestioned for centuries? In other words, how could a North American Constitution be designed? Would it extend the current U.S. Constitution to additional territory, or would different principles underlie its development?

Another emerging sphere of interest encompasses the Pacific. With the Pacific states growing in population, voters, and representation in Congress, presidents and political parties are taking a greater interest in the economic markets and population issues in east and southeast Asia and Oceania. The terms "Pacific Rim" and "Pacific Basin" did not exist two decades ago, but they have become part of the current lexicon of U.S. corporations interested in new markets in China, the Philippines, Indonesia, and Korea. Many of these U.S. initiatives are by Asian-Americans themselves, in particular in California, Washington, and Hawaii. First- or second-generation Japanese and Chinese are among the investors, as are first-generation Vietnamese, Koreans, and Filipinos. These are also individuals who have strong ties with ethnic organizations and who financially support prospective legislators and presidential candidates.

These recent shifts in U.S. foreign policy toward Latin America, the Pacific, and East Asia can be expected to continue. The Sunbelt and West Coast areas are increasing their economic strength in the nation and their political clout in Washington. Their rise is occurring at the same time that the political and economic clout of the Northeastern industrial core is declining. Europe itself is experiencing major economic changes, especially the development of a stronger and larger European Union. It is likely that Europe will continue to be much more "inward looking" in the future than it has been in the past, and its markets, half a billion people, present a variety of political and economic challenges for old and new states.

Where these changes in the world political map will take the United States in the next few decades is somewhat uncertain. What *is* reasonably certain is that the United States will look more toward Latin America and Asia than it has previously; that there will be increased congressional debates and votes on economic, political, and military issues in these new areas of U.S. involvement (for example, immigration, favored nation trading status, and support for specific leaders); that military involvement will be only in selected places, and especially in those places where the United States has major interests or long-standing commitments; that the United States will participate, with Europeans, in international peacekeeping operations in Africa and the Middle East; that human rights issues (such as immigration quotas, family planning, nutrition, and disease ecology) will assume a much greater role in foreign policy and international agreements; and that global environmental issues will also be given a high priority by governmental, intergovernmental, and nongovernmental organizations. That the United States is still redefining its emerging spheres of interest means that the next couple of decades are likely to be a time of a certain amount of uncertainty and unevenness.

REFERENCES

Agnew, J. A. (1987a), *The United States in the World-Economy: A Regional Geography*. New York: Cambridge University Press.

Agnew, J. A. (1987b), *Place and Politics: The Geographic Mediation of State and Society*. Boston, MA: Allen and Unwin.

Agnew, J. A. (1992), "The U.S. Position in the World Geopolitical Order after the Cold War," *The Professional Geographer*, 44, 7–10.

Agnew, J. A. (1993a), "The United States and American Hegemony," in P. J. Taylor (ed.), *Political Geography of the Twentieth Century: A Geographical Analysis*. London: Belhaven, pp. 207–238.

Agnew, J. A. (1993b), "Trading Blocs or a World That Knows No Boundaries? The British–American 'Special Relationship' and the Continuation of the Post-War World Economy," in C. H. Williams (ed.), *The Political Geography of the New World Order*. New York: Belhaven, pp. 132–147.

Agnew, J. A., and S. Corbridge (1989), "The New Geopolitics: The Dynamics of Geopolitical Disorder," in R. J. Johnston and P. J. Taylor (eds.), *A World in Crisis: Geographical Perspectives*. Oxford: Blackwell, pp. 266–288.

Alexander, L. M. (1968), "Geography and the Law of the Sea," *Annals of the Association of American Geographers*, 58, 177–197.

Archer, J. C. (1983), "The Geography of Federal Fiscal Politics in the United States of America: An Exploration," *Environment and Planning C: Government and Policy*, 1, 377–400.

Archer, J. C. (1988), "Macrogeographical versus Microgeographical Cleavages in American Presidential Elections," *Political Geography Quarterly*, 7, 111–125.

Archer, J. C. (1992), "A Medium-Term Perspective on Demographic Change in the American Midlands," in I. Bowler, C. Bryant, and D. Nellis (eds.), *Contemporary Rural Systems in Transition: Vol. 2. Economy and Society*. Wallingford, UK: CAB International, pp. 62–84.

Archer, J. C., G. T. Murauskas, F. M. Shelley, P. J. Taylor, and E. R. White (1985), "Counties, States, Sections and Parties in the 1984 Presidential Election," *Professional Geographer*, 37, 279–287.

Archer, J. C., and F. M. Shelley (1986), *American Electoral Mosaics*. Washington, DC: Association of American Geographers.

Archer, J. C., F. M. Shelley, P. J. Taylor, and E. R. White (1988), "The Geography of U.S. Presidential Elections," *Scientific American*, 259, 18–25.

Archer, J. C., and P. J. Taylor (1981), *Section and Party*. New York: Wiley.

Arnold, J. L. (1985), "Section and Party in Tennessee: An Analysis of Post–Civil War Presidential Voting Patterns." Unpublished M.A. thesis, Department of Geography, University of Oklahoma, Norman, Oklahoma.

Asker, J. R. (1995, March 6), "U.S. Begins to Release Secret Satellite Imagery," *Aviation Week, 142:10*, 64–65.

Barone, M. (1990), *Our Country: The Shaping of America from Roosevelt to Reagan*. New York: Free Press.

Barraclough, G. (1967), *Introduction to Contemporary History*. Harmondsworth, UK: Penguin.

Barry, B. L., and T. R. Dye (1978), "The Discriminatory Effect of At-Large Elections," *Florida State Law Review*, 7, 85–122.

Bartley, N. V., and H. D. Graham (1976), *Southern Politics and the Second Reconstruction*. Baltimore, MD: Johns Hopkins University Press.

Bell, D. (1973), *The Coming of Post-Industrial Society*. New York: Basic Books.

Bellamy, E. (1888), *Looking Backward*. Boston, MA: Houghton Mifflin.

Bemis, S. F. (1957), *The Diplomacy of the American Revolution*. Bloomington, IN: Indiana University Press.

Bensel, R. F. (1984), *Sectionalism and American Political Development*. Madison, WI: University of Wisconsin Press.

Berry, B. J. L. (1991), *Long-Wave Rythms in Economic Development and Political Behavior*. Baltimore, MD: Johns Hopkins University Press.

Beschloss, M. R., and S. Talbott (1993), *At the Highest Levels: The Inside Story of the End of the Cold War*. Boston, MA: Little, Brown.

Bibby, J. F. (1992), *Governing by Consent: An Introduction to American Politics*. Washington, DC: Congressional Quarterly.

Bickford, C. B., and K. R. Bowling (1989), *Birth of the Nation: The First Federal Congress, 1789–1791*. Madison, WI: Madison House.

Billington, R. A. (1944), "The Origins of Middle Western Isolationism," *Political Science Quarterly*, 60, 44–64.

Billington, R. A. (1960), *Westward Expansion: A History of the American Frontier* (2nd ed.). New York: Macmillan.

Black, E., and M. Black (1992), *The Vital South: How Presidents Are Elected*. Cambridge, MA: Harvard University Press.

Blechman, B. M., et al. (1993), *The American Military in the Twenty-First Century*. New York: St. Martin's.

Blouet, B. W. 1987. *Halford Mackinder: A Biography*. College Station, TX: Texas A & M University Press.

Bluestone, B., and B. Harrison (1982), *The Deindustrialization of America: Plant Closings, Community Abandonment and the Dismantling of Basic Industry*. New York: Basic Books.

Boggs, S. W. (1946, December 22), "Cartohypnosis," *Department of State Bulletin, 15:390*, 1119–1125.

Boorstin, D. (1983), *The Discoverers*. New York: Random House.

Borden, A. W., and G. Q. Wong (1994, September) "GIS Supports Election Management," *GIS World, 7:9*, 22–24.

Bowling, K. R. (1991), *The Creation of Washington, DC: The Idea and Location of the American Capital*. Fairfax, VA: George Mason University Press.

Bowman, I. (1928), *The New World: Problems in Political Geography* (4th ed.). Yonkers, NY: World Book.

Bowman, I. (1948), "The Geographical Situation of the United States in Relation to World Policies," *Geographical Journal, 112,* 129–145.

Brady, D. W. (1988), *Critical Elections and Congressional Policymaking.* Stanford, CA: Stanford University Press.

Bridge, S. (1903), *Inside History of the Carnegie Steel Company: A Romance of Millions* (4th ed.). New York: Aldine.

Brinkley, A. (1993), *The Unfinished Nation: A Concise History of the American People.* New York: Knopf.

Brody, D. E. (1978), *The American Legal Systems: Concepts and Principles.* Lexington, MA: D. C. Heath.

Brown, R. H. (1948), *Historical Geography of the United States.* New York: Harcourt, Brace and World.

Browning, C. E. (1973), *The Geography of Federal Outlays: An Introductory and Comparative Inquiry.* Chapel Hill, NC: Department of Geography, University of North Carolina.

Bruchey, S. W. (1975), *Growth of the Modern American Economy.* New York: Dodd, Mead.

Brunn, S. D. (1974), *Geography and Politics in America.* New York: Harper and Row.

Brunn, S. D. (1987), "A World of Peace and Military Landscapes," *Journal of Geography, 86,* 253–262.

Brunn, S. D., and G. Ingalls (1972), "The Emergence of Republicanism in the Urban South," *Southeastern Geographer, 12,* 133–144.

Brunn, S. D., and J. A. Jones (1994), "Geopolitical Information and Communication in Shrinking and Expanding Worlds: 1900–2100," in G. J. Demko and W. B. Wood (eds.), *Reordering the World: Geopolitical Perspectives on the Twenty-First Century.* Boulder, CO: Westview, pp. 301–322.

Brunn, S. D., and E. Yanarella (1987), "Towards a Humanistic Political Geography," *Studies in Comparative International Development, 22,* 3–86.

Bryan, N. S. (1993, March/April), "GIS Helps Produce Clinton's Victory," *Business Geographics, 1:2,* 28–32.

Bureau of Transportation Statistics, U.S. Department of Transportation (1955), *National Transportation Atlas Data Bases: 1995; BTS-CD-06.* Washington, DC: U.S. Department of Transportation.

Burnett, A. (1985), "Propaganda Cartography," in D. Pepper and A. Jenkins (eds.), *The Geography of Peace and War.* Oxford: Blackwell, pp. 60–89.

Burnett, A., and P. J. Taylor (eds.) (1981), *Political Studies from Spatial Perspectives.* New York: Wiley.

Burnham, W. D. (1970), *Critical Elections and the Mainsprings of American Politics.* New York: Norton.

Campbell, A., et al. (1960), *The American Voter.* New York: Wiley.

Cattell, R. B. (1958), "Extracting the Correct Number of Factors in Factor Analysis," *Educational and Psychological Measurement, 22,* 667–697.

Chambers, W. N., and W. D. Burnham (eds.) (1967), *The American Party System: Stages of Political Development.* New York: Oxford University Press.

Chester, E. W. (1975), *Sectionalism, Politics, and American Diplomacy.* Metuchen, NJ: Scarecrow.

Clark, G. L. (1985), *Judges and the Cities*. Chicago, IL: University of Chicago Press.

Clark, G. L. (1994), "NAFTA—-Clinton's Victory, Organized Labor's Loss," *Political Geography*, 13, 377–384.

Cochran, T. C. (1972), *Business in American Life: A History*. New York: McGraw-Hill.

Cohen, S. B. (1973), *Geography and Politics in a World Divided* (2nd ed.). New York: Oxford University Press.

Cohen, S. B. (1992a), "Policy Prescriptions for the Post Cold War World," *The Professional Geographer*, 44, 13–16.

Cohen, S. B. (1992b), "Global Geopolitical Changes in the Post Cold War Era," *Annals of the Association of American Geographers*, 81, 551–580.

Cohen, S. B. (1994), "Geopolitics in the New World Era: A New Perspective on an Old Discipline," in G. J. Demko and W. B. Wood (eds.), *Reordering the World: Geopolitical Perspectives on the Twenty-First Century*. Boulder, CO: Westview, pp. 15–48.

Congressional Quarterly Weekly Report (1993, December 18), 51:50, 3494–3495.

Converse, P. (1966), "The Concept of a Normal Vote," in A. Campbell, P. Converse, W. E. Miller, and D. E. Stokes (eds.), *Elections and the Political Order*. New York: Wiley, pp. 136–157.

Cotter, P. R. (1981), "Southern Reaction to the Second Reconstruction: The Case of South Carolina," *Western Political Quarterly*, 38, 542–551.

Cox, K. R. (1979), *Location and Public Problems: A Political Geography of the Contemporary World*. Chicago, IL: Maaroufa.

Cox, K. R., D. R. Reynolds, and S. Rokkan (eds.) (1974), *Locational Approaches to Power and Conflict*. New York: Wiley.

Crump, J. R. (1989), "Spatial Distribution of Military Spending in the United States, 1941–1985," *Growth and Change*, 20, 50–62.

Crump, J. R., and J. C. Archer (1993), "Spatial and Temporal Variability in the Geography of American Defense Outlays," *Political Geography*, 12, 38–63.

Dalby, S. (1990), *Creating the Second Cold War: The Discourse of Politics*. London: Pinter.

Daniel, C. (ed.) (1987), *Chronicle of the 20th Century*. Mount Kisco, NY: Chronicle Publications.

Davis, S. T. (1981). "Reapportionment: Numerical Politics," *American Demographics*, 3, 24–29.

de Blij, H. (1992), "Political Geography of the Post Cold War World," *The Professional Geographer*, 44, 16–19.

DeCarli, R. C. (1993), "The Constitutionality of State-Enacted Term Limits under the Qualifications Clauses," *Texas Law Review*, 71, 865–901.

DeConde, A. (1976), *This Affair of Louisiana*. New York: Charles Scribner's Sons.

Demko, G. J., and W. B. Wood (eds.) (1994), *Reordering the World: Geopolitical Perspectives on the Twenty-First Century*. Boulder, CO: Westview.

De Seversky, A. P. (1952), *Air Power: Key to Survival*. London: Herbert Jenkins.

Dicken, P. (1989), *Global Shift: Industrial Change in a Turbulent World*. London: Chapman.

Dikshit, R. D. (1975), *The Political Geography of Federalism: An Inquiry into Origins and Stability*. New Delhi, India: Macmillan.

Dillon, J. (1911), *Commentaries on the Law of Municipal Corporations* (5th ed.). Boston, MA: Little, Brown.

Dodd, D. B. (ed.) (1993), *Historical Statistics of the United States: Two Centuries of the Census, 1790–1990.* Westport, CT: Greenwood.

Doenecke, J. D. (1979), *Not to the Swift: The Old Isolationists in the Cold War Era.* Lewisburg, PA: Bucknell University Press.

Donaghu, M. T., and R. Barff (1990), "Nike Just Did It: International Subcontracting and Flexibility in Athletic Footwear Production," *Regional Studies, 24,* 537–552.

Downs, A. (1957), *An Economic Theory of Democracy.* New York: Harper and Row.

Dye, T. R. (1985), "Party and Policy in the States," *Journal of Politics, 46,* 1097–1116.

Dye, T. R., and S. McManus (1976), "Predicting City Government Structure," *American Journal of Political Science, 20,* 257–271.

Easterly, E. S. (1977), "Global Patterns of Legal Systems: Notes toward a New Jurisprudence," *Geographical Review, 67,* 209–220.

Elazar, D. J. (1980), "Political Culture on the Plains," *Western Historical Quarterly, 11,* 261–283.

Elazar, D. J. (1984), *American Federalism: A View from the States* (3rd ed.). New York: Harper and Row.

Elazar, D. J. (1988), *The American Constitutional Tradition.* Lincoln, NE: University of Nebraska Press.

Elazar, D. J. (1994), *The American Mosaic: The Impact of Space, Time and Culture on American Politics.* Boulder, CO: Westview.

Engstrom, R. L., and M. D. McDonald (1986), "The Effect of At-Large versus District Elections on Racial Representation in U.S. Municipalities," in B. Grofman and A. Lijphart (eds.), *Electoral Laws and Their Political Consequences.* New York: Agathon Press, pp. 203–225.

Ettlinger, N. (1992), "Development Theory and the Military Industrial Firm," in A. Kirby (ed.), *The Pentagon and the Cities: Urban Affairs Annual Reviews* (Vol. 40). Newbury Park, CA: Sage, pp. 23–52.

Famighetti, R. (ed.) (1993), *The World Almanac and Book of Facts, 1994.* New York: World Almanac.

Famighetti, R. (ed.) (1994), *The World Almanac and Book of Facts, 1995.* New York: World Almanac.

Faulkner, H. U., and T. Kepner (1944), *America: Its History and People.* Washington, DC: United States Armed Forces Institute, War Department (Published for United States Armed Forces Institute by Harper and Brothers).

Fenton, J. H. (1966), *Midwest Politics.* New York: Holt, Rinehart and Winston.

Ferrell, R. H. (1969), *American Diplomacy: A History* (Rev. ed.). New York: Norton.

Fett, P. J., and D. E. Ponder (1993), "Congressional Term Limits, State Legislative Term Limits and Congressional Turnover: A Theory of Change," *Political Science and Politics, 26,* 211–216.

Finn, M. T., and N. L. Jellison (eds.) (1993), *The American Bench: Judges of the Nation* (7th ed.). Sacramento, CA: Forster-Long.

Fite, G. C. (1981), *American Farmers: The New Minority.* Bloomington, IN: Indiana University Press.

Formisano, R. P. (1993), "The New Political History and the Election of 1840," *Journal of Interdisciplinary History, 23,* 661–682.

Friedman, L. M. (1973), *A History of American Law.* New York: Simon and Schuster.

Gallagher, T. M. (1987), *Paddy's Lament.* New York: Harcourt, Brace, Jovanovich.

Gannett, H. (ed.) (1898), *Statistical Atlas of the United States Based upon the Results of the Eleventh Census.* Washington, DC: United States Government Printing Office.

Garreau, J. (1982), *The Nine Nations of North America.* Boston, MA: Houghton Mifflin.

Gertler, M. (1988), "The Limits of Flexibility: Comments on the Post-Fordist Organization of Production and Its Geography," *Transactions, Institute of British Geographers, 13,* 419–432.

Gertler, M. (1992), "Flexibility Revisited: Districts, Nation State and the Forces of Production," *Transactions, Institute of British Geographers, 17,* 259–278.

Glassner, M. I. (1993), *Political Geography.* New York: Wiley.

Goldstein, J. S. (1988), *Long Cycles: Prosperity and War in the Modern Age.* New Haven, CT: Yale University Press.

Goodchild, M., and B. Massam (1969), "Some Least-Cost Models of Spatial Administrative Systems," *Geografiska Annaler, 52B,* 86–94.

Gordon, D. M. (1977), "Class Struggle and the Stages of American Urban Development," in D. C. Perry and A. J. Watkins (eds.), *The Rise of the Sunbelt Cities.* Beverly Hills, CA: Sage, pp. 55–82.

Gray, C. S. (1988), *The Geopolitics of Super Power.* Lexington, KY: University Press of Kentucky.

Grofman, B. (1985), "Criteria for Districting: A Social Science Perspective," *UCLA Law Review, 33,* 77–183.

Grofman, B. (ed.) (1990), *Political Gerrymandering and the Courts.* New York: Agathon Press.

Grofman, B., A. Lijphart, R. B. McKay, and H. A. Scarrow (eds.) (1982), *Representation and Redistricting Issues.* Lexington, MA: D. C. Heath.

Gudgin, G., and P. J. Taylor (1979), *Seats, Votes and the Spatial Organization of Elections.* London: Pion.

Guinier, L. (1994), *Tyranny of the Majority.* New York: Free Press.

Gunther, J. (1947), *Inside U.S.A.* New York: Harper and Brothers.

Hall, K. (1989), *The Magic Mirror: Law in American History.* New York: Oxford University Press.

Harley, J. B., B. B. Petchenik, and L. W. Towner (1978), *Mapping the American Revolutionary War.* Chicago, IL: University of Chicago Press.

Harries, K. (1995), "The Last Walk: A Geography of Execution in the United States, 1786–1985," *Political Geography, 14,* 473–495.

Harries, K., and S. D. Brunn (1978), *The Geography of Laws and Justice: Spatial Perspectives on the Criminal Justice System.* New York: Praeger.

Harrison, R. E. (1944), *Look at the World: The Fortune Atlas for World Strategy.* New York: Knopf.

Hart, J. F. (1991), *The Land That Feeds Us.* New York: Norton.

Harvison, P. E., R. C. Speaker, and M. L. Turner (1985), "Drawing the Lines—by the Numbers: The Statistical Foundations of the Electoral Process," *Government Information Quarterly, 2,* 389–405.

Henrikson, A. K. (1975), "The Map as an 'Idea': The Role of Cartographic Imagery during the Second World War," *American Cartographer, 2,* 19–53.

Henrikson, A. K. (1980), "The Geographical 'Mental Maps' of American Foreign Policy Makers," *International Political Science Review, 1,* 495–530.

Henrikson, A. K. (1994), "The Power and Politics of Maps," in G. J. Demko and W.

B. Woods (eds.), *Reordering the World: Geopolitical Perspectives on the Twenty-First Century*. Boulder, CO: Westview, pp. 49–70.

Hesseltine, W. B. (1968), *Sections and Politics: Selected Essays by William B. Hesseltine* (R. N. Current, ed.). Madison, WI: State Historical Society of Wisconsin.

Hewes, F. W., and H. Gannett (eds.) (1883), *Scribner's Statistical Atlas of the United States*. New York: Charles Scribner's Sons.

Hickey, D. R. (1989), *The War of 1812: A Forgotten Conflict*. Urbana, IL: University of Illinois Press.

Hicks, J. (1931), *The Populist Revolt: A History of the Farmer's Alliance and the People's Party*. Minneapolis, MN: University of Minnesota Press.

Hirst, M. E., and J. Zeitlin (eds.) (1989), *Reversing Industrial Decline: Industrial Structure and Policy in Britain and Her Competitors*. Oxford: Berg.

Hoffman, M. S. (ed.) (1989), *World Almanac and Book of Facts, 1989*. New York: World Almanac.

Hoffman, M. S. (ed.) (1992), *The World Almanac and Book of Facts, 1993*. New York: Pharos Books.

Hofstadter, R. (1960), *The Age of Reform*. New York: Vintage Books.

Horn, D. L., C. R. Hampton, and A. J. Vandenberg (1993), "Practical Application of District Compactness," *Political Geography*, 12, 103–120.

Hudson, J. (1988), "North American Origins of Middle Western Frontier Populations," *Annals*, Association of American Geographers, 78, 395–413.

Hudson, R. (1992), "Industrial Restructuring and Spatial Distribution: Myths and Realities in the Changing Geography of Production," *Scottish Geographical Magazine*, 108, 74–81.

Huntington, S. P. (1961), *The Common Defense: Strategic Programs in National Policy*. New York: Columbia University Press.

Hurd, C. (1944), "World Airways," in H. W. Weigert and V. Stefansson (eds.), *Compass of the World: A Symposium on Political Geography*. New York: Macmillan, pp. 109–120.

Johnson, C. A. (1976), "Political Culture in American States: Elazar's Formulation Examined," *American Journal of Political Science*, 20, 491–509.

Johnson, H. B. (1976), *Order upon the Land: The U.S. Rectangular Land Survey in the Upper Mississippi Country*. New York: Oxford University Press.

Johnston, R. J. (1979), *Political, Electoral and Spatial Systems*. New York: Oxford University Press.

Johnston, R. J. (1980), *The Geography of Federal Spending in the United States of America*. New York: Wiley.

Johnston, R. J. (1988), "The Political Organization of US Space," in P. L. Knox et al., *The United States: A Contemporary Human Geography*. London: Longman, pp. 81–109.

Johnston, R. J. (1991), *A Question of Place: Exploring the Practice of Human Geography*. Oxford: Blackwell.

Johnston, R. J. (1993), "The Rise and Decline of the Corporate-Welfare State: A Comparative Analysis in Global Context," in P. J. Taylor (ed.), *Political Geography of the Twentieth Century: A Geographical Analysis*. New York: Wiley, pp. 115–170.

Johnston, R. J., F. M. Shelley, and P. J. Taylor (eds.) (1990), *Developments in Electoral Geography*. New York: Routledge.

Jonas, M. (1966), *Isolationism in America, 1935–1941*. Ithaca, NY: Cornell University Press.

Kapstein, E. B. (1992), *The Political Economy of National Security: A Global Perspective*. New York: McGraw-Hill.

Karlan, P. S. (1993), "The Rights to Vote: Some Pessimism about Formalism," *Texas Law Review*, 71, 1705–1740.

Kasperson, R. E., and J. V. Minghi (eds.) (1969), *The Structure of Political Geography*. Chicago, IL: Aldine.

Kendall, M. G., and A. Stuart (1950), "The Law of Cubic Proportion in Electoral Results," *British Journal of Sociology*, 1, 183–196.

Kenkel, J. F. (1983), *Progressives and Protection: The Search for a Tariff Policy*. Lanham, MD: University Press of America.

Kennedy, P. M. (1987), *The Rise and Fall of the Great Powers: Economic Change and Military Conflict from 1500 to 2000*. New York: Random House.

Key, V. O. (1949), *Southern Politics*. New York: Random House.

Key, V. O. (1955), "A Theory of Critical Elections," *Journal of Politics*, 17, 3–18.

Key, V. O., and F. Munger (1959), "Social Determinism and Electoral Decision: The Case of Indiana," in E. Burdick and A. J. Brodbeck (eds.), *American Voting Behavior*. Glencoe, IL: Free Press, pp. 281–299.

Kirby, A. (ed.) (1992), *The Pentagon and the Cities: Urban Affairs Annual Reviews* (Vol. 40). Newbury Park, CA: Sage.

Kleppner, P. (1970), *The Cross of Culture: A Social Analysis of Midwestern Politics, 1850–1900*. New York: Free Press.

Kleppner, P. (1979), *The Third Electoral System, 1853–1892*. Chapel Hill, NC: University of North Carolina Press.

Kleppner, P. (1987), *Continuity and Change in Electoral Politics, 1893–1928*. New York: Greenwood Press.

Klingberg, F. L. (1952), "The Historical Alternation of Moods in American Foreign Policy," *World Politics*, 4, 239–273.

Klingberg, F. L. (1983), *Cyclical Trends in American Foreign Policy Moods: The Unfolding of America's World Role*. Lanham, MD: University Press of America.

Knox, P. L., et al. (1988), *The United States: A Contemporary Human Geography*. London: Longman.

Kodras, J. E., and J. P. Jones (eds.) (1990), *Geographic Dimensions of United States Social Policy*. London: Edward Arnold.

Komarow, S. (1995, June 30), "Base Closings Put Clinton in Tough Spot," *USA Today*, 13:203, 5A.

Ladd, C. E. (1982), *Where Have All the Voters Gone? The Fracturing of America's Political Parties* (2nd ed.). New York: Norton.

LaFeber, W. (1986), "The Evolution of the Monroe Doctrine from Monroe to Reagan," in L. C. Gardner (ed.), *Redefining the Past: Essays in Diplomatic History in Honor of William Appleman Williams*. Corvallis, OR: Oregon State University Press, pp. 121–142.

LaFeber, W. (1989), *The American Age: United States Foreign Policy at Home and Abroad since 1750*. New York: Norton.

Lauria, M. (1994), "The Transformation of Local Politics: Manufacturing Plant Closures and Governing Coalition Fragmentation," *Political Geography*, 13, 515–539.

Leib, J. I. (1995), "Heritage versus Hate: A Geographical Analysis of Georgia's Confederate Battle Flag Debate," *Southeastern Geographer*, 35, 37–7.

LeMay, M. C. (1987), *From Open Door to Dutch Door: An Analysis of U.S. Immigration Policy since 1920*. New York: Praeger.

Leuchtenberg, W. (1993), *In the Shadows of FDR from Harry Truman to Bill Clinton*. Ithaca, NY: Cornell University Press.

Libby, O. G. (1894, June). "The Geographical Distribution of the Vote of the Thirteen States on the Federal Constitution, 1787–88," *Bulletin of the University of Wisconsin; Economics, Political Science, and History Series, 1:1*, 1–116.

Lincoln Journal (1993, September 26). "Russian Nuke Total Surprising," 2B.

Logan, J. R., and H. L. Molotch (1976), *Urban Fortunes: The Political Economy of Place*. Berkeley, CA: University of California Press.

Loomer, S. A. (1993, August 28), *MicroCAM: Microcomputer Automated Mapping, Version 4.0*. West Point, NY: Department of Geography and Environmental Engineering, United States Military Academy.

Lossing, B. J. (1872, November), "The Natural and Political History of the Gerrymander," *The American Historical Record, 1:11*, 504–507.

Mackinder, H. J. (1904), "The Geographical Pivot of History," *Geographical Journal*, 23, 421–444.

Mackinder, H. J. (1919), *Democratic Ideals and Reality*. London: Constable; New York: Holt.

Mackinder, H. J. (1943), "The Round World and the Winning of the Peace," *Foreign Affairs*, 21, 595–605.

MacRae, D., and J. A. Meldrum (1960), "Critical Elections in Illinois: 1888–1958," *American Political Science Review*, 54, 669–683.

Madison, C. (1993, January 9), "Foreign Policy: Juggling Act," *National Journal*, 25:2, 62–65 .

Mair, A. (1993), "New Growth Poles: Just in Time Manufacturing and Local Economic Development Strategy," *Regional Studies*, 27, 207–221.

Mair, A., R. Florida, and M. Kenney (1988), "The New Geography of Automobile Production: Japanese Transplants in North America," *Economic Geography*, 64, 352–373.

Maisel, L. S. (1993), *Parties and Elections in America* (2nd ed.). New York: McGraw-Hill.

Makower, J. (1986), *The Map Catalog: Every Kind of Map and Chart on Earth and Even Some above It*. New York: Vintage Books.

Malecki, E. J. (1991), *Technology and Economic Development: The Dynamics of Local, Regional and National Change*. London: Longman.

Markusen, A. (1986), "Defense Spending: A Successful Industrial Policy?" *International Journal of Urban and Regional Research*, 10, 105–121.

Markusen, A. (1987), *Regions: The Economics and Politics of Territory*. Totowa, NJ: Rowman and Littlefield.

Markusen, A., P. Hall, S. Campbell, and S. Deitrick (1991), *The Rise of the Gunbelt: The Military Remapping of Industrial America*. New York: Oxford University Press.

Markusen, A. R., and J. Yudken (1992), *Dismantling the Cold War Economy*. New York: Basic Books.

Marschner, F. J. (1959). *Land Use and Its Patterns in the United States: Agriculture*

Handbook No. 153. Washington, DC: United States Government Printing Office.

Martis, K. (1989), *The Historical Atlas of Political Parties in the United States Congress.* New York: Macmillan.

Martis, K. C., and G. A. Elmes (1993). *The Historical Atlas of State Power in Congress, 1790–1990.* Washington, DC: Congressional Quarterly.

Massey, D., and R. Meegan (1982), *Anatomy of Job Loss.* New York: Methuen.

Mauro, T., and M. Hall (1995, May 23). "Term Limits Struck Down: Fight on to Change the Constitution," *USA Today 13:176,* 1A–2A.

McCarthy, J. L., and J. W. Tukey (1978), "Exploratory Analysis of Aggregate Voting Behavior: Presidential Elections in New Hampshire, 1896–1972," *Social Science History,* 2, 292–331.

McDonald, R. A. (1995), "Opening the Cold War Sky to the Public: Declassifying Satellite Reconnaissance Imagery," *Photogrammetric Engineering and Remote Sensing,* 61, 385–390.

Meinig, D. W. (1986), *The Shaping of America: A Geographical Perspective on 500 Years of History: Vol. 1. Atlantic America, 1492–1800.* New Haven, CT: Yale University Press.

Meinig, D. W. (1993), *The Shaping of America: A Geographical Perspective on 500 Years of History: Vol. 2. Continental America, 1800–1867.* New Haven, CT: Yale University Press.

Merriam, C. E., and H. F. Gosnell (1940), *The American Party System: An Introduction to the Study of Political Parties in the United States.* New York: MacMillan.

Miller, B. (1994), "Political Empowerment, Local–Central State Relations, and Geographically Shifting Political Opportunity Structures: Strategies of the Cambridge, Massachusetts Peace Movement," *Political Geography,* 13, 393–406.

Milne, S., and S. Tufts (1993), "Industrial Restructuring of the Small Firm," *Environment and Planning, A,* 25, 847–861.

Monmonier, M. (1991), *How to Lie with Maps.* Chicago, IL: University of Chicago Press.

Monmonier, M. (1995), *Drawing the Line: Tales of Maps and Cartocontroversy.* New York: Holt.

Morison, S. E. (1971), *The European Discovery of North America: The Northern Voyages, A.D. 500–1600.* New York: Oxford University Press.

Morison, S. E., H. S. Commager, and W. E. Leuchtenburg (1980), *The Growth of the American Republic* (Vol. 1). New York: Oxford University Press.

Morrill, R. L. (1981), *Political Redistricting and Geographic Theory.* Washington, DC: Association of American Geographers.

Morrill, R. L. (1987), "Redistricting, Region and Representation," *Political Geography Quarterly,* 6, 241–260.

Morrill, R. (1994), "Electoral Geography and Gerrymandering: Space and Politics," in G. J. Demko and W. B. Wood (eds.), *Reordering the World: Geopolitical Perspectives on the Twenty-First Century.* Boulder, CO: Westview, pp. 101–119.

Muehrcke, P. C. (1986), *Map Use: Reading, Analysis and Interpretation* (2nd ed.). Madison, WI: JP Publications.

Muller, P. O. (1981), *The Outer City.* Englewood Cliffs, NJ: Prentice Hall.

Murauskas, G. T., J. C. Archer, and F. M. Shelley (1988), "Metropolitan, Nonmetropolitan and Sectional Variations in Voting Behavior in Recent Presidential Elections," *Western Political Quarterly,* 41, 63–84.

Murphy, A. B. (1992), "Western Investment Patterns in East Central Europe: Emerging Patterns and Implications for State Stability: *Professional Geographer*, *44*, 249–259.

Nie, N. H., S. Verba, and J. R. Petrocik (1979), *The Changing American Voter*. Cambridge, MA: Harvard University Press.

Niemi, R. G., B. Grofman, C. Carlucci, and T. Hofeller (1990), "Measuring Compactness and the Role of a Compactness Standard in a Test for Partisan and Racial Gerrymandering," *Journal of Politics*, *52*, 1155–1181.

Norusis, M. J. (ed.) (1988), *SPSS/PC+ Advanced Statistics, V2.0*. Chicago, IL: SPSS Inc.

O'Loughlin, J. (1982), "The Identification and Evaluation of Racial Gerrymandering," *Annals*, Association of American Geographers, *72*, 165–184.

O'Loughlin, J. (1992), "Ten Scenarios for a New World Order," *The Professional Geographer*, *44*, 24–28.

O'Loughlin, J. (1993), "Fact or Fiction? The Evidence for the Thesis of US Relative Decline, 1966–1991," in C. H. Williams (ed.), *The Political Geography of the New World Order*. New York: Belhaven, pp. 148–180.

O'Loughlin, J., and A. M. Taylor (1982), "Choices in Redistricting and Electoral Outcomes: The Case of Mobile, Alabama," *Political Geography Quarterly*, *1*, 317–340.

O'Loughlin, J., and H. van der Wusten (1990), "Political Geography of Panregions," *Geographical Review*, *80*, 1–19.

O'Tuathail, G. (1993), "Japan as a Threat: Geo-economic Discourses on the USA–Japan Relationship in US Civil Society, 1987–1991," in C. H. Williams (ed.), *The Political Geography of the New World Order*. New York: Belhaven, pp. 181–209.

Pacione, M. (ed.) (1985), *Progress in Political Geography*. London: Croom Helm.

Parker, G. J. (1985), *Western Geopolitical Thought in the Twentieth Century*. London: Croom Helm.

Parks, N. L. (1966), "Tennessee Politics since Kefauver and Reece: A Generalist View," *The Journal of Politics*, *24*, 144–168.

Paullin, C. O. (1932). *Atlas of the Historical Geography of the United States*. New York: American Geographical Society.

Peck, F., and A. Townsend (1984), "Contrasting Experience of Recession and Spatial Restructuring," *Regional Studies*, *18*, 319–338.

Peirce, N. R., and L. D. Longley (1981), *The People's President: The Electoral College in American History and the Direct Vote Alternative*. New Haven, CT: Yale University Press.

Pennock, J. R. (1979), *Democratic Political Theory*. Princeton, NJ: Princeton University Press.

Peters, W. (1987), *A More Perfect Union*. New York: Crown.

Peterson, S. (1963). *A Statistical History of the American Presidential Elections*. New York: Frederick Ungar.

Phillips, K. P. (1969), *The Emerging Republican Majority*. New York: Anchor Books.

Pickles, J. (ed.) (1995), *Ground Truth: The Social Implications of Geographic Information Systems*. New York: Guilford.

Polsby, N. W., and A. Wildavsky (1991), *Presidential Elections: Contemporary Strategies of American Electoral Politics* (8th ed.). New York: Free Press.

Pomper, G. M. (1967), *"Classification of Presidential Elections,"* Journal of Politics, *29*, 535–566.

Porter, D. L. (1979), *The Seventy-Sixth Congress and World War II: 1939–1940*. Columbia, MO: University of Missouri Press.

Potok, M. (1994, October 31). "Disarmament's Risky Business: Putting Bombs to Bed," *USA Today, 13:33*, 7A.

Pounds, N. J. G. (1963), *Political Geography*. New York: McGraw-Hill.

Powaski, R. E. (1991), *Toward an Entangling Alliance: American Isolationism, Internationalism, and Europe, 1901–1950*. New York: Greenwood.

Proceedings and Debates of the Senate of the United States, Eighth Congress, First Session 1852. Washington, DC: Gales and Seaton.

Protocols of the Proceedings (1884), International Conference Held at Washington for the Purpose of Fixing a Prime Meridian and a Universal Day. Washington, DC: Gibson Brothers.

Pry, P. V. (1990). *The Strategic Nuclear Balance: Vol. 2. Nuclear Wars, Exchanges and Outcomes*. New York: Crane Russak.

Raisz, E. (1944), *Atlas of Global Geography*. New York: Global Press.

Reading, D. C. (1973), "New Deal Activity and the States, 1933 to 1939," *Journal of Economic History, 33*, 792–810.

Rees, J. (1981), *Industrial Location and Regional Systems: Spatial Organization in the Economic Sector*. New York: Bergin.

Rees, J., et al. (1985), "New Technology in U.S. Manufacturing Industry: Trends and Implications," in T. Thwaite and R. P. Oakey (eds.), *The Regional Impact of Technological Change*. New York: St. Martin's, pp. 164–193.

Ristow, W. W. (1944), "Air Age Geography: A Critical Appraisal and Bibliography," *Journal of Geography, 43*, 331–343.

Rogin, M. P. (1967), *The Intellectuals and McCarthy*. Cambridge, MA: MIT Press.

Rooney, J. F., et al. (1982), *This Remarkable Continent*. College Station, TX: Texas A & M University Press.

Roseboom, E. H., and A. E. Eckes (1979), *A History of Presidential Elections from George Washington to Jimmy Carter* (4th ed.). New York: Macmillan.

Rummel, R. J. (1970), *Applied Factor Analysis*. Evanston, IL: Northwestern University Press.

Rundquist, B. S. (ed.) (1980), *Political Benefits*. Lexington, MA: Lexington Books.

Sachs, C. (1993, September), "Campaigns and Computers," *Campaigns and Elections, 14:4*, 59.

Scammon, R. M., and A. V. McGillivray (eds.) (1993), *America Votes: A Handbook of Contemporary Election Statistics* (Vol. 20). Washington, DC: Congressional Quarterly.

Schattschneider, E. E. (1960), *The Semisovereign People*. New York: Holt, Rhinehart and Winston.

Schirm, A. L. (1991), "The Effects of Census Undercount Adjustment on Congressional Apportionment," *Journal of the American Statistical Association, 86*, 526–541.

Schlesinger, A. (1933), *The Rise of the City*. New York: Macmillan.

Schlesinger, A., Jr. (1986), *Cycles of American History*. Boston, MA: Houghton Mifflin.

Schneider, W. (1992, November 7), "A Loud Vote for Change," *National Journal, 24:45*, 2542–2544.

Schoenberger, E. (1987), "Technological Change and Organizational Change in Automobile Production: Spatial Implications," *Regional Studies, 21*, 199–210.

Schwartzberg, J. (1966), "Reapportionment, Gerrymandering and the Notion of Compactness," *Minnesota Law Review, 50,* 443–457.

Scott, A., and M. Storper (1986), *Production, Work, Territory.* Boston, MA: Allen and Unwin.

Semple, E. C. (1908), *American History and Its Geographic Conditions.* Boston, MA: Houghton Mifflin.

Shafer, B. E. (1991), *The End of Realignment? Interpreting American Electoral Eras.* Madison, WI: University of Wisconsin Press.

Sharkansky, I. (1969), "The Utility of Elazar's Political Culture," *Polity, 2,* 66–83.

Shelley, F. M. (1982), "A Constitutional Choice Approach to Electoral Boundary Delineation," *Political Geography Quarterly, 1,* 341–350.

Shelley, F. M. (1984), "Spatial Effects on Voting Power in Representative Democracies," *Environment and Planning, A, 16,* 401–405.

Shelley, F. M. (1993), "Political Culture and the Contemporary Restructuring of the American Great Plains," *Proceedings, International Symposium on Contemporary Agriculture and Rural Land Use.* Manhattan, KS: Kansas State University.

Shelley, F. M. (1994), "Local Control and Financing of Education: A Perspective from the American State Judiciary," *Political Geography, 13,* 361–376.

Shelley, F. M., and J. C. Archer (1989), "Sectionalism and Presidential Politics in America: A Twentieth Century Reinvestigation of Voting Patterns in Illinois, Indiana and Ohio," *Journal of Interdisciplinary History, 20,* 227–255.

Shelley, F. M., and J. C. Archer (1994), "Some Geographical Aspects of the 1992 American Presidential Election," *Political Geography, 13,* 137–159.

Shelley, F. M., and J. C. Archer (1995), "The Volatile South: A Historical Geography of Presidential Elections in the South," *Southeastern Geographer, 35,* 22–36.

Shelley, F. M., J. C. Archer, and E. R. White (1984), "Rednecks and Quiche Eaters: A Cartographic Analysis of Recent Third Party Electoral Campaigns," *Journal of Geography, 83,* 7–12.

Shklar, J. (1991), *American Citizenship: The Quest for Inclusion.* Cambridge, MA: Harvard University Press.

Sigal, L. V. (1993), "The Last Cold War Election," *Foreign Affairs, 72,* 1–20.

Smith, H. R., and J. F. Hart (1955), "The American Tariff Map," *Geographical Review, 45,* 327–346.

Speier, H. (1941), "Magic Geography," *Social Research, 8,* 310–330.

Staeheli, L. A., and M. S. Cope (1994), "Empowering Women's Citizenship," *Political Geography 13,* 443–460.

Stefansson, V. (1922), *The Northward Course of Empire.* New York: Harcourt Brace.

Sternsher, B. (1987), "The Harding and Bricker Revolutions: Party Systems and Voter Behavior in Northwest Ohio, 1860–1982," *Northwest Ohio Quarterly, 59,* 91–118.

Storper, M., and R. Walker (1984), "The Spatial Division of Labor: Labor and the Location of Industries," in L. Sawers and W. Tabb (eds.), *Sunbelt/Snowbelt.* New York: Oxford University Press, pp. 19–47.

Strategic Mapping (1992), *Using Atlas GIS: Desktop Geographic Information System.* Santa Clara, CA: Strategic Mapping.

Tax Foundation (1992). *Facts and Figures on Government Finance, 1992 ed.* Washington, DC: Tax Foundation.

Taylor, P. J. (1981), "Factor Analysis in Geographical Research," in R. J. Bennett (ed.), *European Progress in Spatial Analysis.* London: Pion, pp. 251–267.

Taylor, P. J. (1990), *Britain and the Cold War: 1945 as Geopolitical Transition*. New York: Guilford.

Taylor, P. J. (1992), "Tribulations of Transition," *The Professional Geographer*, 44, 10–12.

Taylor, P. J. (1993a), *Political Geography: World-Economy, Nation-State and Locality* (3rd ed.). New York: Wiley.

Taylor, P. J. (ed.) (1993b), *Political Geography of the Twentieth Century: A Geographical Analysis*. London: Belhaven.

Taylor, P. J., and R. J. Johnston (1979), *Geography of Elections*. New York: Holmes and Meier.

Taylor, P. J., and R. J. Johnston (1995), "GIS and Geography," in J. Pickles (ed.), *Ground Truth: The Social Implications of Geographic Information Systems*. New York: Guilford, pp. 51–67.

Thompson, M. M. (ed.) (1987), *Maps for America* (3rd ed.). Washington, DC: United States Government Printing Office.

Thrift, N. (1992), "Muddling Through: World Orders and Globalization," *The Professional Geographer*, 44, 3–7.

Thrower, J. W. (1972), *Maps and Man: An Examination of Cartography in Relation to Culture and Civilization*. Englewood Cliffs, NJ: Prentice-Hall.

Tiebout, C. M. (1956), "A Pure Theory of Local Expenditures," *Journal of Political Economy*, 64, 416–424.

Trachte, K., and R. Ross (1985), "The Crisis of Detroit and the Emergence of Global Capitalism," *International Journal of Urban and Regional Research*, 9, 186–217.

Trubowitz, P. (1992), "Sectionalism and American Foreign Policy: The Political Geography of Consensus and Conflict," *International Studies Quarterly*, 36, 173–190.

Trubowitz, P., and B. E. Roberts (1992), "Regional Interests and the Reagan Military Buildup," *Regional Studies*, 26, 555–567.

Tufte, E. (1973), "The Relationship between Seats and Votes in Two-Party Systems," *American Political Science Review*, 67, 540–554.

Turner, F. J. (1932), *The Significance of Sections in American History*. New York: Holt.

USA Today (1994a, July 21), "Spy Money," *12:217*, 4A.

USA Today (1994b, September 30), "Secret Building," *13:12*, 7A.

U.S. Bureau of the Census (decennial), *Census of Population and Housing*. Washington, DC: United States Government Printing Office.

U.S. Bureau of the Census (various years), *Statistical Abstract of the United States*. Washington, DC: United States Government Printing Office.

U.S. Bureau of the Census (1918), *Negro Population, 1790–1915*. Washington, DC: United States Government Printing Office.

U.S. Bureau of the Census (1947), *County Data Book*. Washington, DC: United States Government Printing Office.

U.S. Bureau of the Census (1975), *Historical Statistics of the United States, Colonial Times to 1970*. Washington, DC: United States Government Printing Office.

U.S. Bureau of the Census (1983a). *Congressional Districts of the 98th Congress: Arkansas*. Washington, DC: United States Government Printing Office.

U.S. Bureau of the Census (1983b). *Congressional Districts of the 98th Congress: North Carolina*. Washington, DC: United States Government Printing Office.

U.S. Bureau of the Census (1991, July). *TIGER/Line Census Files, 1990: Nebraska; CDRM 587600*. Washington, DC: United States Bureau of the Census.

U.S. Bureau of the Census (1992, January), *Census Bureau Teaching Resource 1: Congressional Redistricting. BC-1635A*. Washington, DC: United States Bureau of the Census.

U.S. Bureau of the Census (1993a, May). *Census of Population and Housing, 1990: Summary Tape File 3C; CD90-3C-1*. Washington, DC: United States Bureau of the Census.

U.S. Bureau of the Census (1993b). *Congressional District Atlas, 103rd Congress* (Vol. 1). Washington, DC: United States Government Printing Office.

U.S. Bureau of the Census (1993c). *Congressional District Atlas, 103rd. Congress* (Vol. 2). Washington, DC: United States Government Printing Office.

U.S. Bureau of the Census (1994a, April). *Federal Expenditures by State for Fiscal Year 1993*. Washington, DC: United States Government Printing Office.

U.S. Bureau of the Census (1994b, October), *1992 Census of Governments: Popularly Elected Officials in 1992; Preliminary Report No. GC92-2(P)*. Washington, DC: United States Government Printing Office.

U.S. Congress, Congressional Budget Office (1994, May), *Cleaning Up the Department of Energy's Nuclear Weapons Complex*. Washington, DC: United States Government Printing Office.

U.S. Congress, Office of Technology Assessment (1991, February), *Complex Cleanup: The Environmental Legacy of Nuclear Weapons Production*. Washington, DC: United States Government Printing Office.

U.S. Congress, Office of Technology Assessment (1993, September), *Dismantling the Bomb and Managing the Nuclear Materials*. Washington, DC: United States Government Printing Office.

U.S. Department of Defense (1988), *Atlas/Data Abstract for the United States and Selected Areas, Fiscal Year 1988*. Washington, DC: United States Government Printing Office.

U.S. Geological Survey (1970), *The National Atlas of the United States of America*. Washington, DC: United States Government Printing Office.

U.S. Geological Survey (1987), *Maps of an Emerging Nation: The United States of America, 1775–1987*. Reston, VA: United States Geological Survey.

U.S. Office of Management and Budget (various years), *Budget of the United States Government*. Washington, DC: United States Government Printing Office.

U.S.S.R. Ministry of Defense (1982), *Whence the Threat to Peace?* Moscow: Military Publishing House.

van der Wusten, H. (1992), "A New World Order (No Less)," *The Professional Geographer, 44*, 19–22.

Van Voorst, B. (1990, July 16), "America's Doomsday Machine," *Time, 136:3*, 19.

Wade, L. L., and J. B. Gates (1990), "A New Tariff Map of the United States (House of Representatives)," *Political Geography Quarterly, 9*, 284–304.

Walters, R. (1974), *The Nuclear Trap: An Escape Route*. Baltimore, MD: Penguin.

Ward, D. (1971), *Cities and Immigrants*. New York: Oxford University Press.

Watrel, R. H. (1993), "Sectional Voting Cleavages in Nebraska Presidential Elections, 1892–1992." Unpublished M.A. thesis, Department of Geography, University of Nebraska at Omaha, Omaha, Nebraska.

Wayne, S. J. (1992), *The Road to the White House 1992*. New York: St. Martin's.

Webb, W. P. (1931), *The Great Plains*. New York: Ginn and Company.

Webster, G. R. (1988), "Presidential Voting in the West," *Social Science Journal*, 25, 211–232.

Webster, G. R. (1992), "The Geography of a Senate Confirmation Vote," *Geographical Review*, 82, 154–165.

Weigert, H. W., H. Brodie, E. W. Doherty, J. R. Fernstrom, E. Fischer, and D. Kirk (1957), *Principles of Political Geography*. New York: Appleton-Century-Crofts.

Weigert, H. W., and V. Stefansson (eds.) (1944), *Compass of the World: A Symposium on Political Geography*. New York: Macmillan.

Welch, S. (1990), "The Impact of At-Large Elections on the Representation of Blacks and Hispanics," *Journal of Politics*, 52, 1050–1076.

Whittlesey, D. (1939), *The Earth and the State: A Study of Political Geography*. New York: Holt.

Whittlesey, D. (1956), "The United States: The Origin of a Federal State," in W. G. East and A. E. Moodie (eds.), *The Changing World: Studies in Political Geography*. New York: World Book, pp. 239–260.

Will, G. F. (1992), *Restoration: Congress, Term Limits and the Recovery of American Democracy*. New York: Free Press.

Williams, C. H. (ed.) (1993), *The Political Geography of the New World Order*. New York: Belhaven.

Wilson, W. (1908), *Constitutional Government in the United States*. New York: Columbia University Press.

Wood, G. R. (1969), *Representation and the American Revolution*. Charlottesville, VA: University of Virginia Press.

Wright, J. K. (1932), "Voting Habits in the United States: A Note on Two Maps," *Geographical Review*, 22, 666–672.

Wyman, R. E. (1968), "Wisconsin Ethnic Groups and the Election of 1890," *Wisconsin Magazine of History*, 51, 269–293.

Zagarri, R. (1987), *The Politics of Size: Representation in the United States, 1776–1850*. Ithaca, NY: Cornell University Press.

Zelinsky, W. (1973), *The Cultural Geography of the United States*. Englewood Cliffs, NJ: Prentice-Hall.

Index

INDEX

Note: Page numbers in italics refer to maps, graphs, or tables.